W9-AGX-421

The Holocaust in Romania

RADU IOANID

THE HOLOCAUST IN ROMANIA

The Destruction of Jews and Gypsies
Under the Antonescu Regime, 1940–1944

WITH A FOREWORD BY ELIE WIESEL
AND A PREFACE BY PAUL A. SHAPIRO

IVAN R DEE
CHICAGO 2000

PUBLISHED IN ASSOCIATION WITH THE UNITED STATES HOLOCAUST MEMORIAL MUSEUM

Translated from the French by Marc J. Masurovsky, CyberTrans International.

Published in association with the United States Holocaust Memorial Museum. The assertions, arguments, and conclusions contained herein are those of the author. They do not necessarily reflect the opinions of the United States Holocaust Memorial Council or the United States Holocaust Memorial Museum.

Library of Congress Cataloging-in-Publication Data:
Ioanid, Radu.
    [Evreili sub regimul Antonescu. English]
    The Holocaust in Romania   :   the destruction of Jews and Gypsies under the Antonescu regime, 1940–1944 / Radu Ioanid.
        p. cm.
    Includes bibliographical references and index.
    ISBN 1-56663-256-0 (alk. paper)
    1. Jews—Persecutions—Romania.   2. Holocaust, Jewish (1939–1945)—Romania.
3. World War, 1939–1945—Gypsies—Romania.   4. Gypsies—Nazi persecution—
Romania.   5. Romania—Ethnic relations.
    I. Title.
    DS135.R7I6513   2000
    940.53'18'09498—dc21   99-43229

Contents

Foreword *by Elie Wiesel*   vii

Preface   *by Paul A. Shapiro*   xi

Acknowledgments   xv

Introduction   xvii

Maps   xxvi

1   The Legal Status of the Jews in Romania   3

2   The Massacres Before the War   37

3   The Massacres at the Beginning of the War   62

4   Transit Camps and Ghettos, Deportations, and Other
Mass Murders   110

5   The Massacres in Transnistria   176

6   Life in Transnistria   195

7   The Deportation, Persecution, and Extermination of the Gypsies   225

8   The Survival of the Romanian Jews   238

9   The Fate of Romanian Jews Living Abroad   259

10   Antonescu and the Jews   271

11   A Summing Up   289

Documentary Sources   297

Notes   299

Index   339

Foreword
by Elie Wiesel

I DO NOT hesitate to say it: Radu Ioanid merits the recognition of all those who are interested in that history which has so lamely become known as the Holocaust. His work treats an unfortunately little-known subject: the tragic fate of the Jewish communities in Romania. Only a few historians, such as the great Raul Hilberg or Dora Litani, among others, have addressed it in their works. In fact, Radu Ioanid often leans upon them, but his work explores more fully the Evil which reigned in Transnistria, between the Bug and Dniester, the two great rivers in Ukraine. His work, based as it is on material from unpublished archives, thus constitutes a new contribution to this field.

Of Romanian origin, the author brings a special sensitivity to this subject. He knows the enemy. He follows him step by step in his hunt for the Jews from town to town, from decree to decree, from spontaneous pogroms to organized persecutions, from the traditional hatred to the physical liquidation; he shows the victims first in their homes, then in the ghettos, and finally, in death. One might say that his goal is to confront the enemy with its own crimes which, in a sense, were "more cruel" but more savage for being less structured in their brutality than those of the Germans.

While there were no gas chambers in Transnistria, everything else was there: not one community was spared; all were decimated. Two hundred fifty thousand Jews perished there in thousands and thousands of ways. There was the terror, the threats, the nocturnal death marches, the sealed wagons, the starvation, the plagues, the humiliations, the public executions, the fires: from time to time, the reader, his heart broken and exhausted, will stop in the midst of a page, incapable of absorbing one more image, or one more scream.

The orders came from on high, from Marshal Ion Antonescu himself. All, or almost all, were executed with more or less enthusiasm. Romanians, Germans, and Ukrainians outdid one another in cruelty. Everywhere it was the same. In the towns as in the villages, summer as in winter, being Jewish meant subjection to torment and torture. How can one read the official report of the Romanian General Constantin Trestioreanu without shuddering from horror and disgust? "I hanged (or had hanged) around five thousand people, mostly Jews, in the public squares of Odessa"? You read well: 5,000 gallows, 5,000 human beings swayed by the wind, before the eyes of the whole population. Or the testimonies of the thousands of Jews locked up in furnaces set on fire by Romanian soldiers? "Some Jews appeared at the windows and, to escape the flames, begged the arsonists to shoot them, pointing at their heads and hearts." According to a survivor or a soldier, about 35,000 Jews were burned alive or hanged in the city of Odessa alone. Another source cites a more "charitable" figure: only 25,000 in Odessa and Dalnic.

How to explain so much cruelty, manifested on so many levels, by Romanian society? Why were there so few interventions (there were, but they were rare and weak) on behalf of the victims? From the simple soldier to the most powerful officer, from the anonymous employee to the bureaucrat invested with the superior and implacable authority of the State, the Jews—and later the Gypsies—could not expect any measure of pity or humanity.

To understand the process which led to the paroxysmal violence toward the Romanian Jews during the war, Ioanid supplies us with documented details of the day-to-day anti-Semitism that preceded it. Ancestral religious influences, absurd accusations of deicide, the need for a scapegoat, economic factors, everything is there. But the author does not content himself with an evocation of the past; he insists also on revealing the present in all its ugly and confusing ambiguity. How to understand the popularity of Antonescu after the fall of the Communist dictator Nicolae Ceausescu? Streets bearing his name, statues erected, elected officials observing a moment of silence to honor his memory: has the nation then so quickly forgotten his bloody misdeeds, the atrocities he ordered, his crimes against humanity, and his death sentence?

It takes tremendous force to read this book from cover to cover. But the author had still more to write it. Yes, indeed, Radu Ioanid merits our gratitude.

Preface
by Paul A. Shapiro

IN JUNE 1991, fifty years after Romanian military forces joined those of Hitler's Third Reich in Operation Barbarossa, driving deep into the Soviet Union, and just eighteen months after the fall of the Communist regime of Nicolae Ceausescu, I traveled with Radu Ioanid to Bucharest. Our job was to begin the process of identifying Romanian archival materials relevant for study of the Holocaust. The trip was an early step in the systematic effort undertaken by the United States Holocaust Memorial Museum to identify and collect, generally on microfilm, Holocaust-related archives from all countries. Although the Museum itself would not open for another two years, even then its plan was to facilitate further study of the Holocaust and encourage a more complete and profound understanding of the most unspeakable crime and greatest tragedy of the twentieth century.

The director general of the Romanian National Archives was not encouraging. Romania had been a "haven for Jews," he proclaimed, even if a "few wild men on the periphery" had committed atrocities. Whatever real losses the Jewish community of Romania and Romanian-administered Transnistria had suffered had been "at the hands of the Germans," so we would do better to seek out German archival records.

That director general, his successor, and an "acting successor to the successor" all seemed to do their best to impede access to the wartime holdings of the Romanian National Archives. But Radu Ioanid outdid them, pressing systematically and relentlessly for access to records hidden from view for half a century. Slowly, over succeeding years, important collections were pried into the open and microfilmed for this museum's archives, usually after heated discussions in Bucharest regarding the availability for study, state of organization, and very existence of the respective archival fonds. Here, to cite just a few examples, were recorded the actions of the Romanian police and gendarmerie; the Romanization ("aryanization") of enterprise personnel rolls, professions, and property; the organization and imposition of forced labor on both Jews and Gypsies; and the deliberations and decisions of the presidency of the Council of Ministers aimed at the destruction of the Romanian Jewish community.

Other Romanian institutions, either less wed to preserving the myths and secrets of the wartime period or motivated by other reasons, were more forthcoming. Opening their archives, they often discovered together with Dr. Ioanid and other researchers from the Museum the full extent of what transpired in their own country between 1940 and 1944. The Ministry of National Defense, the Romanian Information Service (successor to the dreaded Communist-era Securitate), the Foreign Ministry, and other institutions eventually provided a treasure trove of materials relating to military command and operational units, the Iron Guard, surveillance of "suspect" individuals, postwar trials, diplomatic fine points, and, tragically, planned and implemented deportations of Jews and Gypsies, mass starvation and killing, and crude political calculations made at the expense of innocent victims.

The effort to identify and retrieve archival materials in Romania itself was paralleled by similar efforts in territories under Romanian administration during World War II but in independent Moldova and Ukraine today. There, in the archives of Chişinău, Cernăuţi, Mikolaev, Vinnytsya, Ismail, Odessa, and other localities where Romanian forces operated, where Romania's governor of Transnistria issued orders, and where Romanian and German occupation zones met, additional collections contributed to the completion of a remarkable picture, more detailed than any I have encountered for any other country. It is a picture of Romania's wartime regime, its bureaucratic and military structures, and its vicious actions to dispossess and deport, concentrate in camps and ghettoes, and in every way imaginable visit death upon Romanian and Ukrainian Jewry, as well as Roma communities. The archival resources on the

Holocaust in Romania that are currently in the archives of the United States Holocaust Memorial Museum as a result of this effort total not hundreds or thousands or even tens of thousands of pages of material, but hundreds of thousands of pages.

The Holocaust in Romania is the first book based on these new archival resources that treats the entirety of Romania's role in the Holocaust. Dr. Ioanid extracts from this mass of new documentation a well-defined picture of the workings of the system of victimization and destruction, clarity about who was responsible for the fate of Jews and Gypsies on Romanian-controlled territory, and a measured but still overwhelming analysis of the cost in human lives and human dignity. All flowed from a clear policy, implemented step by step and on a priority basis, directed and monitored carefully by wartime dictator Ion Antonescu, and aimed at the elimination of Jews and Gypsies from the Romanian lands.

The system is revealed, the responsibility of the Antonescu regime and of Ion Antonescu personally is clear, and the victims are counted. Yet *The Holocaust in Romania* invites future scholars to plumb the archives still further to build on the foundation Dr. Ioanid has provided. There is so much detail in those hundreds of thousands of pages. How to understand the careful consideration given to who would be allowed to remain in the ghetto during mass deportations from Cernăuți? Or the remarkably detailed planning of deportations from the ghetto of Chișinău, planning that included a count of the orphans and mentally impaired, and the special arrangements made for each of them, including the babies? Or the intensity of denunciations made by "normal citizens" targeting Jews spotted outside the ghetto after curfew? Or the razor-sharp economic analysis of the value of Jewish possessions and the lease-value of their homes? Or the fine distinctions of lineage and rights made at times, and not at others, when the fates of Roma were in the balance? Or the ferocity of mass killings in Odessa, violent death in the transit camps and ghettoes of Transnistria, or forced labor and starvation in places like Șargorod, Djurin, Vapniarca, and Kopaigorod? Radu Ioanid's synthesis stimulates the reader to ask such questions, and provides a framework within which to seek answers.

The Center for Advanced Holocaust Studies of the United States Holocaust Memorial Museum encourages research and publication projects that shed new light on Holocaust-related subjects and facilitate access to research materials that provide a basis for further study. *The Holocaust in Romania* succeeds admirably on both counts.

Center for Advanced Holocaust Studies
United States Holocaust Memorial Museum

Acknowledgments

MANY PEOPLE helped me with their advice, financial support, and, most important, time. George Soros personally supported the project with a generous grant, allowing me to work without interruption on the book for a year. Marcus Raskin, director of the Institute of Policy Studies in Washington, D.C., during my 1989 Soros fellowship there, helped me in numerous ways. Raul Hilberg, uncontested dean of Holocaust studies, frequently shared with me his impressive expertise on the Holocaust in Romania. Jean Ancel, who almost single-handedly laid the foundation of Romanian Holocaust studies, eased my work with numerous excellent suggestions and important historical information. Abraham Peck opened the doors of the American Jewish Archives in Cincinnati, where I found important sources. Paul Stahl and Isac Chiva, distinguished French academics, sharpened the manuscript and helped me better situate a complicated subject in a wider context.

Special acknowledgment goes to my colleagues and friends on the staff of the United States Holocaust Memorial Museum, who supported this project for many years with encouragement and access to archival materials acquired all over Europe. Sara Bloomfield, executive director, lent her support to publication, bestowing the prestigious imprimatur of the museum. Brewster Chamberlin volunteered precious time for long discussions of a complicated topic. Both he and Paul Shapiro negotiated agreements of cooperation with various Romanian, Ukrainian, and Moldovan government agencies and surveyed records that included doc-

uments amounting to hundreds of thousands of pages. Michael Beren-
baum, former director of the museum's Research Institute, helped with
numerous kind suggestions. More recently Paul Shapiro, of the museum's
Center for Advanced Holocaust Studies, contributed institutional support
and personal enthusiasm. The staff of the museum's archives and library
made my life as a researcher much easier than it might have been. Michael
Gelb and Benton Arnovitz edited the manuscript with patience, care, and
dedication, contributing in an essential way to the final form of the book.
Leo Spitzer and Vladimir Tismaneanu gave the project early and important encouragement.

Ivan R. Dee, my American publisher, who suffered with grace the
anticipation of this manuscript, deserves special praise. Cindy Nixon
brought a special commitment to the expert editing of the manuscript.

Finally, I wish to thank from the bottom of my heart the hundreds and
hundreds of Jewish and Gypsy Holocaust survivors in the United States,
Europe, and Israel who shared with me their painful memories. This book
is dedicated to them and the loved ones who never returned to them from
the Romanian killing fields.

R. I.

Washington, D.C.
November 1999

Introduction

ROMANIAN NATIONALISM in the nineteenth century evolved in tandem with the increasing economic role of Jews in the country. In February 1866, Romanian Prince Alexandru Ioan Cuza was forced to abdicate, and in May of that year Carol de Hohenzollern-Siegmaringen (later King Carol I, 1866–1914) assumed the throne. Two months later a new national constitution was adopted; Article 7 of this document denied Romanian Jews their political emancipation—a situation that would prevail until after World War I. Romanian Jews thus became stateless, heightening their vulnerability to economic and political discrimination. The motivating resentment against the Jews came both from the boyars, or gentry, and from the new bourgeoisie, who had recently begun to play a political role in the nation's affairs. As long as Jews worked as go-betweens—tax collectors, distributors of manufactured goods, and salesmen of spirits for whose production the boyars held the monopoly—they were allowed a measure of rights. But as soon as they showed a desire to integrate, to gain civil and political rights, they were deemed a "social peril," the "plague of the countryside," and similar epithets.

Jews had long been active in Romania in a wide range of crafts. Their economic competition stimulated the new Christian bourgeoisie to violent opposition and to the advocacy of measures "restricting" Jews in favor of "national labor." Meanwhile, too little land consigned the peasants to lives of misery. Unable to resolve the severe agrarian problem and willing to pander to the nationalist feelings of Christian craftspeople and merchants, the government sought to divert its frustration and anger onto the Jews.[1] Although Article 44 of the 1878 Congress of Berlin had linked international recognition of Romanian independence to the granting of equal political and civil rights to the Jews, the government soon abandoned this aim, substituting for full emancipation a procedure to grant "naturalization" only on an individual basis. From that time well into the twentieth century, Romanian writers expressed hostility toward Article 44.

After World War I, three regions were returned to Romania as agreed upon in the Treaty of Versailles: Bessarabia from Russia, and Bukovina and Transylvania from Austro-Hungary. Political leaders were enthralled with the reunification of historically Romanian provinces under the national flag. Simultaneously, however, that same leadership demonstrated a growing reluctance to grant civil rights to minority groups. Despite strong pressure from Western powers, not until 1923 did Jews in Romania win legal equality.

After 1929, "the Jewish question" acquired an increasingly mass character, with recurrent economic crises serving as background. Anti-Semitic activities were not solely the work of radical organizations. From a desire to restrict "Jewish capital" (partly the consequence of perceived electoral necessities), both the National Liberal party and the National Peasant party adopted anti-Semitic slogans. Mainstream and fascist parties alike exploited anti-Semitic agitation aimed at the lower-middle class, among whom they nurtured the idea of climbing the social ladder and who blamed "Jewish competition" for thwarting their efforts to do so. King Carol II's royal dictatorship (1930–1940) substantially intensified anti-Semitism and economic polarization (spectacular wealth for the few and acute privation for the masses)—all the more reason for the masses to adopt anti-Semitic rhetoric and to make anti-Semitic gestures. As a Romanian scholar observed:

> Anti-Semitic propaganda that the dictatorship's men were unscrupulously conducting together with agitators on the far right every day, every hour, fueled the hatred, the resentment, and the appetite of the petty bourgeoisie. . . . Unscrupulousness . . . and ignorance were instrumental in falsifying reality and transforming social problems, especially those of the lower-middle classes, into a racist issue. The Romanian and Jewish upper classes also benefited [from the direction of resentment at the more visible] Jewish lower-middle class that comprised the impov-

erished population of Moldavian towns and cities [and] suffered deprivations still greater than those of the Romanian population. [It was these people who] had to endure all the humiliations and brutality of relentless persecution. But the underlying truth remained hidden behind the rantings of those who, year in and year out, preached "racial" hatred and pogroms.[2]

In brief, economic problems underscored the rise of Romanian anti-Semitism after 1929, amplifying the political and cultural manifestations of nineteenth-century attitudes toward Jews. External factors also contributed: the influence of theoreticians of anti-Semitism such as Edouard Drumont, Houston Stewart Chamberlain, Charles Maurras, and Alfred Rosenberg, as well as the tolerance of Western governments toward the openly anti-Semitic joint regime of Octavian Goga (a government official in various positions through 1938) and Alexandru C. Cuza (head of the National Christian party).

Before World War II, the Jews of Romania were organized into local communities that oversaw religious life, education, and philanthropy; Romanian law countenanced the existence of Jewish federations. Such a federation existed in Regat ("Old Romania" or the "Old Kingdom" of Romania in its pre–World War I borders) with its own chief rabbi. Regat contained both Ashkenazi and Sephardic communities, most of the Sephardim being concentrated in Bucharest. The Ashkenazim were divided between traditional and liberal blocs. There also were ultra-Orthodox communities in the city of Sighetul Marmației (Maramureș District) and in Sadagura (in Bukovina). Jewish holidays such as Rosh Hashanah, Yom Kippur, Pesach (Passover), and Succoth generally were strictly observed in the smaller Jewish communities, but in the larger cities Rosh Hashanah and Yom Kippur were increasingly the only holidays observed by most Jews.

Virtually every sizable Jewish community had a synagogue, some sort of cultural and administrative center, a communal school, and a home for the elderly. There were several Jewish hospitals: in Bucharest, Iași, and Cernăuți. Two major organizations expressed the interests of this population: the Union of Romanian Jews (Uniunea Evreilor Români, or UER) and the Jewish party (Partidul Evreiesc). Wilhelm Filderman, who headed the former, fought for the civil rights of Romanian Jews; the Jewish party was a Zionist organization led by Theodor Fisher, Josef Fisher, Sami

Singer, and Mişu Weissman. Numerous B'nai B'rith lodges and other
Zionist organizations were to be found throughout the country.

Although the standard of living among Romanian Jews in the 1920s
was higher than that of Polish Jews, many were virtual paupers. In
Bessarabia and Regat cultural assimilation was quite pronounced. For the
most part the Jews read Romanian newspapers, although in Bessarabia the
older generation spoke Yiddish. It was also spoken in Moldavia but not in
Walachia. Most Jews in Transylvania shared affinities with Hungarian
culture.

In 1930, of 756,930 Jews in Romania, 318,000 derived their income
from commercial enterprise, including 157,000 from trade and credit,
106,000 from manufacture or the crafts (twice the rate of the Romanian
population), and 13,000 from agriculture. Nine thousand were self-
employed, and eight thousand worked in communications or transporta-
tion. Romania could claim some very wealthy Jewish families, such as the
Auschnitts, who owned steel factories and iron mines. Jewish banks, such
as Marmorosh Blanc & Company, Lobl Bercowitz & Son, Banca
Moldovei, and Banca de Credit Român, played an imposing role in the
economy. Except for the last of these, however, all went bankrupt during
the depression of the 1930s.

Jews constituted 40 to 50 percent of the urban population in Bessarabia and Moldavia. Fully half the population of Iaşi, the original capital of
Moldavia, was Jewish. The 1930 census shows that Jews made up the following percentages of the total population by region:

Region	Percentage[3]
Bessarabia	7.2
Bukovina	10.8
Dobruja	0.5
Moldavia	6.5
Muntenia	2.1
Oltenia	0.2
Transylvania	10.0

Civil liberties that Jews had worked for generations to acquire were
seriously undermined by the Goga-Cuza government's anti-Semitic laws
of 1938, which, inspired by Germany's Nuremberg Laws, deprived at
least 200,000 Jews of their civil rights. Ion Antonescu's governments of
1940 and 1941 abolished the rights of the remaining Jews. The war and

the pattern of Nazi anti-Semitic policy gave the Romanian "Conducator" (or ruler) the opportunity for a radical "resolution" of the Jewish question in Romania. The numerical aspect of that "question" and how it was answered may be traced in the percentages of Jews as part of the Romanian population from the middle of the nineteenth century until the end of World War II:[4]

Year	Total Population	Jewish Population	Percentage of Jews
1859	4,500,000	130,000	2.9
1877	5,000,000	216,304	4.3
1882	5,000,000	265,000	5.3
1894	5,500,000	243,233	4.4
1899	5,956,690	269,015	4.5
1912	7,234,919	239,967	3.3
1930	18,057,028	756,930	4.2
1941	16,795,900	375,422	2.2
1942	16,805,388	295,084	1.8
1945	17,000,000	355,972	2.1

The dramatic decline in the number of Romanian Jews in 1941 and 1942 is obvious. Yet in a memorandum distributed by the Romanian delegation to the 1946 Paris Peace Conference, only 1,528 Jews were said to have died in Transnistria and 3,750 inside Romania (probably Regat only).[5] Raul Hilberg, however, has concluded that 270,000 Jews died in Romania, a figure that seems to be a reasonable approximation.[6] (This figure does not, however, include 135,000 Transylvanian Jews killed after deportation by the Hungarian administration of northern Transylvania to Nazi concentration camps or the sizable indigenous population living in Transnistria, the area between the Dniester and Bug Rivers, which fell to Romania during the war.)

What indeed was the fate of the Jews who lived under Romanian administration in Regat, Bessarabia, Bukovina, and Transnistria during World War II? How many Jewish victims lived, and in many cases died, under the Romanian administration during those years? To what extent did the German and Romanian administrations cooperate in the destruction of Romanian Jews? And finally, how can one explain the survival of half the Romanian Jewish population at the end of that war?

*   *   *

On December 26, 1942, 196 Moldavian and Walachian Jewish forced laborers in Transnistria were loaded into cattle cars for a nineteen-day journey that took them from Alexandrovka to Bogdanovka. They traveled without food or water in temperatures dropping to forty degrees below zero. Eleven of them died during the trip. Upon arrival on January 14, 1943, they were piled into a pigsty, where they tried to protect themselves from the cold with straw. "The straw is for the pigs, not for the *Jidani* [kikes]," the farm administrator bellowed at them.

This small-scale tragedy is only one of thousands revealed by Romanian wartime documents and the testimonies of witnesses and survivors. At least 250,000 Romanian and Ukrainian Jews perished under the Romanian fascist administration. Transnistria, the part of occupied Ukraine under Romanian administration, served Romania as a gigantic killing field for Jews. Yet the majority of 375,000 survived to the war's end. The question is whether Romania's wartime dictator, Marshal Ion Antonescu, was a murderer or a savior of Jews during the Holocaust.

A post-Communist Romania has recorded a mixed attitude to a history swept under the carpet by the Communists and officially forgotten for decades. On the one hand, upon reaching Slobozia or Piatra-Neamţ, today's traveler may find himself greeted by a statue of Antonescu in a town square; some of these memorials were indeed dedicated with considerable fanfare and the participation of government officials. Many streets have been named after Antonescu. In Oradea one of the city's most important synagogues stands on such a thoroughfare. Yet the country's current president, Emil Constantinescu, has publicly acknowledged Romania's responsibility in the Holocaust, and recently the Ministry of Education has mandated the teaching of the Holocaust in Romanian schools.

The movement to rehabilitate Antonescu may be fueled by the energy of a limited number of nostalgics, but its roots stretch deep into Romania's history. Soon after World War II, the Communists began to impose their own criteria for the writing—or rather, rewriting—of Romania's past. Initially exploited as a propaganda tool for use against their political enemies, the saga of the extermination of the Romanian Jews soon disappeared from the newspapers and from scholarship and classroom instruction; later, study of the fascist period fell victim to a propaganda requiring numerous omissions and distortions. The 1960s in particular saw the emergence of an overtly nationalistic and xenophobic tendency in Romanian historiography, giving rise to a new official scholarship that left

out the destruction of a large part of Romanian Jewry during World
War II.

Openly revisionist books appeared during the 1970s, diminishing the
number of Jewish or Gypsy victims and promoting the notion that the Romanian government was in no way responsible for the killings. Instead,
they were implicitly or explicitly attributed only to "the Germans and
Hungarians." Communist revisionist historians suggested that Romania
had not—as other countries had—cooperated with the extermination
plans of the Nazi regime: an alleged national resistance reflected the Romanian people's militant humanism, a humanism that had prevented in
Romania the monstrous crimes carried out by Germany and other of its allies. Outright lies, such as the assertion that the Romanian government
had not surrendered a single human life to the Germans, found their way
into the works of Romanian historians.

After the fall of Nicolae Ceausescu, Romania's president from 1974
to 1989, revisionist writings multiplied. Many historians characterized
Antonescu's regime as only "moderately anti-Semitic." Some even declared that the fascist regime had approached the solution of "the Jewish
question" only by encouraging emigration. After Ceausescu's departure a
heavily anti-Semitic and xenophobic movement grew in Romania, generated by an alliance of extremist political parties and drawing upon the enthusiasm of unreformed elements from the former Securitate, the secret
police of the Communist regime. The aim of these groups has been to isolate Romania, end political and economic reform, and establish their own
control over the country. They have sought to identify foreigners in general, ethnic minorities in particular, and especially Jews as responsible for
all the difficulties Romania faces. The deep roots of the Romanian anti-
Semitic tradition have brought to this campaign followers from the mainstream parties too, both those in power and those in the opposition. From
the pseudosocialist left to the alleged conservative right, numerous politicians have supported the rehabilitation of Antonescu, citing (as pretext)
his liberation in 1941 of Bessarabia and Northern Bukovina, which had
been occupied by the Soviets in 1940. How could this liberation have
been accomplished except through the alliance with Nazi Germany, and
why would one hold a few abuses of the Jews (perhaps regrettable but un-
derstandable, considering widespread "Jewish assistance to the Soviets")
against the accomplishments of such a national hero?

Extremist politicians have not been the only ones seeking to glorify

Antonescu. Representatives of the Romanian mainstream intelligentsia have also participated indirectly in his post-1989 rehabilitation. Professor Mihai Zamfir, who became Romania's ambassador to Portugal, compared to "a hero" France's Maurice Papon, the onetime Vichy deputy prefect of Gironde who was condemned for the deportation of fifteen hundred Jews. *Romania Literara,* a leading literary weekly, accused Jews of conspiring to cover up the crimes of communism and of exploiting the Holocaust as a way of claiming a monopoly on suffering. Against this majority, the distinguished professor George Voicu, to take only one example of a quite different tendency, has struggled with the "irrepressible anti-democratic, xenophobic, anti-Semitic temptations" of the Romanian intelligentsia. Voicu wrote that "as long as Romanian intellectuals continue to see [anti-Semitism and the Holocaust] as a secondary, irrelevant, embarrassing . . . topic, or even more disturbingly, as an antinational or false issue, . . . Romania will be condemned to remain a peripheral, exotic state, [largely impervious] to the values of European and universal culture."[7]

For those who follow post-Communist politics, Romania's attempt to rehabilitate a World War II fascist government comes as no surprise. Chauvinism, revisionism, and attempts to rehabilitate war criminals are characteristic of most Eastern European countries. Yet the case of Romania is the most egregious: nowhere else in Europe has a mass murderer, Adolf Hitler's faithful ally until the very end, a man who once declared war on the United States, been honored as a national hero, inspired the erection of public monuments, and had streets named for him.

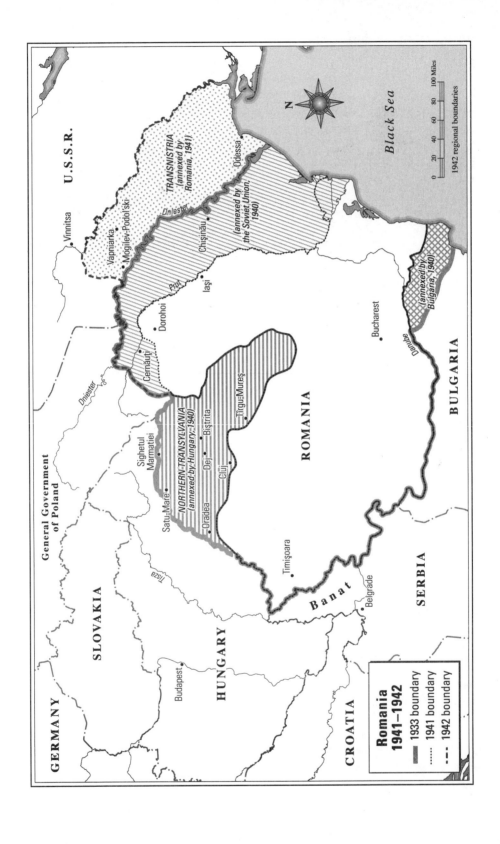

GERMANY

SLOVAKIA

HUNGARY

CROATIA

SERBIA

BULGARIA

ROMANIA

U.S.S.R.

General Government
of Poland

Black Sea

TRANSNISTRIA
(annexed by
Romania, 1941)

(annexed by
the Soviet Union,
1940)

(annexed by
Bulgaria, 1940)

NORTHERN TRANSYLVANIA
(annexed by Hungary, 1940)

Banat

Vinnitsa
Vapniarka
Mogilev-Podol'ski
Odessa
Chişinău
Dniester
Prut
Iaşi
Dorohoi
Cernăuţi
Sighetul
Marmatiei
Satu Mare
Oradea
Dej
Cluj
Bistriţa
Tîrgu-Mureş
Bucharest
Danube
Timişoara
Belgrade
Budapest
Tisza
Dniester

N

100 Miles
80
60
40
20
0

1942 regional boundaries

**Romania
1941–1942**

1933 boundary
1941 boundary
1942 boundary

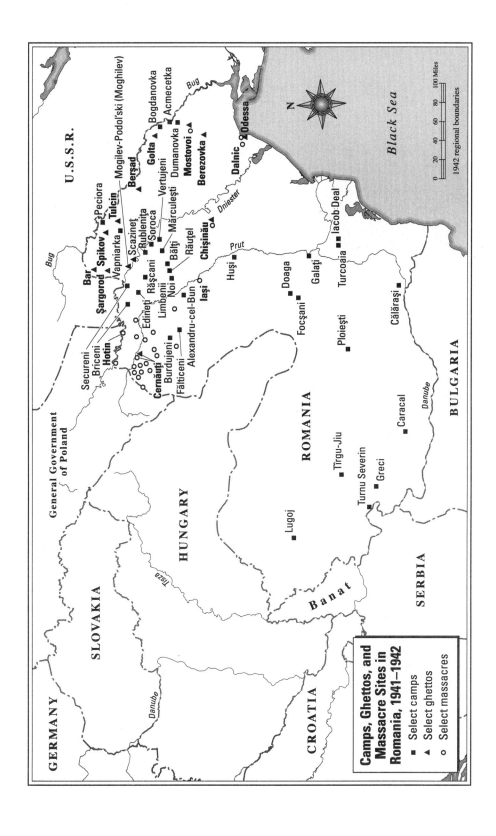

Camps, Ghettos, and Massacre Sites in Romania, 1941–1942

- ■ Select camps
- ▲ Select ghettos
- ○ Select massacres

The Holocaust in Romania

CHAPTER 1

The Legal Status of the Jews in Romania

On a fine spring day in early June 1946, four prisoners were escorted on the grounds of the Fort Jilava prison, near suburban Bucharest. Recorded by a movie camera, one of these men was attired in an elegant double-breasted suit, with a white shirt and a dark tie. A double-peaked white handkerchief could be seen emerging from his breast pocket, and in his right hand he carried a dark hat. Following one-by-one into a forest meadow, the other three prisoners also wore civilian suits, but these looked rather crumpled.

The column halted, and each of the four took his place before a wooden post. Documents were read aloud to the prisoners, already sentenced by the People's Court, and the members of the gendarmerie readied themselves. The prisoner on the extreme right raised high the hat he was carrying, and a rifle volley replied from the firing squad. With a pistol, an officer administered the coup de grace to three of the four—to the man on the right, at least twice. The camera took close-ups.

The war years had been a long season of "Leaders": Germany's *Führer,* Italy's *Duce,* Romania's *Conducator,* all of these in one way or another allied in the perpetration of the Holocaust. Romania's leader until August 1944 was Marshal Ion Antonescu, guided, as were many of his countrymen, by a desire to rid Romania of "foreign elements" and "foreign influence." Proudly tracing the purity of their national ancestral charter back to 101 C.E., when conquering Roman legions garrisoned the territory then known as Dacia, the notion that Jews may well have been among those who entered with these legions summons an ironic note: Ion Antonescu; former Counsel of Ministers vice-president Mihai Antonescu; Gheorghe Alexianu, ex-governor of Transistria; and former Deputy Interior Minister General C. Z. Vasiliu were the only Romanians executed for war crimes following World War II. After the fall of communism a huge cross was erected at their place of execution. It stands today on this government-owned land, and on this monument the convictions about which one reads are Ion Antonescu's—about the eternity of the motherland.

*   *   *

The roots of anti-Semitism in Romania, as in most of Eastern Europe, stretch deeply into history. Exercising their limited authority under the Ottoman Empire of the Turks, sixteenth-century princes of the Romanian Lands already were decreeing restrictions of one sort or another on the Jews as a non-Christian people with nebulous and often suspect external loyalties. But the Jewish community was typically permitted a great deal of cultural autonomy, and its members were allowed to pursue their livelihoods with a minimum of official interference until the mid-nineteenth century. Only then did the status of the Jews become a significant political question, a matter that gained importance with each passing decade during the second half of that century. Modernization brought a movement toward emancipation and secularization, but each step in the direction of the Jews' true integration into Romanian society seemed to trigger a reactionary response. These responses constituted part of a countermovement away from the intellectual and political trends emanating from the Enlightenment, the French Revolution, and the general evolution of Western Europe and America. Collectively they created the milieu that spawned the radical nationalist and xenophobic movements that would one day unite in the fascist parties that came to power in the 1930s, enacting their anti-Semitic programs as law.

PREFASCIST ANTI-SEMITIC LEGISLATION

Roman-era tombstones confirm that as early as the second century Jews lived on the territory of what is present-day Romania. Some historians have speculated that during the eighth and ninth centuries some of the Khazars (a people of Turkic origins who converted to Judaism) established themselves on the territory of Romania. Around the year 1367, Jews who had been chased from Hungary established themselves in Walachia.

The first anti-Jewish juridical measures were taken in Moldavia and Walachia during the fifteenth and sixteenth centuries. Ruling Walachia from 1456 to 1462, Vlad Țepeș, also known as Vlad the Impaler, and the real man behind Bram Stoker's classic Dracula tale, persecuted Jewish merchants. In Moldavia, Ștefăniță (1522–1527), Alexander Lăpușneanu (1552–1561 and 1564–1569), and Petru Șchiopul (1579) promulgated discriminatory measures against Jewish merchants, sometimes later revoking them. Aron Voda (1592–1595) of Moldavia had many of the Turks of that principality killed and almost certainly some Jewish merchants who were Turkish subjects. Mihai Viteazul (1596–1601) also ordered the killing of nineteen Turkish merchants of the Jewish faith. Still, anti-Semitic measures were sporadic, as were measures in which Jews were also intended or collateral victims of Romanian anti-Turkish sentiment; these facts argue against any perception of sustained, ruler-inspired persecution in these territories during the late Middle Ages. The "foreign policy" of the Romanian Lands was based on vassalage to the Ottoman Empire, manifesting itself in particular in the form of a heavy annual tribute to the sultan. Since that empire was rather tolerant toward Jews, indigenous princes generally complied with that policy, requiring only that "Jews from the Principalities adopt organizational structures based on the Ottoman corporatist system,"[1] under which the Jews were required to form guilds. The same applies to the vacillating attitude of the reigning princes of the eighteenth century, some of whom promoted discriminatory measures while others protected the Jewish population.

The legislation of the nineteenth century evolved under the banner of ethnic and religious discrimination. The few demonstrations of goodwill toward Jews, and especially the granting of civil rights, ran against the tenacity of widespread indigenous anti-Semitism.

The "Organic Regulation" of 1831, adopted under Russian pressure, became the first "constitution" of Romania. Chapter 3, Section 94 of the document required each Jew to register with local authorities and to specify his occupation so that "those Jews who [cannot] demonstrate their usefulness [could] be expelled from the concerned localities."[2]

Although the revolutionaries of 1848 in Moldavia and Walachia had requested the emancipation of the Jews, and in spite of the goodwill expressed toward the Jews by Prince Alexandru Ioan Cuza, the nineteenth century brought a new phase in the evolution of anti-Jewish measures. The growing number of such laws and regulations indicated that this attitude was becoming a fundamental purpose of state policy. On May 5, 1851, a commission was established in Iaşi; although its ostensible purpose was to fight against "vagrancy," its actual purpose was to define and restrict the right of Jews to settle in Moldavia. On July 31, 1859, in Focşani, Interior Minister Mihail Kogălniceanu demanded that the committee charged with drafting laws for Walachia and Moldavia bar foreign Jews from entering these territories (although it did proclaim the gradual emancipation of resident Jews). In messages to the legislative bodies on December 7, 1863, and January 1, 1865, Prince Alexandru Ioan Cuza opened the doors for the gradual emancipation of Romanian Jews. But on January 3, 1864, Kogălniceanu publicly contradicted the prince, and in December of the same year Jews were forbidden to practice law. In 1864 legislation gave Jews the right to vote solely in district elections but restricted even this limited franchise only to those who had served or were serving as officers in the army, held a university diploma, or owned an industrial plant.

In 1866 the abdication of Alexandru Ioan Cuza and the beginning of the reign of the Hohenzollern-Siegmaringen family constituted a major setback for those who favored emancipation of the Jews, Prince (later King) Carol I being himself an anti-Semite. As historian Carol Iancu has observed, "Interior Minister Ion Brătianu, a former revolutionary of 1848, inaugurated a systematic anti-Jewish policy in the spring of 1867. . . . Brătianu's circulars anticipated the mass expulsions of Jews from the countryside, and [even] expulsions from the country as a whole were strictly enforced by local officials."[3] In March 1868 draft legislation was presented to the Chamber of Deputies as part of a plan to eliminate Jews from most forms of economic activity in the villages. The proposed law was not accepted, but some local officials enforced its provisions as if the bill had been passed. In July 1869, after the French government protested the condition of Jews in Romania, Kogălniceanu replied that he refused to consider Jews full Romanians; on December 16, I. Codreanu, a deputy from Bîrlad, spoke in a similar vein before Parliament, denouncing the "behavior" of Romanian Jews and the aid they received from the "Universal Israelite Alliance." Iancu has summarized the legal situation of the Jews at the outbreak of the 1877 War of Independence:

> They did not have the right to reside permanently in the countryside and they could be expelled [from the countryside and even cities] on charges of vagrancy following an administrative order. They could own neither house, nor land, nor vineyards, nor hotels, nor taverns in the countryside; they could not possess land for cultivation; they could not sell tobacco; their right to own houses or buildings in the cities was always challenged; they could not take part in any public adjudication; they could not become professors, lawyers, pharmacists, state-certified doctors, or railroad employees; they were obliged to serve in the military, but were barred from becoming officers.[4]

At the Congress of Berlin in 1878, the nations of Europe recognized the independence of Romania but required the country to consider all citizens, including Jews, equal under the law. Article 44 of the Treaty of Berlin stipulated that religion might not be used to exclude anyone from "the enjoyment of civil and political rights, access to public employment, [elevation to] ranks and honors, or the exercise of specific . . . professions."[5] But on January 17, 1879, Parliament revised Article 7 of the 1866 constitution, which had made it impossible for Jews to become Romanians (unless they converted); now an individual petition and parliamentary vote were required for naturalization, a requirement that remained on the books until 1919.

After 1879 the government's course vacillated, anti-Semitic in spirit even if punctuated by occasional democratic gestures. Important political figures such as Interior (and sometimes Foreign) Minister Kogălniceanu and Prime Minister Ion Brătianu maintained before Parliament and abroad that Jews were the enemies of Romania. Parliament itself provided the venue for numerous anti-Semitic declarations. The attitudes they reflected helped ensure, for example, that between 1866 and 1904 only 2,000 Jews would be naturalized. Jewish veterans of the 1877 War of Independence received citizenship, but they numbered a mere 888. Between 1879 and 1911, Parliament naturalized only 189 Jews on a case-by-case basis.[6]

Under Russian pressure, Romania adopted in 1882 a law against "nihilists" and, as the authorities had the power to define these, this made it easier to expel Jews;[7] between 1880 and 1894, 859 individuals were deported, including 163 Jews; and from 1894 to 1906, a total of 6,529, including 1,177 Jews.[8] During one 1890 parliamentary session deputies debated "the Jewish invasion from Russia"; no distinction was made between those Jews born in Moldavia and Walachia on the one hand and those who were actual immigrants from the tsar's territories. In 1891 D. A. Sturdza, the future liberal prime minister, demanded that the government not grant entry to Jews expelled from Russia. On March 1 the Council of Ministers, Romania's chief governmental body, supported Parliament's request to expel Jewish "invaders." Later that year the Chamber of Deputies, under the liberal-conservative government of General I. M. Florescu, appointed a committee to consider new laws discriminating against Jews.

Anti-Semitic discrimination eventually barred Jews from jobs in the railroads, the customs service, the state salt and tobacco monopolies, and the stock market. The 1866 constitution permitted only Romanians (including naturalized subjects) to purchase real estate in rural areas, while an 1869 law forbade Jews to collect taxes there. In 1884 itinerant merchants were barred from the villages, a measure affecting many Jews. Several regulations hindered Jews from obtaining licenses to sell alcoholic beverages in rural settings.

The most dramatic form of discrimination in the rural areas was a series of expulsions that dislocated thousands of Jewish families during the last third of the century—more often in Moldavia than in Walachia, and more often after 1885. While both local and central authorities initiated these expulsions, community councils generally did so only at the prompting of the prefectures or the Ministry of Internal Affairs. How enthusiastic the local bodies were we do not know, but the disbanding of one or two—as when the prefect of Bacău disbanded one of its communal councils for refusing to expel several Jews from the village of Valea Seacă—dissuaded others that might have been considering insubordination.

Those expelled were permitted only a day to leave, even if they were elderly or had been born in the locality, as on August 20, 1885, when twenty-five Jewish families were forced from their homes in Brustureasa Bacău District. In 1889, Kogălniceanu, concretizing plans conceived earlier, drafted nine circulars to hasten the departure of Jews from the countryside, under conditions permitting widespread abuse and robbery. More than twelve hundred men, women, and children were forced from the districts of Roman, Vaslui, Tutova, and Covurlui.[9] Another campaign in late 1876 affected Jews in the district of Vaslui, driving more than eight hundred from their homes in less than twenty-four hours.[10] That spring Jews in Argeş received evacuation orders, though in this case we do not know if the orders were actually carried out. In 1891, thirty-two of the seventy Jewish families in the village of Pueşti (Tutova District) were ordered to leave; this measure was later canceled. In 1897, many Jews living in the districts of Fălciu and Suceava were expelled; in 1899, more than two hundred from Mălini, Dolma, and Broşteni (Suceava District); in 1904 and 1905, others from towns located in the districts of Dorohoi, Botoşani, Neamţ, Bacău, Tutova, and Tecuci; and occasionally still others from more urban settings, as in 1887, when five hundred Moldavian Jews were expelled from Bucharest. During the latter years of the nineteenth century and the early years of the twentieth, anti-Semitism and poverty also combined to prompt the mass emigration of Jews from Romania. Between 1899 and 1904, fifty thousand Jews left, and by the start of World War I, ninety thousand Romanian Jews had emigrated.[11]

For those Jews who remained, discrimination in the fields of medicine and health was also significant. Jews might open a pharmacy only if no Romanian was competing for the license (per a regulation of October 25, 1869). Only Romanians could serve as primary-care physicians at the district level (per a regulation of September 11, 1873). The health law of April 3, 1886, amended in 1893, 1896, and 1898, made Romanian citizenship a requirement for all jobs in sanitary services. "Foreign" pharmacy students or pharmacists' assistants could be hired only if a Romanian student or assistant also was employed. Although the same law made medical care free for poor Romanians, it stipulated that "foreigners can be admitted for treatment in those hospitals [only] for a fee; the number of beds occupied by foreigners can never exceed 10 percent of the total . . . in the hospital in question."[12] Even this minimum service was often ignored: in 1877, a new administrative regulation at the Bacău Hospital excluded Jewish patients; in 1891, the chief physician of Botoşani began refusing consultations to Jewish patients, also barred from that town's hospital; and on June 25, 1892, the *Monitorul Oficial* (Official Monitor) announced that Jews would no longer be admitted to hospitals in Moldavia.

The Primary Education Law and the Secondary and Higher Education Law, both passed in 1893 and amended several times over the next decade, made education free only for the "sons of Romanians." "Foreigners" might enroll, but only to the extent that space was available, and they had to pay tuition. Lyceums and especially universities nurtured powerful centers of anti-Semitic propaganda in the nineteenth century. The universities at Iaşi and Bucharest supplied the cadres for early anti-Semitic organizations and, after World War I, the core of the first fascist organizations.

The anti-Semitic tradition in the Romanian army—which later played such an important role in the killing of Romanian and Ukrainian Jews during World War II—took root in the nineteenth century. In 1868, military service became compulsory for all males in Romania, with the exception of foreigners; since Jews were generally treated as foreigners, this meant that the army might lose a supply of manpower and cannon fodder. An 1876 law on recruitment therefore stipulated that all male *residents* must serve; in other words, only citizens of other nations might avoid service. Jews thus became subject to the draft despite the fact that they were not citizens but "stateless foreigners," as the law defined them, or mere "inhabitants of the country." And this new provision was passed after the Congress of Berlin.

Within the army Jewish soldiers were often mistreated, and persecution drove some to suicide. On December 12, 1891, one soldier killed himself in Bucharest's gendarmerie; on April 14, 1895, a certain Horovitz from Iaşi did likewise. On November 8, 1896, an unsuccessful suicide attempt followed the torture of M. Solomonovici by Captain V. Sinescu, who was sentenced to two months' imprisonment as a result of the incident; on March 6, 1898, another Jewish enlisted man was severely beaten during his military service in the "Rosiori" Regiment No. 4.

In November 1913, delegates to the Extraordinary Congress of Romanian Jews considered the problem and appealed to the king, the legislature, and the cabinet to repeal a confidential military order (reproduced in the October 8 edition of the newspaper *Seara* [The Evening]) mandating discrimination against Jewish soldiers. Company commanders were to monitor the moods among all non-Romanian soldiers, Jews in particular; non-Romanians were to be promoted to officer rank only as an exception, after review by superior authority, and never in the case of Jews. In order to avoid open discontent, officers were asked to keep the contents of the instruction secret.[13]

This was the state of affairs as the Balkans sank into an era of violence that began nearly two years before World War I engulfed the West. In Romania some thirteen thousand Jews were mobilized in 1913 to fight in the Second Balkan War; but, despite valiant efforts on their behalf by such prominent intellectuals and political leaders as Ovid Densuşianu, Constantin Rădulescu-Motru, C. C. Arion, Lascăr Antoniu, and Leon Ghica-Dumbrăveni, even those who served were refused citizenship. At the height of World War I, Romanian security measures further encouraged discrimination when the 1915 Law for Monitoring Foreigners brought the deportation of hundreds of Jewish families from border areas of Moldavia to district capitals, where they could be kept under closer watch.[14] Yet 23,000 Jews served in the Romanian forces, sacrificing 882 dead and 735 wounded; 825 earned decorations for valor. All the while, anti-Semitism continued to thrive in the armed forces.

This state of affairs found reflection in Liviu Rebreanu's short story "Iţic Ştrul, Deserter," which depicted the tragedy of a Jewish soldier harassed by an officer who forced him to choose between desertion and suicide. The hero chose to kill himself. Reality was sometimes more tragic than fiction. The Supreme General Staff unleashed an anti-Semitic campaign leading to the execution of a number of Jewish soldiers accused of spying, as on November 22, 1917, in Company 6 of the Eighth Mountain Regiment, where six Jews were shot (one miraculously survived) by their erstwhile comrades on orders of their commanding officer.[15] A lunatic wave of denunciation of the Jews—soldiers and civilians alike—followed the banning of communication in the Yiddish language in September 1916. One study noted that "entire families were taken to police stations" and that "anywhere from eleven to twelve thousand Jews were arrested in Moldavia, nine thousand of them during January 1917 in the districts of Iaşi, Botoşani, Dorohoi, Bacău and Fălticeni." While most of these "suspects" went free after a brief detention, their jailors robbed, flogged, or otherwise abused many of the rest.[16]

The end of World War I brought temporary refuge from this kind of persecution, especially because the settlement dictated by the Western powers reflected—at least superficially—the intent to foster democratic government throughout the Continent. Although some were encouraged by these measures, those Jews who, exasperated by the abiding anti-Semitism of government and masses alike, had abandoned Romania for the West or for Palestine would be the happy ones. Nearly 100,000 of them, more than one-third of the community, left between 1899 and 1914. Those who later would read in the reforms of 1918 and 1919 the prospect of a genuine and lasting liberalization were doomed to disappointment and tribulation.

On December 29, 1918, Romania abolished the humiliating requirement of parliamentary confirmation for a Jew to become a citizen: proof of birth in the country, and that the individual was not a citizen of another, would henceforth suffice. Even these requirements were waived for those who had fought for the country since 1913;[17] only persons sentenced for treason, desertion, or spying were ineligible. Still, though the law of December 1918 represented an important step toward emancipation, it contained a de jure form of discrimination, ostensibly against "minorities" outside Walachia and Moldavia. By that date Romania had absorbed Transylvania, Bessarabia, and Bukovina, where considerable populations of Magyars, Germans, Ukrainians, and Jews resided. Romania's rulers were happy to own these territories, less so about the minorities they contained. A law of May 22, 1919, supplemented the earlier law by reaffirming that Jews from Moldavia and Walachia were entitled to Romanian citizenship (and even simplifying the procedure) but spelling out the corollary that those from Transylvania, Bessarabia, and Bukovina were not.

Under the St. Germain treaty signed on December 9, 1919, by the Allied powers and Romania, the country agreed to safeguard minorities in its territory, acknowledging that "all Romanian citizens are equal before the law and enjoy the same civil and political rights no matter what their language, race, or religion."[18] In Article 7 of the treaty Romania pledged "to recognize as full citizens and with no formalities the Jews located on all territories of Romania who could not obtain any other citizenship."[19] The new constitution of March 1923 granted Jews and other minorities full citizenship; Article 56 of the Citizenship Law of 1924 extended Romanian citizenship to all inhabitants of Bessarabia, Bukovina, Transylvania, Banat, Crişana, Maramureş, and Satu Mare who had been born there of resident parents.

In a sense the period between 1923 and 1938 represented a golden age of human rights in Romania. But storm clouds began to gather in the mid-1930s, with movements led by such groups as the Christian National

Defense League, the Iron Guard, and other political parties that raised "the Jewish question," brandished anti-Semitic slogans, and agitated for a revision of the status of the non-Christian minority. The legal underpinnings of tolerance would not long survive the arrival in power of the radical anti-Semitic right—represented by the minority Goga-Cuza cabinet of the National Christian party—in December 1937.

*   *   *

The cultural history of modern Romanian Jewry cannot be separated from the history of the various Romanian provinces. When Moldavia (without its northern half, Bessarabia, which was lost to Russia in 1812) and Walachia united in 1859 to create Romania, there were already sizable differences between Jews from the two provinces. Moldavian Jews were the majority and were almost all of Ashkenazi origins. They also belonged to Jewish communities, which had emigrated from Poland and Russia and lately established themselves in Moldavia. The Jews in Walachia had established themselves in the south of the country in earlier times and were of Ashkenazi and Sephardic origins. Most of the Jews from Walachia lived in Bucharest, which was by far the most Westernized city in Romania. In 1899, Regat had a population of 266,652 Jews, representing 4.5 percent of the total population. Of this total, 72.4 percent lived in Moldavia, where they made up 10.5 percent of the population of the province.[20] During the same year Walachia had a population of 60,760 Jews, of which 43,724 lived in Bucharest. One can thus assume that the Jews from Walachia were more assimilated and Western oriented than the Jews from Moldavia. Ezra Mendelsohn reminds us, however, that this assumption nonetheless requires a certain caution, especially concerning the history of Romanian Jewry in the nineteenth century, for "Reform Judaism of the German or Hungarian type never took root in Walachia; nor was the acculturation of Walachian Jewry accompanied by the adoption of a Romanian national identity."[21]

Both of these Jewish communities suffered the consequences of Romanian anti-Semitism:

> Prewar Romania had a well-deserved reputation of being, along with Russia, the most anti-Semitic country in Europe. Despite pressure, at times quite intense, from the great powers of Europe, Romania had

steadfastly refused to emancipate her Jewish subjects. As a result, by the
eve of World War I, very few Romanian Jews had acquired citizenship;
the great majority were considered foreigners and therefore of inferior
legal status. It is instructive to compare this situation with that of Hungary. Unlike the Magyars, the Romanians had no need of Jewish services
in ethnically mixed regions, since the Regat was a homogeneous Romanian nation-state.[22]

After the end of World War I, the demographic composition of
Greater Romania, which reacquired Bessarabia from Russia, and Transylvania and Bukovina from the Austro-Hungarian Empire, changed dramat-
ically. From an ethnically largely homogeneous entity, Romania now
found that 30 percent of its inhabitants were ethnic minorities, of whom
the Jews represented an important fraction. According to the 1930 census,
Bessarabia had 207,000 Jews, or 7.2 percent of its population; Transylvania had 193,000 Jews, or 3.5 percent of its population; and Bukovina had
93,000 Jews, or 10.9 percent of its population.

The history of the Jewish communities in these newly acquired territories was quite different from the history of the Jews in Walachia and
Moldavia. In Bessarabia the very large Jewish community had suffered
severe discrimination under the Russian tsars. The infamous pogrom of
1903 is one well-known historical remainder of many years of savage
anti-Semitic agitation. The Jews in Bessarabia were largely Yiddish
speaking and belonged to the lower-middle class and to the proletariat.
The Jewish intelligentsia in Bessarabia was Russified and looked, as Ezra
Mendelsohn wrote, toward Odessa and not Vienna. But in general the
Jews of Bessarabia felt no regret at leaving behind the tsarist empire or the
chaos of the Russian civil war.[23] According to Mendelsohn,

> The same cannot be said about the Jews from Transylvania, who up until
> World War I, lived in the Hungarian part of the Austro-Hungarian Em-
> pire. As in Slovakia and other parts of the Austro-Hungarian realm, the
> Jews were regarded as useful allies in the heroic struggle for Magyari-
> zation, and in Transylvania as elsewhere they were content to play the
> role of loyal Magyars. . . . In the north the Jewish community was much
> more like that of Subcarpathian Rus—very populous, very prominent in
> the few cities that existed in this backward area, mostly Yiddish speak-
> ing, and very strongly Hasidic (the most famous center of Hasidism

being in Szatmár-Németi or Satu Mare, the home of the famous Satmar dynasty).[24]

In Bukovina, which had been part of the Habsburg Empire, the situation of the Jews was again very different. Outside Cernăuţi, then the capital city, some Jews retained Hasidic and Orthodox traditions, but on the whole the Jews were Germanized and not viewed with hostility by the rest of the population. Emancipated and Westernized, the Jews from Cernăuţi were not unlike a sizable fraction of the acculturated Jewry from Bucharest.

*   *   *

The Jewish political scene in Romania was extremely complex due to the existence of diverse communities such as those from Regat, Bessarabia, Bukovina, and Transylvania. "The leading political organization of Regat Jewry," reports Mendelsohn, "was the Union of Romanian Jews (Uniunea Evreilor Romani, known as the UER) the interwar version of the prewar Organization of Native Born Jews (Uniunea Evreilor Pămînteni) founded in 1910. The Organization of Native Born Jews was chiefly a society of [the] Bucharest bourgeoisie and [the] professional class, which favored the Romanization of Romanian Jewry and which fought for Jewish legal equality."[25] Despite the fact that the UER appeared at first glance as an "assimilationist" organization, fighting for Jewish emancipation and against anti-Semitism, the UER was in fact a pro-Zionist association. The group's most prominent leader was Wilhelm Filderman, an important lawyer from Bucharest.

In the newly acquired territories Jewish nationalism ran stronger than in Regat. For example, the Folkist movement, which proclaimed Yiddish as the national language of the Jewish people, was strong in Bukovina. The Jewish socialist organization Bund was rather strong in Bessarabia, where moderate Orthodox Jews and Zionists also had a strong presence. In Transylvania radical Orthodox anti-Zionist Jews coexisted with a majority of the Neolog (Reform) Hungarian-oriented Jewry. Transylvanian Jewry had its Zionist movements as well.

Immediately after the end of World War I, the strategy of the Jewish politicians in Romania was to ally themselves with the major Romanian political parties that were disposed to show some willingness to fight anti-

Semitism. The UER first supported the National Liberal party, then the People's party, and then the National Peasant party. This political strategy was contested by the Zionists, who in 1928, through four members of the Romanian Parliament (two from Transylvania, one from Bukovina, and one from Bessarabia), created a Jewish national club soon to become a Jewish national party (in 1931). That year the Jewish party received almost 65,000 votes, which sent four deputies to Parliament. Two years later the new party's vote declined by half, which failed to send a single representative to Parliament. On the brink of World War II, Filderman remained the undisputed leader of the Romanian Jewish community. Modern, aggressive, and courageous, he would play a major role in the battle to save the Romanian Jewry during the Holocaust.

But no matter how diverse the Romanian Jews were, no matter how their strategies for survival differed, one common danger confronted them all: anti-Semitism. Widespread, violent, and common, anti-Semitism was by far the largest threat to Romanian Jews.

Common as anti-Semitism was in many Romanian political parties, only two of them used violence when dealing with the Jewish problem. The first was the aforementioned Christian National Defense League (Liga Apararii National Crestine [LANC]) created in 1923 by Professor Alexandru C. Cuza, which advocated a strictly enforced *numerus nullus* (no Jewish representation, participation, or membership) and the revocation of the citizenship of Jews. LANC, which can be described as a "constitutional" fascist party, used the swastika as a political symbol long before Hitler did. More radical in the ways in which it proposed the solving of the Jewish problem was the second party, a splinter of LANC, the Iron Guard, first known as the League of the Archangel Michael, led by Corneliu Zelea Codreanu. Members of both LANC and the Iron Guard were involved in many anti-Semitic incidents in the 1920s. These incidents—destruction of synagogues, burning of Jewish homes, beatings of Jews—were unfortunately only a prelude to the suffering Romanian Jewry would undergo during World War II.

Anti-Semitic politicians fueled the rising hate against the Jews. For example, on July 14, 1926, A. C. Cuza declared: "It is monstrous that the constitution should speak of the rights of the Jews. The solution ought to be to eliminate the Jews by law. The first step ought to be to exclude them from the army. Leases of forests granted to Jews should be canceled. All land held by Jews should be expropriated. Likewise, all town houses owned by Jews should be confiscated. I would introduce a *numerus clausus* (proportional Jewish representation, participation, and membership) in the schools."[26] Attacks against the Jews were not only verbal. Anti-Semitic students staged numerous violent demonstrations during which many Jews were severely beaten and Jewish houses and shops were vandalized and devastated. Personal attacks were frequent as well, as on August 9, 1926, when a number of Jews were attacked at the railway station in Adjud; after being severely beaten, the victims were thrown off the train.[27] Sometimes the incidents had more tragic results. On November 10, 1926, a trial for Cernăuți Jewish students charged with organizing a demonstration against certain anti-Semitic university professors opened "in an extremely stormy atmosphere. . . . When the Court rose and the public had filed out, a young man drew a revolver and shot one of the accused students, the young David Falik, in the abdomen. He fell in a pool of blood. The criminal was immediately arrested. Interrogated as to the motive for his crime, he stated that his name was Nicolae Totu, that he was a pupil of the Iași lycée, and that he had come specially to Cernăuți in order to commit his crime."[28] Shot three times, Falik died after forty-eight hours. Student associations in the city immediately organized rallies during which they expressed solidarity with the criminal.

Totu's trial opened in Cîmpulung on February 21, 1927. His lawyer, Paul Iliescu, a member of the Romanian Parliament, said: "David Falik has been killed by the bullet of Totu and so will die all the country's enemies, by innumerable bullets which will be fired against the filthy beasts. Gentlemen of the jury, the icon of this boy should hang in your homes. You should pray that God may give health and long life to this martyred child who is an honor to our nation. Totu is a martyr and a hero."[29] Cuza also spoke in the defense of the accused, calling him "our dear child Totu."[30] The verdict was not guilty. "Adorned with ribbons of the national colors, Totu was carried in procession around the town on the shoulders of his friends."[31] The following day Octavian Goga, then the Romanian minister of the interior, declared that Totu was a national hero.[32] Nicolae Totu would eventually become one of the leaders of the Iron Guard. LANC merged with Goga's National Agrarian party, creating the National Christian party. At the very end of 1937, Goga ascended to the position of prime minister in an administration that became known in Romanian history as the Goga-Cuza government. This government would enact heavy anti-Semitic legislation. *Numerus clausus* was to become a fact, and approximately 200,000 Jews would be stripped of their citizenship.

On January 21, 1938, King Carol II and Goga, also president of the Council of Ministers, signed a decree mandating the "review" of the citizenship of Romanian Jews. Minister of Justice Rădulescu-Mehedinți cited as the government's motivation the "Jewish invasion" after the unification of the principalities in 1859.[33] In interviews granted to A. L. Easterman of the British *Daily Herald,* Carol and Goga claimed that 250,000 or even 500,000 Jews were "illegals." But if Carol II denied any plan to expel them, Goga spoke of them as "500,000 vagrants" not to be considered Romanian citizens.[34] In an interview with *Paris Soir* on January 10, Goga already had elaborated on his ideas:

> At the end of the last century, the Treaty of Berlin forced us to grant . . . citizenship rights to the Jews. Fortunately, . . . it did not state that they had to be naturalized immediately, and so we could view them as foreigners. Furthermore, at that point there were not that many in Moldavia and Walachia, which made up our country then. For the most part these descended from Jews chased from Spain in the fifteenth century . . . ; these Jews of the pure Semitic type, with olive skin, black eyes, black hair, fairly fine features, and reasonably good looks, have nothing in common with those we call here the "barbaric Jews," with their reddish skin, slanted eyes, and flattened faces, who came later from Poland and Russia. We could accommodate the former if needed. . . . [But] I estimate that about 500,000 Jews [of the latter type] have immigrated here since 1914.[35]

Goga proposed to deport those half million Jews to Madagascar, and he was seconded by his colleague Istrate Micescu, minister of foreign affairs in the Goga-Cuza government, who opined, "it is urgent that we sweep up our courtyard because it serves no purpose to tolerate this garbage."[36]

In spite of Goga's racist comments, Carol II and Goga's Decree No. 169 did not establish legal discrimination based solely on racial criteria: geography, other conditions of birth, and the obligation to possess specific legal documents were also determinants. But if the decree was not strictly racist, it was nonetheless fascist in intent; it embodied the government's own anti-Semitic values, and it was calculated to steal the ground out from under the feet of its political competitor on the right, Codreanu's

Iron Guard, by demonstrating before the public that the Goga-Cuza administration too could be counted upon to "restrict" the Jews.[37] To cite another example of the politics of the time, the constitutional law adopted on February 27, 1938, defined membership in the Romanian nation by blood, legally distinguishing between Romanians "by race" and Romanians "by residence."[38] The government certainly did not overrule Gheorghe Alexianu, royal resident of the territory of Suceava (and three years later governor of Transnistria), when on December 1, 1938, he forbade the Jewish population to speak Yiddish in public places.[39] In the spring of 1940, Carol tried to co-opt the other radical anti-Semites by bringing the Legionnaires (many of whom were now members of the Iron Guard) into his government of royal dictatorship, and during the summer that government adopted a markedly fascist direction. But try as Carol did throughout the entire period from January 1938 (when he dissolved the Goga-Cuza government and installed his own dictatorship) to September 1940 (when he was forced from power by an alliance of the Legionnaires and Ion Antonescu), he failed to beat the Legionnaires at their own game.

FASCIST ANTI-SEMITIC LEGISLATION

Definition of the "Jew"

On August 8, 1940, Carol II approved Law No. 2650, which defined who was to be considered a Jew and delimited three categories of them; it also specified the degree of legal discrimination to which each was to be subjected. The executive decree was signed by Prime Minister Ion Gigurtu and Minister of Justice Ion V. Gruia. A corollary law forbade marriages between Romanians "by blood" and Jews. Though antedating the actual fascist government, these laws constituted additional confirmation of the fascist tendencies that characterized the late royal dictatorship. Because such laws referred to "Romanian blood," the "biological conception of the nation," and "the racial laws of Nuremberg," a brief digression into a short summary of Nazi Germany's anti-Semitic definition of the Jew is necessary.

The November 1935 citizenship law of the Third Reich divided the

German people into Aryans and non-Aryans, many of the latter further subdivided into: (a) "second-degree *Mischlinge*" (literally, "mixed-bloods," or persons with one Jewish grandparent); (b) "first-degree *Mischlinge*" (persons with two Jewish grandparents but not married to a Jew as of September 15, 1935, and not professing the Judaic religion); and (c) Jews (persons with two Jewish grandparents and professing the Judaic religion or married to a Jew as of 1935, or persons with three or four Jewish grandparents). It was only persons defined as Jews who were eventually subjected to extermination. In general, *Mischlinge* could neither be civil servants nor serve in the army; they were not permitted to marry Aryan Germans without official consent. With respect to the *Mischlinge,* two contrary attitudes prevailed among the Nazi officialdom, one tending toward their integration into German society, the other, never fully implemented, seeking their elimination.[40] It is important to note that even in racial Germany, in certain cases the sole criterion for categorizing individuals as either Aryan or non-Aryan was religion.[41]

From mid-1940 to early 1942, a large number of laws and regulations with strong anti-Semitic intent issued from the Romanian government.[42] Specifically, the law of August 8, 1940, defined the following as Jews:

a. persons professing the "Mosaic" faith;
b. persons born to parents practicing the Mosaic faith;
c. persons converted to Christianity, though born to unconverted Jewish parents;
d. Christians born to a Christian mother and a Jewish father who had not been baptized;
e. persons born illegitimately to a Jewish mother;
f. women included in the above subsections, even though married to Christians, if they embraced Christianity less than one year from the establishment of the "Party of the Nation" (June 22, 1939); and
g. Jews "by blood" even if atheists.[43]

The definition of "Jew" in this law was stricter even than in Germany, as demonstrated by items d and e above. Under the Nazis, Christians born to a Christian and a Jewish parent were labeled as second-degree *Mischlinge,* those to a Jewish mother outside of wedlock as first-degree *Mischlinge.*

The Romanian law further categorized Jews as follows: (a) a broad group consisting of those who had settled in Romania after December 30,

1918; (b) a much smaller group consisting of those naturalized before 1918, including those who had served in Romania's wars, the descendants of those individuals, and those naturalized pursuant to the absorption of Dobruja in 1913; and finally (c) all others. Jews in all three categories were barred from adopting Romanian names; none might buy rural property; and any who educated their Christian children in a spirit contrary to "religious or national principles" risked revocation of parental authority. If, on the date of the decree, Jews belonging to the second category were not yet government employees, they could neither enter state employment nor take up military service; those in the first and third categories could in no case work as civil servants, attorneys, merchants in rural districts, purveyors of alcoholic beverages, soldiers, editors, members of national sports associations, or housekeeping personnel in public institutions. The decree stipulated imprisonment of anywhere from one month to two years for violators.

The same decree gave obvious preference to Jews or their descendants who had been naturalized as participants in the 1877 War of Independence and to those naturalized individually by parliamentary vote. The number of such persons was small, no more than two thousand. Combatants in the Second Balkan War and World War I (decorated or not) also received preference. This law constituted a return to nineteenth-century anti-Semitic dicta that put into doubt the citizenship of most Romanian Jews. As the minister of justice acknowledged, this classification constituted a transitional step to a future system.[44] Indeed, twenty-seven days after the passage of the decree, Romania transformed itself into a "National Legionnaire State."

The law prohibiting marriages between Jews and gentiles—the preamble of the document directly citing the 1935 Nuremberg Laws—emphasized that people of pure Romanian blood were "the main element making up the foundation of the country."[45] Later the government provided for waivers to state officials wishing to marry non-Romanians, but not if the latter were Jews. Another law extended the same privilege to commissioned and noncommissioned officers. Despite numerous references to "biological criteria" in defining the nation, Romanian law continued to define Jewishness on the religious basis set out in the August 8, 1940, decree. However, these criteria evolved further under the successor Antonescu governments.

Under Antonescu (then prime minister), the statutory decree of October 5, 1940, defined Jews as "all those both of whose parents, or only one of them, [were Jewish], regardless of whether they or their parents were baptized, . . . whether they are Romanian citizens, or whether they have their residence within the territory of our country."[46] This definition found subsequent confirmation in numerous anti-Semitic laws, including the October 14, 1940, decree concerning access to education; that document classified as Jews those born of two Jewish parents or a Jewish father, without consideration of the confession of that father, and those born to a Jewish mother outside of marriage.[47] That year and the next, other laws dealing with the medical and military professions reflected similar definitions.[48]

The system of law gave expression to the religious criteria upon which fascist legislation was inconsistently based, swerving to the racial definition and back again. A December 17, 1941, decree mandating a census of those "with Jewish blood" required registration at the Central Jewish Office (*Centrala Evreilor*) for all persons having one or two Jewish parents or two Jewish grandparents. Yet in this case Jewish parents or grandparents meant all those who professed or had ever professed the Mosaic religion. Individuals having a single Jewish grandparent did not need to register with the Central Jewish Office, but they nonetheless had to make a declaration to the police,[49] a requirement that was dropped in 1942.[50] The same ambivalence is revealed in the fact that a Jew born to Jewish parents who had converted to Christianity and who had himself been baptized was nevertheless considered Jewish for tax purposes—but Christian regarding his military obligation!

The 1940 anti-Semitic laws of the Gigurtu government under Carol II thus formed the precedent for lawmakers in the subsequent fascist regimes (of Antonescu-Sima and Antonescu). And unlike the situation in Germany, conversion to Christianity continued to be considered valid by the Romanian fascists, as long as it had taken place prior to August 9, 1940. Despite the hostility between Antonescu and Carol II, an undeniable continuity characterized the two governments' anti-Jewish legislation.

Hitler freed some *Mischlinge* from their inferior standing; in 1943, Antonescu likewise legally emancipated a number of fully ethnic but "integrated" or "meritorious" Jews from their inferior status.[51] Such exceptions, however, could have no effect on the great mass of the Jewish population, whose lives were inescapably circumscribed by anti-Semitic legislation. Still, as we shall see below, it was often not the law per se, but geographical and other factors, that determined life or death.

Economic Legislation

In an interview granted on September 28, 1940, to the Italian newspaper *La Stampa* (The Press), Ion Antonescu laid out the underlying conception that would guide Romania's anti-Jewish economic legislation. Jews formed the greatest obstacle to expansion of the Romanian economy, Antonescu averred, promising to solve the problem by "replacing Jews with Romanians—in the first place Legionnaires—who will ready themselves during the interim. Most Jewish property will be expropriated in exchange for compensation. Jews who arrived in Romania after 1913—that is, after the second phase of the Balkan Wars—will be removed as soon as possible, even if they have become Romanian citizens, while the rest . . . will be gradually replaced."[52]

Because the alliance between Antonescu and the Iron Guard lasted only a few months, this "economic program" was carried out both with and without Legionnaire cooperation. The process of expropriation was termed "Romanization" (similar to Aryanization) by the corporatist economist Mihail Manoilescu, who categorized all enterprises as one of three types: (1) foreign-owned (financed abroad, profits repatriated); (2) belonging to Romanian Jewish capitalists who transferred neither profits nor interest abroad but whose enterprise benefited non-Romanians; and (3) owned by Romanian capitalists, in which case all profit remained part of Romania's wealth.[53] Since the first two cases could be equated, the term "Romanization" came to mean that enterprises based both on foreign capital and on Jewish capital would be transferred to "Romanian" ownership. In Manoilescu's words, "we will make no distinction between foreigners and domestic Jews."[54] At the same time, this "theoretical" approach distinguished between "Jewish" and "Romanian" capital strictly on the basis of ethnic criteria.

In further detailing the conception of Romanization, Manoilescu explained:

We do not include among the nonnative forces to be eliminated the German people of Romania. The German national community has a character of its own that cannot be compared to the other ethnic groups in our country. In this part of the world, this community enjoys histori- cal rights comparable to our own and personifies a civilization and cul- ture comparable to those of the German Reich.[55]

In fact, Romanization was the economic expression of state anti- Semitism. The intent was to establish a "Romanian national bourgeoisie" and to cleanse the economy by removing non-native elements, the Jews above all.

During the first stage of Romanization, from September 1940 to Jan- uary 1941, this "economic" initiative proceeded chaotically, often taking the form of simple plundering. Legionnaires forced many Jews to sell their businesses for modest sums or simply took them over without any compensation at all. On occasion, to circumvent this process, some Jew- ish property owners sold to ethnic Germans (who, by agreement with the Third Reich, enjoyed specified extraterritorial rights), thereby causing an increase of German capital in Romania. Ultimately, the Legionnaire ex- propriations caused severe economic disruption and elicited the discon- tent of Antonescu, who, for all his anti-Semitism, believed in adherence to the law.

On October 5, 1940, Law No. 3347 nationalized Jewish rural prop- erty, with Article 2 specifying a very broad definition of a "Jew," held to be a person either of whose parents was Jewish, regardless of whether they were practicing, whether they were citizens or not, or whether they were residents on Romanian soil. No exceptions in the enforcement of this law were to be permitted. A supplementary decree of November 17 or- dered nationalization of forests, mills, distilleries, lumberyards, and gra- naries, as well as nonarable land. In combination with expulsions and deportations, these decrees completed the Romanization of rural areas. On December 4, Jewish-owned boats and barges were confiscated too.

Decree No. 842, published on March 18, 1941 (after the Iron Guard had been removed from power), dealt with "the transfer of Jewish build- ings to state-owned assets." The term "Jew" was defined in accordance with the same Article 2 of the October 5, 1940, law, but here it exempted:

  a. Jews naturalized on an individual basis before August 15, 1916;
  b. Jews who had fought in the Romanian army and had been wounded or decorated;
  c. descendants of Jews who had died fighting for Romania;

d. Jews who had converted to Christianity at least twenty years earlier,
   if they had married Romanians;

e. other Jews who had converted at least thirty years earlier; and

f. descendants of those included in the preceding exemptions.

In the cities a purge of Jewish civil servants had begun even before
the inauguration of the "National Legionnaire" government in September
1940. From August 6 to September 3, nine ministries in Bucharest dismissed a total of 609 Jewish employees. On September 13, immediately
after the fascist consolidation of power, the Iron Guard established "commissars of Romanization" with great power over the manufacturing sector; often corrupt, more often inept, these figures caused significant
damage to the economy in only a few months. As a result, on January 18,
1941, they were removed by order of Antonescu. And on November 16,
1940, Law No. 825 ordered all enterprises of any nature whatsoever to fire
salaried (i.e., white-collar or professional) Jews, excepting only certain
veterans and their descendants, and providing for only two weeks to three
months of severance pay, depending on seniority. Under this law, only the
Council of Ministers retained the right to grant dispensations to certain
public works where skilled Jews were essential.[56]

Further decrees restricted surviving Jewish business activities in late
1940 and early 1941. The government prohibited Jews from engaging in
the sale of products included in the state monopoly—for example, salt,
matches, tobacco—while the Ministry of Labor required Jewish-owned
grocery stores to remain closed on Sundays so they might not take away
business that otherwise would go to Romanian shops the other six days of
the week.[57] And on March 25, 1941, Jewish stockholders in Romanian
companies were required to register their names on all bearer bonds.

The administration and resale of expropriated Jewish property presented particular problems that had to be addressed by law. Statutory decrees of May 3, 1941, and March 6, 1942, crafted a National Center for
Romanization, placing at its head a deputy minister for Romanization,
colonization, and inventory. On August 23, 1941, the National Bank of
Romania was authorized to grant special credits for the acquisition of
commercial and industrial property from Jews; to ease its operations, risks
it assumed were insured through the Ministry of Finance. On March 14,
1942, a decree specified punishments for those attempting to conceal Jewish property through fictitious sales.

While expropriations could be carried out with some degree of effi-
ciency, the same was not true of the replacement of Jews in the workforce.
Although most Jews were fired in 1943, thousands continued to work for
Romanian firms, which were forced to seek every possible sort of waiver
and approval because the Jews' skills remained irreplaceable;[58] even a
"Romanized" economy could not do without their services.

Forced Labor

Another key component of the fascists' anti-Semitic legislation was Jewish forced labor. As early as December 5, 1940, the government decreed
that Jews were obligated to work in the public interest under the Ministry
of National Defense or for other state ministries (such as the Labor Ministry) and institutions in cooperation with the Defense Ministry. Organization of Jewish labor was assigned to the so-called recruitment circles.[59]
During their employment Jews fell under military supervision and law.[60]
The youngest (eighteen to twenty) and oldest (forty-one to fifty-one) of
those imprisoned enjoyed the privilege of working in their cities of residence; those aged in between could be assigned to the so-called external
detachments. Severe sanctions threatened anyone who tried to evade these
coercive measures, as evidenced by this sampling of instructions from a
Supreme General Staff order of June 27, 1942, specifying punishments
for the following violations:

    f. For minor infractions (delay in answering roll call, indiscipline): cor-
       poral punishment.

    g. Deportation to Transnistria, fatigue duty, or transfer to ghettos with
       family awaited those who: repeated infractions mentioned under point
       f; worked carelessly, evaded work through fraud or bribery, were ab-
       sent at roll calls, or suspended work without permission; failed to ad-
       vise the recruitment circle of changes in residence; or cultivated close
       relations with Romanians.[61]

Ultimately, exploitation of Jewish forced labor fell to the Supreme
General Staff of the army, pursuant to Antonescu's Order No. 5295. The
army had the right to use women between the ages of eighteen and forty
as laundresses, seamstresses, and even office workers. Though only adults
were obligated under the law, minors were widely employed. Indeed, a
message sent by the General Staff to the Central Office of Romanian Jews

on January 10, 1943, stated that students were obligated to perform labor from the age of sixteen.[62] Such youths were used to remove snow, perform agricultural labor, or dig out victims of Allied bombings.

The forced laborers' housing typically was unsanitary, often in railroad cars, shacks, and barns. They endured hunger and cold, and lacked proper clothing and medical attention. On the order of Antonescu, on July 8, 1941, General Ion "Jack" Popescu, deputy minister of the interior, ruled that all Jews in the internment camps would have to perform "hard labor." In cases of flight, one out of every ten remaining prisoners would be shot. Those not meeting expectations would suffer deprivation of rations and be barred from receiving food packages.[63] Only toward the end of the war were these draconian regulations sometimes ameliorated as, increasingly convinced of the likelihood of Allied victory, the slave masters grew more willing to countenance evasion—when the appropriate "special taxes" or bribes were forthcoming.

Military Status of the Jews

The military status of Romanian Jews under fascists translated, as we have seen, into the organization of Jewish forced labor under military jurisdiction and the levying of additional taxes. The December 5, 1940, decree that forced Jews to labor "in the civic interest" in accordance with the needs of the state also abolished the military obligation of Jewish males.[64] Those Jews physically incapable of labor service were required to pay a military tax. The modest number of Jewish officers and noncoms still on active duty at the time of the decree were retired, but they were allowed to receive benefits only if they had served at least ten years.

On January 20, 1941, yet another decree increased the military taxes. Even Jews mobilized for labor in various enterprises now were obligated to pay; only those on forced labor projects and retired officers were exempted. Physicians, pharmacists, engineers, and architects conscripted by the armed forces enjoyed better conditions—for a while.

The Health-Care Professions

On November 15, 1940, "Jewish" doctors and other health-care providers, regardless of what religion they practiced or the nationality of their spouses, were excluded from the National Association of Physicians. Jewish physicians were segregated in their own professional associations, based on their specializations, and permitted to care only for Jewish patients. But to join even these associations a doctor was required to have been a citizen living in Romania prior to June 1, 1919. Each such individual was obliged to wear a badge identifying him as a Jewish physician.

The Society of Jewish Physicians fell under the authority of the National Association of Physicians. In addition to limiting Jews' medical practice, their role in medical science was also restricted: Jews were henceforth forbidden to join medical-scientific societies, and they were even barred from publishing in scientific journals. The peculiar wording of the law, openly anti-Semitic and yet peculiarly nonexplicit, would baffle no one: "To be enrolled in the College of Physicians [a doctor] must be of Romanian, Aryan, Magyar, or Turkish ethnicity and [practice either] the Christian or Muslim religion."[65] The practice of medicine was now declared incompatible even with marriage to a Jewish man or woman (although Romanian physicians married to Jewish women before publication of the law were not penalized). Members of the College of Physicians were, as a rule, allowed to provide care "only to Christian Romanian or Aryan ethnic patients and to Turkish patients"; Jewish patients could receive attention only in emergencies.[66]

On October 3, 1940, a new law prohibited the granting of pharmacy licenses to Jews and forbade them from opening drug warehouses or medicinal products laboratories. Clearly these regulations brought disarray to the practice of medicine in Romania, but the great irony is that fascist medical legislation claimed the goals of preserving and improving the health of the ethnic Romanian population.

Education

On August 29, 1940, near the end of the reign of Carol II, the Ministry of National Education, Religion, and the Arts regulated the place of Jews in elementary, secondary, and higher education. Even in Jewish schools, the Romanian language had to be taught, and history and geography had henceforth to be taught by Romanian schoolteachers specially appointed by the ministry. A *numerus clausus* strictly limited Jewish students to no more than 6 percent of any single *gymnasium* class. Jewish students whose parents belonged to the "second category" (i.e., those naturalized before 1918, descendants of Jews naturalized before 1918, and war veterans) were to enjoy preference over other Jews in admissions. Jewish students might be admitted into Romanian classrooms only to fill vacant seats, and they had to pay special taxes. The presence of Jews was likewise limited to 6 percent in higher, professional, and technical education.

Scarcely had these restrictions been adopted when a new decree of October 11, 1940, changed the *numerus clausus* in higher education to a *numerus nullus:* Jews could no longer be teachers or serve as administrators in either state-run or private schools serving the Romanian or other Christian communities, nor could they enroll as students therein. In extraordinary cases the Ministry of National Education, Religion, and the Arts had the right to suspend these rules when employees and students were born to Jewish fathers who had converted and Christian mothers of non-Jewish ethnic origin, provided they themselves had been baptized in the Christian religion before the age of two; certain categories of veterans and their descendants were also excluded.[67]

But even this was not enough: the fascists eliminated the exceptions one month later. Segregated Jewish schools continued to exist, and the system of school apartheid was capped with a prohibition against books written by Jewish authors in public libraries, lists of which were posted there and in bookstores.[68]

Other Anti-Semitic Legal Measures

During the autumn of 1940, dozens of professional, social, and other associations expelled Jewish members; these included the bar associations, the journalists' and writers' unions, the Society of Architects (on its fiftieth anniversary), the Romanian Opera, even the deaf-mute association. Professional and social discrimination went hand in hand with ministerial orders that essentially outlawed the recognition of Jews as human beings. One decision, of September 9, 1940, proclaimed that the Romanian state protected the practice of Roman Orthodoxy (the predominant religion); Roman Catholicism (unified); Latin, Greco-Ruthenian, and Armenian Catholicism; the Reformed (Calvinist) Church; Evangelical Lutheranism; Unitarianism; Armenian Gregorianism; and Islam. The government acknowledged the de facto existence of Judaism, promising that its right to continue to exist would be conditioned by subsequent ministerial provisions; other than these, "religious associations or sects . . . [were] prohibited."[69] Thus the de facto denial of recognition to the Mosaic faith also applied de jure to some of the Protestant "sects," whose persecution ranged up to and sometimes included deportation orders in 1942 and 1943.[70] Nonetheless, the Jews continued to figure as the chief target.

On September 9, 1940, the Ministry of National Education, Religion, and the Arts ruled that synagogues might remain open only with its special approval. In early 1941, Minister Radu Rosetti proposed a ban on conversions of Jews to other religions, for "the ethnic being of our people must be protected against mixture with Jewish blood."[71] By August 26, 1941, the Ministry of Internal Affairs had prohibited Jews access to beaches.[72] Then, less than two weeks later, on September 8, the Ministry of National Education, Religion, and the Arts further required that theaters and opera companies relieve all Jewish personnel of their posts. Jewish theaters and theater companies existed, to be sure, but they could not present the works of Romanian authors and they could present other plays only in the Romanian language. A decree of November 20, 1941, "Romanized" movie companies, movie theaters, and travel and tourism agencies. Meanwhile, local administrative agencies prohibited Jews from owning motorcycles and even bicycles.

Some regulations reflected—or, rather, fostered—the notion that security considerations necessitated restrictions on the Jews. Thus a decree of May 7, 1941, forced Jews to turn in their radios to the police. The minister of the interior justified this action to Antonescu (as if Antonescu had to be convinced) by stating that "Jews possessing radios are receiving propaganda news contrary to the general interests of the country, which they then spread, thereby continually inciting the population."[73] An afterthought of May 1, 1942, generously exempted from the radio law certain Jews who had one gentile parent.[74]

Needless to say, the deprivation of rights left the Jews open to systematic plunder. The state claimed the lion's share: discriminatory tax measures soon touched real estate, enterprises, and liquid capital alike. A law of October 21, 1941 (originating in the Ministry of the Interior but countersigned in Defense), ordered that Jews render the army, according to annual income, varying quantities of new footwear, clothing, and bedding. It is not surprising that the extortion was backed by the threat of violence: evasion would bring up to ten years in jail, not to mention a fine of 100,000 to 500,000 lei.[75] Two months later Jews disabled in World War I from 1916 to 1918 were exempted, but early the next year the government, as if reluctant to be seen as conciliatory, stipulated that the remaining Jews who could not afford the tax in kind would have to pay the exchange value in cash.[76]

These were hard times for all, and the government sought to guarantee that the most miserable gentile Romanian suffered less than the happiest Jew. Restrictions on the supply of food to Jews constituted an early step in this direction; and the childish vindictiveness of some of the laws underscores the fact that insult was just as important to the fascists as was injury. According to Article 4 of Decree No. 1215 (of mid-1941), for example, Jews were permitted to buy bread, but the purchase of pastries was forbidden them. Beginning on August 14, 1942, Jews had to pay a higher price for bread, which they might purchase only with specially marked ration cards.[77] Local administrative measures added to the Jews' humiliation, as illustrated by the edict of March 25, 1942, by which the military prefect of Botoşani District prohibited farmers from selling their produce to Jewish homes or shops and barred Jews from buying at market or from shopping outside the hours of 10:00 A.M. and noon.[78] The mayor of the town of Roman actually prohibited outright the sale of bread to Jews.[79] In other districts as well, similar measures were taken.[80]

Within such a climate why include a "nonpeople" in the nation's census? Thus, by a statutory decree of December 17, 1940, Romanian Jews (for this purpose, those having at least one Jewish parent) were to be counted separately, based upon their registration with local police departments. Decree No. 1257 of April 30, 1942, would later exempt Jews who had converted to Christianity before August 9, 1940, if they had only one Jewish parent—strange proof that somewhere under the surface the regime still wavered (as we will continue to see in subsequent chapters) in its definitions and its intentions.[81]

*   *   *

Wearing the yellow (occasionally black) star—that ultimate symbol of dehumanization—was never systematically required of the Jews of Old Romania but only of those living in Transnistria and certain departments of Moldavia, Bessarabia, and Bukovina. During the summer and fall of 1941, it had seemed, however, that no Romanian Jew would be able to avoid donning the star. Immediately after the declaration of war against the USSR on June 22, and following the Iaşi pogrom, Jews were obliged to wear the yellow star in some communities of Moldavia; for example, on July 4, 1941, the commander of the Bacău police announced that all Jewish men and women would have to start wearing the yellow star (two superimposed triangles, six centimeters per side) over the left breast within forty-eight hours. Only Jews in military uniform were excepted.[82] In a memorandum sent on July 15, 1941, to Mihai Antonescu, a distant relation to Ion and vice president of the Council of Ministers, Wilhelm Filderman, president of the UER, demanded that this "illegal" measure be rescinded. One of the ironies of history is that Filderman and Antonescu were former schoolmates, a fact that gave Filderman a tentative line of communication to the government. Scarcely two weeks had passed, therefore, when Deputy Minister of the Interior Popescu received Filderman; during their August 2, 1941, discussion Filderman was promised flexibility in the interpretation of the law. His disappointment must have been all the more bitter, then, when the measure remained in force.[83]

Filderman persisted in demanding elimination of the yellow star. On August 7, 1941, he gained another audience with General Popescu. Filderman later noted that he had "explained, among other things, that this badge was still being worn [in certain towns of Moldavia], even though the minister had ordered it to be discontinued [which he had not—R.I.]. The general explained to me that wearing the badge would be observed throughout the country and showed me a sample of the Star of David and orders that were ready for dissemination throughout Romania."[84]

In fact, on August 14, 1941, Order No. 1 from the Botoşani Territorial Military Command stipulated that "the Jewish population, regardless of sex or age, is required to wear, visible on the left side of the chest, a six-pointed star."[85] An identical order (No. 25007) was issued by the Third Army in the district of Baia on August 18, 1941.[86] Violation of these provisions was punishable by imprisonment of one month to one year, as well as by fines. In a new memorandum to the Supreme General Staff, Filderman protested these directives and the fact that such orders were already in effect elsewhere, for example, after August 13 in the city of Roman.[87] Still, on August 25, Order No. 3 of the Fourth Territorial Command, with authority in the Moldavian districts of Iaşi, Baia, Botoşani, Roman, Bălţi, and Soroca, mandated the wearing of the yellow star for all Jews. Violation was punishable by a prison term of six months to five years.[88] Worse still, during an August 27 meeting with Popescu, Filderman learned that "the yellow star would probably be extended to the entire country." This matter did not fall within Popescu's authority, he said, but rather within that of Ion Antonescu.[89] And then one week later, on September 3, an order (No. 8368) from the National General Inspectorate of the Police stated that the entire Romanian Jewish population would be required to wear a 6-centimeter black star on a white background contained within an 8.5-centimeter square. Baptized Jews would not be obliged to wear this badge.[90] The Bucharest Prefecture of Police issued the same order in its municipal jurisdiction on September 5, 1941.[91]

Also on September 5, 1941, Filderman sent two memoranda, one to the Ministry of Internal Affairs and the other to Antonescu himself, "strenuously requesting" cancellation and stating that even German Jews were not obliged to wear a star.[92] The memo sent to the head of state declared that Filderman would resign if the measure was not rescinded. The next day Filderman and Chief Rabbi Alexandru Şafran sent another memorandum to Nicodeme, patriarch of the Romanian Orthodox Church, asking him to forbid profanation of the Star of David; there is no evidence that the prelate responded.[93] On September 8, Filderman obtained a meeting with Antonescu himself, who, in a good mood, received him and Dr. Nicolae Lupu (a National Peasant party leader who facilitated the meeting, was a politician on good terms with Antonescu, and was sympathetic to the plight of the Jews); the leader agreed to order Mihai Antonescu "to cancel the wearing of the badge throughout the country."[94] Indeed, on September 10, the prefect of police in the capital, N. Radu, sent a written message to the president of the Sephardic Jewish Community stating that following a decision of Marshal Antonescu, Jews would not be required to wear any distinguishing badge. It is not known how many other persons or institutions received similar notices, but in general, as stated, the star was not imposed outside certain localities in Moldavia, Bukovina, Bessarabia, and Transnistria.[95] Despite all of this, the rescinded order nevertheless was temporarily imposed on the 350 Jews of Piteşti (near Bucharest) on September 12, 1941.[96] As things settled down German diplomats could not refrain from protesting the cancellation of the order for all Romanian Jews, which they did in the pages of the official *Bukarester Tageblatt* (Bucharest Daily) of December 2, 1941, asserting that the yellow star should be essential in the "New Order"; their words produced little effect.[97]

In areas where persecution of the Jews was stronger, however, the yellow star was indeed enforced. For example, as late as February 26, 1943, General Corneliu Calotescu, military governor of Bukovina (wherein, unlike Bessarabia, seventeen thousand Jews remained undeported), issued an edict reinstating the requirement that Jews wear the star. Violation of the order was to be punishable by internment in a labor camp. Those exempted from this order included converted Jews, Jewish women married to Christians, and Jewish women, even if divorced, whose children were the products of marriages with Christians.[98] On August 18, 1943, the fascist newspaper *Porunca Vremii* (Commandment of the Epoch) proposed the introduction of the Star of David in all of Romania as a distinguishing mark for Jews, citing as the model the measure adopted in Bukovina.[99]

Filderman's persistence had become one of the factors leading to the dissolution of the Union of Jewish Communities of Romania and its replacement by the Central Jewish Office, or *Centrala Evreilor.* This *Judenrat,* a government-controlled institution to facilitate the persecution of the Jews, grew out of consultations in October 1941 between Mihai Antonescu and his subordinate Radu Lecca, director of the Office for Jewish Problems.[100] Lecca acted as the governmental official in charge of the Jewish population until 1943, when some of the responsibility was transferred to the Ministry of Labor. Until then Lecca oversaw the new administrative and economic agency established by the law that Marshal Antonescu had signed into effect on December 16, 1941. The Centrala was responsible for, among other things, the following:

- exclusive representation of the interests of Romanian Jewry and administration of the assets of the former Union of Romanian Jews;
- "reeducation" and organization of Jews for "work and trades";
- preparations for Jewish "emigration";
- organization of cultural activities, schools, a newspaper, and self-help;
- organization of Jewish "work projects" and other forms of mobilized labor;
- provision of data required for "Romanization";
- creation and updating of files on all Romanian Jews, including issuance of photo identity cards that Jews had to carry on their persons;
- receipt of all petitions by Jews; and
- general oversight of the legal system governing the Jews.[101]

The Central Jewish Office thus became one of the two main venues through which the course of the Holocaust in Romania played out. The other (and more important) means was the series of government actions—sometimes opening the door to mass anarchy—by which Romanian fascists sought to carry out the elimination of Jews from their country. Later, when the tide of war reversed, these two venues were also the most significant in terms of the attempts to retrace steps in an inglorious administrative retreat from genocide, thereby permitting the survival of a large portion of Romanian Jewry.

*   *   *

The Holocaust in Romania culminated in a series of devastatingly cruel deportations carried out under murderous conditions. The administrative and legal measures authorizing these deportations, as well as the evacuations, expulsions, concentration in ghettos, and resettlements of Jews, will be described in the following chapters. The Jewish population of Bessarabia and almost all that of Northern Bukovina were deported or "evacuated," as was the entire Jewish rural population of Moldavia. "Evacuations" were carried out primarily in northern Moldavia, southern Transylvania, and, to a lesser extent, Walachia. Transit camps and ghettos were established in Bessarabia, Bukovina, and Transnistria. Between June 1941 and February 1942, the internment of thousands of Jews as hostages in camps emerged as a widespread practice. After the German-Romanian defeat at Stalingrad, Antonescu increasingly came to see voluntary emigration of the Jews as a solution preferable to forced deportation. But German pressure, the inertia of Romania's bureaucratic apparatus, and the lack of British and American receptivity impeded hope for a massive voluntary departure. That came only with the end of the war.

Antonescu was able to keep King Michael I in a ceremonial role from September 6, 1940, until August 23, 1944, when the latter took part in the coup during which the marshal was arrested. On December 19, 1944, the king and the minister of justice, Lucrețiu Pătrășcanu, abrogated all discriminatory laws against the Jews, forbidding all practices based on them. They also abrogated all discriminatory measures various public agencies had employed "in the absence of legal foundation."[102]

In Western and much of Central Europe political emancipation had been the product of a long process of mutual reconciliation between Christians and Jews. In Romania emancipation came as the result of external intervention, in the face of strong opposition from both the government and the people.[103] This is what occurred after the Paris Peace Conference of 1856 and the Congress of Berlin of 1878; this was the situation that likewise emerged from the Treaty of St. Germain (1919) and the Paris Peace Conference of 1923. As the precarious equilibrium crafted in Europe following World War I fell apart, Romanian leaders essentially annulled Jewish emancipation, perceived by many as unjustly imposed and detrimental to the interests of Romanians. The behavior of the top officials of Romania's fascist governments attests to this.

CHAPTER 2

The Massacres Before the War

Despite the fact that Romanian anti-Semitism found its most visible and concrete manifestations in the sphere of legislation during the late 1930s and that systematic, state-sponsored violence would not be organized until 1941, widespread popular anti-Semitic violence in the months after the conflict with the Soviet Union in 1941 signaled that a new phase had arrived in the story of the Romanian Holocaust. The timing of these events reflected not only the more general drift in a Central and Eastern Europe dominated by Nazi Germany, but the specifics of the Molotov-Ribbentrop Pact between the USSR and Germany, which permitted the Soviets to occupy territories belonging to Romania. Many Jews regarded the Soviets as potentially better suzerains than the Romanians, while others remained indifferent to them or even hostile. But Romanian nationalists exploited anti-Semitic stereotypes to portray the Jewish community as a whole as a pro-Communist fifth column. Other resentments of the Jews as a capitalist element in a predominantly peasant-worker environment, fanned by unscrupulous fascist publicists, came to the surface. Coupled with the opportunism of criminal and semicriminal elements eager for plunder, these emotions spilled over into bloody mob violence against Jewish communities in some parts of the country. The government largely stood aside from these events, though on paper at least it disapproved of public lawlessness. Still, in some cases participation of soldiers and police officers pointed toward the possibility of deliberate state involvement in the future.

MASSACRES DURING THE SUMMER OF 1940

During the spring and summer of 1940, the Romanian fascist movement expanded at an accelerated pace. By coming to an agreement with the Iron Guard, Carol II hoped to save his throne and compensate for certain failures of his foreign policy. On June 22, Carol founded his Party of the Nation and transformed Romania, in official terminology, from a "corporate" to a "totalitarian" state. The Iron Guard and its new leader, Horia Sima, played a considerable role in this national party.

Also in June 1940, less than a year after the signing of the Molotov-Ribbentrop Pact, the USSR issued an ultimatum demanding that Romania cede Bessarabia and Bukovina. The forced cession of these provinces, along with a number of communities in Dorohoi District in July, was a heavy blow to Romanian prestige and triggered severe reactions in the country's internal political life. In the face of this Soviet aggression Carol made an overture to Nazi Germany by appointing as prime minister a pro-Nazi industrialist, Hermann Goering's friend Ion Gigurtu, and as foreign minister an equally pro-German corporatist theoretician, Mihail Manoilescu.

The Soviets imposed humiliating conditions upon their capitalist neighbor. The Romanian forces were given three days to withdraw, but the Soviets did not respect even this term, entering the country and undertaking their first arrests before June 29. It infuriated Romanian nationalists that many Ukrainians happily greeted reunification with their long-lost cousins and that Jews were pleased with the downfall of the anti-Semitic regime. Whatever the perceptions of the Romanians, however, the great majority of Jews were fearful of the anticipated Stalinist changes; but Communists and other leftists were enthusiastic. Inside their truncated state Romanians sought scapegoats, and who might better fulfill this role than those whom nationalists had traditionally branded traitors and spies?[1]

Jacques Truelle, ambassador of France, reported a picture at variance with that of Romania's fascists: "while numerous incidents did occur during the evacuation of Bessarabia and Bukovina in 1940, it is a fact that the Jews were not the only participants, but that all of the Romanian scum in these provinces, as well as the Ukrainian, Russian, and other minorities, joined . . . in insulting the Romanian regiments withdrawing without a fight."[2] But the notion of the Jewish Communist, saboteur, and enemy of the Romanian people now began to appear more frequently in popular propaganda and official reports. Intelligence agencies reinforced the anti-Semitic trend: one document of July 4, 1940, titled "Jewish Activity: The Jews of Bessarabia and Bukovina During the Evacuation," describes more than twenty incidents, some unverified and others implausible, reportedly provoked by Jewish Communists. "In Bolgrad," ran one account, "the Communists [proudly] wore the six-pointed Jewish star and a red ribbon."[3] But a Jewish witness from Secureni recalls the opposite:

> News of the entry of the Russians spread with the speed of lightning in the town. . . . We were afraid to go out into the street, since we did not yet know what the attitude of our new masters would be. Suddenly, from the opposite direction we saw the arrival of . . . Lipovans [ethnic Russians from Bessarabia and the Danube Delta] wearing their holiday clothes and carrying armfuls of flowers to greet the Russians; then they began to dance to honor the conqueror. . . . We Jews truly felt glad, believing that everything had happened for the best and that we were saved. . . . Time showed us how much we were mistaken. . . . Shortly after the occupation the Soviet authorities began deportations to Siberia. . . . Most of those deported were Jews, but many Christians were too.

Exactly what any of the various demonstrations meant remains elusive, however, for as the same witness recounts, "about eight to ten days after the declaration of war on June 22, 1941, . . . these same Lipovans . . . came out to offer the Germans flowers, bread, and salt."[4]

Massacres attended the Romanian withdrawal. The killings typically were carried out by soldiers but sometimes by Romanian or Ukrainian mobs. The ugliest of them accompanied the withdrawal from Bukovina, the first taking place in the community of Milcoreni (in Dorohoi District). Following orders by an officer named Goilav, soldiers seized and abused the family of Sloime Weiner, including his son, User, and his daughters, Roza Weiner and Fani Zekler (the latter carrying an infant). Leading this group to the Tureatca Forest, the soldiers also caught a lame shoemaker named Moscovici, his wife, and their two children, as well as the wife of Isac Moscovici (apparently unrelated to the shoemaker) and their two young daughters. The mob made all of them line up in front of a ditch and then proceeded to shoot them. Isac Moscovici fell into the soldiers' hands shortly thereafter, to be beaten so badly that he died on the way to the hospital.[5]

Other victims fell too. On June 30, soldiers from the Romanian Sixteenth Infantry Regiment under Valeriu Carp killed eight people in the village of Ciudei, including Moise Schachter; Dr. Conrad Kreis; the Hessman brothers; Herman Gross; and the latter's wife, daughter, and grandson. Kreis was savagely tortured and his body dismembered.[6] Marius Mircu, a Jewish reporter, later explained the incident as revenge for the participation of Kreis and certain others ("the leaders of the Communist organization" of Ciudei) in a delegation greeting the Soviets. Carp ordered the four he considered guilty to be bound hand and foot, and after breaking their legs, he and his men "smashed their skulls, tied them to trees, and dismembered them with bayonettes."[7] On that same day in Suceava a group of eighteen soldiers under a lieutenant broke into the home of the Jew Suhar Lax de Costina. After torturing him they tied him to a horse's tail to be dragged for almost three kilometers to the edge of the village, where his bullet-riddled corpse was later found in the woods.[8]

July 1, 1940, found Commander Carp and his men in action again, this time in the environs of nearby Zăhărești. The men gathered thirty-six Jews from surrounding villages, some whose names have been traced: Leon Hamer, Leib Stekel, Ira Lupovici, Nuta Druckman, Moise Haller, Bartfeld, Herr, and the Edelsteins, mother and daughter. A witness recalled that they were tortured horribly: "Some of them had their tongues torn out, their ears and fingers cut off. Afterward, they were lined up around a pit, shot, and thrown in."[9] Carp forced two of the Jews to take part in the firing squad; we can identify one of these as Fredi Dermer from Suceava. The commander brought his own daughter along to enjoy the spectacle. At his orders the men tossed a dead horse onto the bodies of the dead Jews lying in the pit. In January 1941, surviving Jews exhumed the corpses and gave them a Jewish burial in the Suceava cemetery.

Also on July 1, 1940, in Şerbăuți (Suceava District) the chief of police, Adjutant Bujica, and his friend, the farmer Hapinciu, murdered Şmil Gheller, his wife, Sally, and Leib Ellenboghen with a revolver and threw the bodies into a stream. Their remains were retrieved early in 1941 and given a proper burial, also in Suceava.[10] In his standard compilation,

Cartea neagră (The Black Book), Matatias Carp records numerous crimes committed in early July 1940:

> In Comănesti-Suceava the Zisman brothers were thrown from a train and shot. Rabbi Leib Schactel and his two sons were first tortured, then killed at the edge of the village. The wife of the rabbi was shot while praying. Sloime Medler was killed by a bayonette to the nape of the neck. In Crăiniceni, district of Rădăuți, the Aizic brothers and Burah Wasserman were shot by a group of eight soldiers under an infantry sergeant. In Adîncata the Jews Weinstein, Maratiev, and Feigenbaum were killed. In Găureni-Suceava the landowner Moise Rudich was shot. In Liuzii Humorului (Suceava), Natan Somer was killed; in Igesti, also in Suceava, M. Hibner, his wife and sons, and Iosub Hibner and his four children were killed by soldiers and farmers.

Numerous killings took place in July on the trains, especially in Moldavia. Jewish travelers, especially Jewish soldiers, were shot and their bodies left in the fields. Some died under torture; others were permanently disabled.[11] In Rădăuți Romanian soldiers shot six Jews.[12] Many were thrown from moving trains; other victims were buried along the rail line in unmarked graves. On July 2, for example, Leon Cohn, a hairdresser from Bucharest on his way to service in the Twenty-ninth Infantry Regiment, was thrown from the train in Văculești along with three Jewish friends; farmers buried their bodies, and the local mayor filled out their death certificates weeks later.[13]

The largest massacres took place in the towns of Galați and Dorohoi. Near the Galați train station on June 30, a unit of the Romanian army cut down at least four hundred Jews attempting to flee to the USSR.[14] The July 3 issue of the newspaper *Timpul* (The Times) confirmed another anti-Semitic outrage involving an undetermined number of Jewish dead and wounded in Galați that also took place on June 30.[15]

During its withdrawal from Bukovina the Twenty-ninth Infantry encountered Soviet troops. A Romanian officer, Captain Boroș, and a Jewish soldier, Iancu Solomon, died in the clash. Solomon's funeral was to be held July 1 in Dorohoi. An honor guard composed of ten Jewish soldiers, including Sergeant Emil Bercovici and under the command of a Christian noncommissioned officer, was dispatched to the cemetery. As the coffin was being lowered into the grave, rifle shots rang out. The Romanians in charge ordered the soldiers to leave the cemetery. Several civilian Jews hid in the mortuary chapel. At the cemetery gate another platoon disarmed the Jewish soldiers and shot them. Bercovici's body was positioned near a machine gun, and the troublemakers convinced the mob that had gathered that "the Jews" had opened fire on the retreating Romanian soldiers. Before long the rioters had massacred another forty Jews, including four children: Freida Rudik (seven years old), Tomy Rudik (six), Moise Rudik (two), and Simion Cohn (two)—all neighbors who had lived on Regina Maria Street. All of the victims, with the exception of a ninety-four-year-old man who was struck at the base of the skull, were shot in the head, chest, or abdomen.

The pogrom continued in the city after local residents had marked the houses of the gentiles with painted crosses. Soldiers invaded the homes of Jews, raping, pillaging, and murdering: they shot Avram Calmanovici and cut off his genitals; they shot Eli and Friga Reizel, cutting off Friga's ears to get her earrings. After shooting her soldiers cut off Rifca Croitoru's breasts. A Jewish survivor injured in the incident at the cemetery, Sulimovici, was saved by a police sergeant. At the hospital he found thirty other injured Jews. The mob shot eighty-year-old Hers Ionas on Brătianu Street; Bercu Aclipei, Isac Rabinovici, Manole Wittner, and a Mr. and Mrs. Zeliger were simply shot. Many other Jews found refuge through the efforts of Lieutenant Isăcescu, Captain Stino, Lieutenant Colonel Marino, Colonel Ilasievici, and General Sănătescu.[16]

According to several sources, the Dorohoi pogrom resulted in two hundred deaths.[17] The Romanian historians Ion Calfeteanu and Aurica Simion cite a figure of 160—90 in the city, the others hunted down nearby.[18] Carp counts 136 killed in Dorohoi and its surroundings, but his figure does not include Jews thrown from moving trains, victims whose number can only be guessed. In 109 cases the murderers can be identified as soldiers and peasants; in three cases, policemen and townsmen. We have no information regarding the other killers.

Ambassador Miguel A. Rivera of Chile informed Santiago of 180 victims in the Dorohoi episode, warning that this event was merely a prelude to what was coming.[19] The pogroms in the district of Dorohoi do not appear to have resulted from orders of central military or civilian authorities but, rather, from uncoordinated local military initiatives and from anti-Semitic agitation, in the atmosphere of wartime catastrophe. Chaos was the milieu in which reinvigorated anti-Semitism thrived. In July and

August anti-Semites expelled Jewish families from the rural areas of Moldavia. All Jews from the districts of Dranceni and Răducăneni, for example, were evacuated to Huşi; in that town 120 were arrested (it is not known how many were deportees, how many residents) before being interned in specially established camps.[20]

LIFE AND DEATH UNDER THE IRON GUARD, SEPTEMBER 6, 1940–JANUARY 21, 1941

On September 6, 1940, the Iron Guard and Marshal Antonescu forced King Carol II to abdicate, blaming him for the loss of Bessarabia, Bukovina, and northern Transylvania. Although exhibiting clearly totalitarian features, his rule had been pro-Western; in his dictatorship he had imitated the corporatist model of Portugese dictator Antonio Salazar rather than the populist one of Hitler. Equally hated by the Iron Guard and Antonescu, Carol came to serve as the scapegoat for the failures of the Romanian political class. As we have seen, following the abdication the Iron Guard proclaimed Romania a "National Legionnaire State"; to the new king, Michael I, they allotted a merely symbolic role. Antonescu took over leadership of the government as president of the Council of Ministers, gaining the title of "Conducator." Horia Sima, leader of the Iron Guard, became vice president of the Council of Ministers, making him the second highest-ranked man in Romania. The Iron Guard held portfolios in the Ministry of Foreign Affairs (Mihail Sturdza); Internal Affairs (Constantin Petrovicescu, supervised by Ion Antonescu through his confidant and undersecretary of state for internal affairs Colonel Alexandru Rioşanu); National Education, Religion, and the Arts (Traian Brăileanu); Public Works and Communications (Pompiliu Nicolau); and Labor, Health, and Social Security (Vasile Iaşinschi). Antonescu retained control of the War Ministry, but the three undersecretariats went not to politicians, but to career military men. Legionnaires "seconded" those running the Ministry of National Economy and the National Bank. In addition, Legionnaires controlled all of the prefectures, the press, and virtually all senior-level posts in the ministries, excepting only War, Justice (with titular head Mihai Antonescu, another of Ion's confidants), and Agriculture (headed by conservative Nicolae Mareş).

The change in government led to a new wave of anti-Semitic excesses. The exclusion of Jews from the remaining professional associations that had continued to tolerate them and the graffiti that marked Jewish businesses in the provinces were the least of those measures. And yet on September 14, 1940, the same day that he named the Legionnaire cabinet, Marshal Antonescu met with Wilhelm Filderman, the renowned Jewish leader. Antonescu apologized for "romantic incidents" perpetrated by "exploited young men," agreed to overturn such irresponsible decisions as the "abolition" of Judaism, and even "ordered" an end to the painting of the word "Jewish" on stores and businesses.[21] Antonescu wrote to the UER that if the Jews did not "undermine the government," the community had nothing to fear.[22] Strangely, as we have already seen, Filderman's visit was only the first of a series of meetings and other communications with Antonescu, one of the paradoxes of the Romanian Holocaust: Hitler would hardly have received representatives of German Jewry or overturned anti-Jewish measures.

But whatever Antonescu's gestures of moderation, at the grassroots level all hell broke loose. Between September 26 and 30, 1940, Legionnaire police arrested hundreds of Jews in Buzău, Arad, and Iași, holding some of these people for several days, torturing some, and robbing many. Anti-Semitic activists organized boycotts of Jewish stores, while petty officials closed synagogues in Bucharest and the provinces. On October 11, the Legionnaire prefect of Cîmpulung, Cristea Rusu, simply ordered all Jewish-owned stores closed in his jurisdiction. In the company of Legionnaire chief Erhan and the commander of the local garrison, Colonel Mociulski, Rusu carried out the systematic pillaging of Jewish property the next day. Legionnaires and policemen carried out the looting while the soldiers maintained order—had the mob gotten in on the act, there would have been less for the authorities to destroy. Ringleaders of one mob tortured Rabbi Moses Iosif Rubin in order to extract a confession to the effect that he had used his synagogue to hide dynamite intended for sabotage. They then dragged him through the town, between sentinels aiming revolvers at his head, and finally harnessed him and his sons to one of the carts transporting the goods that had been stolen from him.[23]

Elsewhere too mobs plundered Jewish stores and manhandled their owners. On October 21, 1940, the police arrested ten Jews in Vaslui, releasing one for some reason but subjecting the other nine to torture for several days; one of the latter attempted suicide. Officials, neighbors, or ugly crowds expelled many Jews from their homes or confiscated their businesses. Petty officials and greedy competitors took over manufacturing enterprises owned by Jews, and even the pathetic possessions of itinerant peddlers were looted. On October 29, the eighty-five-year-old traveling salesman Paul Leibovici of Bucharest fell under attack by Legionnaires in the commune of Teişani (district of Prahova). These thugs beat the old man in the town hall, took him to the forest, and threatened to hang him if he didn't deliver the goods he had purchased in the villages—these "valuables" were beans and nuts.[24] In that same month a crowd robbed the shop Herman Naftuli Bringles kept in Cernavodă; the mob then shaved the heads of each member of his family, both men and women, before chasing the Jews from the town.[25]

Filderman sent several memoranda regarding the ongoing anti-Semitic persecutions that had occurred throughout October to Ion Antonescu; to the ministers of internal affairs, justice, and labor; to the director of the State Bureau of Investigation; to the mayor of Bucharest; and to the presiding judge of the Court of Appeals.[26] On October 31, Antonescu once again received Filderman, who recorded the following notes shortly thereafter:

> Prime Minister Ion Antonescu . . . [exhorted] the Jewish population to understand the circumstances, without exaggerating isolated instances of abuse that the government had no intention of tolerating, and to encourage the Jews to continue to tend to their affairs. . . . Jews who had arrived in the country after 1919, even those holding Romanian citizenship, would have to leave Romania, while native Jews could work on a proportional numbers basis.[27]

Filderman's diligent efforts proved fruitless: Antonescu was prepared to protect neither the property nor the lives of Romanian Jews at that time.

November 1940 saw the first Jewish deaths at the hands of the "National Legionnaire" government. On November 2, in Bucharest, the Legionnaire police arrested Lucian Rosen, aged fifteen, charging that he had posted Communist handbills. Dragging him to the prefecture, the policemen savagely beat him with a metal object, strangled him, threw him from a sixth-floor window, and finally (on the chance he might still be alive) shot him.[28] On November 22, Legionnaire police arrested the merchant Solomon Klein and discovered 1.5 million lei on his person. The next day his corpse was returned to his family—minus the money—with the explanation that he had thrown himself out a fourth-floor window at police headquarters.[29] On November 23, Teodor Gerber, sixteen years old, was arrested (for the second time in several days); two days later his lifeless body was returned to his parents.[30]

On November 10, 1940, Legionnaire police in Ploieşti burst into the synagogue at 4 Municipal Street to arrest sixty Jews in the middle of services, charging that the ostensible worshippers had come for a Communist meeting. The police took the Jews to headquarters, where they abused and beat them. On the fourteenth of the month Horia Sima ordered them freed. The Ploieşti police, however, refused to comply. On November 27, in defiance of a renewed release order, they took eleven of their captives to a secret location where they were murdered; their bullet-riddled bodies were found in ditches on the outskirts of town the next day.[31]

The Iron Guard didn't reserve its hatred exclusively for the Jews. On November 26 and 27, 1940, sixty-three Romanian politicians, senior military officers, and policemen accused of complicity in the recent arrest and execution of Corneliu Zelea Codreanu (Sima's predecessor as head of the Iron Guard during the reign of Carol II) were executed by Legionnaires in Jilava Prison near Bucharest. Among the victims were former Bucharest prefect Gabriel Marinescu, Generals Gheorghe Argeşeanu and Ion Bengliu, and former head of the intelligence services Mihail Morusov, who, according to the statement of Codreanu's father, used Sima as an informant.[32] Also on November 27, 1940, Nicolae Iorga, former prime minister, preeminent historian, politician of the right, father of "Romanism," xenophobe, and anti-Semite, was assassinated, as was the economist and prominent National Peasant party member Virgil Madgearu. Former prime ministers Constantin Argetoianu, Gheorghe Tătărescu (saved by Alexandru Rioşanu), and Gheorghe Gigurtu (saved by Sima) and former ministers Mihail Ghelmegeanu and Nicolae Marinescu nearly shared the same fate. These assassinations and attempted assassinations sent shock waves through the Romanian political class: no one was safe, anyone could be arbitrarily executed. Where each feared for his life, who would oppose the Iron Guard over a matter so "trivial" as the persecution of a few *Jidani* (the plural form of *Jidan,* the pejorative term for "Jew")?

Whatever misgivings any Romanians may have entertained, Nazi Germany was enthusiastic. The Legionnaire movement received an especially positive evaluation from the SS for these crimes. As Heinrich Himmler wrote to Sima in early December,

During the initial period of [our] takeover, our enemies were [also] found guilty and shot by the movement, outside the scope of the national justice system. . . . In the case of the Legionnaires who avenged the death of their dear captain [and] innumerable comrades, this kind of action is just, since it could never be carried out under the legal system, which is hindered by judicial provisions and will always be subordinate to their formalities. I send you my best wishes, to you and the Legionnaire movement, which has demonstrated so much self-denial on behalf of your fatherland.[33]

And whatever image Antonescu was trying to project during the audiences with Filderman, perhaps his real attitude toward violence—even against Romanians—came out in other statements. The victims of the Jilava murders, Antonescu learned, had been shot repeatedly: 587 separate bullet wounds were found on the bodies of thirteen victims; others had died from blows to the skull with heavy, sharpened objects (perhaps axes); and still others had died from stab wounds.[34] Upon hearing of the savagery of the killings, Antonescu remarked to General Petroviceanu: "I am not sorry about what happened to them, since they caused so much damage to our country."[35] Ironically, even though there had been no love lost between Antonescu and the Legionnaires' victims (Iorga in particular had been close to Carol II, Antonescu's sworn enemy), Antonescu understood that the assassinations could be exploited one day to discredit the Legionnaire movement, which he did, in fact, do following the abortive "Legionnaire Rebellion," the attempted Iron Guard coup d'état, shortly thereafter. For the time being, however, immunity for the Jilava murderers served as a green light inviting the Legionnaires to yet more audacious mayhem.

One of these events was the January 19 murder of the Jew Alexandru Spiegel in Hîrsova. After beating him with a bullwhip (Spiegel suffered severe injury to his genitals), the Legionnaires tied their victim, naked and barefoot, to a post in the town square. Three Iron Guard farmers stood watch to prevent any rescue attempt. It was so cold that they carried out this duty by turns, replacing one another on two-hour shifts. They contrived to prop up the victim's head so that schoolchildren brought in especially for the purpose might bombard him with snowballs. Spiegel passed away at 9:00 P.M. that night.[36]

Between September 6, 1940, and January 22, 1941, anti-Semites murdered eleven Jews in Ploieşti and three in Bucharest. Physical abuse and robbery accompanied each other, though the sadistic pleasure the bullies derived from torturing a captive apparently was often an end in itself. On November 6, 1940, Legionnaires in Bucharest arrested and beat one hundred Jews at the Iron Guard Center at 1 Traian Street. They then escorted them in columns to Legionnaire headquarters on Roma Street, where they continued to abuse them from noon until midnight; the victims were then released. That same day another group of thugs dragged thirty more Jews to police headquarters, where they were brutally beaten.[37] Hundreds of other Jews in Bucharest underwent similar treatment on November 10.

On November 22, the terror exploded in Călăraşi. Legionnaire goons rounded up forty-five Jewish men in a midnight raid, cramming them into a cellar at their headquarters, where they beat them "almost ceaselessly." Having stretched them out "naked, face to the floor," teams of four Legionnaires at a time beat their victims with wet cords, fresh teams relieving those who tired. Rabbi Moses Faibis Goldenberg was singled out for special attention because he had been accused of attempting to arrange the murder of two key Legionnaires in order to thwart anticipated attacks on the Jewish community. Dr. Silviu Cohn was alleged to have been Rabbi Goldenberg's co-conspirator. Wounded twice during World War I, Cohn was tied to an execution post in the town center, where the pharmacist Duţescu slapped him until blood streamed down his face; children and hoodlums taunted him and pulled his hair. When the Legionnaires had finished the beatings—on November 25—they ordered all the Jews to leave town within five days, holding some back temporarily, however, by order of the mayor, to sweep the streets. Administrative officials complicit in the episode arranged a formal ban on the exiles' travel to Bucharest, Ploieşti, Brăila, or Constanţa. Threats and other forms of pressure forced a number of Jewish merchants to sell all of their property to Legionnaires. The merchant Iancu Lerey, a disabled veteran of World War I (his hand had been amputated after the battle of Tatlogeac), was forced to sell out to his partner, Tudor Velicu, at 20 percent of the value of his share.[38]

Anti-Semitic brutes, officials, and mobs forced Jews to perform humiliating labor not only in Călăraşi. On December 12, the police commissioner of Tîrgovişte, a man named Vătăşescu, ordered the town's Jews, regardless of age, social status, or education, to clean mud from the streets.[39] Similar episodes took place in Brăila, Buzău, Constanța, and Petroșani.[40] In the commune of Pungești (district of Vaslui) the members of the Jewish community—men, women, children, the elderly—were forced to perform labor that included cleaning floors, sweeping streets, and constructing roads; the most powerful landowner in the area, Jack Marcopol, arranged to have them perform labor on his private property.[41]

Eager to criticize Iron Guard "lawlessness," Ion Antonescu expressed indignation about some of these departures from good order at the January 11, 1941, meeting of the Council of Ministers.[42] Nothing the Conducator said or did restrained the outrages of the winter of 1940–1941. The members of the Iron Guard drew their symbol on the heads of their victims; they expropriated their property; they expelled Jews from towns. In their zeal to do harm to the Jews the anti-Semites thought little of the harm their actions might cause the majority population, with only an occasional exception: in Urziceni on November 5, for instance, a Jewish dentist, the only one for miles around, was not only permitted but positively forced to remain.[43]

The expropriations had another unanticipated effect. Besides destroying a large number of businesses and impairing the national economy, as both Marshal Antonescu and even representatives of Germany acknowledged, these seizures sometimes led to a strengthening of ethnic German capital in Romania. The Nazis' racial ideology made the *Volksdeutsch* (German people) abroad virtual countrymen; German diplomacy undertook the advocacy of their interests. In the case of Romania this translated into the definition of the ethnic German minority as a privileged group. The liberal leader Constantin I. C. Brătianu pointed out this situation to Ion Antonescu in a December 18, 1940, letter in which he argued that "the liquidation of Jewish businesses" for which Romanian buyers could not be found and the "terror" fomented by anti-Semitic youth opened broad new opportunities for the German minority to expand its role in the economy. "Instead of nationalization, we are experiencing 'denationalization.'"[44] Ethnic Germans benefited from the support of Germany's foreign investment banks and proved themselves quite capable of exerting influence on the Legionnaires to help them take over Jewish firms. This occurred in November and December 1940 in Petroșani, Sibiu, Mediaș, and Brașov.

In *Cartea neagră* Matatias Carp's analysis of the seizures and sales shows that the number of robberies was low during September 1940 and that there probably were no forced expropriations during that month. October showed a clear-cut increase in the number of such incidents in six localities, half in Moldavia (the only incident in Transylvania took place in Alba Iulia). November saw the greatest number, since cases of pillaging and forced transfers of ownership occurred in about forty-five localities; of this number, twenty-two took place in Transylvania, the remainder being evenly divided between Walachia and Moldavia. In December there was a reduction of about 30 percent in the number of communities witnessing this type of activity, though now Bucharest alone accounted for 10 percent of all incidents. On a regional basis Transylvania continued to lead, followed closely by Walachia and then Moldavia. Just as Bucharest was atypical in December, in that month and in January 1941 the city of Iași demonstrated an anomaly in the other direction: its major Jewish population experienced less suffering than in September, October, or November. But perhaps this had more to do with the soothing effects of the six million lei the community paid to the district's Legionnaire commander, Vlad Sturdza, than to any lack of zeal for persecution in that city itself.[45]

The targets of expropriation and plunder varied greatly: schools, synagogues, even cemeteries were not exempt; above all, commercial and industrial firms attracted "purchasers," with preference going to stores, hotels, and restaurants. Money, jewels, and furs were popular items, and therefore their enthusiasts "Romanized" many a private home. Interested neighbors "bought," "appropriated," or "confiscated" cattle, sheep, horses, timber, firewood, radios, and grain.

On December 9, 1940, the Union of Jewish Communities of Romania submitted a twenty-six-page appeal to Marshal Antonescu, summarizing the arrests, physical abuse, expropriations, and murders thirty-nine Jewish communities had experienced during the preceding months. Antonescu replied by ordering Minister of the Interior Constantin Petrovicescu, a Legionnaire, to open an investigation. But even though this interchange took place a month before the antagonism between Antonescu and the Iron Guard came to a head, his action does suggest the strain that had come to suffuse their relations by year's end:

I will not be able to tolerate indefinitely disorder which shakes the entire country. . . . I do not protect [those] Jews who are primarily guilty of the misfortunes afflicting our nation. At the same time, as head of the government, I cannot tolerate acts that compromise the effort to achieve recovery by means of law and order, an effort impeded daily by the thoughtless actions of people unconscious of the evil they are causing to our nation and to the Legionnaire movement. For the last time I am appealing to those who are supposed to wield authority within the [Iron Guard] and to those who bear governmental responsibilities to repudiate these actions that, while exacerbating our situation, serve no useful purpose.[46]

That a crisis was brewing between Antonescu and the Guard seems further indicated by the fact that his previous order went unheeded. A new thirty-eight-page memorandum signed by Wilhelm Filderman on January 9, 1941, stated that the investigation had as often as not been carried out by the very parties guilty of the outrages, who intimidated the victims into stating that nothing had happened to them. The Union of Jewish Communities of Romania report contained a long list of incidents, beatings, and seizures of property that had taken place in more than thirty localities since December 9: more than 100 arrests, 120 cases of physical abuse, and nearly 300 confiscations of shops or money.[47] And these figures do not represent the whole picture either, since the fear of reprisals held many Jews back from appealing to the authorities, even through the Union of Jewish Communities of Romania.

This was, of course, only one source of the friction between the Conducator and the Guard, but it did contribute to the crisis that soon broke out and to which we will turn our attention momentarily. One should not overstate the importance of differences on the Jewish question: as late as January 10, 1941, Antonescu reproached the minister of the interior for not having interned illegal Jewish immigrants responsible for engaging in commerce, promoting communism, and other alleged misdeeds.[48] But Antonescu did represent a different brand of—or, rather, an approach to—anti-Semitism, one slightly less virulent and slightly more considered than that of the Iron Guard. Despite this, we shall soon have occasion to see how even after his victory other considerations moved Antonescu to countenance, if not urge, far more horrible outrages against the Jews.

THE LEGIONNAIRE REBELLION AND THE BUCHAREST POGROM,
JANUARY 21–23, 1941

On January 10, at the last meeting of the Council of Ministers attended by
Legionnaires, Antonescu expressed his concern over the economic disruption caused by the Iron Guard's anti-Semitic excesses, which, for him,
were emblematic of that organization's general irresponsible radicalism:

> Terrible things are occurring in our country. The country is being bol-
> shevized. Bolsheviks have penetrated the Legionnaire movement. In
> Brăila, for example, [Jewish] intellectuals were made to clean up snow:
> lawyers, doctors, rabbis [alike]. . . . Jewish businesses and stores have
> been seized, thereby destroying both trade and credit. Under such con-
> ditions, after two months we will be confronting an economic catastro-
> phe. Factories are no longer shipping finished goods because the Jewish
> store owners are no longer buying merchandise.[49]

Under the guise of Romanization, the Legionnaires had exploited the state
apparatus—the police in particular—for purposes of outright robbery.
Most businesses that "passed into the hands" of Legionnaires had quickly
fallen into ruin. On a national scale this had produced a dire impact. Antonescu, an army officer who represented what Barrington Moore has
called "the honorable fascism of the clerks," did want the economic dis-
possession of the Jews and their physical removal, but he had considered
this the end result to be realized only gradually and lawfully. In this he had
the tacit agreement of his German friends, who needed a well-functioning
Romanian economy to support their anticipated war effort against the
USSR.

Since at least 1935, Romanian oil had been a preoccupation of the
Berlin authorities; in the summer of 1938, it became a principal interest of
German diplomacy.[50] In an August 8, 1940, letter to Prime Minister Ion
Gigurtu, Goering made the improvement of relations directly conditional
on deliveries of oil.[51] Relations between the Iron Guard and Berlin had not
proven a simple matter. While the National Socialist German Workers'
Party (NSDAP) and its Sicherheitsdienst (SD, or the security service) and
SS—the ideological and repressive organs of Nazism—had encouraged
the Legionnaires, the same could not be said for Germany's Foreign Ministry, the Economics Ministry, and the Supreme Command of the Armed
Forces, which rightly feared that the Iron Guard would disrupt the Roma-

nian economy.[52] Another factor tipped the scales in favor of Antonescu in Berlin: the Romanian army, which, despite certain sympathies of some superior officers for the Legionnaires, was not dominated by the latter.

Berlin had not failed to note the strained relations between the Legionnaires and Antonescu. As early as November 23, 1940, German Foreign Minister Joachim von Ribbentrop had warned his Legionnaire counterpart, Mihail Sturdza, not to allow ideological fervor to jeopardize the requirements of the military.[53] The next day Sturdza received similar advice from Field Marshal Wilhelm Keitel.[54] Antonescu was aware of these conversations and sought to demonstrate his de facto leadership power over the Iron Guard by forbidding Sturdza from trying to directly influence Hitler. Instead, he himself visited the Führer on January 14, 1941, winning him over, as an observer recalled, to his own position:

> the main difficulty [were] elements who do not realize that the revolution is not a condition to be perpetuated but . . . followed immediately by constructive activity. . . . Following his line of thought, [Hitler] recalled, with a certain liveliness in his voice, that he had needed six or seven years to eliminate those elements who had not understood. He added that Marshal Antonescu might be forced to proceed in the same fashion.[55]

In a still less veiled reference to his purge of the Brownshirts in the "Night of the Long Knives," Hitler told Antonescu, "You have to get rid of . . . fanatical militants who think that, by destroying everything, they are doing their duty."[56] Nor did the United States remain totally in the dark, for in early February 1941, the German economic attaché in Bucharest told the American ambassador that "everything accomplished in the name of Romanization of businesses" would have to be undone and that although "the Jews must go away . . . they would be liquidated gradually and in accordance with the law."[57] Antonescu's reining in of the radicals had already gotten under way by January 18, when he eliminated the position of Romanization commissar, an act Iron Guard leaders interpreted as an overt attack. After Antonescu's return from Germany the tension between him and the Iron Guard had intensified; some Legionnaires now began to demand his recall and the establishment of a "pure" Legionnaire government led by Horia Sima.

The murder of a German air force commander, Doering, in Bucharest, probably by an agent of the British Intelligence Service, was used by both sides as a pretext to start hostilities. On January 20, 1941, Antonescu dismissed Minister of Internal Affairs Petrovicescu, who was close to the Iron Guard, ostensibly for having failed to protect Doering. Antonescu also dismissed Alexandru Ghika, director of the police forces, and Constantin Mamuica, director of another department at the Ministry of Internal Affairs. The Guard replied by refusing to accept these dismissals and proceeding to arm its followers. The Legionnaires barricaded the Criminal Investigation Bureau floor at the Bucharest Prefecture of Police, its central headquarters on Roma Street, and the police barracks. By the evening of January 21, the mutiny had spread throughout the country. At first German Ambassador Wilhelm Fabricius tried to mediate, seeking to persuade the Guard to acknowledge Antonescu's authority. Indeed, agents of the SD and the SS in Bucharest initially threw their support behind the rebels; subsequently, they sought to protect the Legionnaires from Antonescu's wrath and helped hundreds escape to Germany. (In his memoirs Walter Schellenberg, acting head of Amt VI [foreign intelligence], even cited Reinhard Heydrich as the instigator of the putsch!)[58] Whatever the Germans' original confusion, however, and despite whatever cross-purposes may have been at work, Hitler's personal order to put German troops at Antonescu's disposal soon reestablished German unity of purpose and tipped the balance in the Conducător's favor. The Führer's phone call reassuring Antonescu of his support came in a sense after the fact: loyalist forces were already mopping up the last rebels.[59] On February 6, Manfred von Killinger, the new German ambassador, would report that Antonescu had emerged in definitive control, thanks to Hitler and the German army.[60]

Suppression of the rebellion cost the Romanian army twenty-one dead and fifty-three wounded.[61] In the country as a whole 374 persons reportedly died and 380 were wounded—Jews, Guardists, soldiers—but these figures may be low.[62] Of equal or greater significance were the repressions carried out afterward. What happened to the Legionnaires after the rebellion? Rank-and-file members not involved were left alone, though Legionnaire activities henceforth came under close secret police surveillance. Some leaders found protection from German diplomats or security personnel, who smuggled them out of the country. Many other rank and file and some of the involved leaders surrendered; the army interned them at first, sending them to the front at the beginning of the war against the USSR.

July 1941 found the following leaders condemned to life sentences at hard labor: Horia Sima, leader of the Legionnaire movement and onetime vice president of the Council of Ministers; his deputy, Traian Borobaru; Vasile Iaşinschi, former minister of labor; Corneliu Georgescu and Constantin Pop, both former undersecretaries at the Ministry of National Economy; Nicolae Pătraşcu, Iron Guard general secretary; Viorel Trifa, president of the National Union of Christian Romanian Students; Dumitru Grozea, head of the Legionnaire Worker's Corps; Ilie Gîrneaţă, head of the Legionnaires' charitable activities; and others. With the exception of a certain Sîrbu, all these leading Iron Guard members escaped, most of them with German help, and ended up in Berlin.[63] Sentenced to prison terms ranging between five and fifteen years were Alexandru Ghika, former director of the police at the Ministry of Internal Affairs; Constantin Mamuica, former departmental director in the Ministry of Internal Affairs; and Mihail Sturdza, former minister of foreign affairs.

Those found guilty of the murder of the inmates at Jilava Prison on November 26 and 27 were sentenced to death: Stefan Zăvoianu, former general secretary of the Ministry of Internal Affairs and former prefect of the Iron Guard police; Gheorghe Creţu, Octavian Marcu, Constantin Savu, and Ioan Tănăsescu, former members of the Legionnaire police; and Dumitru Anghel, a rank-and-file Legionnaire. Sentenced to death in absentia were Dumitru Grozea and thirteen other Legionnaires, most of them former policemen, including the murderers of Nicolae Iorga.[64]

In all 9,352 Legionnaires were arrested for participation in the rebellion, nearly half of them in Bucharest. Of these, 2,980 had been tried by August 1941, 1,842 receiving jail terms.[65] Their grants of protection to the rebels had so compromised the SS and SD in Antonescu's eyes that officially they had to withdraw all their representatives from Romania.[66]

The Legionnaire groups that sought refuge in Germany continued to trouble Romanian-German relations. There is no reason why Hitler might not have kept them as a possible Trojan horse for insertion at a later date, though his first impulse seems to have been to offer their heads to Antonescu as a gesture of support: Hitler wanted to cement the relationship as he contemplated the impending invasion of the Soviet Union. In May the German ambassador told the marshal that not only had "the Führer decided to hand over Horia Sima and all the Legionnaires who are in Germany to [you] if [you] so desire," but that "we have requested in writing from all the Legionnaire refugees in Germany a . . . pledge not to engage

in political activity." More remarkably, Antonescu indicated his indifference, perhaps motivated by the desire to demonstrate the trust he felt toward the Führer, perhaps as a gesture of magnanimity toward the radical
right in his own country: "I thank the Führer for this new act of consideration toward Romania, but . . . it would be painful for me to sentence and
execute men who once collaborated with my government." None of this,
however, meant that the Conducator would tolerate shenanigans: "I do ask
that Herr Hitler keep a close watch over all Romanian political refugees,
[and if] they fail to live by the pledges they have made, I will demand that
they be extradited and brought to justice."[67]

Many of the refugees were soon at work in the Heinkel airplane factory in the Berkenbrüken camp; some of the leaders cultivated their frus-
trated ambitions from their exile in Rostock.[68] It was thence that Sima
slipped away in late 1942, turning up in Italy to embitter relations among
all involved. Hitler in particular already had been angered by political
overtures to him by Sima. Sima's flight may have been facilitated by Kurt
Geisler, the former Gestapo head in Romania, settling an old score with
the Antonescu government that had expelled him.[69] When Sima escaped
Ribbentrop accused Himmler himself of involvement, triggering Hitler's
wrath against the SS chief.[70] Following Sima's escape the Berkenbrüken
Legionnaires were transferred to Buchenwald, others to Dachau; nevertheless, one should bear in mind that in the camps these wayward but basically devoted fascists enjoyed privileged status. In early 1943, a group
of leading Legionnaires disavowed Sima, working for improved relations
with Marshal Antonescu. Sima was eventually extradited from Italy and
was for a while under arrest in Berlin.[71] After Romania broke with the
Axis powers on August 23, 1944, the dream of the ultras came true, and
Hitler permitted them to form a Romanian government-in-exile with Sima
at its head; by that time, however, it was too late.

Back in the spring of 1941, three Legionnaires had been executed for
the murder of a Jew and the attempted murder of another, the acts committed after the coup attempt; this punitive response was the Antonescu
government's attempt to show that it meant to enforce "law and order."
Their sentences were exceptional: few were punished for crimes against
the Jewish population during the Legionnaire Rebellion.[72] And yet the
paralysis of government during those two days had afforded the opportunity for the outbreak of some of the worst anti-Semitic violence that had
so far taken place, the chief focus of the last part of this chapter.

*   *   *

From the start Legionnaire propaganda named the Jews as instigators of their conflict with Antonescu. As such, one flier of a Legionnaire student organization demanded the "replacement" of all "Jewish-oriented persons" in the government.[73] The Legionnaire press organ, *Cuvîntul* (Word), stressed the centrality of "all of the *Jidani* and bandits in our country" as targets in their planned coup.[74] Dumitru Grozea cursed the "Masonic hydra" that showed its strength through government officials who had "sold out to the Jews."[75] Elsewhere, *Cuvîntul Nostru* (Our Word) editorialized that the need to exorcise the "Judeo-Masonic plot" demanded the union of army and Guard, arguing that "if someone has to be shot, let [it not be] our own. . . . We have other targets."[76]

Such propaganda—indeed, the entire political show of the five-month Legionnaire government—constituted a tremendous incitement to pogroms. In the chaos caused by the struggle between the Iron Guard and Antonescu, many saw the moment for the "Great Pogrom." In Bucharest alone at least 120 Jews would pay with their lives for this perception; Carp lists 116 victims by name, along with four unidentified corpses.[77] This list matches almost exactly another published on September 20, 1941, by *The Record* of the United Romanian Jews of America,[78] though the latter adds Teodor Gerber and Lucien Rosen (killed by Legionnaires prior to the mutiny) and Max London (murdered by Legionnaires afterward).[79] The Romanian chargé d'affaires in Washington, D.C., Brutus Coste, acknowledged a figure of 118 in a conversation with Ray Atherton, head of the European Division of the State Department, but apologetically blamed "irresponsible, marginal elements."[80] Raul Hilberg cites German and American sources on the Bucharest pogrom in support of figures of 630 dead and 400 disappeared.[81] Most likely, these sources exaggerate the numbers: the Jewish community of Bucharest was, after all, in a better position to compile evidence regarding the number of victims; this was the source for the figures cited in Carp's book in 1946.

Most of the murders during the three-day rebellion took place in Jilava Forest, the rest at the slaughterhouse at the intersection of the roads of Fundeni and Pentelimon, in Bucureștii Noi District, and in the streets and houses of various residential districts. On January 21, the Legionnaires gathered about two hundred Jews into the basement of their headquarters. The fascists did not forget to take all of the victims' valuables before they set upon the Jews. They next drove the Jews in the basement up to the attic under a rain of blows with truncheons and iron bars. The Legionnaires then beat them with a bullwhip and copper rods on the face, palms, buttocks, and soles of the feet in a room especially set aside for that purpose. Prisoners were finally made to drink from the basin in which Rabbi Gutman had been permitted to wash the blood from his head.

The next morning the prisoners were divided into two groups. The fortunate ones were taken to Strauleşti, on the outskirts of Bucharest, where they were beaten for two more days, had rifle shots aimed just above their heads, and then underwent a last robbery (who knows? perhaps some of those tricky Jews had managed to hide something the first time around); they were then released to walk home in tatters. Other Legionnaires trucked the second group of more than ninety Jews via Giurgiu Road to Jilava Forest, where they shot most of them, generally one to three times, mainly in the head. Some of those in the first truck were dispatched near the bridge over the Sabar River, after which the murderers stole the gold teeth, clothes, and shoes from the eighty-six corpses that they left lying under the trees.[82]

Some of the victims, wounded only, managed to escape, including Rabbi Gutman. After the murderers left, Gutman took the road to Bucharest, upon which he met two Romanian gendarmes, who for some reason let him pursue his journey; German soldiers, however, detained him, taking him to the Jilava town hall, where seven Jews, some of them wounded, were already being held. That evening all were once again taken to the forest and shot, but once again the rabbi miraculously survived. Two Legionnaires stealing clothes from the dead discovered the survivor, considered whether to shoot him, but then decided to return him to the town hall, where he was merely beaten, had his hair and beard torn out, and was informed that he would be shot anyway. However, the gendarmes freed him. One of them even accompanied him back to the forest to identify the bodies of two of his sons.[83] Miguel A. Rivera, the Chilean diplomat, described Rabbi Gutman's martyrdom in one of his reports.[84]

Additionally, thirteen Jews were murdered at the Bucharest slaughterhouse, but two escaped, critically but not mortally wounded. Those killed included Millo Beiler and the Rauch brothers, disemboweled, their intestines hung like neckties on other corpses, which were displayed on meat hooks[85] and labeled "Kosher meat."[86]

Many Jews met their deaths in their own homes. For example, sev-

eral members of the Frînghieru family, including four children, were murdered in their house at 15 Intrarea Colentina. Two other children who were
in bed at the time, Aron and Haia, miraculously survived, even though
several bullets were fired at them.[87] The bullet aimed to kill little
Rodriques Honores Brickman of 9 Mihai Voda Street, however, did not go
astray.[88]

Severe beatings and other forms of humiliation usually preceded the
murders, and indeed it was the physical abuse that constituted the favored
medium by which the Legionnaires and their friends expressed their apti-
tudes. Many Jews were abused at the Bucharest Prefecture of Police,
about three hundred at the Malbin synagogue, and a number of others at
the headquarters of the Union of Jewish Communities and the Fifteenth
Police Precinct on Matei Basarab Street. The women were, by and large,
released after physical abuse, which explains the small number of
women's names that appears on the lists of murder victims.

The goings-on at the police precinct may perhaps be taken as typical
of the episodes of mass physical abuse. There two police commissioners
(Legionnaires, of course) supervised a team of 40 workers from the Par-
comet plant who volunteered to beat 150 captives between early evening
on January 21 and early afternoon on January 23. Guests from other Legionnaire centers came to observe, occasionally getting in a few good
licks of their own. One of the diversions the revelers most enjoyed was in-
venting charges, "convicting" their prisoners, and then administering
them fifty or a hundred lashes with a bullwhip. As usual, the pogromists
had helped themselves to whatever valuables their victims happened to
have on their persons, and after the beatings they sheared their victims'
hair with hedge cutters. Finally, they forced their charges to swallow large
amounts of a homemade purgative consisting of magnesium salt (150–
160 grams) mixed with petroleum, gasoline, and vinegar, and then the Legionnaires crammed their captives into a crowded room to swelter in their
own fecal matter until the guards grew bored and allowed the victims to
leave.[89]

Six synagogues were vandalized and looted in Bucharest: the
Sephardic synagogue on Negru-Voda Street, Congregation Beth Horni-
draș Vechiu at 78 Calea Mosilor, Congregation Podul Mogoșoaia on
Atena Street, the synagogue on St. Vineri Street, "Fraterna" synagogue of
3 Mamulari Street, and "Sinagoga Mare" at 11 Dr. Beck Street. Four were
set ablaze, two of these totally destroyed in the flames.[90]

Carp's *Cartea neagră* lists the names and addresses of 1,107 Jews tormented or murdered during the Legionnaire Rebellion. A majority, 615 people, of the victims of robbery lived (or had lived) in the Dudesti Quarter, known for its high density of predominantly poor Jewish residents. Calea Moşilor and the Moşilor Quarter accounted for nearly 150 victims. In the Văcăreşti neighborhood and at Calea Rahovei and the surrounding area, 136 Jews were robbed. More than thirty victims were registered in other neighborhoods of Bucharest.[91] In all, the anti-Semitic rioting directly touched at least 1,360 Jews.[92]

In his postwar Spanish emigration Horia Sima admitted that "these Jews became the victims of uncontrolled . . . elements at the periphery of the Legionnaire movement . . . while the heads of the Legionnaire units were busy containing the rebellion of Marshal Antonescu." Nevertheless, the Iron Guard leader argued that the number of victims among the Jewish population of the capital "must be attributed to the risk this people brought on itself" when it "plotted to trigger an internal conflict": the recent mayhem should be accounted to the Jews' leaders and only to "peripheral elements" of the Legionnaire movement.[93]

*   *   *

The five months between the Legionnaire Rebellion and Romania's entry into World War II brought Romanian Jews a hiatus of relative physical safety. Nevertheless, Jews still died as a consequence of their ethnicity. The agreement formalizing the Soviet occupation of Bessarabia and Bukovina foresaw the departure of those inhabitants who did not wish to become Soviet citizens and the emigration from Romania of those who preferred to live under the Soviets. Joint Romanian-Soviet committees worked toward that goal. In Bukovina a committee operated in Burdujeni until Romania closed the border in January 1941, which caught by surprise 137 people who wanted to leave, 110 of them Jews and 27 Christians. The latter were sent back to the places in Romania where they had resided; the Jews were detained at the Burdujeni train station. Romanian border guards later escorted the Jews, including women and children, through the nighttime snow to the border, where they forced them at gunpoint to attempt crossing to the Soviet side. The Soviets had just finished mining the border zone, so many of the Jews were killed or injured in explosions. Others fell when the alarmed Soviet border guards fired at them, not having been alerted to the plans of the Romanians. For their part, the Romanian guards fired upon those Jews who tried to return. As of February only fifty-eight of these Jews remained alive, interned under hellish conditions in Burdujeni until May, when they were transferred to the Tîrgu Jiu camp for political prisoners and Jews.[94]

From late June 1940 to the end of May 1941, more than 600 Jews were slaughtered in Romania, at least 450 of them during the summer 1940 events at Galați and Dorohoi. In late 1940 and early 1941, Legionnaires killed 136—in Bucharest 3 were murdered before the rebellion, 120 during, and only 1 after it. Eleven others perished in violence in Ploiești on the eve of the rebellion and one in Hîrsova. The figure of six hundred is probably lower than the actual total, including, as it does, the official (i.e., minimal) number of victims of the Dorohoi pogrom (fifty); other sources suggest something more like two hundred victims during the Dorohoi pogrom. Dozens of Jews were thrown from moving trains, but their number probably never will be known. Neither does the estimate include the fifty-two or so who died in Burdujeni.

The overwhelming responsibility for the murders, robberies, and other abuses must be borne by military personnel and policemen, the latter often Legionnaires, though these galvanized a more diffuse—but much broader—popular malice. Still, it is important to bear in mind that there was no systematic and centralized plan for these massacres; in 1940 and early 1941, the state had not formulated such a plan.

[CHAPTER 3]

The Massacres at the Beginning of the War

THE WORST of the early, popular violence was still to come. The initiation of war against the Soviet Union signaled the opportunity for the mob, bolstered by policemen and off-duty soldiers and now supported by elements of officialdom in the first primitive attempts at forced evacuations, to turn to murder and mayhem in the streets of city, town, and village; for the first time Jews were crowded onto trains and transported from place to place without water, food, or the chance to relieve themselves away from the rolling stock in which they were entombed, a new form of mass murder soon taken over by the central government as part of an overall strategy for handling "the Jewish question." The mob's cruelty and greed took the form of truly shocking torture, rape, killing, and robbery, all continuing earlier precedents but achieving spectacular new heights of barbarism. And yet the widespread occurrence of these episodes, their intimate connection to the war itself, the participation of Germans stationed in Romania, and the experience of murder by transport all combined to point to a new chapter in the history of Romanian anti-Semitism and the Romanian Holocaust that would get under way only as the state itself—under the inspiration of Marshall Antonescu and his cabinet—began to gain sway over events.

THE IAŞI POGROM

In late June and early July 1941, thousands of Jews were killed in one of the most savage pogroms of World War II, the Iaşi pogrom, perhaps the most infamous event in the history of the Holocaust in Romania. What follows in this section recounts an anti-Semitic outburst of immense proportions, one that was neither isolated nor happenstance but, rather, part of a larger pattern of mayhem planned and enacted by Romanism fascists inside and outside the government.

In the view of Matatias Carp, the Iaşi pogrom was a natural culmination of decades of state and popular anti-Semitism, that fervent nationalist bigotry manifested in no fewer than 196 restrictive laws adopted between 1867 and 1913 and given more virulent expression during those years when European fascism was ascendent. But these phenomena were not introduced by the fascists: mass expulsions; social, educational, and employment discrimination; mob violence and the terrorism of hooligans; the existence of social and political organizations for the promotion of the most lurid anti-Semitic propaganda; robbery, rapine, and vandalism; and murder and pogroms—these all developed slowly and grandly over the course of several generations.[1]

The Iaşi pogrom was conditioned by two sets of circumstances. The first, as Carp has emphasized, was historical: the city of Iaşi was steeped in a hoary anti-Semitic tradition stretching back at least a century; Iaşi was to Romanian anti-Semitism what Vienna was to Nazi Jew-hatred. Both A. C. Cuza's violently anti-Semitic Christian National Defense League and its offshoot, Corneliu Zelea Codreanu's Legion of the Archangel Michael (the Iron Guard), were born in Iaşi. The second set of circumstances involved the convergence of those factors conditioning Romania's entrance into World War II. Both official and popular propaganda in Iaşi cast many of the events leading to this ill-considered adventure as part of a struggle against "world Jewry," painting Romania's Jews as "enemy aliens," "Bolshevik agents," "factors of dissolution," and "parasites on the Romanian nation."

On the eve of the war some 100,000 people inhabited the city of Iaşi, 50,000 of them Jews. Since the city was close to the Soviet frontier, it became the focus of many of the anti-Semitic measures that accompanied plans to join Germany's invasion of the USSR. Several days before Romania joined the war Ion Antonescu ordered the compilation of lists of "all Jews, Communist agents, or sympathizers in each region."[2] More ominously, by Order No. 4147, issued at approximately the same time, he initiated preparations for the expulsion of all Jews aged eighteen to sixty from villages located between the Siret and Prut Rivers and their confinement in the camp established at Tîrgu Jiu in Walachia several years earlier for political opponents; trains would be leaving on June 21. The families of these deportees were forced to relocate to urban communities. Forty-eight hours were to be allotted for the operation.[3] That order was counter-signed by General Popescu, deputy minister of the interior, and was sent to the chief of staff of the army, the General Inspectorate of the Gendarmerie, the National General Directorate of the Police, and the administrations of all prefectures.

Several days before the onset of war, during a conference that brought together the leadership of the gendarmerie legions (units) of Romania, General C. Z. Vasiliu, general inspector of the gendarmerie, ordered *curăţarea terenului* (the cleansing of the land), meaning the liquidation of all Jews in rural areas, and the internment or deportation of those living in urban areas.[4] While waiting to be assigned their positions in Bessarabia and Bukovina when the war should get under way, some of the gendarmes were stationed in Iaşi, where they were on hand just in time to take part in "action" against the city's Jewish population. During his trial in 1946, Antonescu would try to justify the concentration and deportation of the Jewish population from Moldavia by citing "a military principle that states that the population living close to the front must be displaced."[5] Antonescu also claimed that there had been "German demands" that the Jews of Moldavia be "organized into ghettos." None of this explained, however, the murderous intent of the population movement imposed on the Jews, nor, indeed, why the leader of Romania would submit to pressure by another country.[6]

It is obvious that the presence of a substantial Jewish population close to the front displeased both Romanian and German military officials. In a deposition of November 12, 1945, Lieutenant Colonel Traian Borcescu, former chief of the Secretariat of the Secret Intelligence Service (SSI), identified the brains behind the operation to remove that population: "the Second Section [i.e., army counterintelligence] under the chief of staff was handling the displacement of the Jewish population of Moldavia . . . under the leadership of Colonel Gheorghe Petrescu."[7] The Second Section included three statistical offices (in Bucharest, Iași, and Cluj) and followed the activities of political parties and ethnic groups. Borcescu may have had an ulterior motive in identifying the military as bearing greater responsibility than the SSI, but in actuality the two cooperated closely. But even when discussing the culpability of his own organization, Borcescu pointed to military complicity, if not leadership: while acknowledging that "the preparation and execution of the massacres at Iași were the work of the first operational echelon [of the SSI]," he reported that when Eugen Cristescu (the SSI's director) returned from Bucharest, "he told me, 'I scored the major achievements in Moldavia by working with [the Second Section], and particularly with Colonel Radu Dinulescu and Colonel Gheorghe Petrescu.'" In any case, Grigore Petrovici, former SSI agent, testified after the war that "in paving the groundwork for the Iași pogrom, Junius Lecca, SSI station chief [of Iași], had played a major role by supplying intelligence concerning Jewish residences and centers."[8]

According to Cristescu's postwar statements, the Iași pogrom had been orchestrated by the German Gestapo, the SD, the Geheime Feldpolizei (secret military field police), and their Romanian agents, but not by the SSI or the Abwehr (Military Intelligence Office of the High Command of the German Armed Forces).[9] Cristescu's statements suggest that those German security agencies had been working secretly in Romania, without the knowledge of Romanian officials; here one must recall that SD and Gestapo representatives had indeed been expelled from Romania for their role in the Legionnaire Rebellion. Cristescu underscored the fact that the only German secret service officially admitted in Romania was the Abwehr,

> whose liaison officer with the SSI was Major Hermann von Stransky. The name of that German officer was often cited in testimony concerning the organization of the Iași pogrom. A nephew of Ribbentrop, married to a Romanian from Galați, after having spent a long time in Romania and speaking fluent Romanian, von Stransky [helped the Antonescu regime by informing] the SSI regularly on the failed attempts by Horia Sima to cross the border in January and February 1941.[10]

But it is not unthinkable that von Stransky might have been an agent not only of the Abwehr but also of other German services. In any case, von

Stransky maintained strong ties with the SSI through the person of Lieutenant Colonel Ionescu-Micandru, chief of the "Germany" branch of the SSI.

Just before Romania's entry into the war the "first operational echelon" of the SSI was created, based on orders of the Office of the President of the Council of Ministers and the Office of the Chief of Staff of the army; its official mission was "to defend the rear against sabotage, espionage, and acts of terror," and the echelon was composed of about 160 men. On June 18, 1941, this unit traveled by motor vehicle to Moldavia.[11] Lieutenant Colonel Borcescu later stated that one of the unit's secret goals had been the elimination, through deportation and repression, of the Jews throughout Moldavia. SSI division director Florin Becescu-Georgescu, working toward that goal, had brought to Iași the files of Jews and Communists before leaving Bucharest. After the Iași pogrom the unit headed for Chișinău, where new versions of the Iași massacres were prepared by the same SSI teams. The echelon also journeyed to Tighina and Tiraspol, where it organized looting, and then to Odessa, where it took part in further massacres.[12] Elements of the operational echelon engaged in systematic looting and murder in Bessarabia and Transnistria.

Events had begun to unfold more rapidly after German and Romanian military operations against the USSR began on June 22, 1941. Soon thousands of Jews from rural areas of northern Moldavia were put aboard trains and then interned in the camps of Tîrgu Jiu, Craiova, Caracal, and Turnu Severin. On that same day a report by Colonel Constantin Chirilovici, police superintendent of Iași, stated that some Legionnaires "were taking a sort of course under the tutelage of two uniformed officers, a captain and a sublieutenant."[13] These were apparently sessions organized by the SSI to prepare former Iron Guards for an anticipated anti-Jewish action. One of the officers was Gheorghe Balotescu, a head of the SSI in Iași; the other was probably Emil Tulbure, also a member of the SSI station there. Both held identification papers from the chief of staff of the Romanian army, indicating that not only the SSI was involved.

On June 24, the Soviet air force conducted a raid against Iași (in the Rîpa Galbenă area and the train station), producing minor damage and only a few casualties. But this provided the spark the fascists were able to fan into widespread anti-Semitic hysteria, which could be exploited by opportunists ready for plunder and by bullies afraid to fight the Soviets but prepared to assault defenseless civilians. Iron Guardists deliberately spread the rumor that the entire Jewish population of Iaşi was working for the Red Army and had signaled the Soviets where to drop bombs. The next day the menace gathered strength as the municipal police department systematically contacted home owners with an invitation to paint the sign of the cross on their windows and doors so that mobs would know which homes to spare.[14]

Things soon got worse. On June 26, a second—and this time devastating—Soviet air raid took place, hitting the headquarters of the Fourteenth Infantry Division, the telephone company, and St. Spiridon Hospital. Six hundred people were reportedly killed (including 38 Jews); other sources give a figure of 111 killed and hundreds wounded.[15] This bombing further fueled the anti-Semitic fever. Romanian military reports claimed that Jews from Iaşi had been found among the Soviet air force crews that had been shot down. Soviet paratroopers and saboteurs were allegedly active in the city. Anti-Semitic activists and opportunists exploited such kindling to stoke the fire.

That same day soldiers from the Fourteenth Division were in Iaşi, including a company of one hundred men from the division's Thirteenth Regiment and a battalion of three hundred gendarmes.[16] Another three hundred policemen were in transit from other localities, ready for action not only in Iaşi but also in Bessarabia and Bukovina. German troops belonging to the 198th Division of the Thirtieth Army Corps, as well as SS and Todt Organization troops, were also ready for action against unarmed civilians.[17]

As important as the Soviet attacks may have been in setting off the violence, the still more important fact is that government officials had been plotting against the Jewish community for several days. According to the Jewish reporter Marius Mircu, local military authorities on June 20 sent Henry Staerman, the head of one of the compulsory labor camps (110 young Jewish men were already there), urgent orders to dig two long trenches (two meters wide and two meters deep; one of the ditches thirty meters in length, the other fifteen) in the Jewish cemetery of Păcurari; *these measurements already had been formulated by the city government!* The trenches were completed on June 26.[18] The trenches also appear in the testimony of Braunstein, one of the leaders of Iaşi's Jewish community; his report differs from Mircu's only in that he places the order *two weeks* before the pogrom.[19]

On the twenty-sixth too, Major von Stransky arrived at the German command in Iaşi together with Ionescu-Micandru; several hours later they moved on to Holboca: it would seem the Germans were actively involved.[20] According to witness Lieutenant Colonel Constantin M. Rădulescu-Siţa, Ionescu-Micandru and von Stransky recalled their own roles in the Iaşi events while discussing plans to "take care of" the Jewish community of Bucharest by the same means (at a December 1942 feast in honor of SSI chief, Eugen Cristescu).[21]

June 26 therefore marks the real beginning of the Iaşi pogrom. In its report for that day the Dorobanţi Thirteenth Regiment (a unit of the Four-teenth Division, named in honor of the infantrymen of the War of Inde-pendence) recorded its arrest of Iosub Cojocaru, Leon Schachter, and Herşcu Wolf, allegedly for having signaled to the Soviet air force the lo-cation of buildings housing Romanian troops. Officers at division head-quarters interrogated and then released them; but since they now knew where headquarters was located, their escort, the Legionnaire Sergeant T. R. Mircea Manoliu, took them to the garrison firing range to shoot them. Schachter fled unharmed; seriously wounded Wolf lost conscious-ness but survived; Manoliu did manage to murder Cojocaru.[22]

On that same day five unidentified Jews were sent to locate unex-ploded bombs in the courtyard of the same headquarters. Although they had been sent by Commissioner Nicolae Crăciun of the Fifth Police Precinct, they were not released after the task.[23] That afternoon the lead-ers of the Jewish community were convened at Central Police Headquar-ters, and "the Jews of Iaşi" were accused of having collaborated with Soviet Jewish aviators. Police Superintendent Chirilovici ordered that within the next forty-eight hours Jews had to hand over to the police all binoculars, flashlights, and photographic equipment.[24] At four o'clock in the afternoon Colonel Dumitru Captaru (the district prefect), Colonel Constantin Lupu (garrison commander), Police Superintendent Chir-ilovici, Police Inspector Giosanu, and Chief Physician Cosma met in the prefect's office to map strategy, assigning to each police sector a detach-ment of gendarmes to conduct house searches and arrest "saboteurs" and "spies."[25] Between 5:00 and 9:00 that evening the first searches took place, engaging 140 policemen and 677 gendarmes organized into forty teams. These placed 317 Jews under "temporary" arrest, detaining another 207 who owned flashlights or who owned decorative or clothing items made from red cloth as more serious suspects.[26]

On Friday the twenty-seventh sporadic rifle fire could be heard throughout the city; shortly after 11:00 A.M. Chirilovici called Lupu to tell him that large groups of Legionnaires had gathered, singing, in the Jewish cemetery; he then made his way (supported by a platoon of soldiers) to the cemetery, where, alarmed at the arrival of the law, the armed Legionnaires began to scatter:

> In the building where they had assembled, I [Chirilovici] found two crates filled with weapons. Two of the Legionnaires . . . said that they had been sent by the [army's secret service] to arm all those Legionnaires who might soon find themselves behind enemy lines [i.e., possibly the same men who may have been involved in preparing the Iron Guards for the pogrom]. I asked . . . why they had not reported this measure to us. I returned to the city military command with my soldiers, but about one hour [later] the two individuals showed up in officer uniforms and apologized, stating they had been preparing for an abortive secret assignment. These two officers [then] showed me the order from the Supreme General Staff.[27]

The two commanders turned out to be the aforementioned plainclothes SSI officers Gheorghe Balotescu and Emil Tulbure, who, wearing uniforms, had already organized one of the anti-Semitic training episodes of June 22.[28] The explanation that they were preparing volunteers to remain behind the Soviet lines appears strange too: their "agents" had behaved so boisterously that they had roused the entire neighborhood. Just as strange was the behavior of Chirilovici, who had allowed the Legionnaires to be armed (they were still officially enemies of the state) and had allowed them to leave, even though he had enough soldiers to handle them.

The most significant events of the day represented various overt and covert preparations for a pogrom. Nevertheless, the day did not end without the spilling of Jewish blood: Dr. Marcu Caufman's father, a resident of the Nicolina Quarter, had been shot by a "sergeant of the artillery."[29] That same evening the still captive five Jews, now charged with spying, were detained by the Thirteenth Regiment Dorobanți; these men were handed over to Manoliu, the same sergeant who had murdered Cojocaru. This time Manoliu once again led the prisoners to the firing range and, aided by one Corporal Nicolau, lined up the "suspects" and shot them.

The five corpses were found the following day, when the district prefect reported six (!?) casualties to the commander of the Fourteenth Division (near the border, Iași was under military jurisdiction).[30]

The Pogrom Unfolds

On Saturday morning, June 28, a group of thirty soldiers from the Thirteenth and Twenty-fourth Artillery Regiments abused and robbed several Jews on the pretext that the former were looking for a wireless transmitter set. German soldiers got in on the action in the Tătărași neighborhood, on Răchiți Street, around the slaughterhouse, and on Aurel Vlaicu and Vasile Lupu Streets. The police superintendent arrived with the garrison commander, the city's chief prosecutor, the military prosecutor of the Fourteenth Division, and a platoon of gendarmes to "investigate." At about the same time Sergeant Manoliu was arrested, apparently for the record, because he was released soon after by the military prosecutor, Major Nicolae Scriban.[31]

Meanwhile, freshly printed posters incited the citizenry of Iași to take matters into their own hands: ROMANIANS! FOR EACH *JIDAN* THAT YOU KILL, YOU LIQUIDATE A COMMUNIST. THE MOMENT FOR REVENGE HAS COME.[32] Civilians joined men in uniform to terrorize the Jews. That evening Police Inspector Gheorghe Leahu ordered the Iași police "not to interfere with what the army is carrying out inside the city."[33]

At nine o'clock in the evening an airplane, apparently a Soviet one, fired off several flares, followed immediately by rifles of different calibers. Panic spread among troops heading for the front. There was shooting in the Păcurari, Toma Cosma, and Sărărie neighborhoods, and shots were fired on Carol, Lazăr Catargiu, and Lăpușneanu Streets. Military units were deployed and "returned fire."[34] But there were no casualties, and no bullet holes were found on the walls of houses the next day. Shells from old-fashioned hunting weapons, however, were found.[35]

Rumors of "Soviet paratroopers" spread. Soon groups of Romanian and German soldiers, gendarmes, and civilians took advantage of these rumors to justify the widespread assaults on the Jews that began the robbery and mayhem to which they gave themselves over for the rest of the night. An eyewitness later recalled,

> On the night of June 28–29, 1941, a group of young Christians led by the coachman Lepioskin and accompanied by [soldiers] entered . . . the

slaughterhouse neighborhood and engaged in massacres and plunder. . . . Air-raid sirens went off at nine and lasted until eight the following morning. . . . A group of soldiers accompanied by paramilitary reservists . . . shot the owner of the Minca textile store, Iosif Smilovici. Another group entered the courtyard of the Binder Hotel on Lăpușneanu Street and under the pretext that they had discovered a machine gun in the attic, arrested the owner, Blau, together with his wife, infant daughter, sister-in-law, and mother-in-law; following summary judgment these were executed by machine-gun fire. . . . Later it was learned that the machine gun from the attic had been placed there by Legionnaire soldiers guarding [a tax office].[36]

The authorities, steeped in the anti-Semitism of their culture (and some sympathizing with the mob), did nothing to restore order. Many were inclined to blame the Jewish victims, as appears in the report by Police Inspector E. Giosianu of June 29 to the General Police Directorate in Bucharest: "On the evening of [June] 28–29 at approximately 10:30, Communist Jews and Romanians fired an unknown number of shots with automatic weapons throughout the city of Iași in order to induce panic among the people and to slow troops on the way to the front. . . . The police [and representatives of] the Romanian and German armed forces . . . mounted house searches."[37] Another June 29 police report to Bucharest indicated that late on June 28 the garrison commander (Colonel Constantin Lupu) met at Central Police Headquarters with the military prosecutor of the Third Army (Colonel Gheorghe Barozzi), the inspector of the gendarmerie (Colonel Gheorghe Bădescu), Police Inspector Giosianu, and the military prosecutor of the Fourteenth Division (Major Scriban) to discuss the situation. They made the decision to reinforce the "patrols" already sent out to the scenes of reported "diversionary" activity and to gather "suspects" at police headquarters.[38]

The following day shots could be heard throughout Iași as goons—in and out of uniform—shot down Jews. Other Jews were lined up and marched through the neighborhoods of Tătărași, Păcurari, Sărărie, and Nicolina to Central Police Headquarters. Some columns stopped at the National Lyceum, the Dorobanți Regiment site, the Wachtel School, and the Regional Police Inspectorate, but all were eventually herded to central headquarters; men constituted the majority of these parties, but they also included women, children, and senior citizens, many still in their pajamas.

Beaten and bruised, they were forced to march in step, arms raised above their heads. Their captors, Romanian and German, as well as the mobs lining their path, spat on them; pelted them with rocks and bottles; and struck them with sticks, bars, and rifle butts. Those who could not walk because of injury or ailment were shot, so that the streets were soon strewn with corpses.[39]

In the neighborhood of Păcurari one Dr. Piker was shot in front of his wife. The manufacturers Fall, Holzman, Schneer, and Pulferman were murdered along with their sons and sons-in-law. In the Brătianu neighborhood the merchant Milu Goldner was also shot down in front of his wife, as was Dr. Manole Solomon. On Brătianu Street the laryngologist Solomonovici, who had been visiting his daughter, was similarly murdered. On Ştefan cel Mare Street someone murdered a little girl, Tauba Grünberg, leaving her disemboweled in front of Hirschensohn's store. On the corner of Ştefan cel Mare and Lozonschi Streets the family of Samuel Leibovici was machine-gunned: father, daughter, and son died on the spot, the mother subsequently in Gelehrter Hospital. The hosteler Herman Rottman was shot on University Street.

Many of the perpetrators of these crimes apparently were motivated not so much by the lust for blood as the lust for lucre: the actor Vinovschi of the National Theater, a participant in the murder of the Leibovici family, managed to seize their business after the crime.[40] If Vinovschi had to wait, other perpetrators robbed their Jews as soon as they had been rounded up. This is what happened to the baker Herscu Marcu of 27 Zugravi Street, forced to Central Police Headquarters with his wife and two children early in the morning by an opportunistic Gypsy from Iaşi's outskirts. Forbidden to lock their doors, all of the family's possessions were looted during their absence. Avram Ihil, a twenty-four-year-old office clerk, was turned out of his house with his family; he was severely beaten, his father struck by a man named Racoviţă, a mortician from St. Spiridon Hospital, and his mother dragged by her hair into the street. After chasing Jews away, the mob looted their homes. Solomon Steinberg of 24 Păcurari Street had rented a room to Colonel Mihail Niculescu-Coca, whose aide robbed the family's valuables while the Steinbergs were being held by the police; when they complained to the colonel upon their release, he slammed his door in their faces.[41]

German soldiers took part in an outrage at 3 Xenopol Street, in which the merchant Jean Olivenbaum and his family were slaughtered together with the three members of the Marcusohn family. The soldiers draped the corpse of Olivenbaum over a machine gun, photographed it, and thus created "proof" that the Jews had fired on German troops; the photograph was reproduced in the German magazine *Der Adler* (The Eagle). Near the intersection of Stroescu and Vovidenie Streets German soldiers executed the pediatrician Cozac Averbuch. They had asked people in an air-raid shelter if there were any Jews among them, and having received a negative reply, they left; someone denounced Averbuch, however, and the Germans, furious at having been tricked, returned and shot him.[42]

Often the civilians, emboldened by the company of soldiers, gendarmes, and policemen, proved the most violent pogromists; very often they were armed, highly unusual for Romanian workers or peasants in peacetime or wartime. "Henry Staerman (7 Ipsilante Street) was taken from his house [to the prefecture]," one testimonial reported, "by several railroad employees who lived in the neighborhood. They carried revolvers just like the guards who accompanied them."[43] "Leon Davidovici (8 Pînzăriței Street) was evicted from his house with his father by the watchman Roman, . . . who lived across the street from them," said another account. Though Roman arrived at Davidovici's doorstep in the company of a German officer, it was the civilian who struck the father on the head with an iron bar; he died in his son's arms.[44] Many other testimonials in files of Bucharest's Office of War Criminals recount similar events:[45] Stefan Scobai, a Legionnaire, is reported to have shot and killed Iție Burstin and Herman Mihailovici;[46] Dumitru Constantinescu killed several Jews by bludgeoning them;[47] the shoemaker Dumitru Rusu killed five Jews by gunning them down.[48] Other Jews died several hours after being beaten by Scobai and another civilian, Rudolf Lubaș (who, "working" with policemen Leon Cristiniuc and Constantin Blînduț, had already murdered three Jews with a bayonet).[49] Still other Jews were severely abused by the shopkeeper Dumitru Dădîrlat; the white-collar employee Nicolae Rusu; the teamster Vasile Velescu; the Legionnaires Dumitru Andronic, Ion Laur, and Dumitru Dumitriu; the student Aurel Gramatiuc; the policeman Mihai Anițulesei; and other civilians identified as Gheorghe Tănase, Nicolae Lupu, Ion Mănăstireanu, Gheorghe Bocancea, Gheorghe Grosu, and Dumitru Ciubotaru.[50]

German and Romanian, cop and robber, civilian and soldier, the rioters soon transformed the streets of Iași into Brueghel canvases. Survivors of the Jewish groups that were led to police headquarters later recorded the visions that accompanied their passage: those who left the Fifth Police Precinct at 5:00 P.M. were greeted by the corpse of an old man on Apeduct Street, a few paces beyond that of a child (of the plumber Suchär); in front of the Chamber of Commerce building and the Ghemul Verde Store on Cuza-Vodă Street, two heaps of dead people (in which they discerned the bodies of women and children) awaited them. The following image decorated the front of the police station on V. Alecsandri Street: the corpses of Şmil Idelovici, Moise Şebraru, and the latter's son-in-law lay on top of one another and thus provided the backdrop for a German soldier murdering an old man with a bullet to the back of the neck.[51] Another group of Jews being marched down Smîrdan Street by soldiers ran into an old Jew coming from Central Police Headquarters bearing the pass marked "free," to prove to vigilantes that he had already been cleared of suspicion, just in time to witness his murder by a German soldier unconvinced of his clearance. In front of Sirata Grossu's dental practice lay the bullet-riddled corpses of the tavern keeper Schneider, a boy, an old man, and a few steps away, still others. At the Jelea pharmacy in Sărărie more dead Jews had been tumbled, one on top of the other.[52]

History may judge the Romanians kind in comparison with the Germans in occupied Poland or Ukraine, for two Romanian officers persuaded the guards of Isidor Sulemer's group to let their people go.[53] Others slated for the police station roundup managed to escape by bribing their Romanian guards. Mendel Sacagiu escaped the worst by treating the soldiers who mobbed his house at 55 Smirdan Street to one thousand lei apiece and each of the civilians who followed to fifty.[54] However, to characterize all these Romanians as kinder than their German counterparts would be to deny them their due: the patrol headed by the shoemakers Munteanu, Cucu, and Turilă (armed only with sticks and a hoe, though backed up by jeering neighbors) marched a group of eighteen Jews—eighteen at first—some three kilometers to an airfield. Those who grew exhausted marching with their hands above their heads were bayoneted right in the street; the eleven who made it past the mobs taunting and spitting at them fell before the soldiers' machine guns upon arrival at their destination.[55]

Some massacres in the making miscarried at the last minute: a convoy of eight hundred to one thousand men, among them Iosub Weissmann, David Iţic Meier, and Iţic Moriţ, was forced to lie facedown along several large trenches near the bank of the Bahlui River. There many were beaten by some laborers, clerical employees, and shopkeepers. But these Jews got off easy: their tormentors were forced to satisfy themselves with merely drowning a rabbi from Buhusi. Police Chief Chirilovici's driver, witnessing the scene, called his boss, who arrived shortly thereafter with an aide. Chirilovici ordered a sergeant who was about to shoot some of the Jews to release them and thereby defused this particular situation.[56] The director of the Dacia Mill, Grigore Porfir (later recognized by Israel as a "righteous gentile"), managed to save about one hundred Jews working at his business (some at hard labor, others recent recruits, still others regular employees); and he did so despite the fact that soldiers threatened to kill him if he interfered in their anti-Semitic revelry.[57] The pharmacist Beceanu saved dozens of Jews at similar great peril to his own life.[58] Commissar Şuvei of the Second Police Precinct freed a group of 350 being herded toward Central Police Headquarters, and Commissar Mircescu and Police Officer Sava saved many Jews by advising them to leave their homes or taking them into protective custody.[59]

But other rescuers fared less well. An engineer by the name of Naum, known to his friends as something of a left-wing activist, tried to protect a Jew who was about to be killed on Păcurari Street; an officer gunned him down too with the cry, "Die, you dog, with the Jew you're protecting." The priest Răzmeriță was shot on Sărărie Street trying to save several Jews. Enraged railroad workers murdered the machinist Ioan Gheorghiu when he stood in the way of their rampage on Zugravi Street.[60]

And all this time very large numbers of Jews were being corralled into the courtyard of Central Police Headquarters. One official report of 9:30 A.M. had one thousand people in the courtyard, though its author confessed that "we do not know all the details."[61] And yet a report signed by Chirilovici said that there were already close to 1,800 on hand by 9:00.[62] The superintendent of the Iaşi police counted 3,500 at noon, a figure District Prefect Dumitru Captaru gave the Ministry of the Interior at 1:00 P.M.[63] Chirilovici estimated that by sunset some five thousand Jews had been arrested.[64]

General Stavrescu, commander of the Fourteenth Infantry Division, appeared at the courtyard of the station several times during the course of that day, indicating the involvement of the highest military authorities. By 11:00 A.M. Police Commissars Dumitru Iancu and Titus Rahoveanu had begun the process of sorting the arrestees, by identification papers, by their looks, or by whatever criteria struck them and their assistants as valid. Between two hundred and two thousand individuals, most of them women, were released with papers identifying them as having been cleared. Some made their way safely home, others were slaughtered before they got there, and still others were rearrested and brought back. Ironically, just as some Jews were leaving the courtyard, slews of others were arriving. Indeed, many came of their own free will, hoping for the now famous ticket bearing the word "free" with which they hoped to ward off the numerous self-appointed street patrols.

But around noon SS troops and other German soldiers from the Todt Organization created a perimeter stretching along Vasile Alecsandri, Cuza-Voda, Brătianu, and Piața Unirii Streets to funnel the rows of Jews entering the courtyard. By 1:30, Romanian gendarmes and policemen had joined them, as had civilian "volunteers" such as Ghiță Iosub.[65] All were armed with iron bars or sticks, with which they struck the Jews with all their might, primarily on the head. Among those who died from these blows were Iancu Şoicat of 22 Mîrzescu Street; his nineteen-year-old son, Sami; and his seventy-five-year-old grandfather, Haim Segal.[66] According to witnesses, by midafternoon the situation seemed to have escaped all control. Around 2:00 P.M. the captors opened fire on their prisoners with machine guns, other automatic weapons, and hunting rifles. One of these was the Legionnaire Dumitru Dumitriu, who owned an adjoining mechanic shop.[67]

A crowd of panicked Jews broke through the enclosure and sought refuge in buildings and alleys around the nearby Sidoli Movie Theater. They were mercilessly hunted down and liquidated, as one of the leaders of the Iaşi Jewish community later reported:

In Alecsandri Street, toward the Zarifopol garage . . . I saw the crowd flee in total chaos, fired on from rifles and machine guns. I fell onto the pavement after two bullets hit me. I lay there for several hours, seeing people I knew and strangers dying around me. . . . I saw an old Jewish man, disabled after the war of 1916–1918 and wearing the Bărbătie si Credinţa decoration on his chest; he also carried with him papers that officially exempted him from anti-Semitic restrictions. However, bullets had shattered his thorax, and he lived his last moments on a garbage can like a dog. Farther down the young Segal, son of a leather merchant who had been killed with his two other sons, was dying and sobbing,

"Mother, Father, where are you? Give me some water, I'm thirsty." . . .
Soldiers . . . stabbed [the dying] with their bayonets to finish them off.[68]

The corpses at the police station and in the neighboring streets were then
relieved of watches, pens, and anything else of value. The massacre at the
station and in the streets continued intermittently until around 6:00 that
evening, easing off somewhat after the arrival of General Stavrescu at
4:30. It is not known exactly why the killing slowed down and stopped,
but according to Police Inspector Leahu, at the time the massacre began
about 2,500 Jews had already been gathered and taken to the train station—indicating that earlier plans for these Jews had already been implemented before the pogrom started; we will return to this point later.[69]

It is difficult to estimate the number of victims of the Iaşi pogrom.
The moderate estimate of Mircu suggests nine hundred were killed (five
hundred inside the police station, four hundred around the movie house).[70]
The day after the police reported only three hundred.[71] A more forthright
estimate comes from the witness Captain Constantin Darie: three thousand to four thousand Jews killed or injured.[72]

But how could anyone have counted? We know that at least 254 were
buried in mass graves in the Jewish cemetery soon after the events of the
pogrom, but we don't know how many more and how many elsewhere.
The bodies were slowly removed in four trucks and a couple dozen horse
carts over a two-day period. Uncounted corpses were simply taken to the
garbage dumps of Copou District, though not abandoned until stripped of
their clothes. Many mortally injured were tossed in with the corpses,[73] but
if a few here and a few there walked away or were quietly saved, it seems
unlikely that the overall numbers would be very different. To these totals
must be added the tallies from other less well-documented slaughters at
the waterworks and the electrical plant. We do not know the number of
these victims.[74]

And it was precisely during that afternoon—the afternoon of that
bloody Sunday, June 29—that the decision was made to "evacuate" the
Iaşi Jews who were being held as suspects at the police station. Chirilovici
later assigned the decision to Stavrescu, who was allegedly working with
representatives of the district prefecture,[75] an unidentified "high-ranking
German officer," Police Inspector Leahu, Stănciulescu (the director of the
police station), Commissar Anghel, Major Scriban, and—of course—
Chirilovici himself.[76] District Prefect Captaru apparently conveyed some

kind of signal to these gentlemen, for he had already been in telephone contact with Mihai Antonescu at the Interior Ministry, who told him that the ministry wanted to "evacuate" the "suspects" and ordered him to keep Bucharest informed of the measures this ad hoc council decided upon.[77]

Thus did the "transfer" of some 2,500 Jews who had survived the massacre get under way. Their movement to the train station began at 8:00 P.M. One police subinspector, two police officers, two police section chiefs, and twenty patrolmen escorted several convoys, bolstered by a group of German officers and soldiers with two tanks and two motorcycles.[78] After a lengthy head count during which the guards made the Jews lie facedown on the ground, their captors packed them onto an ordinary freight train. During the boarding the German soldiers crammed the greatest possible number of suspects into each berth, though the train was not scheduled to depart until early Monday morning. At around 4:00 A.M. on June 30, another contingent of 1,900 Jews formed at the police station, to be loaded onto a second train. A summary report sent by Captaru at 9:20 A.M. referred again to the fact that Mihai Antonescu and the Ministry of the Interior were behind the project.[79] The destination of the trains and what became of their unhappy passengers will become clear presently, but the continued events in Iași must detain us for the moment.

For the bloodletting of the twenty-ninth had only tapered off on the thirtieth: it did not cease. Dawn found forced laborers toiling to bury the previous day's corpses—along with "moribunds" who were just going to die anyway—in the mass graves previously prepared at the Jewish cemetery. Labor to bury all of the dead was unavailable; the crowds so enthusiastic for beatings and robbery were nowhere to be found when heavy, less emotionally satisfying work required doing. Mircu tells us that "the Germans" forced temporary Jewish funerary workers to throw corpses into the Bahlui River, along with, again, some of the mortally injured.[80] According to the same testimony, as late as six in the evening that night, when a white-bearded Jewish stonecutter named Rotmann arrived with a young assistant to bring food to the exhausted "undertakers," the killing was still going on: three gendarmes ordered the arrivals at gunpoint to hand over their clothes and then executed the two, the old man dying instantly, but the youth begging for a second shot, which finished him off. They were then tossed in with the others already lying in the trenches.[81]

While this work was going on, yet more ghastly events continued elsewhere. It seems that sometime on Monday one hundred Jews who had earlier been set to hard labor at the tramway electrical plant disappeared without a trace.[82] We don't know what happened to this entire group, but we do know what happened to one family: on Monday morning the tramway ticket taker Constantin Ifras is reported to have killed with a crowbar the Segals (father, mother, and two children), who happened to pass him on the street.[83] And the massacre continued throughout Monday in various parts of the city, less impressive in scale than Sunday's efforts but producing a hefty total of fifty dead, not including those at the power plant. Nearly half of this figure derives from one incident, triggered around 1:00 P.M., when a group of tank crewmen claimed that they had come under rifle fire near the pharmacy on Brătianu Street. Some reports say the tank was German, others Romanian. Regardless, it is known that these men searched the building, assembled eighteen or twenty Jews in St. Spiridon Square, forced them to lie on the ground, and then murdered them with the tank's machine gun.[84] We also know by name some of the victims: Kunovici, owner of a hat store on Ştefan cel Mare Street; Filip Simionovici, a baker from Brătianu Street; an engineer named Nacht; and the tavern keeper Mille. A surviving photograph captures the body of a four- or five-year-old child lying among half a dozen older victims.[85]

So too, as the garbage crews carted away corpses and municipal crews washed blood from the streets, did the photographer's lens surprise a new group of Jews set to cleaning, stone by stone, the courtyard of Central Police Headquarters.[86] One of these laborers, eighty-year-old Leia Moise of 6 Apeduct Street, left verbal images as vivid as the photographer's:

> I went to look for my son [whom she never found—R.I.], who had been drafted for civil defense labor at the electrical plant. [Not finding him here,] I then went to Central Police Headquarters but was detained and forced to scrub the courtyard. . . . We were forced to clean the blood that had dirtied the courtyard and [thus] the traces of the crimes that had been committed. I removed spattered brains, and I rinsed away the blood-stains that speckled the stones. I remained there without food for three days. On the third day a general arrived to tell us that we were free, admonishing us that whatever had happened there was because of the Jews who had fired on the Romanian-German army.[87]

No further episodes took place that day in the city of Iaşi. The deportees on the two trains, however, continued to die.

The Death Trains

The first of the two death trains consisted, by varying accounts, of between thirty-three and thirty-nine cars bearing 2,430 to 2,590 passengers. The cars were designed to transport freight and had no windows. With rifle butts and bayonets, the captors drove between eighty and two hundred Jews into each car. Many of the unfortunates began their journey already mortally wounded. The guards nailed slats over the small ventilation shutters, so that even breathing became increasingly difficult as the hours passed. The fascists decorated the cars with signs informing their countrymen that inside were COMMUNIST JEWS or KILLERS OF GERMAN AND ROMANIAN SOLDIERS. The leaders had originally designated the town of Tîrgu Frumos as the site at which the deportees were to be concentrated; they soon changed this to Călărași, and this was only the first of numerous changes in the itinerary. The first train left Iași somewhere between 3:30 and 4:15 A.M. on Monday the thirtieth, under guard of a police detachment led by Sergeant Ion Leucea.

Contradictory directives originating in the Ministry of the Interior, the Office of the Chief of Staff, and the district prefecture sent the train on an indecisive but deadly route. At 7:00 A.M. it crawled past Tîrgu Frumos, some forty kilometers from Iași. The train continued on to Pașcani and then Lespezi, only to return to Pașcani and thence to the town of Roman, where it remained from 11:45 A.M. to 4:00 P.M. It then set out once more for Tîrgu Frumos, arriving at 9:30 that night. Thus seventeen hours after departure it remained the same forty kilometers from Iași.

The guards had forbidden anyone to open the doors, to air out the cars, or to offer the inmates anything to drink. So densely packed in most wagons that they could not move, people went mad in the sweltering heat and drank their own urine or the blood that streamed from their wounds. The socialist Carol Drimer and the capitalist Solomon Kahane, the technologist Ghetl Buchman and the Talmudist Haim Gheller—all shared one experience alike: they went mad and died raving.[88] Others who retained their reason shortened their agony by committing suicide. Perhaps the most fortunate were those who simply lost consciousness for hours at a stretch.

One of the few to survive this and subsequent horrors, Israel Schleier, testified later that in one of the cars only eight children and three old men disembarked in Tîrgu Frumos. The majority of the bodies, however, remained, stiffened in the positions in which their previous owners had departed from them: "intertwined and immobile, they seemed to form a single . . . uninterrupted mass." The stench, Schleier recalled, was unbearable, "a horrible blend of blood, corpses, and feces."[89] Just before arrival, during a brief stop at the Săbăoani train station, some of the inmates had managed to break the slats covering the vents on their wagons, but the guards had opened fire.[90] Upon arrival at Tîrgu Frumos the cars boarded last reportedly contained only "forty or fifty people who were still alive, but [they were] in precarious physical condition." In the third car there was one dead person, "an old man with a white beard."[91] The two hundred Jews in the last car were escorted to the town synagogue, according to one witness.[92] Before anyone else could disembark, a German captain and the Romanian commander of a railway battalion, Danubiu Marinescu, arrived to forbid the opening of the other wagons. A telephone conversation ensued between Marinescu, who wanted to execute the survivors, and the district prefect, who was reluctant to receive either the corpses or those yet living because he had received no instructions from the Ministry of the Interior.[93] Meanwhile, the trains stood still, serving as ovens slowly baking their human cargo.

At the same time Police Commissar Ion Botez and guards escorted the disembarked Jews to the town synagogue, making sure "under penalty of death" that none of the townsfolk gave any aid to the "dangerous" internees.[94] Nor might the internees help themselves either: when some of the captives fell on the puddles along the muddy road hoping to quench their thirst—many had not had a drink since Sunday morning—Botez shot them.[95] Survivors long recalled the blows and injuries they received from their hosts, some with bayonets.[96] At the synagogue guards and others freed the captives of their unnecessary pens, jewelry, watches, and money. The town schoolmaster, Dumitru Atudorei (a lieutenant in the reserves), is reported to have participated in the plundering. For refusing to hand over their valuables, a noncommissioned officer shot the two sons of David Blondel on the spot. The president of the local Jewish community, Freitag, arrived at the synagogue to succor the arrivals, but he himself was beaten and robbed.[97]

Someone somewhere in the administration had kept his head: at dawn on July 1, a truck came from Iaşi loaded with gendarmes under Second Lieutenant Aurel Triandaf to take control of the train, order the doors opened, and arrange for the corpses to be removed. The survivors were ordered "from afar" to throw the corpses out of the cars—those in charge approached only after "covering their noses with kerchiefs"—but the squad from Iaşi did call in the local peasants "to see the Communists who had fired on Romanian and German troops."[98] The mayor of the town later reported that it had proven impossible to unload the dead bodies relying solely upon the weakened survivors, so "I ordered the police to bring in some Gypsies to complete the operation. The latter agreed, anticipating the chance to steal some shoes or an article of clothing." The piles of corpses filled some of the railway cars halfway to the roof, however, prolonging the task far beyond the two hours originally anticipated: "in some there were 140 to 145 people, 80 to 90 of them dead."[99] Many of the corpses "had broken heads, hollowed-out eyes, or deep indentations produced by blows, so I guessed some had been loaded dead at Iaşi."[100] Thus Jew and Gypsy loaded some 650 cadavers onto trucks or carts to take them to their final resting place in the town's Jewish cemetery.[101]

The previous night the policeman Gheorghe Tănase seemingly had grown bored, so he reportedly amused himself by firing his revolver into the windows of the cars; now, as the deathly procession arrived at the cemetery, he climbed onto the mounting "heap of corpses" to hasten the local Jews he had brought to the cemetery, beaten, and forced to dig trenches.[102] The most stupendous of these excavations, a trench twenty-five meters long, two and a half deep, and just as wide, had been started on June 29—one day before the train arrived.[103]

The priest Paul Teodorescu from Răsboieni heard screams coming from one of the mass graves, argued with a German noncom, and finally gained permission to pay the Gypsies to extract the buried survivor—"not an easy task," as Teodorescu testified after the war, "because the survivor had been brought in the morning and was at the bottom of the grave, covered up by corpses." Naked and covered in filth, "the man who returned from the dead" was permitted to wash, have a glass of milk, and put on some clothes removed from the dead. He was allowed to return to the train on the truck that had just unloaded a new pile of corpses.[104]

Back at the station the torment of the living dragged on. Some cars, indeed, were not opened. Some captives tried to get a drink by tying many strips from their shirts into a kind of rope, which they then tossed from the railcars toward nearby puddles to sop up water. At first the Romanian and German guards had prevented the mayor of Tîrgu Frumos from bringing bread and water to the Jews, but after a while they relented. However, "when we tried to open the doors of the cars," a merciful witness later recalled, "those inside themselves asked us to close them because the soldiers in the train station were stoning them."[105]

Delayed at the town's Ruginoasa boarding dock, the train and its inmates just sat there. Nathan Goldstein describes the following scene he witnessed from his cattle car in Tîrgu Frumos:

> Being so close to water and thirsty for so long, most could not resist: they would jump out through the small opening of the car to go drink the water. Most were murdered by the soldiers; . . . an eleven-year-old child jumped out the window to get a drink of water, but the [deputy of the train's commander] felled him with a shot aimed at his legs. The child screamed, "Water, water!" Then the adjutant took him by his feet, shouting, "You want water? Well, drink all you want!," lowered him headfirst into the water of the Bahlui River until the child drowned, and then threw him in.[106]

Finally, under Second Lieutenant Triandaf, his gendarme adjutant (Anastase Bratu), and the thirty other gendarmes who had just arrived from Iași, the death train resumed its journey to Călărași just before 4:00 P.M. When the train arrived at Mircești, forty kilometers from Tîrgu Frumos, the following morning, 327 corpses had to be unloaded and buried near the village of Iugani.[107] A group of Jews frantic with thirst jumped off the train and ran to some ponds close to the railroad track. Triandaf reportedly ordered their execution on the spot, himself taking part by emptying his revolver into the unfortunates.[108] The train passed through Săbăoani, ten kilometers down the road, on July 3, continuing on to Roman, whose authorities refused to let it stop because of its stench. On orders from the Supreme General Staff of the Romanian army, temporarily located in Roman in connection with the invasion of the USSR, the train was then sent back to Săbăoani, where three hundred more corpses were deposited.[109]

Triandaf had given strict orders to allow the Jews no water; at various train stops guards fired on the prisoners to keep them from piling out of the cars, while at others Germans and Romanians pelted with rocks any who tried to leave. At Roman and subsequent stops, however, railroad workers sold buckets or hats filled with water to the internees at fantastic prices. For unknown reasons the military authorities at Săbăoani ordered a check by military physicians, after which the train returned to Roman.

Here fifty-three more corpses were unloaded. The local Red Cross washed and deloused some of the living but, having condemned their infested garments, left them completely without clothing.

The following day the Jews were transferred to other cars, and the train left Roman with fifty kilograms of sugar, presumably to feed the inmates. During the night of July 4–5, the train remained at Mărășesti (120 km from Roman), where ten corpses were removed; the next night, at Inotești (100 km from Mărășesti), forty more were unloaded. At Ploiești the inmates received water and bread. On July 6, the train finally reached Călărași, its original destination, where 1,076 survivors, including the 69 moribund, emerged; 25 more corpses were removed from the cars.

And here ended the mission of the thirty armed gendarmes who had escorted the dangerous "subversives." The guards returned to Bucharest, where their chiefs had arranged an expression of appreciation after their mission: bread and cheese, two glasses of wine, and seventy lei apiece.[110]

Here also ended the journey of the first train that left Iași on the morning of June 30 with 2,530 Jews, finally arriving at Călărași on July 6 with 1,011. The captives had covered some five hundred kilometers over a period of six and one-half days of tropical heat, most of that time without water. The train had yielded 10 corpses at Mărășesti, 654 at Tîrgu Frumos, 327 at Mircești, 300 at Săbăoani, 53 at Roman, 40 at Inotești, and 25 at Călărași.[111] With the shootings of those trying to get water at the stops, the total fatalities on the first death train amounted to some 1,400 Jews.

The first death train had stopped, but of course the story had not. At Călărași the Romanians detained the "suspects" at a makeshift camp in the courtyard of the Twenty-third Infantry Regiment. The death rates soon dropped, though during the first several days ninety-nine more internees died, including the sixty-nine who had been near death upon arrival. Two-thirds were stark naked or nearly naked during the first several days. The authorities kept them there to little purpose—some were set at forced labor in Gheorgheni or Pia Petrea—for nearly two months, until August 30. One of the reasons that conditions improved was that these guards were willing to accept bribes. The Jewish community of Bucharest in particular made strong efforts to improve the lot of the inmates. Those in charge also allowed the synagogues of Călărași to shelter one hundred of the children and one hundred "intellectuals," though why they would have shown such mercy to precisely that latter element most likely to be identified with communism remains a mystery.[112] Between sixty and ninety-five inmates received hospital treatment, though they did not receive a reprieve from their labor assignments.

At the end of August 1941, the government decided it would be safe to allow the surviving Jews to return to Iaşi; this time, however, their military escort protected them from the hooligans infesting a number of the train stations on their way home. The actions of the lieutenant in charge were particularly commendable, but history has not discovered his name.[113]

The second death train had a briefer history. At 6:00 A.M. on June 30, 1,902 Jews boarded eighteen cars. The last car contained eighty corpses removed from the station at Iaşi, people killed by gunfire, disemboweled with bayonets, or bludgeoned with sledgehammers. Six policemen under orders of Commander Ciuhat guarded the train.[114] The transport took eight hours to reach its destination at Podul Iloaei, twenty kilometers from Iaşi, moving so slowly that the guard was able at times to follow it on foot. Some cars arrived with as many as one hundred dead and as few as three or four half-dead survivors; in some of the wagons a prisoner had died, on average, every two or three minutes.

At one of the stops a Dr. Peretz, whose father and son were on the verge of death from dehydration, slipped through a hole in the planks to get some water. A German soldier shot and killed him. Moments later his father and one of his brothers died of exhaustion and dehydration (another brother survived). Tili Şmilovici paid a soldier 100,000 lei for a glass of water; the soldier failed to return with it, so Smilovici jumped out of the car to get a drink from a nearby pond, where he was cut down by the guards' gunfire. Married only three days before, the dentist Friedman paid twenty thousand lei for a glass of water. Gulping the liquid greedily, he realized too late that it was lye, thereupon suffering the inevitable agonized death. Another dentist, Goldman, tried several times to shorten his suffering by attempting suicide, but fellow riders stopped him.[115] At one stop the inmates were permitted to drink from a pond where pigs wallowed; several fainted and drowned right there, others perished later from the ensuing gastrointestinal infections. Upon arrival in Podul Iloaei the 708 surviving passengers were locked up in synagogues or assigned to Jewish residences in the community; the 1,194 dead were buried in the local cemetery.[116]

The total number of victims of the Iaşi pogrom and its aftermath can

never be determined. The sources vary the count from 3,200 to 13,000, the
lesser of these two figures coming from revisionist Romanian historians,
approximately as trustworthy as their Western revisionist counterparts.[117]
Raul Hilberg cites German diplomats accredited to Bucharest, who estimated four thousand dead.[118] Curzio Malaparte, a fascist Italian war correspondent who later switched from justification of the pogrom to its
condemnation, would report seven thousand victims.[119] The Communist
historian Gheorghe Zaharia (with every reason to discredit the fascist governments that preceded his own authoritarian regime but also not eager to
emphasize Jewish losses and thereby justify one ideological underpinning
of Zionism) cited documents from the archives of the Ministry of the Interior of the Romanian People's Republic indicating more than eight thousand victims.[120] These were the same sources that bolstered the charges at
the Antonescu trial, proffered in an indictment that proclaimed the orga-
nizers of the pogrom responsible for ten thousand deaths. And yet an SSI
report, dated July 23, 1943, and based on lists of the dead prepared by the
synagogues of Iași, took perfectly seriously the figure of 13,266, including 40 women and 180 children; cited recently by scholars working in Romania, this figure seems not unreasonable.[121]

Many circumstances contribute to the difficulty of establishing the
exact number of victims of the Iași pogrom. Such documentation is almost
inevitably by nature incomplete and not fully accurate; much of what we
know derives from testimony at the postwar tribunals. At those trials
nearly all of the accused sought to minimize their own roles; but by the
same token, some tried to buy the sympathy of the court by exaggerating
those of others. Whether an element of hyperbole distorts survivors' accounts is debatable; but in any case, they cannot be used to accurately
gauge the number of deaths. The historian's task is thus challenging; but
whatever doubts remain as to the details, the following pictures seem
more or less certain:

The SSI played a leading role in preparing the pogrom, though as an
institution it apparently did not play the leading role in its execution. Still,
many of its agents did get involved in the bloodletting. SSI Lieutenant
Colonel Traian Borcescu acknowledged in 1946 that although it was not
the "mission" of the operatives "to implement . . . the slaughter," teams
headed by Inspector Petrovici, Captain Balotescu, Major Tulbure, and
Gică Cristescu (the brother of Eugen) rolled up their sleeves to participate
in the work. Members of Petrovici's team in particular confirmed their

own involvement in the events that took place in the courtyard of Central Police Headquarters on June 29.[122] All these teams were set into motion by one of the SSI's top officials, Florin Becescu-Georgescu.[123]

It is especially noteworthy that the SSI supplied arms and provided leadership to the Legionnaires who incited the pogrom. But how could SSI head Eugen Cristescu arm the enemies of the Antonescu regime? This question remains unanswered. All we know—and those who testified may have been lying—is that former SSI agents claimed in 1946 that Cristescu was reporting to both Mihai and Ion Antonescu about events in Iași; the SSI's first operational echelon (which some evidence suggests was comparable to the Germans' Einsatzgruppen [Mobile Killing Units]) may have even sent to the Interior Ministry a photo album depicting the pogrom.[124]

The Second Section of the army, as well as local military authorities who, in the absence of explicit instructions, took the initiative to "go beyond the call of duty," bore a large share of the responsibility. Chief among them was Colonel Constantin Lupu, commander of the Iași garrison. Though not actively involved himself, Lupu did nothing to disarm the troops under his command when they participated in looting and violence against civilians. Colonel Dumitru Captaru, district prefect, received and executed the order to evacuate the Jews of Iași by train; he had asked for and obtained approval to do this from the Ministry of the Interior and from Mihai Antonescu (for the moment replacing Ion Antonescu, then directing military operations, as head of state).[125] Addressing the Ministry of the Interior on June 29, 1941, Captaru reported that "some individuals argued that the Jews themselves were to blame for the mass murder unleashed against them by the German and Romanian armed forces and the Christian population."[126] On July 2, 1941, in a second report to the same ministry, Captaru again blamed the Jews for the pogrom, branding them Communists and saboteurs and accusing them of firing on the Romanian and German forces.[127] Colonel Chirilovici, the superintendent of the Iași police, had prevented some outrages, but at the same time he participated in the arrest—and therefore indirectly in the torture—of the Jews. General Stavrescu, who commanded the Fourteenth Division, also took part in all major decisions concerning the Jews. German complicity is obvious throughout.

To return to the chronology, at 11:00 P.M. on June 28, Ion Antonescu telephoned Colonel Lupu, who reported to him about the situation in Iași. The head of state ordered the "evacuation of the Jewish population," considering it "necessary" to include the women and children.[128] The morning of June 29, Mihai Antonescu ordered the city prefecture "to evacuate the Jewish population from Iaşi . . . one transport to Tîrgu Frumos and the other to Podul Iloaei."[129] And the next day Ion Antonescu himself ordered that "all Communist Jews . . . who were caught with red flags or weapons be executed that same night."[130]

A communiqué issued on July 1 by the Office of the President of the Council of Ministers acknowledged that five hundred Jews had already died, but it rationalized the fact in such a way as to make it appear that the Romanians had only been defending themselves: "The Soviets try to generate acts of sabotage [and] disorder . . . in our rear [by parachuting] spies and terrorists who contact agents living [among our] Judeo-Communist populace. . . . Some of them were caught, and the acts of aggression that they tried to carry out were severely punished. Five hundred Judeo-Communists who had fired shots at German and Romanian soldiers were executed in Iaşi."[131] In an order sent to all prefects on July 4, Marshal Antonescu accused the Jews of having "insulted and attacked" the Romanian army. Nonetheless, even at this moment he staked a claim on behalf of the government's monopoly on the right to punish the "guilty": it is a "great shame," he said, "when soldiers [take] their own initiative and often only to plunder or abuse, attack the Jewish population and kill at random, as was the case in Iaşi. . . . Only the government has the right to take the necessary measures."[132]

Perhaps such statements were intended to leave Antonescu a means to evade possible future accountability. In 1946, he explained that he had known that "at least two thousand [Jews] had been thrown into wagons and asphyxiated. It is because of those two thousand that I left for Iaşi— I was even bombed at the Nicolina train station—and I mentioned this to the German general. I expressed the opinion that an investigation [of the pogrom] should be launched to find out who the perpetrators were; perhaps the German Gestapo? I uncovered only one Legionnaire [Sergeant Manoliu], whom I brought before justice, but he was acquitted."[133] Actually Manoliu survived the war and was one of the very few Romanians tried during the war for crimes committed during the Iaşi pogrom.[134]

General Leoveanu, general director of the police and state security, headed the Antonescu-launched investigation into the Iaşi events. As early as July 2, he presented Antonescu with a memorandum specifying that there had indeed been no casualties among either Romanian or German military units; that teams composed of Romanian policemen, gendarmes, and German soldiers had engaged in "strict searches" of Jewish homes; that in spite of the fact that Romanian policemen at the central station had released men more than sixty years old, women, and children, the Germans protested and rearrested some of them; and that the Germans had instigated the overcrowding of the train cars. He reported also that ninety-nine Romanian civilians and nine military personnel had been arrested for acts of plunder and that "the Inspectorate and the Central Police Headquarters of Iaşi [had] fulfilled their responsibility by setting up liaisons with local . . . authorities to ensure that order would be maintained and to prevent looting."[135]

For his part, Leoveanu would state after the war that

> following my observations I concluded that [the pogrom] had been a provocation engineered by the Germans through fake shots fired at the army. This fact was demonstrated by the cartridge casings found in the street, [cartridges that] came from starter's pistols bearing the "Flobert" brand. They could not reach a target more distant than three or four meters. . . . No soldier died in the street, and . . . no one was wounded either. . . . The city police rounded up all the Jews . . . from their homes and led them to Central Police Headquarters during the days of the slaughter, aided by troops from the city garrison. . . . I concluded, based on my research, that during the pogrom of the Jewish population Legionnaire elements who cooperated with the police and units stationed in the city were implicated.[136]

Whatever the Romanian leadership thought it was doing, the entire world soon became aware of its actions. In particular the Iaşi pogrom produced a notable outcry among the various diplomatic corps. Ambassador Rivera of Chile announced at a press conference in Montevideo, Uruguay, that "it is very difficult to describe what the Nazi bands and the Romanians did to the Jews in Romania. Human language is too poor. . . . The Jews of Romania were stripped of their possessions, subjected to blackmail, brutally attacked, and many of them slaughtered in the most horrible fashion."[137] In a letter to Admiral Darlan, vice president of the Council of Ministers of Vichy, France, Ambassador Jacques Truelle maintained that "the horrors that took place in the city of Iaşi last July . . . could [never] be outdone."[138]

As early as 1940, American chargé d'affaires Franklin Mott Gunther had warned Prime Minister Gigurtu "of the consequences that the anti-Semitic legislation of August 8, 1940, might bear on the image of Romania around the world."[139] In 1941, he reported to the secretary of state that "I often talked about these outrages with my colleagues" and that the latter were "as disgusted as I am by their hideous nature. . . . The papal nuncio alleges that he [commented on them] to the Ministry of Foreign Affairs. . . . [The Brazilian, Portuguese, and Swiss ministers] asked me to recommend to my government that a joint international protest be filed."[140] The author wrote that he had related on several occasions to Antonescu and other Romanian officials the American horror at the "indifference" to human life in Romania.[141] As late as August 19, Cloyce K. Huston, second secretary of the American legation, expressed astonishment at the official Romanian release acknowledging the execution of five hundred Jews in Iași, the death trains, and the widespread massacres in the zones of military operations.[142] The U.S. legation and the Department of State had another reason for their interest: Iacob Nimovitz, a permanent resident of the United States, and Joseph M. Hirsch and Nathan Spitzer, both naturalized citizens, had been killed during these events.[143]

EARLY MASSACRES IN BESSARABIA AND BUKOVINA

The Iași pogrom was no isolated episode. Romanian military units, Romanian gendarmes, and Romanian as well as Ukrainian peasants murdered Jews in many places during the following weeks.

At the very end of June Ion Antonescu had issued the instructions that gave the go-ahead to numerous central and local authorities to establish what was in effect a state of emergency in regard to the treatment of the Jewish population. What this meant essentially was that as far as the government was concerned, the Jews were outside the protection of the law. That the source of this stance of the Romanian government at all levels was indeed Antonescu himself becomes apparent in such documents as his order subjecting the Jews in principle to martial law, forbidding them to leave their homes between the hours of 6:00 P.M. and 6:00 A.M. His order also mandated rounding up Jews and concentrating them in appropriate "larger buildings." To keep the most suspect Jews under observation and "to punish immediately any signs of trouble," Antonescu's order insisted on the taking of "hostages" from among "the Jewish leadership," to be "immediately" executed in the event of any "civil rebellion."[144] The army transmitted this order to units stationed in various localities on June 30, as did the Ministry of the Interior to the police prefectures.

Nearly two weeks earlier other governmental agencies had already undertaken administrative initiatives that similarly placed the Jews outside the protection of the law. On June 17 and 18, 1941, the leadership of the gendarmerie organized regional conferences in Galaţi (for the Chilia, Ismail, and Cetatea Albă gendarme legions) and in Roman (Orhei, Lăpuşna, and Bălţi), at which the inspector general of the gendarmerie, General C. Z. Vasiliu, ordered local agencies to "cleanse the land" of Jews, entailing "the extermination on site of all Jews found in rural areas," concentration into ghettos of all Jews in the towns, and the arrest of all "suspects," Communist party members, and those who had held office under the brief Soviet regime.[145] Though the order in some regions was transmitted downward in writing, in others regional bosses orally conveyed it to their subordinates, possibly to make sure that the spirit of the order is what got through rather than its letter: few were willing to leave a paper trail connecting themselves directly to the events most had reason to know would soon take place.[146] Elsewhere, Vasiliu himself amplified his point (expressing himself in bureaucratic language rather than the more explicit words those who orally conveyed the order may have used): the government had to devote every effort to keeping the Jewish population under surveillance, he said, since everyone knew "that the Jews have for the most part collaborated with communism and have been hostile to the Romanian armed forces, authorities, and people." Not one Jew, it was stressed, should be permitted "to escape the fate that he deserves."[147] Since Bessarabia and Bukovina were the areas that had been under Soviet rule since 1940, the gendarmeries in these areas in particular were prepared to enact Vasiliu's orders, with the purpose of realizing the anti-Semites' old dream of *curăţarea terenului*.

On July 3, Mihai Antonescu (as vice president of the Council of Ministers, he was responsible for leading the state when Ion Antonescu was at the front) sponsored a conference of administrative inspectors and military prosecutors being sent to Bessarabia and Bukovina. There he declared that the time had come for "complete ethnic liberation" and "purification of our lineage":

Elements that are foreign to our [nation's] soul have grown like a plague
to darken our future. Let us be ruthless so as not to miss this opportunity.
No one should allow himself to be seduced by humanitarian philosophy,
which masks the interests of a most aggressive race . . . behind which we
find a rapacious religion. . . . The act of ethnic cleansing will involve removal or isolation of all Jews in labor camps, from which they will no
longer exert their nefarious influence, along with all others who are foreign to our lineage and whose behavior is suspicious. . . . The provincial
governments will advise on the . . . foreign elements that must be transferred beyond the border, all those who have no reason to be in Bessarabia and in Bukovina.[148]

At the meeting of the Council of Ministers on July 8, 1941, Mihai
Antonescu spoke in the same vein, stressing in particular his intent to reject any traditionalist humanitarian objections to the forced "migration" of
the Jews from Bessarabia and Bukovina. He also supported the cleansing
from those lands of "the Ukrainian element," which would also have "no
reason to be here" any longer. Romanians who had "strayed" into "the
darkness of Bolshevism" would be "annihilated without pity."[149] To put a
fine point on things, Antonescu told his auditors they should be "indifferent if history adjudges us barbarians. The Roman Empire committed acts
deemed barbaric by contemporary standards, and nevertheless it established the greatest political system. This is the most opportune moment in
our history. If need be, use machine guns."[150]

"Cleanse the soil of Communists," "eliminate the Bolsheviks, all suspicious individuals, and Jewish provocateurs," "rid the villages of all
Jews"—such were the subsequent orders from Mihai Antonescu.[151] And
such were the orders elaborated at the next rung of the Romanian bureaucracy. The chief military prosecutor, General Ion Topor, ordered his subordinates "to have all Ukrainians and Romanians who took part in
Communist activities taken across the Dniester River and to take all minorities [i.e., Jews] falling into the same category to be executed."[152]
Vasiliu instructed Colonel Meculescu of the Chişinău Gendarme Inspectorate to "identify and arrest all Jews, irrespective of gender and age, who
can be found in rural areas."[153] As early as July 9, the governor of Bessarabia, General Voiculescu, began to receive reports on the gendarmes'
"cleansing activity."[154] On July 11, Lieutenant Colonel A. Ionescu, chief
of the Second Section, reported to his superiors that his section had al-

ready designed and implemented a plan "to eliminate the Judaic element from the territory of Bessarabia by organizing and activating teams to operate ahead of the Romanian troops." The link from government to administration to the masses emerges clearly in his boast that teams were fostering in the villages "an environment hostile to Judaic elements so that the population will try to eliminate them on its own with the most appropriate means suited to the circumstances."[155] As General Topor put it on July 17, "This country does not need Jews."[156]

Those rounded up faced dire prospects indeed. On July 19, Deputy Minister Popescu conveyed the following order of the leader to the General Inspectorate of the Gendarmerie: "All Jews who are in labor camps or who are imprisoned must be subjected to hard labor. If any flee, one out of ten [remaining] will be executed. If they do not work as required, do not feed them, do not allow them to receive food or purchase it."[157] Many Jews in Bessarabia and Bukovina being held as hostages were executed, killings that did not require any ex post facto justification.

The taking of Jewish hostages was widely practiced in Moldavia, Bessarabia, and Bukovina.[158] Theoretically, for each Romanian or German soldier killed in the regions under Romanian control, fifty Jews were supposed to be liquidated. Mere orders issued by Romanian or German officers produced mass executions. Yet the hostage-taking and land-cleansing orders attest to the fact that responsibility for the murder of Jews also belongs to the central authorities. That the gendarmerie's systematic massacres of Jews (and others) resulted from the determined purpose of the government clearly emerges from the account of the gendarme adjutant Vasile Ivanoiu during his January 1950 trial:

> I reached my station at Gosinu in the district of Hotin on the night of July 10, 1941. Three to four days later I was called in by the section chief of Clişcăuţi, Dumitru Gheorghe, together with the nine gendarme station chiefs located in the area, . . . [who] told us that the time had come to cleanse the soil of all that was noxious to the Romanian state, adding that *those elements had to disappear.* He then read to us the names of those who had to be eliminated, . . . most likely . . . from lists [of] Soviet officials we had found when our troops had arrived. . . . I was given the names of people in two communes. When I heard the names of people who had to disappear, I informed my section chief that some of those people were not guilty of anything and that after their execution we

would be hard-pressed when the relatives came to us for information about them; I let him know that I would not carry out such an action. [Thereupon] the section chief told me that we were at war, that the order had to be carried out without further discussion, and that if I refused, he would personally execute me. When I took my leave, the adjutants from the other sections asked me for advice on the matter. I told them that we were not execution squads and that each and every one of them had to act according to what his conscience dictated, and I added that I would not carry out those orders.[159]

Although the massacres under discussion got under way in July, in some sense they represent a continuation of executions of Jews on the west side of the Prut River, the previous Soviet-Romanian border. When Sergeant Manoliu signaled the beginning of the Iași pogrom by shooting at a group of six Jews on June 27, 1941, he may not have known that analogous events would immediately break out in other localities near the former border.

In the village of Sculeni, for example, Romanians and Germans were engaged in fierce fighting against Soviet troops. The Romanians belonging to Colonel Ermil Matieș's Sixth Mountain Regiment, whose command elements had been garrisoned at Bălți (Bessarabia), had allegedly been humiliated and attacked with guns and grenades by the local Jewish population during the unit's withdrawal from Bessarabia in 1940; they now obtained from the German command an assignment to "assault" a sector centered on Sculeni. This would afford the Romanians an opportunity to take "revenge" on those same Jews.

The overall commander in the area at this time, the German Colonel Buck, ordered the evacuation of the civilian population of Sculeni, who were to be taken to Stînca Roznovanu west of the Prut. Here Captain Ion Stihi and Second Lieutenant Eugen Mihăilescu supervised the sorting of the evacuees, proceeding with the active participation of the former Legionnaire mayor of Sculeni, Gheorghe Cimpoesu (now on leave from the Twenty-third Artillery Regiment). The Christians were taken to the villages of Cârlig and Copou, but the Jews were held back. Mihăilescu, a former theology student and Legionnaire, forced forty of the Jews to dig ditches, he and his comrades then helping themselves to whatever gold, jewelry, or other valuables the Jews had carried with them.[160] Next, together with Sergeant Vasile Mihailov, he killed at least 311 Jews with machine guns and automatic weapons. Cimpoeşu and Paraschiva Barla-conschi Moroşeanu, another civilian from Sculeni, then searched the bodies for remaining jewelry and salvageable clothing.[161]

It would seem that this "action" raised some eyebrows at headquarters because we find Matieş justifying it later that month. In a report to the Fourteenth Division on July 20, the colonel acknowledged that he had ordered Captain Stihi to arrest and execute "all the suspect Jews in Sculeni."[162] On July 30, Matieş responded to further questioning: "It is surprising that we are revisiting a case when soldiers from that regiment in Sculeni had to endure so much because of all those Jews who remained in the town. That is why they were executed *pursuant to orders from our superiors.*"[163] On the following day Matieş maintained in a report to the division chief of staff that, "in my opinion, the regiment's approach was too feeble. . . . Following [orders] Captain Stihi executed all those scum."[164] This detail was confirmed during Matieş's postwar trial by Lieutenant Andronic Prepeliţă from the company commanded by Stihi (who placed most of the blame on Sergeant Mihailov, even though Stihi and Mihăilescu in fact wielded the submachine guns). "The Jews were standing in front of them in a triangular formation," Prepeliţă recalled, "men, women, children. The three . . . fired at them. I saw it with my own eyes."[165]

The 311 corpses buried at Stînca Roznovanu were exhumed from three mass graves during the second half of September 1945 in the presence of a delegation from the Jewish community of Iaşi, the coroner of the Iaşi court, and the new gendarme station chief of the commune of Holboca. It is likely that the number of victims exceeded the above figure: the eyewitness Alexandru Zaharia testified that another mass grave had been dug near a road that had since been relocated.[166] German prisoners of war performed the excavation under Soviet guard, turning up, among other discoveries, thirty-three children between the ages of one and twelve, including seven under one year old and fourteen under six years old. Some corpses were clothed in two or three shirts, suits, shawls (indicating they had anticipated deportation), while others still wore pajamas or nightgowns, especially the women in the second mass grave. Most of the men in the first grave were barefoot, scantily dressed, with their sleeves rolled up. The pockets of their clothing contained everyday objects such as keys, combs, handkerchiefs, and cologne flasks. Some of the corpses still bore identification papers or wore jewelry.[167] The corpses generally displayed signs of gunshot wounds to the chest, but some of them also exhibited cranial fractures. One child between two and four years old probably had been buried alive.[168]

The findings of the exhumation as they appeared in the original report tell us much about the way in which the Jews from Sculeni had been rounded up and executed:

- The three mass graves included the corpses of men and women of all ages.
- Papers found on the corpses, plus additional evidence of circumcision, indicated that these were the corpses of Jews.
- Forensic investigation indicated that the typical corpse bore signs of multiple wounds, predominantly produced by firearms, to the chest and abdomen; less frequently these wounds were located on the head.
- Wounds to the head included not only gunshots, but cranial fractures; reconstruction of the skeleton of one two- to four-year-old indicated no injuries to healthy bones.
- The first grave yielded mostly men of middle age; the second grave contained mostly corpses of women and old people; the third grave produced large numbers of infants, women, and the elderly; only six men of middle age were found there.
- Clothing was usually simple—home wear and night wear; many of the men and women were shoeless.[169]

An obvious and inescapable conclusion emerges: the victims had generally been rounded up very suddenly, to be shot and/or have their heads smashed.

Troops of the Sixteenth Infantry Regiment occupied the village of Ciudei in Bukovina on July 3, 1941; under the command of Valeriu Carp, they had murdered dozens of Jews there after their withdrawal before the Soviets. Now the same men undertook the murder of the entire Jewish population of the area. The number of victims ranged somewhere between 450 and 572. The following families appear in the lists of those murdered: Babat, Grünberg, Schachter, Moses, Rosenblatt, Kula, and Hartman.[170] Peasants aided their soldier brothers. Some of them broke Nathan Schuller's hands, chained him, and led him through Ciudei. A peasant murdered the schoolmaster Sumer Saltinger in front of his house; the mob then forced his wife to place him in a wheelbarrow, take him to the cemetery, and bury him.[171] Peasants armed with axes, pitchforks, hoes, and pickaxes killed Smil Katz's family in the village of Crâsnișoara Nouă. Jews were accused of blowing up the bridge at Crasna, though in fact Soviet troops had destroyed it. Fifty Jews were executed in Crasna Forest; this number included Puiu Hamer, Iacob Katz, Emanuel Hamer, Haim Besner, Hers Besner, and Adolf Katz.[172]

Romanian troops occupied the city of Storojineț on July 4 and began their massacre right away, killing two hundred Jews in two days.[173] Some of those slain included Solomon Drimer and his daughter-in-law; Moritz Loebel's wife, an eighteen-month-old infant whom she held in her arms, and her mother—Moritz Loebel survived but later committed suicide; Mendel Schmeltzer, his wife, and their son-in-law; Mozes Iuhrman and his wife; and the Scheflers (three people), the Sieglers (mother and daughter), the Flinsteins (three people), the Liebermans (two), the Surchises (three), and the Rosners (three).[174] A one-year-old infant was the only survivor from the Schmeltzer and Iuhrman families. The mob chopped up the merchant Leon Elicher and his father at the Margulius windmill; they cut off Roza Karpel's arms in her own house, and though she was later hospitalized, she died while being carried on a stretcher during one of the deportation transports to Transnistria.[175] The pogromists humiliated the old woman Sonntag by draping a cartridge belt on her before murdering her; a photograph of her wearing the belt was proffered as evidence that the eighty-year-old woman had fired at the army.[176] Her daughter found her body in a ditch next to a dead chicken and a dead dog.[177]

The four thousand Jews whose lives were spared were locked up inside two school buildings, where they remained for three days without food or clean water. However, their captors did allow them to drink from the nearby ponds. The recently appointed mayor, the attorney Petru Bruja, wanted to send the Jews home, but Colonel Alexandrescu, who commanded the recruitment district, and the powerful landowner Șerban Flondor opposed him. The mayor resigned, and a man named Dimitrie Rusu replaced him. Under his leadership the authorities converted Grădiniți, Ieronim, Malcinschi, and Lumea Noua Streets into a "ghetto" (after the mob had been permitted to loot Jewish residences). Deputy Mayor Stefan Tomovici (a former Liberal party senator) issued an order requiring the Jews to sweep the streets every day. Certain figures responsible for the Jews—for example, the commander of the gendarme legion of Bîrzescu and the mayor's chief of staff, Isidor Palade—sought to minimize the suf-

fering of their charges, but this did not prevent the transfer, in alphabeti-
cal order, of Jewish families to the Edineţi transit camp in the district of
Hotin. With the exception of eleven of these families, all were eventually
deported to Transnistria.[178]

The occupation troops were just as active in the neighboring villages.
Matatias Carp provides details of the murders of some of them: the soldiers who had occupied the village of Ropcea rounded up the entire Hass
family and forced them on foot to the Siret River. Eugen had to carry his
father for much of the nine kilometers. The soldiers drove all onto a narrow bridge, off of which they shot them one by one. The elderly Osias,
blind, amused them with his unstable gait; he was the first to be felled. His
daughter, Rifca Schneider, followed him into the river, and it is most
likely that the baby she carried in her arms was still alive when it hit the
water. Eugen Hass, his wife, their son, and their daughter were shot and
fell into the current, but the daughter had only been wounded, and locals
rescued her from the river. But when she regained consciousness she
begged an obliging soldier to kill her. The Meer brothers, Osias Rosen
(brother of the martyred Rabbi Mark Rosen of Cernăuţi), and Rosen's
wife were also killed in Ropcea. The locals of Iordăneşti authored a massacre under the command of their small-time leader, Halache Telefon.
Michel Donnenfeld, a man named Haller, and the latter's two boys,
Woloch and Heinich, were among those the crowd brutalized and then
killed.[179]

One of the most horrible massacres took place at Banila on the Siret,
whose inhabitants—urged on by the mayor, Moscaliu, and the self-
proclaimed leader, Barbaza—slaughtered fifteen Jews. The victims included M. Satran, an eighty-year-old blind man, Iacob Fleischer, Iacob
Brecher, and Brecher's daughter. Iacob Brecher's body was cut into pieces
and the blood used to grease cart axles. The parish priest Ştefanovici refused to perform Sunday services the next day,[180] telling his congregation,
"I am ashamed to enter this church, when my coreligionists commit such
crimes."[181] Dr. Salzberg was dragged out of internment in order to attend
to the difficult delivery of a child, but his reward was to be savagely
beaten afterward by the woman's father, a certain Ciornei; one of the soldiers prepared to execute Salzberg, but at the last moment he relented. The
doctor attempted suicide after being returned to internment.[182] A mob of
peasants led by two locals, Ioan Colodelo and Alexe Mateiaş, slaughtered
170 people in the Jewish cemetery of Banila pe Ceremuş (in Storojineţ).[183]

On July 5, massacres took place in all villages of Storojineț District where Jews lived. A group of Ukrainians, Ruthenians, and Romanians (civilians and soldiers) shot or beat to death between eighty and eighty-eight Jews in the village of Stăneștii de Jos; forty more died in the village of Stăneștii de Sus.[184] As early as 1945, Marius Mircu was able to give the names of forty-seven of those killed in his *Pogromurile din Bucovina si Dorohoi* (Pogroms of Bukovina and Dorohoi). Then they started gathering Jews from Băbești, Nepolocăuți, and Călinești, driving them to Stănești. The Count of Scala, a landowner from Călinești and an officer in the army, convinced the gendarme chief not to send the Jews from his village to the newly established transit camps. The count thus managed to spare the latter many hardships, but they ended up being deported to Transnistria just the same.[185]

In the village of Jadova Veche local pogromists dragged Rabbi Ghinsberg around by his beard, struck him on the head, and wounded him with bayonets, but his life was spared; others such as Eli Schnitter, his wife, and Bubi Engel, however, were murdered. Many of the girls were raped; pogromists cut off the beards of all the old men. It is impossible to know for certain how many perished there: all we do know is that only 80 people out of the 543 Jewish residents survived the massacres in their hometown, the convoys to the camps of Edineți, and deportation to Transnistria.[186] In Costești Ukrainian villagers and former Legionnaires rounded up the Jews and then called upon the Romanian army to execute them in a field near the home of the peasant Honceruc. Between 360 and 420 Jews fell there; Mircu was able to identify the names of 33 families, accounting for 105 of the people murdered in Costești.[187] "Of the eight Jews residing in Budineț, six were killed, including Isidor Berghof, secretary of the Jewish community of Storojineț, whose murderers finished him off only after gouging out his eyes."[188]

None of the above crimes were in any way atypical for Storojineț, and analogous abominations proceeded in other villages of the district. In Cires all twelve Jewish families were killed, including Haim Avrum Baruh, a very poor Jew, and his seven or eight children, as well as the farmer Krugman's family (two people). Citizen Buhatir, a visitor from Budineț, is reported to have lent a hand. He harnessed Mrs. Iungman and her sixteen-year-old daughter to a cart with the help of some other peasants and then whipped the horses so that the two victims were dragged, head against the ground, for four kilometers to the bridge of Ciudei. Also in Cires the peasant Burlă was said to have bludgeoned to death seventy-five-year-old Stein Avram, forcing his daughter to dig a grave and throw him in. He then reportedly killed her too, shoving her in with his foot. He then excreted on the corpses.[189] Eleven Jews were killed on the same fifth of July in Vilavca.[190] Still another slaughter took place in Milie, where Ukrainians killed nearly the entire Jewish population, somewhere between 110 and 180 people. These included Dr. Iakob Geller of Cernăuți, who had sought refuge in Milie (his wife's hometown) in order to evade deportation by the Soviets. Geller, his wife, and their twelve-year-old daughter were cut in half on a sawhorse.[191]

In Vijnița twenty-one Jews were killed shortly after Romanian troops entered the town on July 5.[192] The Romanian army took nineteen Jewish hostages in Văşcăuți, executing them shortly thereafter.[193] A massacre took place on that same day in Rostochi-Vijnita (Răstoace): the local residents joined with soldiers to kill at least seventy Jews, among them refugees from Seletin and from Şipote in Rădăuți District.[194] Seventy to 80 Jews were killed in the villages of Căbeşti, approximately 120 in Dracineț, 100 in Broscăuți, and a like number in Bobeşti.[195] Nearly the entire Jewish population of Siret had been deported to a brick factory at Calafat in southern Romania on the eve of the invasion of the Soviet Union, leaving behind only a few old Jews and their families. Now eight old men, including the schoolmaster Meir Hers Schechter and the blind Moise Soihăr, the latter's wife, and the tailor Merdler's twenty-one- and thirty-one-year-old daughters, were all stripped and taken nude to a meadow, where soldiers raped two of the women and then killed everyone. Most of the village watched these events.[196] The Romanian army also executed eighteen Jews in Tereblecea and ten in Oprişani, in Rădăuți District.[197] Jews were abused and tortured but not murdered in Lucavăț (Storojineț District) and a few other villages.[198]

Units of the Seventh Infantry Division, in particular Police Company 7, commanded by Major Gheorghe Vartic, made up some of the forces that entered the city of Herța on July 5, 1941. Vartic ordered the creation of a "Civic Guard" composed of Herța's residents; thus Civic Guards Panait Chifu, Mihai Ştefănescu, Ilie Steclaru, and Iancu Alexandrescu compiled lists of Jews. About fifteen hundred were herded into the city's four synagogues and one cellar. Some of these were next forced to dig a trench, and many were executed there at four o'clock in the afternoon. About one hundred were executed at the Kislinger windmill and thirty-two in a park behind the prefecture. A soldier guarded the heap of bodies at the windmill and fired at any that moved. There were also many rapes. A five-year-old girl, Mina Rotaru, who was still breathing after having been shot, was thrown alive into a trench; a woman carrying a baby in her arms was also executed, as were two ninety-year-old men.[199] Sergeant Major Motrici killed thirty-five Jews by himself.[200] Sulim Leibovici, whose father had already been murdered, was harnessed to a cart laden with the corpses of Soviet soldiers and a dead horse and was forced to pull it (perhaps with other Jews) around town as the townsman Ignat Costica beat him and taunted him with the name "Stalin."[201]

Schoolmaster Victor Rusu proclaimed himself commander of the Civic Guard of the town of Sadagura on the night of July 5–6, initiating the murder of more than one hundred Jews there and in Jucica Nouă and Rohozna; he and his band of peasants raped the girls and looted everyone before killing virtually all of them in the forest. Several Jews survived this massacre by fleeing or remaining still among the corpses. Mircu identifies thirty-two victims representing thirteen families. One witness testified that a baby's sobs could be heard coming from the mass grave for quite some time.[202] Several days later a patrol of Romanian soldiers accompanied by Mayor Novac arrested four surviving Jews in Jucica Nouă, tied them together, executed them, searched their persons for any valuables, and then dumped them into an open ditch, where they remained for more than a month until permission was granted to bury them.[203]

One of the largest slaughters on that day took place in Cernăuți, the capital of Bukovina, where two thousand Jews were killed by Romanian soldiers working in league with local residents, gendarmes, and German soldiers.[204] Two mass graves at the Jewish cemetery received 250 corpses each, a third somewhat fewer.[205] German troops executed another four hundred Jews on July 9, setting fire to the main synagogue with incendiary grenades.[206]

Further mass killings took place between July 9 and 12 in Cernăuți, Hotin, and Soroca Districts. Specifically, German SS and Romanian troops executed 162 Jews in Zoniachie and Răpujineț (both in Cernăuți District) on July 9, another twenty-seven in Coțmani.[207] The same Romanian unit under the command of Ermil Matieș that had killed the Jews of Stînca Roznovanu, near Mărculești, now robbed and killed, under the command of Colonel Matieș and Captain Stihi, another four hundred to five hundred in Gura Căinari, including a number of newborns.[208] A similar massacre occurred in Mărculești proper.[209] An officer who witnessed this testified after the war that on a procurement visit to Mărculești, many of the corpses he discovered in the streets "had been disemboweled" and that some of the women "had had wooden stakes shoved into their genitals." According to the deposition of Colonel Romulus Mureșanu preparatory to one of the postwar trials, more than one thousand Jews had been killed in Mărculești and Gura Căinari.[210]

A group of soldiers from the Fourteenth Infantry Division came upon a group of fifty Jewish refugees on the Fălesti-Chișcăreni road between the villages of Tăura Noua and Tăura Veche, among them at least half a dozen children from Bălți. The soldiers looted their victims, herded them into a pond, and shot them. Two wounded survivors, thirty-four-year-old Dina Frankel and thirty-two-year-old Leica Lambert, dragged themselves onto the road, where a Romanian officer discovered them and sent them to Chișcăreni Hospital. The Ninth German Army protested this incident that "diminished the prestige of the Romanian and German armies."[211] General Tătăranu, deputy head of the Supreme General Staff, ordered an investigation; it led only to the burial of the victims left behind in the pond.[212]

The Romanians reentered Hotin on July 8. The entire Jewish population there was locked up on that very day in two school facilities. Fifty Jewish hostages were selected on July 10 for execution by Romanian policemen and gendarmes.[213] The military police executed 12 more in nearby Lipcani the next day, 40 in Lincăuți, and all 160 Jews in Ceplăuți.[214] Ten people were executed for political reasons in Milovăț (also in Hotin District) during that month.[215]

And so it went elsewhere in the newly reoccupied territories. Three hundred Jews—men, women, children—were killed in Climăuți (Soroca District) on July 12, 1941;[216] gendarmes of the Lăpușna legion under Colonel Nicolae Caracas executed 250 in Călărași in early July;[217] 500 were slaughtered in Edineți on July 6 and 7. Many women were raped, some committing suicide afterward. The corpses were buried in three mass graves, and the Jewish gravediggers too were executed.[218] On July 6, Romanian officials ordered the execution of sixty Jews being held in the recently created camp at the distillery in Noua Sulița.[219] Major Vartic requested in writing from his superiors permission to execute fifty Jewish hostages in Noua Sulița on July 8.[220] The Ninth Mountain Assault Battalion under Colonel Vasile Cîrlan killed 880 Jews in the streets and homes of the town; at least 100 more were killed by troops from the Thirty-seventh Infantry Regiment under orders from Second Lieutenant Savin Popescu.[221] Police Company 7 executed at least 227,[222] Romanian gendarmes killing another 30 to 40 Jews from Noua Suliță in nearby Marșenița.[223]

Massacres occurred around the city of Bălți on July 11. In Buciuluieni Second Lieutenant Mihăilescu of the Sixth Assault Troops Regiment, coauthor of the slaughter at Stînca Roznovanu, executed the only Jewish woman in the village.[224] Ten Jews were killed that day in Soborul Vechi Park in Bălți, where Jews had been imprisoned in two camps under the German occupation, on orders from a Colonel Koller and his aide, Captain Prast. Carp's *Cartea neagră* contains two photographs of the victims.[225] Forty-four Jews from the city were loaded onto two trucks and taken to the village of Slobozia near Bălți, where they were executed after having dug three mass graves. At the last minute the police superintendent, Dumitru Agapie, saved the life of Bernard Walter, president of the ghetto committee. According to Walter's later testimony, Prast took part in the execution.[226] German soldiers executed Soborul Vechi and another twenty Jews in the same park during the night of July 15–16.[227] Several people provided support to the German troops during the slaughter of Bălți on July 12–15: Police Superintendent Agapie; the secret police station chief, Gurie Filipenco; and the gendarme legion commander, Mihai Boulescu.[228] The following eyewitness account could apply to almost any one of the aforementioned massacres:

> The Jews were handed over to the sergeant major by a police representative whose name I do not recall; Sergeant Major Vasile Spintecatu gave each Jew a shovel and ordered them to deepen the trenches. [Next] the sergeant major ordered them to drop the shovels, and the police representative took down all their names. Then [Spintecatu] screamed, "On your knees," and the Jews obeyed, facing the ditch, back to the platoon. [He] whistled a signal, and the gendarmes discharged their weapons. Nine [of the] Jews dropped into the ditch, but the tenth was [temporarily] spared because the weapon destined for him had malfunctioned. Major Boulescu, who attended the execution along with Police Superintendent Dumitru Agapie, sent me to check why the weapon had misfired. When I examined it, I noticed that the hammer had not been properly adjusted. They replaced the weapon and executed the tenth Jew.[229]

A total of seventy-six Jews were executed as "hostages" in Bălți from July 10 to July 17, according to the list of names that the Bălți police compiled, including the ten from the first execution.[230]

German and Romanian troops entered the historic capital of Bessarabia, Chișinău, on July 18, 1941, almost immediately giving themselves over to the mass slaughter of its Jews and those of its environs: it is estimated that about ten thousand ultimately died.[231] This is how the "purification of the Romanian land" proceeded in the neighboring Orhei District. The Orhei gendarme legion, under orders from General Vasiliu, headed by train from Roman to Ungheni at the very onset of the war, crossing the border where they commenced the "cleansing of the land." Commander Filip Bechi, now in charge of the Orhei legion, his deputy (Captain Iulian Adamovici), and his second deputy (Lieutenant Constantin Popoiu, prefect of Orhei under the Goga-Cuza government) implemented Vasiliu's land-cleansing instructions (as described earlier).[232] On July 16, 1941, Bechi ordered the execution of more than one hundred Jews in the new ghetto camp of Telenești, an order carried out at dawn on July 17 by Popoiu and fifty other gendarmes; twenty women and an unspecified number of children were executed the next day at Telenești on orders from Adjutant Filip Mincu.[233] Five other Jews were murdered in Telenești after July 18, four of these transferred from other gendarme stations.[234]

The new Orhei legion commander took up residence in the town on the evening of July 19 and immediately began preparations to exterminate Jews imprisoned in three locations of the city: six hundred in the industrial school and another two hundred or three hundred in the synagogue and a large private house. Yet five hundred other Jews remained in the police courtyard. The first massacre involved those incarcerated at the synagogue and in the house: thirty-six Romanian gendarmes murdered them in the village of Siliștea on the afternoon of July 21.[235] Those in the industrial school were escorted that same evening to the suburb of Slobozia Doamnă. A platoon of German soldiers (who, on the way there, had already executed sixty or seventy elderly Jews) accompanied the Romanian gendarmes. Of the six hundred Jews now in Slobozia Doamnă, about five hundred were executed. The same Romanian gendarmes who murdered them shot down another group of Jews (we do not know if they were from the school, the synagogue, or the house) on the Răuț Bridge.[236] One of the murderers, Sergeant Major Andrei Croială, was subsequently seen opening the mouth of a corpse with a bayonet to extract the gold teeth and cutting the finger off another to steal a ring.[237]

The gendarme section commanded by noncommissioned officer Ion Stoenescu settled down in the village of Bravicea (also Orhei District), where he reissued the land-cleansing orders. Thereupon, a group of seven gendarmes (including Vasile Mihalache, Adjutant Nicolae Burada, Sergeant Major Nicolae Stoian, and Privates Andrei Blech and Nicolae Vintiloiu) shot twenty-five Jews at nearby Delineu in the same jurisdiction.[238] A few days later peasants in the village of Onişcani brought four Jews into the local gendarme station with the request that they be shot: Private Blech was the executioner. The next day the gendarme Vasile Anghel obeyed an order to execute two women, but he refused to shoot a girl in the village of Hagiesti.[239] Thus spared, the twelve-year-old wandered aimlessly for one day and one night, but having no one to turn to, she came back to the Onişcani station. Adjutant Burada handed her over to Blech, who slit her throat with his bayonet and finished her off with a bullet.[240]

Twenty-two Jews were executed in the village of Chirova on orders from Adjutant Florea Glugojanu.[241] Another mass murder took place in Tibirica, where Adjutant Carol Urzică served, aided by Sergeant David Călugăru. Having just arrived with the conquering armies, these men had no sooner begun to exercise their responsibilities than the first military unit arrived with twenty-five Jewish arrestees. New on the job but by no means irresolute, Urzică led these prisoners one by one to the village market, where, with the help of Călugăru and conscripts Ion Oprean and Mihai Maurer, he rifled their belongings and then exterminated them. Maurer was responsible for checking whether the victims were indeed dead; at one point he fired a bullet into a child's head because he was still moving ("even though," according to our source, "seven bullets had already entered his body").[242] Adjutant Mihai Băhnăreanu executed fifteen Jews in Saharna all by himself.[243] In contrast, the priest of the Orhei village of Morozeni gave asylum to a Jewish couple and their young daughter (hoping they would agree to baptism), but a gendarme station chief, Gheorghe Bâra, and Sergeant Major Ioachim Stoian took them to Vatici Forest and murdered them. Bâra, Adjutant Ion Budica, and the village notary raped four of the Jewish girls locked up in the gendarme station.[244]

Adjutant Budica, Sergeant Major Tasache Ciutac, Sergeant Ion Isbota, and Private Dumitru Popescu shot thirty-one Jews (including women, old people, and children) two kilometers from Vârzava (Orhei District) but buried them in graves so shallow that stray dogs soon were seen dragging around their remains.[245] The Onesti station chief, Adjutant Andrei Sârbu, ordered Private Aurel Roşu to execute a Jewish woman who had lost both hands and one leg, as she was deemed a "dangerous element." After this execution Roşu shot a twenty-year-old Jewish man.[246] Romanian gendarmes in Bravicea (Adjutant Radu Barbu, Sergeant Major Panait Dinu, and Privates Blech and Nicolae Paraschiv) murdered three Jews; three others belonging to a family that had evaded the murderers in July were killed at the end of August, pursuant to new orders by Adjutant Major Grigore Stavarche.[247] Sergeant Constantin Miran of the First Tank Regiment, left behind by his unit in order to guard a few damaged tanks, executed a group of ten Jews in Cabâlea (Orhei District) and threatened to shoot gendarme Ioan Soare because he refused to fire at these Jews. Their execution took place on orders from Adjutant Ivan Rusca, the gendarme station chief.[248]

Innumerable other Jews perished in the Orhei District sphere of operations: three Jews in Budăi (denounced by the village priest),[249] sixteen in Negureni,[250] three in Soldăneçti,[251] four in Alcedar, four in Tarasova,[252] and twenty-two in Ghirova, sixteen of these latter women, including one with babe in arms.[253] Eleven Jews were killed in Sărăţeni.[254] A total of twenty-one Jews were exterminated in Crăsnăeţeni, Chiţcani, and Suhuluceni—twenty shot, one drowned.[255] Also murdered in Orhei were fourteen Jews in Leuşeni, thirty in Chiperceni, seven in Horodiştea, six in Busovca, twenty-five in Tiribica, seven in Minceni, twelve in Crăsnăuţi, three in Răspopeni, two in Trifeşti, twenty-seven in Cineşeuţi, eight in Cobilca, two in Furceni, two in Oniscani, five in Beresloci, three in Zăhăicani, two in Cucuruzeni, and twenty-five in Delineu.[256] Juveniles were raped at three sites—Mateuţi, Echimăuţi, and Chiperceni—before being shot.[257] Generally the murderers shot their victims, but thirteen were drowned (three in Zăhăicani, ten—including one infant—in Peresecina).[258]

The slaughter of the Jewish population also took place in Cetatea Albă District; 360 Jews from the rural parts of this district were jailed together with 2,500 from the town proper in preparation for the mass executions at the end of July and the beginning of August. According to several witnesses, these took place near a stone quarry on the outskirts of the city. Alexandru Ochişor, leader of a military unit in Cetatea Albă, commanded the execution squads. Others involved were Major Virgil Drăgan, Colonel Marcel Petală (military prosecutor of the Eighth Army), and Horia Olteanu of the SSI (according to some witnesses, the latter was a lieutenant colonel in the Supreme General Staff of the army). Olteanu subsequently acknowledged "having taken part in the mass slaughter of a group of eight hundred to one thousand Jews" between July 28 and 29, 1941.[259] According to the former gendarmes, the 360 Jews from rural areas perished in early August at the hands of the above-named Captain Ochișor.[260]

The mass murders in Bukovina continued to the end of July 1941. On the night of July 20–21, more than 150 Jews from Sișcăuți, Iujineți, Stănceni, and Babin were brought to Sișcăuți under the pretext of being deported. Once local peasants finished digging a large grave, however, Romanian gendarmes executed the Jews. Adjutant Major Marin Pavel caught five hiding in a large wine vat in Tarutino. According to fellow gendarmes Nuțu Toma and Ion Budisan, Pavel killed them with a stake right in the vat.[261]

The postwar investigation revealed that approximately 250 political suspects and 500 Jews were executed in the territory of the Chilia legion, victims of "political and racial intolerance."[262] Those arrested for political reasons were liquidated in the same way as the Jews, most often en route between two villages, typically at the edge of a ditch prepared in advance. Escorting one such group from the gendarme station in Dumitrești, Sergeant Major Andrei Sîrbu and two other policemen executed six political prisoners (their names were all either Romanian or Ukrainian) near the village of Cișmele.[263] Non-Jewish political suspects also were killed in Cetatea Albă District. On September 4, 1941, Adjutant Stavar Balmoș executed seventeen Romanians for allegedly collaborating with Soviet officials in Fărăoani.[264]

During the massacres in Bessarabia and Bukovina, Romanian soldiers and policemen operated independently of German tutelage. But in some instances the "brotherhood-in-arms" of Romanian and German soldiers found expression in joint operations against defenseless civilians. According to its own documents, Einsatzgruppe 10b was responsible for the murder of 682 Jews in Cernăuți, 551 in Chișinău, 155 in Tighina, and a total of 4,425 between Hotin and Iampol.[265] It has already been noted that German troops participated actively in the massacres of Bălți. Hundreds of Jews were killed by the so-called paramilitary Civic Guards composed not only of Romanian but also of Ukrainian and Ruthenian towns-people and villagers.

All this anti-Semitic internationalism notwithstanding, relations be-tween the Romanian and German armies were sometimes strained. As we saw earlier, following the execution of forty-eight Jews at a pond between the villages of Tăura Noua and Tăura Veche, the Ninth German Army protested the disorderly action. German experience in joint operations with the Romanians throughout Bessarabia and Bukovina had brought the Germans to the conclusion that although the Romanians had the right idea, they were sloppy in their work.[266] A report of Einsatzgruppe D from July 21, 1941, clarifies the sources of German dissatisfaction:

> The Romanians take action against the Jews without any preconceived plan. There would be nothing to criticize about the many executions of Jews had their technical preparation and their manner of execution not been inadequate. The Romanians leave the bodies of those who are exe-cuted where they fall, without burying them. The Einsatzkommando [Mobile Killing Squad] has enjoined the Romanian police to be more or-derly from that standpoint.[267]

Raul Hilberg estimates that more than ten thousand Jews were mur-dered in Bukovina and Bessarabia during July 1941.[268] Most of these were killed by Romanian and German military units acting on superior orders. Others, however, fell victim to Romanian and Ukrainian peasants who wanted (or even felt it their duty) to murder (and, of course, rob) their Jewish neighbors.

*   *   *

World War II transformed what might otherwise have remained a period of severe anti-Semitic outbreaks into a true Romanian Holocaust that, while part of the broader German-European Holocaust, remains at the same time a specifically Romanian story. As in Germany, the immediate background to Romania's Holocaust tapped archaic anti-Semitic tradi-tions and was crafted by the militant agitation of anti-Semitic parties, it-self followed by state legislation and then compounded by wartime circumstances. Bloody mob violence was the result, but now, drawing in government elements, the riot took on the character of a social enterprise and thus invited takeover by the state. This transitional phase, when mass robbery and mass murder evolved from a societal to a governmental enterprise, took place in the months immediately preceding and immediately following Romania's entrance in the war. The tempering of the Romanian-German diplomatic alliance into one of wartime fraternity augured more deliberate and more systematic ill for Romania's Jews. Finally, during this time the Antonescu regime became more directly involved in encouraging the violence, though still more in the sense of indirect inspiration. Soon, however, it would openly take things over, as will be seen in the following chapters.

CHAPTER 4

Transit Camps and Ghettos, Deportations, and Other Mass Murders

With the undertaking of systematic deportation of Jewish populations from and within Romania and occupied Ukraine, Ion Antonescu and his lieutenants became architects of untold sufferings for hundreds of thousands of innocent victims and the death of at least a quarter of a million of them. Their story falls into two halves, the first being their expulsion from their homes and livelihoods, the second their misery and often death in Transnistria. This chapter examines the first half of the story, itself a complex web of events falling into several categories. Overall the experience of the Jews in the territories temporarily occupied by the Soviets in 1940 (those suspected of Communist sympathies) was far worse than for those inhabiting the Old Kingdom, or Regat. The process of concentration in ghettos before ultimate deportation involved unique humiliations and physical sufferings; this was especially so for Jews from rural or small-town Romania, who sometimes had to be moved several times before final deportation. For many thousands, the transports—whether by rail or by march—amounted to murder by deprivation, as the various phases of the process offered numerous opportunities for the majority population to despoil their defenseless victims. Pogroms and outright massacres accompanied events. A few thousand Jews in Regat fell victim to one or another deportation too, and 1941 and 1942 witnessed serious discussion at the government level of plans to clear Regat of its Jewish population in its entirety, just as Bessarabia, Northern Bukovina, and other lands were being cleared of their Jewish populations. It seems that only the turn of the tide at Stalingrad convinced government leaders that they might eventually have to answer for their crimes, which is probably why the deportations were never systematically applied in Regat.

MOLDAVIA AND WALACHIA

In Moldavia, Walachia, and southern Transylvania Jews suffered less at the hands of the Romanian fascist governments than did their fellows at the hands of these same regimes in Bessarabia, Bukovina, and Transnistria. Yet this is a generalization to which there were exceptions: about thirteen thousand Jews were murdered during the pogrom in Iași, then the Moldavian capital. The district of Dorohoi had been transferred in 1938 from Bukovina to Regat, delimited by the country's pre–World War I borders. During deportations from Dorohoi about twelve thousand Jewish inhabitants were sent to Transnistria, at least one-half of which perished. By and large, however, conditions in Regat (and that part of Transylvania remaining after the north was transferred to Hungary in 1940) remained significantly better than those in Bessarabia, Bukovina, and Transnistria.

These tribulations were nevertheless horrendous in and of themselves. As early as June 21, 1941, Ion Antonescu ordered that all able-bodied eighteen- to sixty-year-old Jewish males in all villages lying between the Siret and the Prut Rivers be removed to the Tîrgu Jiu camp in Oltenia and to villages surrounding that camp. Their families and all Jews in other Moldavian villages underwent evacuation to the nearest urban districts.[1] In addition to Tîrgu Jiu, the Ministry of the Interior and certain military garrisons set up camps in Craiova, Caracal, Turnu Severin, and Lugoj.[2] Matatias Carp has estimated that more than forty thousand Jews were uprooted in Moldavia and Walachia during the first two weeks of the war, nearly half of them transported hundreds of miles from their homes. In Carp's words, "entire populations (in Constanța, Siret, Dărăbani), able-bodied men (in Galați, Ploiești, Huși, Dorohoi), or majorities of the men (in Piatra-Neamț, Focşani, Fălticeni, Buzău, etc.)" found themselves interned. Throughout Moldavia and in much of the rest of the country, hundreds more were interned as hostages against anticipated "actions" by other Jews. These internments would last only until January 23, 1942, when the policy of taking hostages was abandoned.[3]

We do have the following victim's testimony of one of these events, the June 19, 1941, deportation from Dărăbani District to Dorohoi District. It took place even before Antonescu's order, one of a few in northern Moldavia under way even before Romania entered the war:

> At 9:00 A.M. we got the order to evacuate the community in thirty minutes . . . and to move toward Havâna Gara Vorniceni, thirty-five kilometers away. . . . We locked our houses, where we had left all of our possessions, without being permitted to bring [even] clothing, shoes, or linen. . . . We were placed on freight cars at the station in Vorniceni, about sixty to seventy persons per car. . . .
>
> We spent a night in the fields in the rain and cold. . . . The chief of police of Vorniceni, Găluşcă, confiscated cows, horses, and carts belonging to some among us, giving no receipt in return; others were forced to sell their animals at ridiculous prices.
>
> Two days later we arrived famished at . . . Dorohoi, where two hundred Jews from that town [joined us]. Between Dorohoi and Tîrgu Jiu we spent six days, suffering atrociously and . . . forbidden to buy provisions in the villages we passed. . . . At the station of Bucecea in the district of Botoşani the Jews who had come to distribute bread to the children were . . . beaten and taunted by the police. . . . At almost every station soldiers and civilians . . . insulted, threatened, [or] stoned us. On the other hand, some soldiers took pity and gave bits of bread to the starving children.[4]

From other evidence we can imagine details of experiences elsewhere. One needs only to read between the lines of messages such as that which the Iaşi prefect, Colonel Dumitru Captaru sent to the Ministry of Internal Affairs a few days later to fill out the picture. He recounted the concentration of Jews from northern Moldavia in the southern part of Romania: 829 Jews (275 adult men, 377 women, 98 boys, and 79 girls) in twenty-four railway cars (twelve passenger cars for the women and children, twelve freight cars for the men). But with the exception of sixteen admitted to the Jewish hospital in Iaşi, all were deported to Giurgiu. Ironically, this cohort was lucky: they suffered nothing worse than forced labor, and nearly all of them survived the war.[5]

On November 12, at Marshal Antonescu's request, the Supreme General Staff offered statistics showing that 47,345 Jews were then employed in "socially useful"—or, more precisely, forced—labor,[6] the luckier at projects in their own communities, others in "external work detachments" hundreds of kilometers away. An undated list from the Supreme General Staff shows that these assignments sent more than seventeen thousand Jews to twenty-one districts.[7] Engaged in enterprises such as breaking rocks and repairing roads, these Jews toiled in a state of pronounced exhaustion.[8] A letter from the General Staff to Radu Lecca, the governmental representative charged with oversight of the Jews, noted that internees were often minimally clothed and shod: "a recent inspection," Lecca was informed, "uncovered a highly precarious situation: 50 percent of the Jews had torn clothes and shoes; 80 percent had no change of underwear."[9]

In the sketchy bureaucratic parlance of another official report, this one dating from November 1943, we can discern something of the conditions on a dike-building project, the prisoners/laborers of which—1,400 to 1,800 of them—had been at work for anywhere between one and two years:

> *Housing:* In wooden barracks or partially buried huts. The workers are not sheltered from rain, cold, and so on. Most sleep on the ground.
>
> *Food:* Insufficient, since foodstuffs do not reach the kitchen in sufficient quantities in accordance with allocations.
>
> *Clothing:* Most of the workers are completely naked. A fragment of a sack or an old rug is used to cover their genitals, and they walk around barefoot.
>
> *Work:* Excessive, since those who can get out of work by giving money can go home, while those miserable persons who remain are forced to perform the work of the others as well as their own.
>
> *Sanitary conditions:* Catastrophic, given the conditions described above. Parasites proliferate. Parasite extermination cannot go forward because of a lack of materials (. . . pesticides, but especially linen . . .).

> *Doctors:* Have no authority. The sick [formally] exempted from labor
> are nonetheless forced to work, and even struck. Doctors' reports
> are met with derision.[10]

Even the management of the Army Supply Corps acknowledged the harsh
circumstances of Jewish artisans at army shops in their hometowns: "They
work nine hours per day. Because they earn nothing . . . they are forced,
after carrying out their duties, to work in town to earn their living. For this
reason they come to work exhausted, and their productivity is often less
than mediocre, although not from any lack of goodwill on their part."[11]
The tragic experience of the forced laborers would later emerge in the
indictment against Second Lieutenant Nicolae Crăciunescu of the Sixty-
eighth Fortifications Infantry Regiment, who had commanded the detachment in Heleşteni. Crăciunescu had often struck his charges with his
riding crop. Those who had money could purchase his benevolence and
go home at the end of the week; others could not. The workers ate beans
mixed with oil and moldy bread. When the irregular food consignments
arrived, the commander "confiscated" them.[12]

The advantage that Jews in Regat enjoyed over those living in the territories that had been lost to and then regained from the Soviets reflected
a distinction the government made between the two categories of Jews.
Nonetheless, through the first half of the war, numerous laws and regulations ate away at whatever relative security membership in the first category entailed. Most important, a series of orders in the summer of 1942
sought the elimination of all Jews suspected of Communist sympathies, a
purpose explicitly formulated in the July 24 instruction of the Office of
the President of the Council of Ministers to the Ministry of Internal Affairs. *All* Jews who were Communists or Communist sympathizers were
to be deported to Transnistria; as a result 1,045 Jews were sent to Transnistria in July.[13] On September 3, the Bucharest Prefecture of Police arrested 395 Jews, many of whom were suspected of being Communists,
including three who, in December 1940, had petitioned to go to Soviet-
occupied Bessarabia under the exchange of populations arrangement;
their petitions had just been unearthed in the archives of what had been the
Soviet legation in Bucharest.[14] A mere five days after their arrest, all of
them were deported to Transnistria. During their trip their number grew to
578 as more Communists, sympathizers, suspects, and would-be émigrés
arrested in provincial towns were boarded onto the trains. Another 407

who had already been interned in Tîrgu Jiu were likewise packed into the freight cars. Yet a further 554 Jews from still other towns, all suspected of Communist activity but not previously arrested, and 85 others already sentenced and imprisoned soon joined the caravan.[15]

Suspected Communist affiliation was not the only justification for deportations from Regat. On July 11, 1942, the Supreme General Staff ordered evacuation to Transnistria as punishment for violations of the forced labor regime.[16] Thus on September 22, 1942, a new group of 148 Jews and their families were sent to Transnistria following reports by General Cepleanu of their evasion of forced labor.[17] Another group was arrested on October 2, 1942, but these Jews were freed eleven days later and not deported.[18] However, 126 Jewish youths working on a farm belonging to the aforementioned Radu Lecca were transported. Long "treated like slaves," they had been harshly exploited, crammed into overcrowded quarters, and inadequately fed. Lecca's wife in particular was known for abusing them.[19] When these boys petitioned for transfer to another camp, Lecca arranged through headquarters their deportation to Transnistria, where most died.[20]

Non-Jews too suffered torture, beatings, and exhausting labor in the Tîrgu Jiu camp.[21] The General Staff coordinated and oversaw the forced labor of these other minorities. Just as the Hungarian authorities in northern Transylvania had dragooned Romanians into forced labor gangs, Ion Antonescu ordered able-bodied Magyars to be brought into his own forced labor detachments.[22]

As late as May 13, 1943, a detachment of 250 Jews was sent from Bucharest to perform labor in Balta, Transnistria,[23] but this appears to have been the final "deportation" from Regat.

BESSARABIA AND BUKOVINA

The Massacres

In the chapters that follow there will be ample occasion to recount massacres in many contexts; but it was the war, including the events immediately preceding it, that set the stage for mass murdering. As we saw in the case of Iași, panic associated with the outbreak of war in Romania triggered some of the most horrific events; one should bear in mind, however, that the increasing likelihood of ultimate defeat following the battle of Stalingrad seems both to have cooled Romanians' ardor for anti-Semitic excess and to have made them more receptive to foreign rescue initiatives. The early months of the war saw numerous smaller-scale events analogous in many respects to those in Iași. One of the earliest—only a month after the outbreak of hostilities—was also one of the worst. On July 25, 1941, Romanian troops led a convoy of 25,000 Romanian Jews beyond the Dniester River to German-occupied Ukraine (the province of Transnistria was formed only later), apparently in the hope that the Germans would swiftly dispatch them. They arrived at Coslar, where they were forced to wait in a field. One eyewitness recalled how an adult Jew and his three children were shot merely for edging away from the group.[24] However, the German military authorities refused the convoy, which had to return to Bessarabia. But even before their return crossing, the Germans did manage to cull about one thousand of the "old, sick, and exhausted" on the pretext of interning them in a home for the elderly; after the others had moved on, all were murdered and buried in an antitank trench.[25] On August 13, as the original convoy approached the crossing at Iampol (a small town just east of the river), the Germans killed another 150 who had stopped in the woods without permission. The Germans shot eight hundred more on the banks of the Dniester for "holding up the operation."[26] Of the 25,000 Bessarabian Jews originally herded beyond the Dniester, only 16,500 returned: more than 8,000 had perished between July 25 and August 17. The Germans reported on what appears to be a massacre at the Iampol crossing: Einsatzgruppe D claimed that while returning 27,500 Jews to Romanian territory, it had shot 1,265, mostly young people. But the report included another 3,105 Jews murdered at Cernăuți, clearly a separate incident.[27]

These weeks saw a number of comparable episodes. On August 1, Germans stationed in Chișinău rounded up 450 Jews, mostly intellectuals and young women, whom they then took to the suburb of Vistericeni to murder. All but thirty-nine were murdered, and these few were returned to the ghetto. We don't know why Germans, not Romanians, perpetrated these deeds, why those categories were selected, or why those few were spared.[28] On August 3, the Office of the Police Inspectorate of Chișinău reported that five Jews had died in the Răuțel-Bălți camp because of "hemorrhaging."[29] The next day a group of three hundred Jews driven from Storojineț under Sergeant Major Sofian Ignat and Privates Vasile Negură and Grigore Agafiței was barred by German soldiers from crossing the Dniester. Near the village of Volcineț the Romanians stole their valuables, drove them into the river, and began shooting. Ninety of those who knew how to swim saved themselves.[30] Another massacre took place near the river on August 6, when a Romanian military gendarme battalion shot two hundred Jews and threw their corpses into the Dniester.

A week later the Chișinău police office laconically reported on another incident of this sort: "the Jews from the Tătărași-Chilia camp [whom we mobilized for field labor] refused to work and, when they became unruly, were shot."[31] This massacre had taken place on August 9 after Captain Ion Vetu presented himself to the apparent commander of the camp, invoking an order from Marshal Antonescu that was for some reason transmitted to him by SS Second Lieutenant Heinrich Frölich to execute 451 Jews in the camp. Having obtained the approval of the district gendarmerie commander (the camp commander—if one even existed—seems to have been irrelevant), Vetu and Frölich prepared a "protocol," a copy of which still exists, and carried out the mass murder with German and Romanian soldiers.[32] Captain Vetu later served as scapegoat in one of the regime's rare but sporadic attempts to demonstrate enforcement of law and order, when he was convicted of robbing corpses.[33]

On August 14, two hundred Jews returned to the Chișinău ghetto after a week-long stint at the Ghidighici work site—minus 325 others who had set out with them a week earlier. Two weeks later Romanian Police Battalion No. 10 completed a report stating that while "a Jewish detachment" had been working at the train station, a "skirmish" took place and "some *Jidani* were slightly wounded";[34] this killing was actually the handiwork of the Tenth Machine-Gun Battalion of the Twenty-third Regiment. The officers in charge included Colonel Nicolae Deleanu, Captain Radu Ionescu, Lieutenants Eugen Bălăceanu and Mircea Popovici, and Police Lieutenant Emil Pușcașu.[35]

The Transit Camps

The deportation of Jews from Bessarabia and Bukovina entailed a systematic, wide-ranging process that Marshal Antonescu and his immediate collaborators put in place and that was implemented largely by the Supreme General Staff. While the Antonescu administration pretended

that this was an orderly evacuation of a civilian population, it was in fact
one of the major atrocious crimes of the Holocaust. But the official version remained the same from beginning to end. A memorandum from
the general secretariat of the Council of Ministers on January 24, 1944,
for instance, offered the following official justification for the deportations:

> The deportations [from Bessarabia and Bukovina] were carried out
> to satisfy the honor of the Romanian people, which was outraged by (a)
> the Jewish attitude toward the Romanian army during its retreat from the
> territories ceded [to the USSR] in June 1940; and (b) the Jewish attitude
> toward the Romanian population during the occupation. . . .
>
> Deportations of Jews from Moldavia, Walachia, Transylvania, and
> Banat occurred after Marshal Antonescu ordered [on July 17, 1942] that
> all Jews who had violated laws and provisions then in effect regarding
> prices and restrictions on the sales of certain products—that is, the Jews
> of Galați regarding the sale of sewing thread, the Jews of Bucharest re-
> garding the sale of shoes, and others [regarding] similar infractions—
> would be deported beyond the Bug [River].[36]

The intention "to satisfy the honor of the Romanian people" was, however, by no stretch of the imagination a determinative factor in actual
events. The historical record proves that baser motives were at play: the
desire to find scapegoats for Romanian failures; the eagerness for revenge—on anyone—for Romanian sufferings; the boundless, violent
greed of both state and mob; unrestrained sadism; and blind, unquestion-
ing, boundless bigotry. Between the lines even Antonescu hinted that lust
for revenge was central, when, for example, he spoke of "Jewish agents
who exploited the poor until they bled, who engaged in speculation, and
who had halted the development of the Romanian nation for centuries";
for him, the deportations meant satisfying the ostensible "need to get rid
of this scourge."[37] On July 8, 1941, the dictator's kinsman, Mihai Antonescu, expressed the leadership's intent still more explicitly when he
stated his indifference about whether history would consider his regime
barbaric, and that this was the most propitious moment to deport the
Jews.[38]

Pronouncements and directives over the following weeks continued
to foster the vindictive attitudes that would spell destruction to hundreds
of thousands of Romanian Jews. Two days after Mihai Antonescu's state-

ment, the Conducator himself explained to government inspectors and military prosecutors being sent to Bessarabia and Bukovina that ethnic cleansing would require deportation or internment of Jews and other "dubious aliens" so that they might "no longer be able to exert their injurious influence."[39] By the very date of Mihai Antonescu's statement, following directives issued by the National General Inspectorate of the Police and the Ministry of Internal Affairs, the Office of the Police Inspectorate of Chișinău had already ordered the arrest of all Jews living in rural areas in Bessarabia; strangely, this followed even earlier (mid-June) orders to kill them. Ten days after this Marshal Antonescu ordered that all Jewish prisoners be put to hard labor.[40] On August 5, the Council of Ministers ordered the Jews of Moldavia, Bukovina, and Bessarabia to wear a seven-centimeter-wide yellow star on a black background; Colonel Radu Dinulescu, head of the Second Section of the Supreme General Staff of the Romanian army, transmitted the order to the prefectures.[41] On September 5, 1941, General Ion Popescu at the Ministry of the Interior issued a different order to the governors of Bukovina and Bessarabia: exempting converted Jews, all others were required to wear a black star measuring six centimeters on a white background.[42] The central military authorities, following Antonescu's instructions, renewed the order to employ Jews at hard labor projects such as road repair; garrison commanders were made responsible for strict enforcement.[43]

Let us look now in greater detail at some of the incidents already mentioned briefly. As early as the end of July 1941, the Romanian military began assembling Jews from Bessarabia and Bukovina for deportation across the Dniester River, succeeding in sending across tens of thousands before the Germans became aware of what was going on. However, Romanian soldiers and police soon met resistance from the Germans, who thought their program "precipitous." Transit camps would have to be created because the Germans did not want the Jews in what was still a war zone. Raul Hilberg describes the situation:

> During the last week of July the Romanians, acting upon local initiative, shoved some 25,000 Jews from northern Bessarabian areas across the Dniester into what was still a German military area and a German sphere of interest. . . . The Eleventh German Army, observing heavy concentrations of Jews on the Bessarabia side, . . . attempted to block any traffic across the river. The order was given to barricade the bridges.[44]

On July 29, the Ortskommandatur (German Military Administration) of Iampol reported to his superiors the unexpected arrival of several thousand Jews, left to their own devices under minimal supervision. They could not buy anything to eat, and they sheltered in abandoned buildings. On August 5, the Germans returned an initial convoy of three thousand to the river town of Atachi.[45] On August 6, a Romanian-German dispute became overt. The Germans prohibited their Romanian counterparts from bringing those Jews previously concentrated in Noua Suliță and Storojineț into Ukraine; the Romanians escorted them instead to Secureni, soon to emerge as one of the major transit camps.[46] On August 7, the Germans attempted to send another 4,500 of the Romanian Jewish deportees back across the Dniester into Bessarabia, but now it was the Romanians' turn to refuse them. The Germans took them instead to Moghilev (Mogilev-Podol'skiy). In the meantime, Lieutenant Colonel Poitevin ordered reinforcement of the checkpoint at Iampol, anticipating that the Germans might try to send the Jews back.[47]

On August 6, 1941, an alarmed General Popescu telegrammed General Tătăranu at army headquarters that the Germans would not allow Jews from Cernăuți, Storojineț, Hotin, and Soroca to cross the Dniester, demanding that the army intern them in camps in each department and asking that Tătăranu keep Marshal Antonescu informed.[48] That same day General Palangeanu, chief of the Fourth Army (in whose sphere these events were taking place), worried that "thousands of *Jidani* . . . have been forced to cross the Dniester without guard and without food." He ordered the operation halted for "military" and "public health" reasons.[49] On August 7, Sonderkommando (Mobile Killing Unit) 10b prevented a large contingent of Jews from entering Moghilev. Members of Einsatzgruppe D in Bessarabia observed "endless processions of ragged Jews" turned back by German troops and security police; they thought the Romanians were playing a deliberate game, driving the Jews back and forth until the elderly collapsed in the mud.[50]

August 9, Carp reports, found one group of two thousand Bessarabian Jewish refugees, escorted by Germans toward Bessarabia, "huddled on the roads in Ukraine in a state of terrible destitution on the left bank of the Dniester at Rascov, near the Vadu Roșu Bridge. The Romanian military authorities sent an officer and twenty soldiers with orders to send the convoy as far as possible into Ukraine."[51] A stalemate was the temporary result.

All of this was becoming a major problem, one that worried the Germans. On August 12, German intelligence informed Berlin that Ion Antonescu had ordered the expulsion of sixty thousand Jews from Regat to Bessarabia; assigned to "building roads," German intelligence warned that these Jews might actually be slated for deportation across the Dniester. The Germans began to discern the specter of more than half a million Jews driven into the rear of a thinly stretched Einsatzgruppe D, already staggering under the task of murdering the Jews of southern Ukraine with only six hundred men. The German legation in Bucharest made haste to ask Deputy Premier Mihai Antonescu to eliminate the Jews only in "a slow and systematic manner." The latter replied that he had already recommended to the marshal that he revoke his order since the Conducator had overestimated the number of Jews "capable of work"; indeed, police prefects had already been told to stop enactment of the measure.[52]

On August 14, another Romanian-German misunderstanding erupted. Sonderkommando 10b asked the Office of the Police Inspectorate of Cernăuți to supply twenty-seven Jews from the Secureni transit camp; perhaps this was for some sort of labor detail. The police inspector did not know what to do and asked for the opinion of the Supreme General Staff, which replied a week later that "to approve the request, we must know its precise reasons."[53] The matter seems to have died in the bureaucracy, but what is clear is that even at the dawn of their collaboration in Jewish matters, the Romanians did not automatically comply with every German request.

On the evening of August 16, despite the opposition of Romanian units, the Germans forced 12,500 Jews back from their territory across the bridge at Cosăuți into Bessarabia; the Romanians hastily interned them in the camp at Vertujeni.[54] Soon thereafter the Germans escorted back a large mass of Jews whom the Romanians had deported to Ukraine on July 25; the Romanians had taken them there in disorganized fashion, after which the Germans had had to gather them in Moghilev on the Dniester, short of four thousand of those who had been shot or had died of exposure, exhaustion, and hunger.[55] One phase of this particular operation was the slaughter of the elderly and the sick at the town of Scazineț on August 6. The survivors remained in Moghilev until August 17, when the Germans sent them to Bessarabia via the crossing at Iampol. Coordination among the Romanian police, the Romanian army, and the Germans had never been complete, and as late as August 19, Colonel Meculescu,

commander of the Bessarabian gendarmerie, was still ordering—unsuc-
cessfully—that Jews be deported to the other side of the Dniester.[56] At the
same time the Germans were returning the last of the Romanian Jews: 650
were escorted to Climăuți in Bessarabia on August 20 and were subsequently interned in Vertujeni.[57] On August 29, Einsatzgruppe D calculated
that it had sent back about 27,500 Jews.[58] Ultimately, as we have seen,
only about sixteen thousand Jews survived all phases of this three-week
ordeal.[59]

In Tighina on August 30, 1941, the chief of the German military mission in Romania, Major General Hauffe, and a representative of the Romanian Supreme General Staff, General Tătăranu, signed what would be
called the Hauffe-Tătăranu Convention for Transnistria; this agreement
stipulated that Romanian authorities would govern Transnistria, and it
gave them jurisdiction over any Jews living there. But the document also
stated that deportation beyond the Bug River would no longer be allowed;
consequently, Jews would have to be concentrated in labor camps until the
completion of military operations could make further evacuation to the
east possible.[60]

In outline, two stages of the deportation of Jews from Bessarabia and
Bukovina can be distinguished. The first phase occurred during the summer and early fall of 1941, when the Jews living in rural areas were herded
into transit camps and urban Jews into ghettos. The second stage took
place from September to November, when Bessarabian and Bukovinian
Jews were systematically deported to Transnistria to complete implementation of Ion Antonescu's orders.[61] These expulsions were accomplished
by administrators selected by Mihai Antonescu as "the bravest and tough-
est of the entire police force."[62]

The preparations for the deportation of Jews from Bessarabia and
Bukovina included an intense press campaign. In a typical diatribe, the editor of the fascist newspaper *Porunca Vremii* wrote:

> The die has been cast. . . . The liquidation of the Jews in Romania has
> entered the final, decisive phase. . . . Ahasverus will no longer have the
> opportunity to wander; he will be confined . . . within the traditional
> ghettos. . . . To the joy of our emancipation must be added the pride of
> [pioneering] the solution to the Jewish problem in Europe. Judging by
> the satisfaction with which the German press is reporting the words and
> decisions of Marshal Antonescu, we understand . . . that present-day Ro-

mania is prefiguring the decisions to be made by the Europe of tomorrow.[63]

Meanwhile, the internment of Jews in transit camps accelerated. The Jews of Bessarabia and Bukovina were assembled in Secureni, Edineți, Mărculești, Vertujeni, and other, smaller transit camps. To reach these camps, the gendarmerie dragged the Jews in all directions over the Romanian countryside's rutted roads, most often without water and food; at least seventeen thousand died in August alone during these forced marches.[64] Young children were among the first victims. On the road to Secureni, Roza Gronih of Noua Suliță saw her former neighbor, Mrs. Sulimovici, carrying the corpse of her child for a week, having completely lost her mind.[65] Rabbi Horowitz of Banila on the Siret covered an excrutiating serpentine route on foot: Banila-Socolița-Banila-Ciudei-Storojineț-Stănești-Vășcăuți-Lipcani-Secureni (Bârnova)-Atachi-Volcineț-Secureni (Bârnova)-Atachi-Volcineț-Secureni (Bârnova)-Edineți. On the first day his group numbered 30 persons; one day later there were 1,000; and by the time they reached the Edineți transit camp they numbered 25,000.[66]

Though many cases of criminal abuse took place, some of the guards on this route behaved relatively humanely. On July 6, between Banila and Ciudei, Adjutant Roșu thwarted hooligans' attempts to rob and humiliate the expellees.[67] In two cases, on July 4 in Socolița and on July 5–6 in Vășcăuți, Romanian officers saved Jewish lives by prohibiting mass executions planned by lower-ranking officers.[68] Unfortunately, such guards were the exception. Others refused the Jews permission to sleep or go to the toilet when nature called. Food was not provided, and the prisoners were forced to sell watches or other personal valuables to obtain bread.[69] In Storojineț the Jews encountered Colonel Alexandrescu, commander of the local recruitment center; he struck some of them, forced all to perform various forms of harsh labor, and encouraged the populace to plunder them.[70] Many Jews sought edible plants growing near the roads, and often they were reduced to drinking rainwater from ditches and puddles.[71] In Edineți they were herded into stables, where hunger and exhaustion claimed seventy to eighty per day.[72] On July 7, a camp was created at Vășcăuți to hold 1,500 "undesirable, suspect, and Communist" Jews. Three days later another transit camp with a capacity of 2,500 persons was created at Storojineț.[73]

Also in July 1941, another group of thirty thousand Jews traveled a similarly complex route from Secureni to Cosăuți-Vertujeni. Villagers eagerly awaited the procession in order to "purchase" well-dressed Jews for a few hundred lei, then to kill them for their clothes and shoes. In the village of Bârnova, near Lipnic, this trade took place on a significant scale.[74]

Some of the newly created transit camps were short-lived. For example, on July 20, 1941, the camp at Văşcăuți was evacuated and the internees driven eastward to other camps. Thousands of Jews were concentrated in urban ghettos as holding centers until they too could be deported. On that same July 20, the Storojineț ghetto, enclosing two streets, was established. There Jews were robbed and made to perform forced labor. Four days later the Chişinău ghetto was set up, where eleven thousand Jews were interned.[75] On July 27, this ghetto was reportedly sealed. Pillaging committed by Romanian soldiers reached extraordinary proportions, prompting Ion Antonescu to later order an investigation. Military police reports both before and after this date confirm the widespread chaos that reigned in the transit camps during the deportations. On July 17, 1941, for instance, the chief military prosecutor, General Topor, reported to the Supreme General Staff on about three thousand Jews recently sent to some of the centers (1,546 to Fălești-Bălți; 1,235 to Bălți; and about 700 to the concentration camp at Limbenii Noi), saying that "there is no one to guard them. There is no one to feed them. Please tell [us] what to do with these Jews." Topor's message was more desperate than his words alone suggest: the Eighth Division was about to send another five thousand Jews.[76] Also on the seventeenth the Chişinău police reported that in Bălți District 3,725 Jews had been assembled: 1,540 in Fălești; 1,535 in Bălți; 450 in Chirileni; and 200 in Tîrgu Cernești.[77] (Bălți and Fălești-Limbeni later became transit camps.) The next day Topor, still not having received instructions from headquarters, telegraphed the Ministry of Internal Affairs: "[The Jews] have nothing to eat and there are no troops to guard them. . . . Their stay in Bessarabia is inadvisable. . . . Please transport them to the interior to perform labor. . . . Please send us orders."[78]

On July 22, Topor ordered the Chişinău police office not only to send Jews to forced labor, but to continue interning them all over Bessarabia.[79] Accordingly, on July 27, 1941, 1,904 Jews were interned in the Limbeni camp in the district of Bălți.[80] On August 7, 1,200 Jews from southern

Bessarabia were assembled at Tarutino and transferred to the Cetatea Albă gendarmerie legion's jurisdiction.[81] Between July 22 and July 31, 2,452 Jews were interned in the camp at Răuţel.[82] On August 2, 4,043 Jews were deported from Hotin and 2,815 from Noua Suliţă to be interned in transit camps.[83] On August 4, 8,974 more Jews were interned in Limbeni (3,000), Rășcani (3,024), and Răuţel (2,950);[84] in early September 9,141 Jews from these camps were deported to Mărculești (2,633 from Limbeni; 3,072 from Rășcani; and 3,436 from Răuţel).[85] On August 8, the Hotin police reported that "the Jews brought together from . . . Hotin (3,340), Rădăuţi (4,113), Storojineţ (13,852), Vijniţa (1,820), [and] Cernăuţi (15,324)—a total of 27,849 [in fact 38,449!]—are being held between Secureni in the district of Hotin and Atachi in the district of Soroca."[86]

Conditions in the newly created transit camps grew increasingly harsh—in large part reflecting the virtually complete lack of planning that went into the deportations, a problem we can observe, for example, between the lines of an August 8 report by the Soroca gendarmerie legion to the chief military prosecutor: "About 25,000 Jews in the northern part of the district (Lipnic, Atachi) have come from the Cernăuţi Inspectorate, which no longer has any Jews in its territory." The Soroca legion had neither food, nor housing, nor staff to organize camps for its prisoners. The earlier elimination of the local Soroca Jewish community deprived the authorities of even the hope of supporting a camp by plunder. The authors of the report therefore pleaded with the military to force the Cernăuţi Inspectorate "to organize camps [for the Jews] in the district of Hotin."[87]

The August 8, 1941, temporary solution to the German-Romanian dispute over transit across the Dniester River spelled further overcrowding of the deportees, as evidenced in communications from Romanian military authorities warning subordinate agencies that all "evacuated" Jews would have to remain in the camps:

> The camps must incorporate a medical aid service organized by the Jewish physicians. . . . Jews are to be fed using foreign financial resources collected by the camp inmates or using assistance extended by the community. Guard duty will be set up to prevent escapes. This will be a temporary arrangement lasting . . . until new orders are issued.
>
> Jews transferred to [our] side of the Dniester by German troops must [be] interned. . . . Those from Bessarabia and Bukovina whom the German troops are returning to Bessarabia and persons who earlier fled

to the other side of the Dniester with [the evacuating] Soviet troops will
be interned in camps kept separate from the other Jewish camps.[88]

This order—Order No. 528—from the chief military prosecutor then provides information regarding the systematic organization of the transit
camps.

The response was not long in coming. On August 9, the military prosecutor of the Third Army, Lieutenant Colonel Poitevin, reported that in the
community of Edineți (Hotin District) ten thousand Jews were being
made to live in abandoned houses; no soap having been supplied, the Jews
were as filthy as their new domiciles.[89] More disturbing—from the point
of view of the military—was the fact that the Jewish camps might soon
become the source of typhus epidemics among the Romanians themselves. And the numbers of internees were growing so quickly as to become unmanageable. On August 10, the Office of the Police Inspectorate
of Cernăuți reported to the chief military prosecutor the internment in Secureni of seventeen thousand Jews; in Bârnova three thousand; and in
Berbeni some two thousand. All Jews in the district of Hotin were interned, though we have no precise numbers. The remaining Jews found
themselves under the jurisdiction of the Soroca police, whose area of jurisdiction included the crossing point at Atachi. About ten thousand Jews,
the authors of the report estimated, remained under the control of the Germans beyond the Dniester. "Despite all measures taken by the administrative and communal authorities," the report stated, "and despite the efforts
of the gendarmerie to supply the camps, it was impossible to meet the
growing needs of such a large number of persons. . . . The lack of food
was very pronounced, bread in particular. Many Jews had no money and
faced death from hunger. Measures were taken to have peasants from the
surrounding areas bring food to the Jews."[90]

On August 11, 1941, the Cernăuți Gendarme Inspectorate reported to
the chief military prosecutor that the camp set up at Secureni in Hotin already held thousands of Jews from a variety of sites:

Locality	No. of Jews
Cernăuți District	977
Herța-Dorohoi	1,200
Hotin (town)	3,800
Hotin District	6,625
Noua Suliță	2,800

Rădăuți (town)	520
Rădăuți District	580
Storojineț (town)	1,100
Storojineț District	3,180
Total	20,782

"Medical assistance for these people has been assured," the report said, but "given the excessive numbers, supply [of food] is impossible. To this end, we suggest setting up a second camp in Edineți" (in the same district). The report then warned that the Germans were about to transfer back to Romania some twelve thousand Jews currently waiting in Moghilev, and that the inspectorate could not assume responsibility for them.[91]

On that same day the Cernăuți Gendarme Inspectorate asked higher authorities "to speed up the solution to the problem of the Jews in the Secureni camp, who, because of a lack of food and hygiene, are exposed to an epidemic that could threaten the entire region."[92] On August 15, the Office of the Chief Military Prosecutor relayed its concerns to the Supreme General Staff, and as a consequence, a camp was established in Edineți. Twenty thousand Jews had been herded there, the Cernăuți Gendarme Inspectorate having received Order No. 518/1941, though not necessarily the means, from the General Staff to supply food and to guard the prisoners.[93]

Another order from the Second Section, signed by Colonel Dinulescu and sent to the Office of the Chief Military Prosecutor on August 17, called for setting up a camp at Vertujeni:

> The thirteen thousand Jews transferred by the Germans west of the Dniester to Cosăuți (opposite Iampol) will be interned. . . . Lieutenant Colonel Palade, chief of the Military Statistics Office in Iași, is assigned to carry out this operation. To this end, we ask that you order the Flamura Military Prosecutor's Department to help with the supervision and transfer of those interned. The assistance of the Soroca Prefecture should also be required in order to ensure transport, supplies, and so forth. . . . The Chișinău Gendarme Inspectorate should, through the Soroca legion, give full support to Lieutenant Colonel Palade in carrying out the mission.[94]

Dinulescu and Palade then established that camp (in 1945, Palade would declare that the camp had been set up by the General Inspectorate of the

Gendarmerie on orders from army headquarters).[95] In fact, all three statistical offices—those of Bucharest, Iaşi, and Cluj—under the Second Section, played a role in monitoring and persecuting those whom they described as "subversive elements."[96]

Along with Secureni, Edineţi, and Mărculeşti, Vertujeni was one of the four principal transit camps. As we have seen, the military, anticipating the forced return of the Jews deported over the Dniester to Romania, had first proposed the creation of the Vertujeni camp.[97] It eventually harbored the 13,500 surviving Jews earlier taken by the Romanians to the forest of Cosăuţi on the other side of the river and sent back by the Germans on August 17.[98] And they comprised only the first group of internees. Measures were taken on August 19 to intern at Vertujeni 1,600 Jews from the Alexandru cel Bun camp (Rediu) in Soroca; also on that date 2,000 able-bodied persons from the Rubleniţa camp were interned. The following day 1,500 of the disabled, the elderly, and women and small children from Rubleniţa were also transferred.[99] In all, Vertujeni received 23,009 inmates.[100]

The numbers were growing steadily from the middle of August through late September. By the second half of August the Jews in the Bessarabian transit camps were distributed as follows:

District	Camp/Ghetto	No. of Jews
Bălţi	Răuţel	2,960
	Limbenii Noi	2,622
	Răşcani	3,032
Orhei	Orhei	315
Secureni and Edineţi		11,000
Soroca	Rubleniţa	7,772
	Alexandru cel Bun	3,000
Total		30,701

Approximately twenty thousand Jews from the other side of the Dniester—Jews whom the Romanians had refused to accept in spite of pressure from the Germans—were now confined by the latter in Skariuci (probably Scazineţ). A contemporary report gave different figures:

District	No. of Jews
Bălţi	8,614
Lăpuşna	9,984

Orhei	648
Soroca	22,969
Tighina	65
Total	42,280

Of the 9,984 prisoners in the Chişinău ghetto of Lăpuşna, 2,200 were under sixteen years of age; 3,872 were aged seventeen to fifty; and the remaining 3,912 were fifty-one or older. In the Vertujeni camp in Soroca District, 8,182 of the total number of prisoners were women; 8,540 were men; and 6,247 were children.

We note from the above information that by the summer of 1941 Vertujeni was already the most populous camp.[101] This observation is supported by a report of the Chişinău Gendarme Inspectorate presented at about the same time, which offers a further breakdown by category (note that the figures for Vertujeni are identical in both tables):[102]

Camp/Ghetto	Men	Women	Children	Total
Limbenii Noi	877	908	869	2,654
Răşcani	795	1,164	1,113	3,072
Răuţel	706	1,469	1,060	3,235
Vertujeni	8,182	8,540	6,247	22,969
Total	10,560	12,081	9,289	31,930

Still further information from a report of August 19 of the same inspectorate shows the following distribution of Jews among Bessarabian transit camps:[103]

Legion	Camp/Ghetto	No. of Jews
Bălţi	Limbenii Noi	3,000
	Răşcani	3,024
	Răuţel	2,950
Cahul	Cahul	475
Cetatea Albă		0
Chilia Nouă		0
Ismail	Ismail	6
Lăpuşna		0
Orhei		0
Soroca	Rediu Mari	2,500
	Rubleniţa	5,700

	Vasilcău	3,000
Tighina	Emental	127
	Tighina	100
Total		20,882

As of August 23, there were 22,960 Jews interned in the Vertujeni camp, 10,356 Jews in the Secureni camp, and 11,762 Jews in the Edineți camp.[104]

According to the report of the Bessarabian gendarme inspector, Colonel Meculescu, the statistical breakdown of the Jews in the Bessarabian camps differed somewhat by August 30:[105]

		No. of Jews by Category			
Legion	Camp/Ghetto	Men	Women	Children	Total
Bălți	Limbenii Noi	877	908	849	2,634
	Rășcani	795	1,164	1,143	3,102
	Răuțel	706	1,469	1,060	3,235
Cahul	Cahul	0	0	0	0
Cetatea Albă		0	0	0	0
Chilia Nouă		0	0	0	0
Ismail	Ismail	0	0	0	0
Lăpușna		0	0	0	0
Orhei		0	0	0	0
Soroca	Vertujeni	8,162	8,540	6,847	23,549
Tighina		0	0	0	0
Total		10,540	12,081	9,899	32,520

Mărculești was not even mentioned in the above because it was in Bukovina, not Bessarabia; but according to Carp, there were already about ten thousand Jews there at that time.[106] A government census of Jews in Bessarabia and Northern Bukovina on September 1, 1941, produced the following overall figures: 20,909 in Secureni and Edineți; 24,000 in Vertujeni; 10,096 in Chișinău; and 10,737 in Mărculești.[107] To these we must add the 49,497 Jews confined as of October 11 in the ghetto of Cernăuți.[108] The census gave a total of 65,742 Jews in the camps and ghettos of Bessarabia as of September 1.[109]

Yet another report, this one from August 31, gave slightly different figures for the number of Jews in Bessarabian camps:[110]

District	Men	Women	Children	Total
Bălți	688	944	851	2,483
Cahul	74	300	150	524
Cetatea Albă	n.a.*	n.a.	n.a.	n.a.
Chilia Nouă	217	56	43	316
Ismail	96	0	0	96
Lăpușna	3,630	4,787	2,086	10,503
Orhei	110	159	65	334
Soroca	8,182	8,540	6,247	22,969
Tighina	12	39	14	65
Total				37,290

*n.a. = data not available.

The Cernăuți Gendarme Inspectorate reported to the Office of the Chief Military Prosecutor on September 1 that there were 12,248 Jews in Edineți and 10,201 in Secureni.[111] Note No. 7438 of September 11 from the same inspectorate to the provincial administration of Bukovina gave the same exact numbers, which leads us to believe that they were simply copied from the earlier report.[112]

On September 4, General Topor reported to headquarters on the number of Jews in the camps of Bessarabia and Bukovina and in the ghetto of Chișinău, pursuant to the Second Section's Order No. 5023/B:[113]

Legion	Camp/Ghetto	No. of Jews
Bălți	Limbenii Noi	2,634
	Rășcani	3,072
	Răuțel	3,233
Chișinău	Chișinău	10,400
Hotin	Edineți	11,762
	Secureni	10,356
Soroca	Vertujeni	22,969
Total		64,426

The number of Jews in Bessarabian camps peaked around September 25, after which the major deportations got under way. At that point the numbers were as follows:[114]

District	No. of Jews
Bălți	9,061
Cahul	524
Cetatea Albă	0
Chilia Nouă	316
Ismail	96
Lăpușna	11,323
Orhei	333
Soroca	22,969
Tighina	68
Total	44,690

According to Hilberg's assessment, "more than 27,000 Jews died in July and August 1941 in Bessarabia and Bukovina, in August alone 7,000 in the transit camps and 10,000 in Transnistria."[115] An unpublished document by Romanian historians Ion Calfeteanu and Maria Covaci pushes this figure up to 27,500 deaths over the same time period.[116] We shall now explore some of the stories behind this massive number of victims.

*   *   *

The quantitative picture is terrible enough, but the testimony of survivors, perpetrators, and witnesses paints an almost surreal canvas that more clearly conveys the horror of the transit camps. The Răuțel camp, for example, established in the woods twelve kilometers from Bălți on July 17, amassed Jews from the city ghetto into dilapidated cottages and antitank ditches, all surrounded by barbed wire.[117] Between 2,600 and 2,800 competed for the six cottages, which together could hold 100 people at the most; those forced to seek shelter in the ditches covered themselves with makeshift roofs of branches.[118] A Romanian officer stated that fifty or sixty prisoners died of hunger and maltreatment every day and that "the entire population of Bălți spoke with horror of the camp." Behind the Pămînteni train station the same witness watched as a convoy of inmates swept mud off the streets: "Most were barefoot with no head wear; all were dressed in rags, dying of hunger." At one point workers from a restaurant took the inmates a crate of potato peelings and other garbage, upon which "the poor Jews . . . flung themselves like animals." Some of the local roughnecks tossed them table scraps in the hope of starting scuffles. The witness himself tried to give a pack of cigarettes to a man he knew among the "convicts," but "the sentinel threatened to hit me with his rifle butt, even though I was wearing a military uniform and was armed."[119]

The transit camp of Secureni opened at the end of July 1941. Initially, Jews from Hotin District were interned there, as well as some from Noua Suliță and other Bessarabian localities. According to Joe Gherman, the Hotin prefect, eating raw cereal grain caused the death of 30 or 40 percent of the internees during the first several days, though this later decreased to one-tenth of that rate. The Jews in Secureni, however, were generally in a better financial position—they came directly from the surrounding district—than those in Edineți, who had come from Cernăuți, Storojineț, Noua Suliță, and Rădăuți, totally destitute after having been plundered during previous transportations across the Dniester River and back again.[120] At Edineți conditions were so atrocious that in October 85 percent of the children perished.[121] Whatever their differences, though, the features common to all the camps were more important, as M. Rudich's description of life as he knew it in one of the major transit camps shows:

> The little houses [were] abandoned, ruined, [their inmates] sheltered between walls eaten by the rains. . . . Dirty because they could not wash and did not have a change of clothes, in rags, almost naked, [the new residents] haunted the alleys or lay in their dirty rooms, . . . covered . . . with tatters that the wind lifted, making it seem as if their skin had been torn off.
>
> Then the epidemic came. People suffered for days on end because of their illnesses, with no help, burning with fever, eaten away . . . by suffering that drained them . . . on frames with no bedding. People died like flies. . . . In tiny huts, . . . in barracks, or wherever they could find some shelter for limbs overwhelmed by exhaustion, the Jews sought refuge, . . . leaving behind them, by the roads or in cemeteries, loved ones whom they had cherished. . . . Food? What they could carry with them in their bags, what people sent to them, what they could beg. . . . Misery stalked at the gates . . . and gradually seeped into the alleyways, the crumbling hovels, the courtyards, and the barracks.[122]

In Secureni rape became frequent as the Romanian guards took advantage of their life-and-death power over the imprisoned women and girls; suicides sometimes followed.[123]

The Cernăuți Gendarme Inspectorate reported to the chief military prosecutor on September 1 that it had arranged "good housing" in Edineți and Secureni, but it conceded that the Jews lacked all means and that in Edineți scarlet fever, mumps, dysentery, and typhoid fever had appeared. In Secureni 1,698 Jews from Lipcani had been confined in a "deplorable [state], having not eaten for four days, in rags and covered with parasites."[124] The same inspectorate reported to the governorship of Bukovina on September 11 on these camps, particularly on Vertujeni, in which

> there are a lot of old people, children, and women. . . . Housing conditions are presently acceptable; they will [however] need to be prepared for winter. Despite . . . measures that we take to prevent it, it is easy to escape; for that reason we need barbed wire and lumber. . . . The Jews say that they have no more money with which to buy food. [This will get worse] in the winter when we will not be able to provide any transportation and the residents of neighboring villages will no longer be able to come to the market with foodstuffs. . . . The little wood there once was is gone, and now they make fires with wood from fences or with pieces of the roof. Most of them have no clothes or anything to cover themselves. Most were transferred into Ukraine, then sent back by the Germans, [having] lost everything [they once had]. . . . They suffer a shortage of medication.[125]

One recently discovered document provides a list of rules that governed the transit camps in Bukovina, suggesting something of the conditions in these camps:

a. No one may enter the camp.
b. No one may leave the camp without the approval of General Calotescu; such approval will be communicated by the inspectorate of the Hotin legion.
c. The prefectures can handle supplies, housing, and medical assistance, but they cannot be empowered to release [inmates] from the camps.
d. The prisoners may not communicate with anyone [from outside] under any circumstances.
e. The internal policing is to be conducted by the prisoners, and the legion commander is to intervene when there is a lack of discipline.
f. No one may receive or send any mail.

g. It is forbidden to purchase or sell valuable objects belonging to those who are imprisoned in the camps.

h. Those who have been slated by the prefecture for civic duties must clearly be identified in order to prevent the substitution of other persons.[126]

The testimony of a survivor from the Edineți camp reveals even more:

> The Bessarabian Jews suffered the worst fate. While the Jews in Bukovina still had enough that they could sell or trade (clothes, silver, gold), those from Bessarabia were already in rags. They did not have the right [even] to leave the houses. They were allowed to go out for only two hours [a day]. There was a shortage of water, [and what there was] was polluted. They paid with their life if they left the ghetto; sometimes they were abused. . . . Then there was the typhoid epidemic. The camp commander warned us that if typhoid spread, he would be forced to execute everyone in the ghetto.[127]

As noted earlier, the Vertujeni transit camp had been established in mid-August to house the Jews returned by the Germans, along with the contingent from Soroca District. On August 19, the Bessarabian governor's office cabled the Soroca Prefecture instructions to undertake the creation of this and other camps.[128] There were 22,884 Jews in Vertujeni on September 6, guarded by 248 soldiers.[129] One man assigned to a subsidiary road gang later recalled conditions in the new camp:

> Sanitary conditions were horrible. . . . Water came from four or five wells. There were about 25,000 people. There were endless lines to the wells, where we spent entire nights waiting for a little water. Each family received a small iron pot to cook meals in; we would take that pot to get water. The bread that we were sold was made from [substitutes]. People became so ill from eating fat and [ersatz] bread and from drinking dirty water that they died by the hundreds every day. One day I went to the ditches to move my bowels. . . . As I got closer, I heard moaning . . . and I saw men who had been thrown alive into the latrine.[130]

Lieutenant Colonel Alexandru Constantinescu, the first commander of Vertujeni, came from the Second Section. During the postwar trial of all the commanders of the Vertujeni and Mărculești camps, Constantinescu, an honest man who had requested to be relieved of his commission, testified as a witness rather than as an accused criminal.[131] He termed the crowding of the Jews from Bukovina and Bessarabia into the Vertujeni camp a "horrific concentration" for whom "we could not even guarantee a place to rest." The overcrowding was almost "indescribable," he re-called, "women, children, young girls, men, the sick, those who were dying, and women in labor—all having no way to feed themselves."[132] Four or five hundred Jews were forced to stay in one building designed for seventy or eighty. The Jews reached Vertujeni "covered with lice and abscesses, so worn out that . . . before we could take charge of them, some died, others fainted, and pregnant women gave birth. . . . The suffering of the officers, especially mine, just to see them produced such a state of ten-sion that I could neither eat nor sleep."[133] A former guard, Gheorghe Petrişor, seconded his chief: "Jews died every day and didn't even have the chance of receiving a proper funeral."[134]

Colonel Vasile Agapie replaced the malcontent Constantinescu as commander of Vertujeni on September 8. Though he and his deputy, Cap-tain Sever Buradescu, remained for a mere three weeks, they wasted little time in exploiting the opportunities this assignment offered.[135] One sur-vivor recalled that their cruelty was equaled only by their greed:

> They made us pave the streets of the village, but where could we find the stones? From the banks of the Dniester! To satisfy this whim they set us to task: people weakened by hunger, women, teenage girls, children. Imagine a column of thousands of people [almost naked because their things had been stolen] all carrying stones that weighed twenty to thirty pounds, prodded with rifle butts.[136]

The gendarme station chief for Vertujeni, Ion Oprea, stated during a 1941 inquiry into abuses in the Chişinău ghetto that Captains Buradescu and Rădulescu had often raped Jewish women in the camp.[137] The prisoners were beaten on the slightest pretext. Agapie and Buradescu systematically looted the prisoners. A two-lei fee was levied on prisoners who wanted to make purchases from peasant marketers allowed in the ghetto.[138] The Jew-ish community of Iaşi sent aid totaling 300,000 lei on September 9, but Colonel Agapie pocketed the sum.[139] Some of the inmates improvised the manufacture of soap, but although the soap was successfully marketed, the camp commander kept the money.

The horrors of what was going on also affected the majority popula-tion. For example, soldiers guarding the camp began to suffer from lice.

Drunk with his power, Colonel Agapie began to abuse the Romanian villagers as well. Agapie's men looted the village salt storehouse and even helped themselves to its roofing. Buradescu went so far as to take a coat and bed linen from some peasants who had temporarily lodged him.[140] It hardly comes as a surprise, therefore, that upon the camp's liquidation on October 8, its staff didn't even bother to clean up the remaining corpses, simply leaving them for the villagers to remove.

The transit camp at Mărculeşti was established on September 1. Initially, Jews from the immediate vicinity were confined there. Later in the month Jews from Bălţi District were brought, following the liquidation of camps at Răuţel, Limbenii Noi, and Răşcani on orders from General Topor and the Second Section.[141] A few weeks later some of the Jews from Cernăuţi and Rădăuţi on their way to Transnistria also transited through Mărculeşti.[142] A qualified specialist by now, Colonel Agapie was transferred with his subordinates to Mărculeşti on September 28.[143]

On October 5, Colonel Radu Davidescu, chief of Marshal Antonescu's military cabinet, conveyed his superior's order (No. 8507) to the governors of Bessarabia and Bukovina to coordinate with the National Bank of Romania "the exchange of jewelry and precious metal owned by Jews who have been evacuated from Bessarabia and Bukovina."[144] The order required payment in reichsmarks in the camps or at crossing points in Ukraine.[145] Ion Mihăiescu, official representative of the National Bank for these matters, reached the Dniester River on October 9, 1941, working at the crossing points at Rezina and Orhei until October 14, when he moved on to Mărculeşti.[146] Mihăiescu soon recorded his first impressions in a report to the bank: "thousands of mice scampered about the streets and houses. More than once did they climb up our pants. There was an unusual number of flies that were extremely annoying. . . . As you know, our mission was to collect jewelry and specie and exchange them."[147] Even though a representative from the Ministry of National Defense dispatched to Bucharest three train cars full of rugs, sewing machines, bedding, soap, and fabrics in November 1941, Mihăiescu complained that similar loot worth millions of lei had been left in abandoned houses, protected by neither window nor door, in Mărculeşti.[148] Mihăiescu and his National Bank team thus looted 18,566 Jews in Mărculeşti, even paying a midwife 12,000 lei to conduct body searches of the women for them.[149]

Scolnic Mayer later recounted how, upon his own arrival at the train station in Mărculeşti, "we were greeted by Colonel Agapie and Mihăiescu, who fired pistol shots in the air and waved a stick—threatening to kill those who did not hand over their valuables and surplus clothing";[150] those who refused were shot right then and there.[151] At his subsequent trial Mihăiescu declared that it had been "a representative of the army" who "confiscated" personal possessions and that these possessions had consisted only of "identification papers and diplomas."[152] (In 1941, when Camilia Tutnauer's husband asked Mihăiescu to leave him his credentials because he was an attorney, the latter replied, "Now you are a dog, and you no longer need documents.")[153] Berura Mehr's mother underwent one of Mihăiescu's beatings and died a few days later; according to Henriette Harnik, Mihăiescu enjoyed beating elderly women. Harnik also witnessed Mihăiescu savagely beating a Jew who had requested a receipt for his stolen belongings; the man died several days later from his injuries. Ruhal Kamar's father died the same way. Mitea Katz's seven-year-old granddaughter denounced her grandmother to Mihăiescu for having hidden jewelry, after which both "disappeared forever." Aron Clincofer stated that Mihăiescu confiscated shoes from deportees, while others reported that he ripped earrings from female prisoners' ears.[154] Ella Garinstein, soon to be orphaned in Transnistria, later recounted how Mihăiescu took the coats her family had been wearing, brutally hitting her mother on the ears with a stick to force her to hand over her earrings; when Ella's fifteen-year-old brother refused to give him his boots, Mihăiescu beat him so brutally that he died an hour later.[155]

Stefan Dragomirescu testified that he had seen "thousands of deportees" living in Mărculeşti "in a state of misery that defied description." Corpses lay "in cellars, ditches, and courtyards. You could always find Ion Mihăiescu with his truncheon, beating up [even] deportees who had done nothing wrong. He pushed bestiality beyond the limits."[156] One might sometimes find corpses floating in the camp's only well.[157] Brutes such as Mihăiescu and his men confiscated everything down to baby cribs "for the benefit of the state."[158] The looting of Agapie, Buradescu, and Mihăiescu certainly reached extraordinary proportions, but since an insufficient amount of the booty made its way to the appropriate state coffers, the Supervisory Board of the Defense Ministry undertook an investigation in the spring of 1942.[159]

Unfortunately, as the following sections of this chapter make clear, conditions in other ghettos were similarly awful.

The Ghettos of Chișinău and Cernăuți

The ghetto of Chișinău was the largest in Bessarabia, in operation mainly from July to November 1941, after which time only a few hundred Jews remained. It had been established on July 24 by Order No. 61 of General Voiculescu, the provincial governor, and eventually housed as many as eleven thousand Jews;[160] on August 19, somewhere between 9,984 and 10,578 residents inhabited the ghetto, of whom 2,200 to 2,300 were children and 5,200 to 6,200 were women.[161] Throughout its short existence the ghetto never quite sealed its inmates hermetically from the outside. Some of the guards helped the Jews get food from the outside in return for any valuables the prisoners could offer. Voiculescu worried that the authorities maintained only an "illusion" of control, and at one point he warned that if measures were not taken to assert control, "we will be surprised and overwhelmed by the *Jidani,* or see them flee." To minimize commerce between the guards and the inmates, he ordered the former to be changed every ten days.[162]

As heartless as his attempts to suppress the "black market" may seem, Voiculescu nevertheless worried about certain elements of the situation that were detrimental to his inmates. In an August 31 report to the president of the Council of Ministers, for instance, he stated that Chișinău had the capacity to employ only eight hundred Jews to earn their daily bread; indeed, even their semilicit trade with the locals provided sustenance for only "a small group." The majority of them had no means whatsoever and had to rely on handouts from an overtaxed ad hoc ghetto committee. Reflecting his own anti-Semitic prejudices—and perhaps a cynical understanding of world politics—Voiculescu proposed that the government approach the Hebrew Immigrant Aid Society (H.I.A.S.) in the hope of obtaining aid from the United States.[163]

In the early days of the Chișinău ghetto Jews were permitted to exit with passes from the city's military commander, facilitating soldiers' and gentile civilians' exploitation of their plight. Colonel Meculescu reported on August 20 that guards here allowed Jews to leave without a pass or without donning a star in exchange for wedding bands and other valuables.[164] When Marshal Antonescu learned of this business early in 1942, he was so angered that he demanded the names of those involved.[165] To reimpose control, Colonel D. Tudose, military commander of the city of

Chişinău, addressed the problem by reducing the area of the ghetto on August 29 to better "isolate the Jewish population."[166]

But further overcrowding meant a further reduction in the quality of life. An SSI report covering the period August 20–31, 1941, stated that hygiene in all the camps and ghettos was worsening from day to day because of a lack of soap and underwear, presaging a possible typhoid epidemic. Another report stated that in the Chişinău ghetto—with a population base of 5,377 families (as of September), or 11,380 individuals—the Jews lacked clothing and bedding, and ten to fifteen were dying every day.[167]

Mandated by Antonescu and the Council of Ministers on December 4, a commission investigating the conditions that produced these statistics determined that 11,525 Jews lived in the ghetto at its peak, 3,000 of whom had been utterly destitute. The commission's findings indicated that 441 Jews had died there, 20 of them suicides.[168] Most had died from "natural" causes, especially the elderly or the very young. The commission assembled the following mortality figures:[169]

Date	No. of Deaths*
August 16	4
August 18	3
August 19	4
August 31	5
October 2	12
October 3	9
October 4–5	14
October 9–10	18
October 11	16
October 12	10
October 14–15	14
October 15–16	11
October 18	10
October 21	12
October 22	5

*These numbers do not match the commission's findings. Consistency was not a priority for the Romanian bureaucracy.

Though deportation of nearly the entire surviving population of the ghetto took place during the fall, some flaw in the system permitted a reprieve for about 150 sick prisoners; others exempted for various reasons totaled fewer than this figure.[170]

The second ghetto under discussion here, that in Cernăuți eventually attained a population of about 55,000 Jews, 30,000 of whom were deported in the fall of 1941 and 5,000 the following summer.[171] Those remaining survived in the ghetto until the end of the war.

The Bukovina administration served under three governors during the war: Colonel Alexandru Rioșeanu, who died on August 30, 1941; the aforementioned General Corneliu Calotescu, one of the chief authors of the 1941 and 1942 deportations; and General C. I. Dragalina, who became governor in 1943. After Romanian troops reoccupied Cernăuți in the summer of 1941, Rioșeanu organized a banquet attended by the king, Marshal Antonescu, Dr. Nicolae Lupu (the pro-Jewish leader of the National Peasant party), Colonel Mardare, General Topor, and representatives of Germany. Topor would testify on April 26, 1945, that he had heard Antonescu tell Rioșeanu at this dinner to "get rid of the Jews of Bukovina or I will get rid of you"; Antonescu reportedly told Topor more or less the same.[172] General Ioanițiu was said to have confirmed the same message shortly thereafter during a conversation with Topor on Antonescu's train.[173]

Thus, over the course of a nine-hour operation on October 11, the entire Jewish population of Cernăuți was locked inside the ghetto.[174] But it was earlier, under Rioșeanu, that the system of segregation in the region had been initiated. It was Rioșeanu who signed Order No. 1344 on July 30, 1941, barring Jews from circulating outside their quarters except during the hours between 6:00 A.M. and 8:00 P.M. (an order by the government of Bukovina changed this permitted span in late 1942 to the period between 10:00 A.M. and 1:00 P.M.). Rioșeanu also signed (on orders from the central authorities) a directive requiring Jews to wear a yellow star. The stars turned into a source of income for the local authorities under Calotescu's administration, which issued further regulations governing the Cernăuți ghetto on October 11, 1941, placing the Jews under military jurisdiction and establishing penalties ranging from terms in concentration camps to execution for refusing to wear the Star of David or inciting others to do likewise.[175] It is not known if the death penalty actually came into play over this issue, but hundreds of people were certainly sent to the concentration camp at Edineți for having been caught without the star.[176] Several thousand Jews were permitted to remain there subsequently, the only such locale in Bukovina. During the 1944 retreat General Dragalina suspended the requirement of the yellow star for the Jews at Cernăuți because he feared the Germans would press for mass executions. If evasion of deportation spelled life for many, circumstances nevertheless remained hard; it is indicative of the struggle that only those holding special permits enjoyed the right to work and that these numbered only one thousand out of the fifteen thousand residing in the ghetto as of 1943–1944.[177]

THE DEPORTATIONS FROM BESSARABIA AND BUKOVINA

Bessarabia

Ion Antonescu stated on October 6, 1941, at a meeting of the Council of Ministers, "I have decided to evacuate all [of the Jews] forever from these regions. I still have about ten thousand Jews in Bessarabia who will be sent beyond the Dniester within several days and, if circumstances permit, beyond the Urals."[178] The Bessarabian Jews were deported from the Chișinău ghetto, the Vertujeni camp (where the Soroca District Jews were imprisoned), and the Mărculești camp (where the Bălți District Jews, previously imprisoned in the Rășcani, Limbenii Noi, and Răuțel camps, were interned). The Jews from the ghettos of Orhei, Cahul, Ismail, Vâlcov, Chilia Noua, and Bolgrad were also deported.[179]

The Supreme General Staff organized and supervised the expulsions. Gheorghe Alexianu, governor of Transnistria, later recalled during the Antonescu trial how

> two colonels whose names I do not remember came to Tiraspol in mid-September [insisting] that Marshal Antonescu had sent them to organize the deportation to Transnistria of Jews from Bessarabia and Bukovina and that those from Moldavia and Walachia would soon follow. . . . The Supreme General Staff had sent them, and they showed me [a] map, stating that all the transports of Jews would be under the jurisdiction of the army and the gendarmerie and that the administration [of Transnistria] had to . . . obtain housing and food for them.[180]

Alexianu specified twice during his testimony that the initial order indicated that the Jews were supposed to only cross through Transnistria, their final destination being Ukraine, beyond the Bug River.[181]

General Topor, the chief military prosecutor, ordered the Transnistria

Gendarme Inspectorate to lay the groundwork. It planned to begin on September 6, sending groups of one thousand people to the crossing points of Criuleni-Karantin and Rezina-Râbniţa,[182] even though the Transnistria legion warned on September 3 that the deportations should begin only on the fifteenth.[183] The Second Army Territorial Command ordered the UER to collect resources for the Bessarabian Jews, but no supplies could ever be delivered.[184]

General Topor sent the following order to Colonel Meculescu on September 7, 1941:

1. The operation to evacuate the Jews must begin on September 12 with the Vertujeni camp toward Cosăuţi and Rezina, pursuant to directives from the Chişinău Gendarme Inspectorate.
2. Groups of not more than 1,600, including children, will cross the Dniester at a rate not exceeding 800 per day.
3. Forty to fifty carts should comprise each group.
4. The groups are to leave Vertujeni every other day.
5. At each crossing a legion gendarme officer should be posted.
6. Passage of the groups should occur with no formalities.
7. Itineraries are to be drawn up by Lieutenant Colonel Palade, with the help of the legion commanders.
8. Two additional platoons [of gendarmes] are to be assigned for assistance.
9. The territorial station gendarmes will help cleanse the land [i.e., of Jews] and bury the dead with the help of locals.
10. *The way to handle those who do not submit? ALEXIANU.*
11. Do not take the prisoners through customs. Those who loot will be executed.[185]

What was the meaning of "ALEXIANU" in Topor's order? Lieutenant Augustin Roşca, in charge of deporting the Jews interned at Secureni and Edineţi, clarified the term when he stated on December 23, 1941, to a commission formed by Antonescu to investigate irregularities in the Chişinău ghetto and the deportations, that he had received the following order from the Supreme General Staff via Lieutenant Eugen Marino and Commander Drăgulescu:

The Jews from the Edineţi and Secureni camps will be evacuated beyond the Dniester. [We were ordered to] form groups of one hundred per day, supply them, and request a cart for every one hundred persons, and we [were given] the special task of executing those who could not keep up with the convoy because of weakness or sickness. . . . I was ordered to send two to three days before the departure of the convoys . . . a [blank space in text] which had to be presented to the station chiefs of those localities [on the itinerary] and to request paramilitary personnel and tools (shovels and picks) to dig ditches for about one hundred people at appropriate places, specifically away from the villages so that no one hears the screams and the rifle shots, and not on a hillside so that the water does not wash away the bodies. The ditches must be dug every ten kilometers. . . . *For those who could not reach the ditches, the standard code word for on-site execution was "ALEXIANU."* I was told to transmit this order to Edineţi and also to Lieutenant Victor Popovici in my own company.[186]

During his trial in 1945, Drăgulescu confirmed that he had transmitted General Topor's order, which had been previously conveyed by Marino to Roşca, an order specifying that "all evacuees who could not follow the convoys for reasons of illness or exhaustion must be executed."[187]

On September 11, 1941, Colonel Meculescu ordered the evacuation of the Vertujeni camp. His report that day to the Office of the Chief Military Prosecutor emphasized that this operation would be carried out with the participation of Lieutenant Colonel Palade, who, you may recall, was chief of the Military Statistics Office of Iaşi (directly subordinate to the Second Section of the Supreme General Staff).[188] This order is so telling that it deserves reproduction in full here:

> Pursuant to the order of the chief military prosecutor, please carry out the evacuation of 22,150 Jews from the Vertujeni-Soroca camp as of September 12, 1941, [starting] at exactly eight in the morning so that they can be transferred beyond the Dniester into Ukraine. . . . We have selected the following two itineraries:
>
> a. An itinerary the crossing point of which is Cosăuţi, leaving from Vertujeni, along which route we go to the west of the village of Cremenea, then on the Gura-Camenca-Soroca-Cosăuţi route.
> b. The second itinerary will consist of the Rezina crossing point and the following route: Vertujeni-Temeleuţi-Văşcăuţi-Cusmirca-Rezina.

The Jews in the camps will be rounded up in groups not exceeding 1,600, including children. . . . Those convoys [will be] under the direct supervision . . . of the camp officers and gendarmes. . . . Subsequently, the camp leadership will provide an officer for each itinerary as well as the gendarmes required for supervision.

The march will pace itself at thirty kilometers per day, and each journey will include stages, as follows:

- Itinerary a—Cosăuți, the first stage of the march from Vertujeni to the village of Rediu located on the Gura-Camenca-Soroca route, the second stage from the village of Rediu to Soroca, and the third stage from Soroca to Cosăuți.
- Itinerary b—Rezina, the first stage of the march from Vertujeni to the village of Voinova, the second stage from Cuhurești to Mateuți, and the third stage from Mateuți to Rezina.

The camp officers will lead those convoys and will accompany them, especially on the first itinerary to Soroca and the second itinerary to Mateuți, and from there the convoy will be led by legion officers.

Captain Victor Ramadan's responsibility is to lead the convoys from Soroca and Mateuți on the Soroca-Cosăuți itinerary, and Lieutenant Popoiu's responsibility is the Mateuți-Rezina itinerary. Those officers will be in Soroca and Mateuți at eight at night on September 14 in order to organize the departure on the next day to the crossing points.

The crossings will not require any [bureaucratic] formalities. Eight hundred people will be transferred on September 15, [resting] before the crossing points so as not to block the bridges, and another eight hundred people will be transferred on September 16.

This operation should be carried out as follows: every other day two convoys equal in size (1,600 people) will set out along the same itineraries, stop at the same locations, and be handed over to the legion officers at those localities. The legion officers will be aided by [local] gendarmes, who will receive the Jews at the crossing of the Dniester so as to keep watch over them. Two legion officers will therefore be located at the Mateuți-Soroca-Cosăuți and the Rezina crossing . . . points, taking into account the fact that those convoys will leave Vertujeni every other day and the time needed for one transport, and they will [conduct the deportees over the river], thereafter returning immediately to receive other convoys. The commanders [of the gendarmerie] legions and administrative officials will outfit each convoy with fifty carts that will carry part of the baggage and those who cannot walk. [The number of carts per convoy was soon drastically reduced.—R.I.]

The commanders [of the gendarmerie] legions will also be responsible for giving orders to the posts along the itineraries to help with the *curatarea terenului* [cleansing of the land], burying of the dead, and setting up in timely fashion lodgings at village outskirts, inside barns, in shacks, and the like, so as to keep any epidemic in check. . . .

Jews may not be robbed by the escorts; those who commit such acts will be executed. *With those who disobey, we will proceed according to standards set forth in the law.*[189]

On October 10, Colonel Meculescu ordered the deportation of the Jews from the Chişinău ghetto and southern Bessarabia. The order was sent to the Gendarme Inspectorates of Cahul, Ismail, and Orhei and to Police Companies 23 and 82. Order No. 2830 stated that an interim ghetto had to be established at Tarutino[190] and that the Jews from Chişinău were going to cross the Dniester at Rezina and Tighina, those from southern Bessarabia at Tighina. Other instructions pertaining to the Chişinău cohorts mandated the following: convoys of 1,500 people proceeding primarily by foot; 100–120 carts per convoy for the sick, the elderly, and the children; a starting date of October 12, 1941; and two itineraries—one consisting of four stages (one between Chişinău and Peresecina [28 km], one from Persecina to Orhei [14 km], one from Orhei to Chiperceni [20 km], and one from Chiperceni to Rezina [18 km]) and a second consisting of three stages (one from Chişinău to Mereni [18 km], one from Mereni to Bulboaca [22 km], and one from Bulboaca to Tighina [16 km]). The crossings were to be carried out at a rate of 750 Jews per day.

With regard to the Jews from southern Bessarabia, the same Order No. 2830 anticipated that from Cahul, Ismail, Bolgrad, Chilia, and Vâlcov, one convoy to Tarutino from each locality would suffice, envisioning three or four stages of eighteen to thirty-four kilometers each. In Tarutino all would merge in a single column heading for Tighina, sixty carts having been provided for the sick and the children. The order included specific instructions to consider this a "land cleansing," exact times of departure for all convoys, and very specific itineraries with maps.[191] Colonel Meculescu signed another order on October 23 elaborating more precise instructions for handling the Jews after arrival in the interim ghetto at

Tarutino. At that time there were 2,270 Jews there, then slated for two convoys, one on the twenty-fifth and the other two days later, each divided into three twenty-four-kilometer marches to the crossing point of Iaska.[192] Yet another order, No. 24206, pertaining to the same deportation of Jews from Bessarabia was issued by the army's Third Corps on October 26.[193]

The Bessarabian Jews were systematically fleeced—and not only by peasants in the villages they crossed, official orders to the contrary notwithstanding. Indeed, it was Governor Voiculescu himself who charged a committee of the National Bank of Romania in Chişinău with confiscating gold and other valuables from the Jews.[194] All furniture from the deportees' homes was distributed to local civilian and military officials.[195] According to General Tătăranu, a similar committee of the bank in Atachi robbed the Jews, assisted by officers of Police Company 60.[196] As General Tobescu reported on November 20,

> [when the] deportees arrived at the Dniester, large quantities of luggage remained in the train stations or in the fields. The local authorities ordered the luggage stored in private homes [!] and depots, but the measures taken to guard it were inadequate. We began to inventory [the possessions] today, and we will proceed with their distribution to the army, hospitals, Red Cross, and Patronage Society [i.e., Comisia de Patronaj, a national charity run by Ion Antonescu's wife, Maria]. So far the Fourth Territorial Command of Mărculeşti has taken ten railroad cars [of the Jews' property] and the Ministry of National Defense another three.[197]

The deportations to Transnistria signified death for thousands, and the roads leading to the Dniester River were soon littered with corpses. Sometimes the convoy guards executed Jews who wore the best clothes and then "sold" the corpses to neighboring peasants for their clothes at prices varying between 1,500 and 2,000 lei.[198] The report of the committee set up by Marshal Antonescu to examine irregularities in the Chişinău ghetto contains details of the instructions to the convoy gendarmes and their manner of fulfilling them. Lieutenant Roşca, for example, carried out the orders in a manner that produced the death of five hundred of the Jews evacuated from Secureni to Cosăuţi. Roşca himself provided the following images:

> On the road peasants waited like crows to steal something. At the first ditch, which was about five kilometers [into our journey], we ordered six

gendarmes to guard fifty or sixty [Jews] until the evening came [when they were shot]. The columns were moving . . . in disorderly fashion because of the children, the women, and the elderly. In other ditches we buried 120 Jews from the first convoy. We executed 120 persons in each of the last three convoys, . . . or a total of about 500 [sic].[199]

The Jews from the Secureni camp had been organized into two large cohorts on October 2 in preparation for departures for Transnistria stretching through October 5. Abused and robbed during preparations for departure,[200] they were again humiliated and their increasingly meager possessions pillaged at various way stations along the roads. Riva Leivadman, a survivor, testified that

> while other prisoners of the Secureni camp were being transferred toward Atachi on the other side of the Dniester, we were being robbed by the convoying soldiers and forced to sing embarrassing songs [while] the women with small children . . . who initially were given permission to ride in the horse carts were thrown off. In the night a gendarme officer . . . told all those who could not continue . . . that they would be executed. About five hundred elderly people, women, and even children were executed in groups of ten.[201]

A survivor of the last convoy, a member of a group originating from Hotin recalled:

> We were told that the sick who could not leave the camp would be executed. It was impossible to describe how people, consumed with typhoid fever, dragged themselves through the mud or mothers carried agonizing babies in their arms. Throughout the journey we learned that the convoy before us had been robbed and partially eliminated by the escort. Our numbers diminished as we were forced, day and night, through hills, valleys, and swamps, under the rain and during the first frost of the fall. On the road we abandoned everything we had because we were so exhausted that we could not carry any luggage. At the Dniester, before entering Atachi, we were told under threat of execution to hand over all identification papers and documents.[202]

The same conditions prevailed among the Edineți-Cosăuți convoy, directly under Lieutenant Popovici and indirectly under Lieutenant Roșca.[203] The Edineți camp was evacuated in two phases, on October 10 and 13, 1941. In one of the convoys one hundred people were executed because they could no longer move.[204] Right after that, on October 15, the convoy reached the outskirts of the village of Corbu, where it spent the night in an open field. "Exhausted, famished, with bones broken by the blows from the guards, drenched through and through by the rain," one survivor recalled, "we had to rest that unforgettable night in the mud of the field. The strong wind, the icy night, the first snow killed 860 people."[205]

Observing the digging of ditches and the burial of corpses, peasants living along the route of the Edineți Jews figured out what was going on and began to hide in nearby fields or simply wait openly by the roadside "before rushing to the corpses to rob them."[206] Among the Jews from the Edineți camp was one group originally evicted from the villages of Bukovina that had already endured a torment of two months' pointless wandering just to get there and that then had to endure the Edineți camp regime itself. One hundred from this group were executed near Atachi on November 15, too exhausted to proceed further, including Rabbi Iehosua Frankel of Seletin and his entire family, Rabbi Frankel of Nepolocăuți, Eti Birnbaum, Eti Wagner, Sura Schertzer, Erna Sin, Zlotschewer, and another man by the name of Reinis.[207] Dr. Siegfried Wittner was part of the last convoy from Edineți, dubbed "the convoy of death." He later testified:

> The people at the rear were executed. The order was given to round up in a shed all the sick, convalescent, those falling behind. Our protests, as doctors, were greeted with these words: "Yes, once upon a time you were doctors, but today you are disgusting *Jidani,* and if you do not obey I will shoot you like dogs." The carts at the rear came back empty, and the sergeant, weapon in hand, said, "I got rid of the excess weight." On the road to the left and the right lay the corpses of Jews murdered on previous convoys.[208]

The deportation of the Vertujeni camp was originally planned to extend over three weeks, from September 16 to October 8, 1941. But, as the Soroca gendarme legion would soon report (in Telegram No. 5433), the operation had begun only after delays caused by the defective state of the bridges at Cosăuți-Soroca and Rezina-Orhei; 22,969 Jews had been deported from Vertujeni between September 22 and October 4 (i.e., ahead of schedule) in seven groups of approximately 3,200 Jews each.[209] The Jews were forced to walk thirty kilometers a day, though the number of carts was much smaller than planned—anywhere from four to eight per convoy instead of the fifty required. In the chaos, and as those too weak to keep up fell behind, many families were separated, their members never to see one another again.[210] During one of the postwar trials, one witness, Captain Stoleru, described the progress of the deportees:

> The people had no food when they left the camp, no carts to accommodate all the elderly, the sick, and the children. The route led across open fields; there was not enough supervision, which enabled the civilian population to steal from the Jews throughout the journey. So did the convoys of those unfortunate deportees—exhausted by hunger, misery, and sickness, [and] robbed by everyone—follow their path, . . . harassed by the shouts and blows of the gendarmes, until they could find some rest, either in Cosăuţi Forest or in the "regions of death" beyond the Dniester. The road from Vertujeni to Cosăuţi Forest was lined by the corpses of those who no longer had the strength to reach the crossing point.[211]

Another survivor recalled arrival with a group of evacuees at the Mărculeşti-Cosăuţi Forest on November 4, soaked to the bone by the rain that dogged their trek. No sooner had the wretches huddled together for their night's rest when "someone let out a terrible cry. He had found a ditch, filled with the corpses of men, women, and children."[212]

A report dated September 30, 1941, of the Chişinău Gendarme Inspectorate sent to the government of Bessarabia mentioned that 3,150 Jews had been transferred on September 27, 28, and 29. Another similar report dated October 2, 1941, pointed out that 2,981 Jews had been transferred beyond the Dniester on September 30 and October 1, 1941.[213]

The deportation of Jews from the ghettos of Cahul, Ismail, Bolgrad, Vâlcov, Chilia Noua, and Orhei began in the first half of October and continued throughout November 1941.[214] Some 367 (alternate figures range from 300 to 400) Jews then in Orhei were deported to Transnistria when the ghetto next to the Church of St. Nicolae was liquidated on November 6.[215] General Voiculescu worsened their circumstances when he ordered the Orhei gendarme legion on October 24 not to waste too many carts on them.[216] The gendarmes escorted convoys of Chişinău Jews from Orhei to the crossing point at Rezina. After the war one of these soldiers, Anghel Lungulescu, admitted at his trial that anywhere from fifteen to twenty Jews were missing when each convoy arrived, murdered by their escorts.[217] Gendarmes regularly beat, robbed, raped, and killed their charges.

Peasants and soldiers who were not part of the escort attacked the convoys and looted deportees. Enterprising escorts occasionally sold corpses wrapped in covers to peasants as "clothing packages." In Rezina Traian Saftenco used a big stick to hit Jews. By mistake he struck one of his fellow gendarmes, Ion Ciurea, who fell to the ground. Lieutenant Constantin Popoiu, the same man responsible for killing many Jews earlier in Orhei District, now orchestrated their fleecing in Rezina.[218]

As early as September 29, Colonel Meculescu could report that his men had deported to the other side of the Dniester well over 3,000 Jews: the Bălți legion accounted for 816, the Orhei legion 1,589, and the Soroca legion 770.[219] Between September 27 and October 16, 1941, the legions of Orhei and Soroca escorted 28,903 Jews beyond the Dniester.[220] Three thousand were deported through the Cosăuți crossing point between November 8 and 15.[221] The daily breakdown for two of these gendarme legions suggests something of the tempo of operations:

Date (1941)	*Gendarme Legion*	*No. of Jews Deported*
September 27	Orhei	794
September 28	Orhei	759
September 28	Soroca	650
September 29	Orhei	380
September 29	Soroca	567
September 30	Orhei	739
September 30	Soroca	744
October 1	Orhei	784
October 1	Soroca	717
October 2	Orhei	764
October 2	Soroca	700
October 3	Orhei	666
October 3	Soroca	700
October 4	Orhei	787
October 4	Soroca	800
October 5	Orhei	700
October 5	Soroca	598
October 6	Orhei	800
October 6	Soroca	730
October 7	Orhei	795
October 7	Soroca	800

October 8	Orhei	771
October 8	Soroca	1,000
October 9	Orhei	800
October 9	Soroca	1,000
October 10	Orhei	800
October 10	Soroca	1,200
October 11	Orhei	554
October 11	Soroca	1,190
October 12	Orhei	807
October 12	Soroca	1,190
October 13	Orhei	795
October 13	Soroca	2,001
October 14	Orhei	0
October 14	Soroca	2,195
October 15	Orhei	785
October 15	Soroca	977
October 16	Orhei	547
October 16	Soroca	76

The inmates of Limbenii Noi, Răuțel, and Rășcani were transferred to Mărculești on September 28, before being sent to Transnistria.[222] Some of the Jews from Edineți also transited through Mărculești. Every day convoys of two to three thousand people were transferred to Rezina on the other side of the Dniester.[223] From October 8 to December 16, 1941, the commanders of the Mărculești camp were Colonel Vasile Agapie and his deputy, Captain Sever Buradescu, formerly together at Vertujeni. One unique feature of the "evacuation" of Mărculești was that certain gendarmerie officers protected the Jews against robbery;[224] unfortunately, those instances were rare. The last 1941 deportation of the Bessarabian Jews started from Mărculești on November 10.

Preparations for the deportation of the Chișinău ghetto began on October 4, 1941. The Chișinău Jews sent desperate letters to Ion Antonescu, Mihai Antonescu, and General Voiculescu requesting postponement; they went unanswered.[225] According to Colonel Eugen Dumitrescu, Colonel Tudose's successor as military commander of Chișinău, there were no lists of names for the 1941 deportation of his district (the Romanians seem not to have begun relying on lists of names until 1942).[226]

The first convoy of 2,500 Jews left the city of Chișinău at 10:00 A.M.

(they had been roused at 6:00) on October 8.[227] On the previous day the civilian population had been allowed to purchase the Jews' belongings, but on the eighth only military personnel could do so. A rumor circulated among the Jews that they would be executed or thrown into the Dniester.[228] Convoys of seven hundred to one thousand Jews left the city on foot or in carts, frequently assaulted and robbed; those falling behind were executed. The 1941 deportation ended on October 31.

Through Order No. 15035, Marshal Antonescu exempted from deportation on October 22, 1941, Jews married to Christians and their children.[229] As a result of that order, 57 men, 123 women, and 477 children living in the rural areas were allowed to remain in Bessarabia even in 1942.[230]

On October 28, 1941, General Voiculescu ordered a cart for every seventy people so as to transport the elderly and the invalids, he demanded that the number of escorts per each seven hundred–person transport be doubled to forty men, and he asked that the National Bank conduct its exchanges during the daytime only, presumably to render pilferage more difficult.[231] In some convoys such as those escorted by Captain Brotea, however, the elderly and the sick were not allowed to ride. Brotea even beat gendarmes who tried to stop three Jews from slitting their wrists.[232]

A total of 1,004 Jews were evacuated from Chişinău on October 29, another 882 on the thirtieth, and 257 more on the thirty-first.[233] Colonel Dumitrescu reported: "Jews gone as of October 31: 10,225. . . . On Monday, November 3, 1941, about seventy to seventy-five Jews will leave with the children of the orphanage. Those from the hospitals [will be deported] after they recover. . . . There are still about two hundred Jews for deportation in Chişinău."[234] Another of Dumitrescu's communications specified further: "I am honored to inform you that the last transport of Jews left on October 31. We also need to evacuate the children's orphanage of thirty-eight children, including four newborns and the rest between one and six years of age, as well as the nurses and support staff."[235] On November 14, Dumitrescu sent to the government of Bessarabia a list of Jews exempted from these deportations: former members of the local parliamentary body, which had proclaimed the unification of Romania in 1918; veterans of World War I; and spouses of Christians.[236] Four days later General Voiculescu proudly reported to the Council of Ministers that despite the fact that 118 Jews remained in the Chişinău ghetto—fifty-three of them in the hospital and all soon to be sent off—"the Jewish question has been resolved in Bessarabia."[237]

On January 3, 1942, as a result of an order issued by Voiculescu, fifty-five Jews from the Chișinău ghetto were interned in the Onesti Noi camp in Bessarabia.[238] The deportation of the last Bessarabian Jews to Transnistria was planned according to Order No. 462/CBBT issued by Ion Antonescu. In direct application of that order Voiculescu decreed on May 7, 1942, the review of all permits granted to Jews who remained in Bessarabia.[239] He mentioned in a letter sent to the government of Transnistria his intention to deport the remaining Jews of Bessarabia in four transports, the first one containing 250 people.[240] Governor Alexianu of Transnistria approved these transports, provided they were escorted to Vradievka by Bessarabian gendarmes.[241] On March 29, the Chișinău gendarme inspector, Colonel Meculescu, even suggested to the Bessarabian administration that the 314 Jews remaining in Bessarabia who had converted to Christianity or were married to Christians should be deported.[242]

Through Order No. 2141/1942, Marshal Antonescu approved in May the deportation of 425 more Jews from Bessarabia.[243] Meculescu drew up the plan. The chief of the escort was Adjutant Grigore David of the Lăpușna gendarme legion. The first transport, containing 156 Jews, had already left Chișinău on May 20.[244] This transport included forty-eight mental patients from Chișinău Hospital, but five critically ill and untransportable Jews were exempted.[245] A train of nine merchandise wagons thus arrived at Vradievka Station at 6:00 P.M. on May 22. The 206 Jews placed on those wagons were confined in the Bogdanovka camp.[246] Voiculescu told his colleagues later at a meeting of the Council of Ministers that a final transport with two hundred Jews had left Bessarabia for Transnistria shortly thereafter.[247] But in actuality, yet one more transport—with nine Jews—left Chișinău on July 10.[248] The Bessarabian administration nevertheless informed the Council of Ministers on June 30, 1942, that the Chișinău ghetto no longer existed, the last Jews having been deported on June 25 (!) to Vradievka.[249]

As a final note concerning the deportations from Bessarabia, it is important to mention that members of other minority religious sects were also persecuted in Bessarabia. Thirty-nine members of the Milenaristi (an Orthodox Christian) sect were confined to Onesti Noi in December 1941.

As late as 1943, Jehovah's Witnesses were still interned in that same camp, as were seventy-four Baptists.[250]

Bukovina

Colonel Gheorghe Petrescu of the Second Section, responsible for "displacement of the Jewish population of Moldavia,"[251] and General Topor arrived at the Bukovina Military Command and informed General Vasile Ionescu, military commander of Cernăuţi, and General Calotescu, governor of Bukovina, that they had a telegraphic order concerning the deportation of Jews from Bukovina. Petrescu would declare in 1945 that this had been a follow-up to Marshal Antonescu's order that all Jews from Bukovina be transported east of the Dniester, an order countersigned by Colonel Dinulescu, chief of the Second Section.[252] Indeed, on October 4, 1941, the Supreme General Staff sent Order No. 6651, signed by Dinulescu, to the Cernăuţi Military Command: "All Jews from Bukovina will be sent east of the Dniester within ten days, in accordance with instructions by Marshal Antonescu."[253] On October 9, the Bukovina administration ordered the military authorities of Cernăuţi to set up strict surveillance on the outskirts of the city to prevent Jews from leaving that municipality.[254] Traian Popovici, mayor of Cernăuţi, met on the following day with General Calotescu and later recalled: "I was aghast. All I could do was mumble as I spoke to the governor: 'You have gone this far, Governor?' to which he responded: 'What is there to do? The marshal gives the order, and here we have the representatives of the General Staff.' General Topor, who was the chief prosecutor of the army, and Colonel Petrescu of the General Staff, witnessed the exchange."[255]

The discussion among the men took place in the office of General Calotescu, during which Popovici told the high-ranking officers:

> "You are sending fifty thousand human beings to their death in early winter." As I [Popovici] pointed to General Topor and Colonel Petrescu, I said, "Those men will set up shop in several days at Dragomir Niculescu's and will congratulate each other for their exploits in Bukovina, and you, you will remain here in your capacity as governor of a province that was handed to you so that you could take care of it and protect it. You have no right to take the lives of anyone. How do you wish

to be remembered by history, at Robespierre's side? As for me, I do not wish to see history tarnish my name. Think of what you are doing. You still have time. Talk to the marshal and ask him to postpone this measure until at least the spring."

I was the only one who spoke up like an idealist, and I was shaking from emotion. They were all standing upright. Leaning against a stove, the two [officers] and the governor [Calotescu] at his desk listened to me, in stony silence. After a pregnant moment the governor said: "Mister Popovici, I said the same thing to those gentlemen, I feel the same concerns, but these gentlemen were sent here to supervise the enforcement of this order; I will think about it more." At that moment Colonel Petrescu turned to me and said, "Mister Mayor, who will write this history, the *Jidani* perhaps? I have come here to pull out the weeds from your garden, and you are against this?" I replied in a cutting way: "Colonel, I pull the weeds out of my garden by myself; as concerns history, not only will the *Jidani* write it, because the world does not belong to them; history will be written by historians belonging to all people; we will write it and sooner than you think." . . .

General Vasile Ionescu entered the office, amid this heavy atmosphere. Looking somber, deeply saddened, he saluted us all, then said to the governor: "I ask you not to do this. It is a scandal, what you intend to accomplish. It is a shame, it is awful. It would have been better for me not to have come to Bukovina to witness such barbaric acts." The governor hesitated and decided to take his time, in order perhaps to relent somewhat.

I left the governor's office with General Ionescu. While going down the steps, he told me: "I have refused them categorically, I have asked them for those orders in writing, but they did not want to give them to me. Can you believe it? No written orders. They assert that these types of operations are carried out on the basis of verbal instructions, so that there is no evidence. Dear, Traian! Let's try to convince Calotescu that he should not do something this stupid; it is truly shameful. Furthermore, I am sure that you shattered their conscience. Well, I will talk to him about it again this afternoon."[256]

However, Calotescu issued the following order on October 10, 1941:

I have the honor to announce that we have decided to evacuate the Jewish population from Bukovina. . . . The Jewish population of the municipality of Cernăuți will first be rounded up inside the ghetto set up by the mayor, and from there it will be gradually transported on Romanian railroads. The operations aimed at rounding up the Jews, supervising the ghetto, boarding them, and transporting them to the border points are incumbent upon the Command and Inspectorate of Gendarmes of Cernăuți. You have at your disposal the First Gendarme Battalion, which will be assigned control over the ghetto and transport escort; the 430th Infantry Battalion; and another infantry battalion brought to Cernăuți to safeguard the exits from the city [and to maintain] internal order and security. After the roundup in the ghetto all troops that are present in the Cernăuți garrison will assist in control.

Two trains with fifty cars each, departing from the Cernăuți railroad station, will be used every day. The roundup in the ghetto will take place on October 11, 1941. . . . All security measures will be taken on that day, at dawn, to prevent any actions that might disrupt order. . . . All Jewish assets become the property of the state as of that moment.[257]

Calotescu also signed the following roundup schedule:

7:00 A.M.: The assembling of [leading] members of the Jewish community of Cernăuți and the suburban Jewish communities at the Military Command (to be announced between 5:00 and 7:00 with the assistance of the Regional Police Inspectorate of Cernăuți). The enclosed notification (Order No. 38 and the ghetto regulations) will be given to them. We announce that all permits to engage in civic employment are revoked and [that] the entire Jewish population is to enter the ghetto.

8:00 A.M. to 9:30 A.M.: The members of the community make the announcement to all the Jews of Cernăuți. Meanwhile, Regional Police Inspectorate agencies also announce [the order to] the Jewish population by reading the notification at intersections.

9:30 A.M. to 6:00 P.M.: Time allotted to move into the ghetto.

6:00 P.M.: Sealing of the ghetto.[258]

On the basis of this order more than fifty thousand people were forced into a space adequate for only twenty thousand.[259] National Bank teller windows were set up inside the ghetto on October 12, 1941, where Jews were required to exchange money and valuables for rubles.[260] Calotescu signed the regulations for the Cernăuți ghetto and stated that

Jews could leave it only with the written approval of the Bukovina Military Command. Any exchange with the surrounding society was forbidden; violators could be executed.[261] The Cernăuți Jews were permitted to take only warm clothes and food supplies with them.[262] Calotescu was quite right when he declared, on April 26, 1945, that all orders on the deportations from Bukovina had been drafted by Petrescu, but Calotescu issued them and therefore bore a more-than-criminal responsibility for their implementation.[263]

Storojineț was not the only place whence deportations started on October 13;[264] deportation of the Jews of Cernăuți began as well on that date.[265] The homes of the latter had already been looted by the Ukrainian and Romanian residents, as noted in a memorandum of the Siguranța (the Romanian security police).[266] The first train left from the nearby Sadagura camp with four hundred families brought there for that purpose, but the nineteen other trains left directly from Cernăuți. Half of the trains left at 9:05 each night for the Mărculești camp; the other half left at 2:05 each afternoon for Atachi.[267] The Jews who had not received permission to remain in Cernăuți were removed from the ghetto there (one witness recalled how it "smelled of stale sweat, urine, fecal matter, mildew, and dampness" due to the shortage of water and the overcrowding).[268] "The people who were to be deported were sorted out in groups of two thousand and then driven through mud to the loading docks at the main train station," runs one account:

> Forty to fifty were packed in each car; at Atachi and Mărculești they crossed the river into the empire of hell. Heartbreaking scenes unfolded at the loading areas and at train departures. Members of families were separated, children leaving, parents staying, or vice versa; brothers losing their sisters, husbands losing their spouses. The air was filled with wails, and this broke the hardest hearts. The separation often was forever, some leaving to suffer and die, others staying to feel pain and endure slavery.[269]

While the Cernăuți Jews were transported beyond the Dniester, the mortality rate was high. According to one witness, "In one transport all but one of the sixty infants perished."[270] It was said that the only people who evaded this deportation purchased the favor for very large sums of money, usually in foreign currency.

Popovici tried to oppose the deportations, and he managed to win—with the help of the governor of Bukovina—the approval of Antonescu (who was in Tiraspol at the time) to retain in the city some 15,600 Jews as "specialists," along with some 4,000 others to whom he himself had issued "temporary permits."[271] Popovici stated that after Antonescu made this grant on November 15, 1941, General Calotescu assigned the mayor and General Ionescu the task of deciding who would stay. The German consul Schellhorn declined participation.[272]

Deportation of the remaining Jews of Southern Bukovina in 1941 continued for several weeks after the end of the Cernăuți deportations. Dorohoi District officially had been absorbed in 1938 into Southern Bukovina, an administrative measure still in force in 1941. Southern Bukovina had not been occupied by the USSR in the summer of 1940; hence, the charge of "collaboration" should not have been leveled against its Jews. But with the exception of four or five thousand Jews from Dorohoi deported in the summer of 1941 (after the onset of the war) to Tîrgu Jiu and Craiova in southern Romania and later brought back, as well as the exception of several hundred Jews killed at the beginning of the war in the region of Herta, the entire Jewish population of Southern Bukovina was deported to Transnistria on that basis.[273] According to Carp's estimates, based partly on the last census, 39,000 Jews had lived in Southern Bukovina. Of them, 24,000 lived in the districts of Suceava, Cîmpulung, and Rădăuți, the other 15,000 in the district of Dorohoi.[274] The number of Jews deported from Southern Bukovina is fairly easy to estimate, because the Jews of that region had not had the opportunity to evacuate with the Red Army (nor, of course, had any been deported by the Soviets). Owing to the fairly long distance from these areas to the Dniester River, the deportations were by train up to the crossing points. In addition to the above-mentioned districts the following localities were affected by the deportations: Solca, Burdujeni, Iucani, Gura Humorului, Vama, Vatra Dornei, Siret, and several rural communities.

The deportations proceeded from October 9 to 14. Suceava was evacuated in eight hours, Iucani in four. The 8,000 Jews in Rădăuți were deported in four transports of about 2,000 Jews each between October 12 and 14 (the trains were numbered K3501 through K3504). There were at least four suicides among the deportees.[275] On October 13, "of the 2,000 Jews of the three southern departments (Rădăuți, Cîmpulung, and Suceava), there remained only 179 Jews. Permission for 76 Jews to re-

main in Cîmpulung, 72 in Rădăuți, and 31 in Suceava was granted on the
insistence of gentiles who could not live without their services, mostly in
the sawmills. Dr. Schurtzer, the only gynecologist in Rădăuți, stayed, and
Dr. Teitelbaum was recalled from Atachi, as its only dentist.[276]

Dr. Meyer Teich, head of the Jewish community of Suceava, later
recorded his impressions of the deportation, worth quoting at length due
to its immense detail:

> On Thursday, October 9, 1941, at 5:30 A.M., I was awakened by a
> bailiff from the prefecture, who told me to come immediately to the
> deputy prefect's office. In the street I met several Jews who were crying
> and who informed me that all the Jews of Suceava were to be evacuated
> that same day. I did not believe them, and I asked them not to spread
> panic. I reached the office of Deputy Prefect Ioachimescu at around
> 6:00, where I found Major Botoroagă and the mayors of Burdujeni and
> Iucani from the district of Suceava.
>
> The deputy prefect opened an envelope, as if he had received it at
> that very moment. He read it to me and showed me the evacuation order
> according to which the Supreme General Staff stipulated that all Jews
> were going to be evacuated from Suceava in two shifts: those of Burdu-
> jeni, Iucani, and half of the town of Suceava in two hours and the other
> half of the town of Suceava on the following day. The order set forth the
> death penalty for any attempt to evade, especially those who refused to
> leave, those who attempted to leave valuables behind with Christians,
> and Christians who would keep valuables belonging to the Jews. Later,
> the CNR [National Center for Romanization], the prefecture, and even
> the judicial bodies of Suceava, selling valuables left behind by the Jews,
> wrote (I found sales publications in the Bucharest newspapers being sold
> in Transnistria) about valuables that the Jews had "abandoned," as if
> they had left them there of their own free will. Prefect Stroiescu later or-
> ganized a kind of bazaar to sell such "abandoned goods." The attorney
> Popiniuc and the clerk Païs sold our items. [Others were involved too.—
> R.I.]
>
> Major abuses . . . were reported by the police chief, Apreutesii,
> under Governor Calotescu. A commission of inquiry arrived on site, con-
> sisting of Prosecutor General Andruhovici and Appellate Court Coun-
> selor Iliescu. However, the government did not adopt any measures.
> Prefect Stroiescu and the people cited above continued to sell our assets

and dispose of them as they saw fit, distributing furniture and various items to their friends.

The order stated that we were allowed to bring only small bags and food for eight days. When I asked why they were adopting a measure that would lead to our death, Major Botoroagă replied, "The higher interests of the state." He asked that the leaders of the community inform the population of these decisions. I refused, arguing that I no longer considered myself to be the leader of the Jewish community and that each official had to take care of his own family first and foremost. The evacuation order was announced to the population through the roll of drums. The first transport left several hours later on that day, the second one on the following day. Perhaps because there were not enough cars, about 1,200 Jews remained in the town of Suceava, for whom a third transport was organized on Saturday, October 11. Pursuant to the published order, large quantities of valuables, jewelry, gold, silver, and the like, were deposited at the town hall, in the presence of a representative of the BNR (National Bank of Romania) and the mayor, Ion Janca—the one who later invited the population to a mass meeting where he congratulated the Germans and Antonescu for the . . . evacuation and thanked God for having freed Suceava of the Jews. As a reward he received the "Order of the Black Eagle" from Hitler. . . .

We were promised that the seriously ill, the elderly, and in general those who could not be transported would remain in Suceava. The police chief assured me that all of them would be assembled and cared for. He then told me that if the prefect had been in Suceava, not all the Jews would have been evacuated but . . . only [those who were no longer productive] and that Deputy Prefect Ioachimescu and Colonel Zamfirescu were guilty of an excessive display of zeal. . . . Despite the threat of the death penalty contained in the deportation order, Deputy Prefect Ioachimescu, Major Botoroagă, Police Chief Apreutesii, and other officials received many valuable items from Jews to safeguard them, hoping that no one would come back.

When I asked the mayor to preserve the archives of the Jewish community and especially the civil registries, the communal official Foit told me, "You are not coming back. And even then, you would not be needing such a thing."

I left with the third transport. We were packed into cattle cars that had not been cleaned. When our train was about to start off, Colonel

Zamfirescu arrived and postponed the departure. Police Chief Apreutesii and Major Botoroagă stated that Zamfirescu had ordered that even persons unfit for transport should be evacuated. . . . Indeed, old and sick people appeared, wrapped in hospital linen and without any baggage. The chief physician of the hospital, Dr. Bona, was evacuating all the sick Jews from the hospital, even those who were in serious condition; the coachman Isac Mayer, whose leg had been amputated a few days before, was in agony. He died one hour after we left; his corpse was removed at the train station of Cernăuți. Dr. Bona evacuated even his [former] colleague at the hospital, Dr. Bernard Wagner, who was more than seventy years old, seriously ill, and no longer capable of enduring his suffering and who committed suicide upon his arrival in Moghilev. The worst is that Dr. Bona and Colonel Zamfirescu put us into the train together with some of the patients who had been sick with *typhus abdominalis,* for instance, Isac Terrenhaus, who died upon arrival at Moghilev. I then told Colonel Zamfirescu that the fecal matter did not distinguish between races and that those who had been sick with *typhus abdominalis* not only placed the Jews in grave danger but also other travelers. Colonel Zamfirescu began to laugh and told me that he did not care, that they were all supposed to leave, and that not one Jew must remain in Suceava. . . .

We also were forced to take on board several mentally ill passengers, and since it had not been possible to identify all of them with certainty, two mentally ill Christians were assigned to the transport. Colonel Zamfirescu even wanted to bring Jews from the penitentiary to send them off with us. The head of the penitentiary, who had to request the advice of the Ministry of Justice by telephone, successfully opposed it. Zamfirescu brought to the station [Jewish] women who had been baptized after marrying Aryan men, but at the last minute the governor's office canceled this move. Zamfirescu screamed that there should not be any traces left of Jews: sick with infectious diseases, crazy, whatever; nothing could disturb his plans. Everything occurred as a result of his own initiative. . . . He screamed, threatened, terrorized everyone. There were horrible scenes: the lunatics screamed, the sick cried; their families no longer knew what to do with them. Next to Isac Mayer, who was dead, his daughter held a candlestick [and prayed]. During the transport the cars were locked, and at several stations military personnel fired rifles at the trains, and this is how we journeyed to the station of Volcineț, near Atachi, on the evening of October 12.

We learned there that the . . . first transport had been robbed by the soldiers and gendarmes; many of them had been executed. [This was the case too with] the second transport, which indicated that . . . we would also be victims. I then intervened with the station chief and a border guard officer, and, by bribing them, I was able to arrange a layover at Volcineţ until the following morning. I discovered a living hell in Atachi: several thousand people from various transports coming out of Bessarabia or Bukovina, no organization, a complete lack of shelter and food. The new arrivals were led into ruins of homes with no doors or windows, most often lacking a roof, exposed to wind and rain. Bread cost up to two thousand [lei] a loaf.

On October 13, a convoy came from Edineţi—people beaten, barefoot, in a state that defied imagination. We gave them what we could and realized that [their fate] was what was awaiting us. Some lost their minds in Atachi (e.g., the widow of the attorney Dr. Stein). The sick and many elderly people died (e.g., Schaje, Langer, Golda Beiner, Scheindel Kraft, the widow of Dr. Feingold). There were corpses everywhere: in the streets, houses, cellars.

Then, with Dr. Abraham Reicher, a man endowed with tremendous energy, we began to get organized. We obtained a special permit for Dr. Reicher from Captain Popescu of the Third Regiment of Border Guards, so that he could go by himself to Moghilev to arrange better conditions for us. Indeed, Dr. Reicher returned with promises from Moghilev officials that we would not be interned there. Then a representative of the National Bank of Romania converted our lei at a rate of forty per ruble, which meant actually that four-fifths of their value was confiscated. . . . We decided that some of the deportees should take lei to Moghilev in order to safeguard their wealth in currency. We opted for this course of action, primarily because the representative of the National Bank had told us that he had no more rubles and that he was going to send us the rubles several days later in Moghilev, but we knew that this would never happen. After exchanging the lei there came the body searches and those of the luggage. During these searches two officers alternated, accompanied by military personnel and gendarmes, especially Second Lieutenant Marino, whom I knew quite well because he was the counselor of the Appeals Court of Cernăuţi, and Prosecutor Gorovei, son of Arthur Gorovei of Fălticeni.

Our group was searched by Marino, who converted the money that we had not yet exchanged. . . . He gave small change from his profits to the gendarmes. . . . He pocketed from me 12,000 lei, even though he knew me quite well, and took from my wife's handbag loan titles and other effects worth about 25,000 [lei].

Following this search [we were] led to the banks of the Dniester and taken across on several rafts. The guard soldiers also did their share of stealing, and when many people begged [the troops] to leave them something, they threatened to throw [the Jews] into the water. . . . [One] joked that he'd like to see if these Jews could cross the Red Sea without being harmed. Later I learned that this "joke" had been put into practice several times.[277]

In 1947, the Bucharest court (in Decision No. 4501/947) confirmed the murders of the Jews from Suceava that Romanian gendarmes had committed at the Dniester. Many survivors of the first convoys were finally able to testify against torturers such as Vasile Mihailiuc:

Witness Aron Lazarovici states that the accused bloodied his head with his rifle butt and stole from him two suitcases packed with possessions. The same witness declares that . . . Vasile Mihailiuc took women and children from the convoy in order to intimidate those from whom he intended to steal. Witness Dora Hirschhorn declared that after her convoy had arrived in Atachi she and her husband were beaten by Vasile Mihailiuc until unconscious [and] their three suitcases robbed of 500,000 lei in addition to clothing. The accused threw Dora Hirschhorn's mother into the Dniester, whence she was barely saved. [Rubin Hermann testified] that Vasile Mihailiuc stole money and jewelry from him and executed the Jews Goldhammer and Krakover. Another witness, Moses Summer, told how the accused had savagely abused his father, Berl Summer, who died from his injuries and whose belongings he stole. The Jews Chaim Gross and Avram Friedmann also were abused, the latter being threatened with execution. The accused took 17,000 lei and a gold watch from Chaim Gross and a 42,000-lei watch from Avram Friedmann after having intimidated him by firing a shot that almost hit him. Finally, Mina Gross, the last witness, said that on the convoy the accused shot a child, who died instantly.[278]

On October 22, approximately eight thousand Jews from villages surrounding Cernăuți and from Rădăuți District were concentrated in

Cernăuți and immediately deported to Transnistria by way of Mărculești.[279] Like Atachi, Mărculești was an important transit point on the
Dniester. Gendarmes and soldiers committed many instances of plunder
there. Memoranda dated October 31 and November 11 describe in detail
the depredations organized by Captain Titus Popescu of the Supreme General Staff and by Lieutenant Augustin Roşca of Police Company 60. During the searches many Jews lost their last remaining valuables.[280]

The deportation of the Dorohoi Jews began on November 7 (other
sources give the twelfth and the thirteenth), before they had been robbed
of their money and jewelry. At that time there were 12,238 deportees, half
of whom had been brought from rural districts. A Dorohoi police report of
October describes conditions there: "unhealthy houses; men, women, and
children with miserable and inadequate food; watery soup and nothing
else. Fifteen to twenty sleep in a single room with no light, naked and in
rags."[281]

The Jews of Dărăbani were deported on the same day. None were allowed to stay, "neither the aged, the sick, infants, lunatics, [World War I]
heroes, invalids, war widows, reserve officers, physicians, attorneys,
pharmacists, nor dentists," in one victim's words.[282] The Dărăbani deportees were robbed again at the train station in that town before embarka-
tion. "At the train station . . . they were loaded onto freight cars, piled in
by groups of fifty or sixty, and then locked in. Since they had been originally evacuated from their rural homes in June, most of them had only the
shirt and torn summer clothes they had then worn; infants and old people
overcome by the cold offered a tragic sight that made people cry when
they saw them."[283]

The Jews of Săveni and Mihăileni were deported under the same circumstances on November 8. Some twelve hundred other Jews, who had
been deported to the southern part of the country for hard labor in the
summer of 1941 and then brought back, were also deported from Dorohoi. The deportation of the Jews from Dorohoi ended on November 14,
1941. According to the attorney Musat, sent to Dorohoi by the Union of
Romanian Jewish Communities, about 12,238 Jews had been deported
during those few days, leaving only 2,500. Some Jews froze to death on
their way to Atachi; those who survived were robbed again.[284]

A new wave of deportations befell the Jewish population of Bukovina in 1942 (many of these victims had been able to remain in their
homes in Cernăuți as a result of the protection Mayor Popovici had ini-

tially been able to secure). During a meeting of the Council of Ministers on May 28, the governor, General Calotescu, announced that he had decided to deport four to five thousand Jews from Cernăuți, after having discussed the matter with Governor Alexianu of Transnistria.[285] In June some four thousand were indeed deported, along with several hundred others from Dorohoi. The expulsion was carried out in this fashion: on June 7, Calotescu put his chief of staff, Major Stere Marinescu, in charge of a new round of deportations from Cernăuți. "It would appear as if this project envisioned the deportation of about four thousand people who had been given permits to remain in the city during the selection in November 1941 by the former mayor, Traian Popovici, who had since fallen out of favor," says Carp.[286] Thousands of Jews were brought to the Macabi sports field, rigorously searched (including body searches of the women), and deported in sealed cars to Transnistria, among them former Polish citizens who should have been protected by Chilean passports, sixty-six mental patients, and medical staff from the hospital.[287] The first of these transports left Cernăuți on June 7, 1942, with 1,781 Jews. Another 76 from Cîmpulung, Hotin, Storojineț, Suceava, and Rădăuți were deported on June 8;[288] a group of 308 from Dorohoi on June 11;[289] another 450 from Dorohoi on June 14 (most of them men from external labor detachments whose families had been deported in November 1941);[290] 1,151 from Cernăuți and Hotin on June 15; and finally, 1,162 more from Cernăuți on June 29. In all, between 4,100 and 4,300 Jews were deported from Cernăuți in June 1942, 750 from Dorohoi.[291]

The story of the most defenseless victims highlights the character of Romania's administration. Police Commissioner Ioan Albu's mission was to deport the patients of the hospital. "He came into the hospital and ordered the men under his command to remove twenty-three Sisters of Mercy," recalled one witness after the war, "and then [followed] all the patients, even the seriously ill," a total of thirty; these were individuals whom the government had earlier reprieved. This operation proceeded with extreme brutality: patients were removed from their stretchers in the hospital courtyard, thrown onto trucks, and transported to the Macabi field.[292] When one woman carrying a baby in her arms begged Major Marinescu not to send her to die in Transnistria, he shut her up with a kick.[293] In contrast, when a soldier sent to arrest six Jewish women found four suicides inside the bedroom, along with a terrified elderly woman and a six-month-old baby, he broke down in tears: he too had children and an old mother. But his commander, the same Major Marinescu, punished him with ten days in the stockade.[294]

Lesner Herman, former administrator of a local asylum, later testified about the "arrest" of the old Jewish men there, previously exempted by the government of Transnistria, "now eighty to ninety-five years old, partly blind, and incapable of walking unaided." Commissioner Albu led his policemen to forcibly remove the old men. Albu personally dragged an elderly dying man from his bed and threw him onto the floor of the morgue. Herman stated that, despite his admonitions, "Commissioner Albu behaved like a savage, striking the old men on the head as they pleaded for mercy."[295]

In March 1943, another group of Polish Jews holding Chilean passports had crossed the border clandestinely, seeking refuge from Nazi-occupied Poland. In Cernăuți they were handed over to the Gestapo by Police Commissioner Romulus Cojocaru; the Gestapo ordered their execution. "Romulus Cojocaru did not care that some of these Polish refugees were still recovering after operations and that others were seriously ill," recalled one eyewitness. "Without exception, they were piled into trucks, like animals. . . . Sick people were piled into the truck with their hands and feet tied. . . . Some tried to commit suicide and were thrown into the trucks bleeding from their open veins."[296] Cojocaru confiscated all passports, but not all of his colleagues shared his zeal. Polish refugees who fell into the hands of Security Inspector Mihai Păun were not handed over to the Gestapo.[297] On August 28, 1943, General Dragalina, governor of Bukovina, ordered the expulsion to Poland of 139 Jewish families holding Chilean passports, but their ultimate fate is not clear.[298]

Traian Popovici was perhaps the only high-ranking civil servant in the Antonescu regime to condemn directly and explicitly the deportation of the Jews. In a memorandum to Ion Antonescu on July 14, 1942, Popovici did shield himself from any possible accusation of philo-Semitism, conceding that it was necessary to settle the Jewish question; but this had to be done "legally and in a civilized manner," relying on "European methods." The problem, however, was that

we have stripped the Jews of their belongings and of many billions through highly questionable methods, property that was supposed to end up in the national patrimony but instead became the booty of those who carried out the deportations; because of those methods, useful and irreproachable people, who were known to be perfectly loyal, have been deported, women who were more than seventy years old, the sick, invalids, pregnant women, and the insane.[299]

After denouncing the corruption of the Cernăuți officials and the conditions under which many Jews had died in Transnistria, Popovici continued:

> Because of those cruelly barbarian principles that have guided the executioners of the order that the marshal handed down, the settlement of the Jewish question in Romania, this act of historical significance, the most important act of the current government, this act that was supposed to be the foundation of the resurrection of our national life, this act that could have become a source of national pride for centuries to come, has become one steeped in the basest felony, an act of eternal shame, which brings together all the elements that can expose us to the contempt and hatred of all humanity, perhaps forever.[300]

Realizing that many of Bukovina's Jewish families had lived there for hundreds of years, long before Bukovina was incorporated into Austria, Popovici felt it unacceptable that they "should be decimated, collectively blamed without exception and without the faintest hint of an investigation or judgment, like herds of animals."[301]

Since the deportations from Bessarabia and Bukovina amounted to a massive displacement of population, they could not escape the attention of diplomatic corps. Franklin Mott Gunther, American minister in Bucharest, wrote on November 4, 1941, to Secretary of State Cordell Hull: "I have it on good authority that Marshal Antonescu has stated to, or within the hearing of, the Spanish minister (who is particularly interested in the problem because of the Spanish Jews in Romania) that 'this is wartime, and a good time to settle the Jewish problem once and for all.' "[302] Gunther continued:

> I have constantly and persistently held before the attention of the highest Romanian officials the inevitable reaction of my government and the American people to such inhumane treatment, and even outright slaughter, of innocent and defenseless people, citing at length the atrocities committed against the Jews of Romania. My observations have elicited from Marshal Antonescu, and from Acting Premier Mihai Antonescu,

voluble protestations of regrets for past excesses committed "through error" or by "irresponsible elements." . . . The program of systematic extermination is continuing nonetheless, and I see little hope for the Romanian Jews, as long as the present German-controlled regime continues in power. Its policy is admittedly to drive from the reconquered provinces of Northern Bukovina and Bessarabia, and perhaps also from Transylvania and the Old Kingdom [Regat] as well, every Jew, excepting, of course, those that are or may be useful to it, after taking from them practically all their worldly possessions.[303]

Jacques Truelle, Vichy France's minister to Bucharest, provided a very accurate description of the deportations from Bessarabia and Bukovina.[304] On November 10, 1941, he reported to the French Ministry of Foreign Affairs:

On the set day the Jewish population of those regions was ordered by the local authorities to show up at the train station within four to six hours with supplies for several days. In some cities the highest amount of money that each person could take was set at two thousand lei, or about two hundred francs. No exceptions were made for the elderly, the sick, or children; during the departure the sick were carried on the backs of their coreligionists; some Jews, filled with despair, committed suicide; since the death sentence would be pronounced for anyone carrying gold or money exceeding two thousand lei, some tried to buy food in exchange for jewelry; others burned their banknotes. Those granted the exceptional permission to return home from the train station and retrieve a few items found their houses already looted. In Cernăuți, the area that was made available to the Jews while they waited to leave was too small, and they were forced to sleep under the open air. Then they were loaded into cattle cars, sixty to eighty per car. The trains headed for Moghilev, which they reached after three or four days. There already were victims among those being deported, [some of] the sick who had died during transport or people [who] had died from exposure.

In Moghilev all the houses had been destroyed during the fighting, and the Jews were forced to sleep under the open air again. Then they were ordered to leave on foot, toward an unknown destination, [covering] close to two hundred kilometers, or about fifteen to twenty kilometers per day. They were not given any food, of course, and since they had no money left, they could not buy anything. Some officers forced young girls to become prostitutes in exchange for a piece of bread. The roads were lined with corpses, and only the strongest men and women could endure these travails.[305]

*   *   *

It is difficult to arrive at an accurate figure for the number of Jews murdered by the Romanian and German armies in Bessarabia and Bukovina because it is unclear how many were deported from the two provinces between July 1940 and June 1941 by the Soviets and how many of them had withdrawn with the Red Army or with the Soviet civilian authorities. The last Romanian census prior to World War II (1930) gave a figure of 756,930 Jews—at that time the third largest Jewish community in Europe. Of these, 205,958 lived in Bessarabia, 7.2 percent of the regional population; and 107,975 lived in Bukovina, 10.9 percent of that region's population. Hence, approximately 315,000 Jews lived in Bessarabia and Bukovina in 1930. According to estimates from the Romanian Central Institute of Statistics, 278,943 Jews were included in the population of the USSR as a result of its occupation of Bessarabia and Bukovina.[306] The difference of 36,000 may reflect the number of Jews who lived in Southern Bukovina (which remained Romanian), as well as certain demographic modifications (e.g., migrations, differences between births and deaths). In Dorohoi District, later incorporated in Bukovina, there still lived fifteen thousand Jews. Tens of thousands of Jews from Bessarabia and Bukovina were killed during July and August 1941; on September 1, 1941, officials counted 126,634 still alive.[307]

According to the estimates of Matatias Carp and Jean Ancel, during July and August 1941, about 150,000 Romanian Jews were killed in Bessarabia, Bukovina, Herța, and Dorohoi.[308] As Carp acknowledged:

We might object that those figures are not an accurate reflection of reality since they do not take into account the number of Jewish refugees during the beginning of the war. According to corroborated information, the number of those who tried to save themselves by fleeing was very small. There were several hundred in Cernăuți, several thousand in the region of Chișinău, and almost the same number in southern Bessarabia through the city of Cetatea Albă."[309]

Carp cites in support of that assertion the swiftness of the advance of German-Romanian troops, as well as two Romanian documents attesting to the August 9–17 capture of about 14,500 Jews trying to escape the Soviet troops.[310] On the other hand, for a postwar Romania heavily controlled by the Soviets, Carp was unable to publish any information on the number of Jews deported by the Soviet authorities. For instance, in early June 1941, wealthy Jews from Cernăuți were deported to Siberia. Those known to have engaged in or were suspected of Zionist activities were arrested and deported.[311] More precisely, during the night of June 12–13, 1941, approximately three thousand Jews were arrested and deported, among them the former presidents of various Jewish communities and many others who had been politically active. Even after the outset of war, on June 22, 1941, further arrests and deportations devastated the Jewish population: some ten thousand more fell into the hands of the Soviet police.[312]

Ancel's examination of the evidence has led him to conclude that "the number of Jews deported by the Soviets before the outbreak of the war, mobilized into the Red Army, or otherwise escaping the German-Romanian armies did not exceed thirty to forty thousand."[313] Conversely, Raul Hilberg estimates that in 1941 more than 100,000 Jews from Bessarabia and Bukovina were deported by the Soviet authorities, were incorporated into the Soviet army, or fled the advancing German and Romanian troops.[314] Hilberg claims that more than 45,000 Romanian Jews were killed during the first months of the war: over 10,000 as part of the July killings; another 7,000 in the transit camps that summer; 10,000 who "disappeared" in Transnistria (i.e., those transferred to the rear by the Germans in August before the Hauffe-Tătăranu Convention defined the borders of Transnistria); and about 18,000 who died in the transit camps in September and October.[315]

A report from the U.S. embassy in Stockholm (one of America's de facto listening posts) estimated that about 130,000 Jews from Bessarabia and Northern Bukovina had been allowed by the Soviets to retreat with them in 1941. Therefore, when the Romanian army showed up, it found about 220,000 Jews in both provinces.[316] An Office of Strategic Services (OSS) estimate based on a Canadian source says that "between 100,000 to 130,000 Jews fled from Bessarabia and Bukovina before the invaders."[317]

It is now possible to estimate with greater accuracy how many Jews left one way or another with the Soviet authorities and thus how many were deported by the Romanians. During the spring of 1943, the gendarmerie station chiefs from the two districts of Bălți and Soroca in Bessarabia reported the number of Jews who had been deported and the number who had voluntarily left Bălți and Soroca with the Soviets in 1941:[318]

District	No. of Jewish Settlements/ Population (1930)	No. of Jews Leaving with the Soviets	No. of Jews Deported by the Romanians
Bălți	44/31,695	5,684	7,311
Soroca	18/29,191	1,135	3,119
Total	62/60,886	6,819	10,430

The 17,249 Jews deported by one party or the other constituted 28.3 percent of the Jewish population of Bălți and Soroca, 8.3 percent of the total Jewish population of Bessarabia. This suggests in rough proportions that for every sixty Jews deported by the Romanians, forty had already left with or been deported by the Soviets (in the case of Bălți 56 percent had been deported by the Romanians; in the case of Soroca, 73 percent). The Jews who had left Bălți (i.e., those deported by either the Romanians or the Soviets or those who had left voluntarily with the latter) constituted 41 percent of the town's Jewish population, those from Soroca just under 15 percent of that town's. In 1940, there were seventy thousand Jewish residents in Cernăuți, but Mayor Popovici stated that when Romanian troops retook the city from the Soviets in 1941, there were only fifty thousand, a deficit of 29 percent.[319] (Popovici also estimated that Romanian troops found about 65,000–70,000 Jews in Northern Bukovina in 1941—that is, a considerable reduction from the prewar 100,000.)[320]

If we accept as fact that throughout all of Bessarabia and Northern Bukovina 40 percent of the Jews left (willingly or not) with the Soviets, it would seem likely that (a) a total of 124,000 Jews (81,000 from Bessarabia, 43,000 from Bukovina) left with the Soviets; (b) about 190,000 Jews from Bessarabia and Northern Bukovina found themselves under Romanian administration afterward; (c) at least 123,000 Jews were deported from Bessarabia and Bukovina to Transnistria (i.e., 118,000 during the fall of 1941 and 5,000 during the summer of 1942); and hence (d) about 65,000 Jews from Bessarabia and Bukovina were killed during the first months of the war (in mass murders, at transit camps, during deportations). These estimates are very close to Eugen Kulisher's with regard to the Jews who fled with the Soviets (a 5 percent difference) and fairly close to Hilberg's estimate of the number of Jews killed in Bessarabia and Bukovina (before or during the deportations).

The report of the military committee that investigated the "irregularities" in the Chișinău ghetto indicated that the difference between the number of Bessarabian Jews who were interned (between 75,000 and 80,000) and those eventually "evacuated" (about 55,000) amounted to some 25,000 who had "died of natural causes, fled, or been killed."[321] The mortality rate during the subsequent deportations appears to have been 27 percent. Except for approximately sixteen thousand Jews remaining in Cernăuți, the entire surviving Jewish population of Bessarabia and Bukovina was deported to Transnistria.

How many was this? Fortunately, we have numerous sources on the matter; unfortunately, these sources correspond only roughly. But a survey of the available estimates suggests not only the quantitative side of events but the complexity of documenting them that dogs any attempt to produce a precise picture. A report signed by General Calotescu on April 9, 1942, put the number of Jews deported from Bukovina to Transnistria at 91,845.[322] Somewhat later, on September 7, the governor broke this down into 57,849 deported from rural areas in July and August 1941; 28,341 from Cernăuți in October of that year; and another 4,094 from Cernăuți in summer 1942.[323] The total from this breakdown (90,284) was somewhat lower than that he provided in April, but it was reconfirmed in a final report by the governor dated December 12, 1942.[324] Calotescu's reports do not seem to take into account the Jews from Bukovina who died in the transit camps, but they probably include the thirty thousand deported from Dorohoi and Southern Bukovina. A Chișinău Gendarme Inspectorate report contemporary with Calotescu's first estimate suggests that 55,687 Jews had been deported from Bessarabia;[325] however, this figure equals only the number who reached Transnistria alive. An unsigned Ministry of Foreign Affairs report dated October 12, 1942—one quoted in the August 8, 1943, edition of the newspaper *Bukarester Tageblatt*—stated that 185,000 Jews had been deported to Transnistria by that date.[326] The same source reported that 78,000 of these Jews now survived in Transnistria (25,000 men, 33,000 women, and 20,000 children).

These figures may well be too high: other official Romanian statistics range between 100,000 and 120,000. During his postwar trial Antonescu estimated that no more than 150,000–170,000 Jews had been deported.[327] A December 9, 1941, report over the signature of General C. Z. Vasiliu indicates that 108,002 Jews had been deported from Bessarabia and Bukovina by then.[328] A November 11, 1943, Ministry of Foreign Affairs report signed by the same general increased the total slightly to 110,033 (55,687 from Bessarabia, 43,798 from Bukovina, 10,368 from Dorohoi, and a few stray others), noting that another 2,200 had been sent from Moldavia and Walachia; as of that date 50,741 still survived.[329] The committee that investigated the Chişinău ghetto concluded that 101,405 Jews had been deported from Bessarabia and Bukovina.[330] The American OSS estimated 155,000,[331] and more recently a Rand Corporation analysis gave a figure of over 110,000.[332] Julius Fisher, the author of an early study of the matter, estimated 140,154 Jews deported (though this figure includes the 8,000 killed during the abortive deportations of summer 1941, which other studies do not).[333]

On November 26, 1941, Colonel Broşteanu, Transnistria's gendarme inspector, reported that 110,002 Jews had been received, also indicating the points at which they had crossed: Moghilev, 45,545; Iampol, 30,891; Râbniţa, 27,113; Tiraspol, 163; and Iaska, 2,200.[334] Later, in January 1942, Broşteanu gave an updated figure of 118,847. The crossing points were attributed numbers different from those in the previous report: Moghilev, 55,913; Iampol, 35,276; Râbniţa, 24,570; Tiraspol, 872; Iaska, 2,216.[335] A September 9, 1942, report of the Transnistria Gendarme Inspectorate indicated that 119,065 Jews had been received: 55,913 at Moghilev; 35,276 at Iampol; 24,570 at Râbniţa; 2,216 at Ovidopol; and 1,090 at Tiraspol.[336]

On December 9, 1941, after all but a few thousand of the Jews from Bessarabia and Bukovina had already been sent to Transnistria, General Vasiliu gave an early—and minimal—figure of 108,002.[337] A more detailed accounting from the Civilian-Military Cabinet of the Administration of Bessarabia, Bukovina, and Transnistria (CBBT, i.e., Ion Antonescu's office for these provinces) stated in 1943 that 90,334 Jews had ultimately been deported from Bukovina and 56,089 from Bessarabia, a total of 146,423.[338] My own best estimate is that at least 125,000 Jews, possibly 145,000, reached Transnistria alive. Reliable official Romanian wartime statistics indicate that of these, only fifty thousand would survive to the end of 1943.

*   *   *

Romania never embarked, as did Germany, on a formal program of outright slaughter. But by enacting age-old anti-Semitic fantasies of "driving the Jews out," by systematic depredation and expulsion, the Romanians nevertheless enacted one of the major chapters of the Holocaust of European Jewry. In one sense at least their program was crueler than that of the Germans: as opposed to the Nazis' experiment in impersonal, bureaucratized, industrial killing, the Romanians made their Holocaust a "hands-on" experience. In part this reflects the relative backwardness of Romanian society and government, both hardly capable of organizing systematic extermination and even less capable of carrying them through properly. Indecision, contradictory orders, bureaucracy (in all the negative senses of the word), and the conflicting interests of a variety of instances and figures, as well as the personal motivations of thousands of individual perpetrators, all combined to bring an element of outright chaos to the Romanian Holocaust. In some senses events in Romania during World War II have more in common with the chaotic killing process in Cambodia under Pol Pot or the ethnic cleansing during the Yugoslav civil wars than with the industrial killing processes of the Third Reich.

Botched deportations across the Dniester River convinced Romania's German allies of the Balkan country's incompetence and doubled the suffering of the Jews; the same may be said of the de facto "planlessness" of many phases of the Romanian deportations. As we shall see in the next chapter, outlandish administrative incompetence considerably intensified the misery of Jews deported to Transnistria, causing tens of thousands to die who might otherwise have stood a chance of surviving an already cruel banishment. But the overall disorganization of the Romanian Holocaust also guaranteed a fighting chance for at least the most physically vigorous to survive until the second half of the war, when changed circumstances would bring renewed hope of an ultimate return home or emigration to the United States or Palestine.

[CHAPTER 5]

The Massacres in Transnistria

As LURID as earlier episodes appear in hindsight, the saga of the Jews who actually made it to Transnistria is the centerpiece of the Holocaust in Romania, for here hundreds of thousands perished in outright massacres—sometimes involving German participation—and as a result of deprivation. While the following chapter will describe the living—and dying—conditions that prevailed in the land sprawling between the Dniester and Bug Rivers, this chapter focuses specifically on the mass murders in this region in which tens of thousands of Romanian and German soldiers, professional executioners from the SS, and representatives of the indigenous Romanian, Ukrainian, and German populations indulged their vicious greed and their sadistic lust for blood. Not only Romanian Jewish deportees perished in these killing actions; so did a huge number of the indigenous Jews who inhabited the region on the eve of the war.

Transnistria had belonged to Soviet Ukraine before Romania was given control of the region by Germany in 1941. Thereafter the territory was governed by Gheorghe Alexianu, who directly answered to Marshal Ion Antonescu. On August 19, 1941, a decree proclaimed his administration, even though Soviet troops held on to Odessa for another two months. Soon, however, Transnistria would become what Alexander Dallin, one of the first Western scholars to consider the subject, called "the ethnic dumping ground of Romania."[1] Raul Hilberg estimated that 135,000 Jews from Bessarabia, Bukovina, and Dorohoi reached Transnistria (out of the 160,000 originally seized for deportation).[2] Of the 300,000 indigenous Jews (a majority of them in Odessa), perhaps one-third failed to evacuate with the Soviets[3] (though Hilberg estimated more than one-half, or over 150,000). Only fifty thousand of the Jews deported from Romania, along with an unknown though probably comparable number of indigenous Jews, lived to see the end of the war; all in all, at least a quarter of a million Jews died in Transnistria (not all directly murdered). Even excluding the participation of the SS and German soldiers, Romania was the only country besides Germany to be involved in massacres on such a grand scale.[4]

As we will see in what follows, only on the microscale does the true picture emerge, however; in the postwar words of the survivor Mehr Berura, who lived in Transnistria for two and one-half years, "of the 1,500 deportees with whom I arrived, only 10 percent survived."[5]

ODESSA

In October 1941, one of the largest slaughters of civilians during World War II took place in Odessa. Romanian and German troops occupied the city on October 16, after resistance that had lasted longer than in the neighboring areas, with the last evacuations of military and civilian personnel occurring by sea since the city was by then encircled. The exasperated Romanian Military Command vented its frustration on the "guilty," the Jews.

Relevant in this respect is the following excerpt from a reply by Ion Antonescu to Wilhelm Filderman, who begged the Conducator to show clemency toward the Jews. "In response to the generous reception and treatment granted your Jews among us," the leader wrote, the Jews "have become Soviet commissars" and have urged the Soviet troops in Odessa into senseless resistance, "for the sole purpose of making us suffer losses."[6] According to Dora Litani's estimates, between eighty and ninety thousand Jews lived in Odessa at the moment of its occupation, and "thousands of them, especially intellectuals, were killed during the initial twenty-four hours."[7] Dallin thought that as many as 100,000 Jews or more remained in Odessa, a figure possibly too high.[8] A diplomatic note sent by

Vyacheslav Molotov to all foreign legations in the USSR shortly after the fall of Odessa stated that the German occupiers had killed eight thousand Jews there, a number probably representing only the massacres of the initial days. Vasily Grossman and Ilya Ehrenburg's *Black Book* estimates that three thousand to four thousand Jews were killed during the first days of the occupation.[9]

On October 22, a mine left in a booby-trapped safe destroyed the building housing the Romanian Military Command in Odessa. Located as it was near the old NKVD (Narodnyĭ komissariat vnutrennikh del, or the People's Commissariat of Internal Affairs) headquarters, the Romanians had been warned by local civilians that the building had been mined. During his trial Ion Antonescu admitted that they had been told twice.[10] The explosion killed General Glogojanu, sixteen other officers, nine noncoms, and thirty-five soldiers.

Antonescu's responsibility for events in Odessa also emerged during his postwar trial, in the following dialogue among the marshal himself; another defendant, General Pantazi; the president of the tribunal; and the public prosecutor:

PRESIDENT: What can you tell us about the massacres at Odessa?

ANTONESCU: I was informed of those massacres much later, in July [1944]. General Pantazi's memory is good, he must remember that. He came to me in July 1944, I think, and told me: "I took measures to make the corpses disappear." [As the Red Army neared, the Romanians worried that the remaining evidence of the 1941 massacre would be discovered.—R.I.]

PANTAZI: That is not so.

ANTONESCU: I cannot recall by heart. The fact is that he came to me and told me about some corpses, not about the massacre, and I asked him what he meant. Pantazi did not talk to me about a massacre. In July [October] 1941, when the Odessa command went up in smoke, he asked me to approve some reprisals. I approved them. I even gave him the figures.

PUBLIC PROSECUTOR SĂRACU: Who signed the order to execute two hundred people for every officer and one hundred for every soldier?

ANTONESCU: I gave that order, because I also did it in Romania, and I promulgated many more repressive laws, as did all states during that period. . . . We did not execute any Jews, we did not execute any youth; I did give the order for reprisals but not for massacres.[11]

Telegram No. 561 of October 2, 1941, sent by Colonel Davidescu, head of Antonescu's military office, indeed ordered severe reprisals in Odessa.[12] This command was elaborated on October 23 (at 12:30 P.M.), in Marshal Antonescu's Telegram No. 562 (through Davidescu), to take and execute hostages:

> In view of the action at Odessa that was plotted by local Communists and because any similar type of action must be eliminated in the future, the marshal orders that severe reprisals be enacted:
>
> a. For every Romanian or German officer who died as a result of the explosion, two hundred Communists will be executed; for each soldier who died, one hundred Communists; the executions will take place on this very day.
> b. All Communists in Odessa will be taken as hostages, as well as a member of each Jewish family.[13]

Also on October 23, at 7:45 P.M., Colonel Stănculescu, deputy commander of the Fourth Army, reported to the Supreme General Staff in the person of General Tătăranu that he had ordered immediate reprisals, including "the elimination of eighteen thousand Jews in the ghetto and [the hanging of] at least one hundred Jews for each regimental sector."[14] At the division level similar reports were generated, for example, General Constantin Trestioreanu's of the Thirteenth Infantry: "I hanged in the public squares of Odessa about five thousand people, mostly Jews."[15] That same evening General Ion Iacobici, commander of the Fourth Army, informed Marshal Antonescu's cabinet (in Report No. 302827) that "a number of Jews and Communists were hanged in reprisal."[16] Several historians agree on the figure of five thousand people executed on October 23.[17] Over the course of the same day the gendarmerie and the police jailed more than twenty thousand others, again mostly Jews.[18] On October 24, the Romanian Military Command in Odessa received Telegram No. 563 from Colonel Davidescu:

> To General [Nicolae] Macici [commander of the Second Army Corps]: Marshal Antonescu has ordered [further] reprisals:

1. Execution of all Jews from Bessarabia who have sought refuge in Odessa.

2. All individuals who fall under the stipulations [of Telegram No. 562] of October 23, 1941, not yet executed and the others who can be added thereto will be placed inside a building that will be mined and detonated. This action will take place on the day of burial of the victims.

3. This order will be destroyed after being read.[19]

Three days later Colonel Davidescu asked if this order had been carried out; the Fourth Army reported immediately (in Telegram No. 3218) that it indeed had been executed.[20]

According to Colonel Rodler, chief representative of the Abwehr in Romania, "about nineteen thousand Jews were shot that morning in a square surrounded by a wooden fence in the harbor area. Their bodies were covered with gasoline and burned."[21] Jacques Truelle of the Vichy legation in Bucharest stated that "as reprisals following the October 22 explosion (my Telegram No. 883), . . . 25,000 Jews were crammed into barracks and were shot and shelled before Romanian troops set fire to them."[22] On October 24, 1941, the Jews in the Odessa jail were escorted to the Company 2 of the Tenth Machine Gun Battalion at Dalnic. Along a three-kilometer stretch, those who lagged behind the convoys were shot. The first forty to fifty were tied to one another and executed in an antitank ditch; the others were crowded into three sheds.[23] At the war crimes trial Chief Prosecutor O. A. Bunaciu summarized what ensued:

A great massacre began here. In a most horrible fashion . . . 25,000 to 30,000 peaceable residents of Odessa were murdered. As witnesses stated, those in the first rows were placed in antitank ditches . . . and were shot in the head, forty to fifty at a time. The executioners felt that the system was too slow and costly, since one bullet cost too much for each individual. The commander of the Tenth Battalion found a faster and more cost-effective solution: . . . slots were cut in the walls [of the sheds] through which machine-gun barrels would fit. You can imagine the horrible scenes there, where the young, children, women, old men, and the sick had been crammed.[24]

Here is a related excerpt from the deposition of Alexe Neacșu, a reserve second lieutenant from the Twenty-third Infantry Regiment:

They proceeded to machine-gun those inside the four [*sic*] sheds, and I think that Colonel Deleanu gave the order to fire, or perhaps it was Colonel Niculescu-Coca. The sheds were handled one at a time, and the operation lasted until nightfall. . . . On the following day the sheds where these operations had not been finished were blown sky-high, symbolically and as an example; this operation took place, I believe, at the same time [of day] as the command blew up. After having machine-gunned those sheds for several hours, the commanders of that operation . . . complained that this was the only way that they could liquidate those who were inside; they were visibly annoyed at not having found a faster way to complete these operations. They resorted to oil and gas and then sprayed and set the sheds ablaze.

When the fire broke out, those inside who had escaped the bullets or who had been lightly wounded tried to escape through the windows or by the roof. The soldiers were given the general order to shoot anyone who managed to get out. Some of those who had been inside appeared at the windows and, in order to escape the flames, begged with hand signals to be shot and pointed at their head or their heart.

[They turned] their backs [to the soldiers] in order not to see them shoot. The operation lasted till nightfall; those scenes . . . under the glimmer of the flames seemed even more horrible. The people appearing in the windows were naked, because their clothes had caught on fire. Some women threw their children through the window. I remember one particular scene: a four- or five-year-old child was thrown out of a window and convulsed for about five or ten minutes, his hands above his head, among corpses, because the Romanian soldiers refused to gun him down.[25]

This massacre indeed took place under the leadership of the two above-mentioned military gendarmerie colonels, Nicolae Deleanu and Mihail Niculescu-Coca.[26]

In addition to General Trestioreanu, temporarily in command of the Tenth Infantry as well as the Thirteenth, General Macici and General Iacobici were also implicated. Others who participated directly in the massacre were Captain Radu Ionescu and Lieutenants Eugen Bălăceanu and Eustațiu Mărculescu (these three had taken part in the massacre at Ghidighici, Bessarabia, in August 1941).[27] Lieutenant Colonel Traian Borcescu of the SSI (whose first operational echelon had participated in the Chişinău massacre as well as those of Odessa) testified to the involvement of yet others: "The file [i.e., proving his responsibility—R.I.] on the Odessa exploits was personally handed to me by Grigore Petrovici."[28] Right after the explosion Colonel Radu Dinulescu of the Supreme General Staff's Second Section, who had been involved in many previous anti-Jewish operations, appeared in Odessa, though we cannot trace his subsequent involvement.[29]

As stated in Indictment No. 221/1945, which contains the deposition of witness Alexandru Răcescu, German soldiers probably belonging to SS units also participated in the massacres at the Odessa suburb of Dalnic.[30] However, in his statement at the trial growing out of the indictment, Captain Ovidiu Onca maintained that SS troops had participated in the massacres only in the city of Odessa proper.[31]

According to survivor Izu Landau, about seven thousand Jews were spared in Dalnic and sent on to Bogdanovka (Golta District);[32] the mayor of Odessa, Gherman Pintea, was behind this move.[33] The number of those slaughtered in Odessa and Dalnic differs in various sources but is nonetheless appalling: Litani estimates that several thousand Jews were killed in Odessa immediately after the Germans occupied the city: 24,000 Jews were killed by Romanian troops during the morning of October 23 (19,000 in the harbor and 5,000 in the city) and 16,000 in Dalnic, which brings the total to 40,000 dead.[34] The German officer Rodler referred to forty thousand Jews killed in Dalnic itself.[35] During the trial of the first group of Romanian war criminals, 25,000 to 30,000 were claimed killed in Dalnic.[36] The figures mentioned by Romanian officers present in Odessa vary between 19,000 and 23,000 dead.[37] At his trial Eugen Cristescu, former head of the SSI, stated that 25,000 to 26,000 people had been executed in Odessa.[38] Finally, the handwritten postwar testimony of one survivor also estimated the number of victims burned alive or hanged in Odessa at 35,000.[39] In the final analysis it is quite likely that at least 25,000 Jews were killed in Odessa and Dalnic.

GOLTA DISTRICT

Another large-scale massacre in which the Romanian military authorities of Transnistria were implicated took place in Golta District one month after the events at Odessa. At the first Romanian war crimes trial the fact emerged that the order to exterminate the Jews interned in the Golta ghettos of Bogdanovka, Dumanovka, and Acmecetka came from the prefect of the district, Modest Isopescu; Ukrainian policemen and Romanian gendarmes under his command carried out the mass executions. Most of the victims were Ukrainian Jews, but thousands of Bessarabian Jews also perished there. According to a Romanian officer, at the end of 1941 a dog's existence was worth more than a Jew's life in Bogdanovka.[40]

To flush out any hidden money, the Jews' captors opened a "bakery" to sell the famished victims bread at five gold rubles per loaf. As was reported in the prosecutor's statement at the postwar trial:

> Once there was no more flour, the bakery could no longer operate. But hunger could be appeased only with bread. The indigenous population that came from time to time and sold various foodstuffs to the camp inmates was prevented from selling directly to them. The food was confiscated by Gheorghe Bobei and Izu Landau and resold to the inmates for gold and valuable items at the price that we mentioned. Hence, the inmates were stripped of their belongings in a short period of time, even of the clothes that they wore.
>
> After the looting ended, the accused, Isopescu, committed the most horrendous crime of all: the mass murder of the entire camp population of 48,000 at Bogdanovka. The order for the execution was given to the accused Aristide Pădure, the deputy prefect of Golta District, an accomplice who was just as vicious and whom Modest Isopescu could trust implicitly, [and who was] convinced that the extermination would be total and in the shortest period of time—which is what happened. . . . Pădure was known by the inmates and the district's population for the plunder and the ferocity that he displayed during that whole period. Pădure transmitted the order for the execution to the district prefect of the Dumanovka Raion [province], Vasile Mănescu, who took the initial measures to implement this order. In order to carry out the massacre, they brought in from the city of Golta and the entire district all the policemen under the express orders of Prefect Modest Isopescu.
>
> The massacre began on the morning of December 21, 1941. The inmates were split into two groups: in several stables [were] the sick and disabled who could not go to the forest where the execution was to take place outside the camp; those who could walk were piled into the other stables. The first lot to be massacred consisted of the sick and the dis-

abled; after having scattered hay on the roof of the stables and in front of the entrances, they poured gasoline. The order rang out, "Light the fire!" and in several minutes the two stables and the four to five thousand inmates went up in smoke, under the watchful eye of the police sent by Modest Isopescu, to help them complete his criminal task.

It is not difficult to imagine the torment, the anxiety of 43,000 Jews locked up in the other stables, awaiting their turn. For them, the accused had chosen another site for the massacre: a ravine close to a bog in the vicinity of the camp, each area playing a specific role—the bog, for the looting from the inmates of what they held to be most precious; the ravine, for the execution itself and incineration. While the two stables burned, the ambulatory inmates were led to the execution site. Horrible scenes unfolded: mothers took their children in their arms and asked to be spared; fathers encouraged their children and their wives when the deepest feeling of despair overtook the inmates. They could still hear the desperate screams coming from the stables, which collapsed on the corpses.

In the forest, after having been robbed and stripped, they were made to kneel, naked, on the edge of the ravine: they were shot in groups of three to four hundred people, with explosive bullets. The massacre proceeded at that pace on December 22 and 23, 1941. It was interrupted from December 24 to December 28.

In view of the large number (43,000–48,000) of people who were massacred, the accused, Modest Isopescu, gave the order to cremate the corpses, hoping to erase all traces of what had happened. For that, he chose the strongest two hundred men from among the inmates. The cremation took two months: January and February 1942.

The cremation took place as follows: they formed a layer of straw and wood, upon which they laid down the corpses, then they placed on top of them another layer of straw and another layer of corpses, so that the stacks were two meters tall and four to five meters wide. The corpses were set up in the following order: a thin corpse next to a fat corpse, so that the latter's fat helped burn the thin corpse more quickly. That is how two hundred inmates spent their time trying to erase all signs of this crime for two months. Afterward 150 of those 200 inmates were executed, the pretext being that they had not carried out fast enough the cremation of the corpses.[41]

Vasile Mănescu also participated in the plunder and executions at Bogdanovka, and he further ordered the murder of the Jews detained at Dumanovka. The evidence was advanced at one of the post–World War II trials. Mănescu received his directive from Deputy Prefect Pădure, who himself had received it from Prefect Isopescu. Told to exterminate the inmates of Bogdanovka, he further transmitted the order to Adjutant Vasile Melinescu, but when Melinescu refused to carry out the criminal act, Mănescu took the measures himself. The postwar trial records show that Mănescu "was personally responsible for the massacre, for the fire that was set in the two stables, and for the cremation of the 43,000 inmates after their execution. . . . Vasile Mănescu [was] guilty of the mass execution of eighteen thousand inmates at Dumanovka, for sadistically having carried out Modest Isopescu's order, and for having been present at all times at the execution sites."[42] The executions in Dumanovka lasted for a long time from the perspective of prisoners waiting their turn. Again, the trial records bear witness to the torture:

> Isopescu instructed a small group of trusted murderers and told them to conduct the operation in series: executions for a day, then rest for two or three days. That explains why the executions lasted almost two months, in groups of 100–150 people requiring two to three days per group. For "undesirable and dangerous" Jews, Modest Isopescu established a "death camp." Acmecetka was a farm and a sort of hospital, and according to some of those tried later, the Jews who were brought there were survivors of various ghettos from Transnistria and Romania. In Acmecetka the deportees were subjected to a slow and horrible extermination.
>
> First of all, the inmates were prohibited from getting food supplies. People remained for days on end stretched out on the ground or on beds, unable to move. Modest Isopescu would come and say, "Give them each a cup of corn flour every day" [i.e., food that could have been eaten only if cooked]. They ate it raw, because they could not light a fire.
>
> Isopescu showed up drunk. He relished the torments of the surviving inmates and their children. He looked at them and photographed them. Isopescu took photographs, always took photographs. . . . Witnesses stated that four to five thousand inmates died at Acmecetka, deprived of any food.[43]

A survivor confirms in general terms the figures attributable to the first batch of Romanian war criminals—namely, 48,000 dead in Bogdanovka, 14,000 dead in Dumanovka, and 14,000 dead in Acmecetka.[44] But according to the same survivor's notes, one has to add another five or six thousand to the number given at the trial, for although the number of dead at Bogdanovka is the same, the number at Dumanovka is smaller by four thousand, and at Acmecetka the total is nine or ten thousand greater. Nevertheless, based on the trial records and the survivor's estimates, one can state that at least seventy thousand people were exterminated in the three localities between December 21, 1941, and the end of February 1942.

The Germans' complicity seems to have consisted of pressuring Isopescu: on the other side of the Bug River they feared a typhus epidemic if the inmates weren't liquidated quickly. Melinescu stated during his trial that at 10:00 A.M. on December 24, 1941, Isopescu arrived at the site of what would be the massacre of Bogdanovka with two German officers.[45] Basing her account on the Carp archives in Yad Vashem, Litani relays: "the order for the operation was given by the governor of the Golta District, Modest Isopescu, who acted on advice from Fleischer, a German official on the other side of the [Bug]. The executioners of the order were Romanian district administrators, the Ukrainian militia under the command of and members of the SS Volksdeutsche."[46] In the course of his own trial Radu Lecca declared that the Golta executions were carried out by the Ukrainian police under orders from the Germans, confirming Isopescu's role. But Lecca also admitted that the valuables of the executed Jews remained on the Romanian side of the river.[47] During the Antonescu trial Filderman asserted that the authors of the Golta massacres were both German and Romanian.[48]

A survivor said that during the massacre at Bogdanovka both Romanian and German officers looked on and that Romanian gendarmes executed the Jews aided by Ukrainian policemen. At the trial of the executioners in Ukraine on February 12, 1976, twelve former Ukrainian policemen were condemned; all but one, however, bore ethnic German names.[49] But the commander of the detachment of seventy killers was confirmed as Andruşin, a Ukrainian.[50] Adjutant Melinescu declared at his own trial that he had seen the order for the Bogdanovka executions, dated December 13, 1941, and signed by Deputy Prefect Pădure, in Andruşin's possession.[51] Melinescu further declared that the policeman Mihail

Cazachievici (or Hazachievici) at Dumanovka personally took part in the slaughter of five thousand Jews.[52] On March 10, 1942, 810 Jews remained at Bogdanovka and 1,900 Jews at Dumanovka, under the supervision of Cazachievici and six guards. Thirty to forty Jews died each day in those two ghettos.[53]

THE GERMAN CONTRIBUTION

The extermination of the Jews in Golta District and the elimination of the surviving Jews of Odessa in Berezovka District in early 1942 followed another killing operation, one that involved Einsatzgruppe D, under the command of Otto Ohlendorf. This murder formation had operated briefly in Transnistria and Bukovina and was now attached to the Eleventh German Army under General von Schobert (the army later under Erich von Manstein). From August 9 to August 15, 1941, Einsatzgruppe D operated throughout the regions of Nicolaev and Kherson, moving east of the Dnieper River after October 1.[54] More broadly, between June 1941 and June 1942, Einsatzgruppe D liquidated about ninety thousand people: Jews, Gypsies, Ukrainians, partisans, intellectuals, mental patients.[55] At the same time the Romanians were quite aware of what the local ethnic Germans were doing on their territory in Transnistria under separate and autonomous SS command. According to a report from the Supreme General Staff to Antonescu in March 1942, German policemen subjected the Jewish population of the district of Berezovka to mass executions:

> I. (1) In the district of Berezovka (Transnistria), German policemen executed 4,067 [*sic*] Jews, who had been interned in that district's camps, specifically:
> 1,725 Jews on March 10;
> 1,742 Jews on April 20;
> 550 Jews on April 22;
> 30 Jews on April 24.
> (2) Following the execution the German police burned the corpses and donated the clothes to the German population without having disinfected them, which occasioned typhoid cases in one particular town.
> II. The Supreme General Staff wishes to find out if the German police-

men can conduct such undertakings under Romanian administration.[56]

Marshal Antonescu wrote in response that "it is not the responsibility of the Supreme General Staff of the army to worry about such things."[57]

A report of the Aid Committee of the Central Office of Romanian Jews indicated that by March 22, 1943, one year later, only 185 Jews still survived in southern Transnistria: 425 in the district of Berezovka and 60 in Odessa.[58] A survivor's testimony estimated that in Mostovoi District the SS and policemen from the German communities at Rastadt, Lichtenfeld, and others had killed fifteen thousand Jews.[59]

The status of the ethnic Germans in the new Transnistria was established through an agreement negotiated by Mihai Antonescu and Manfred von Killinger on November 14 and 15, 1941. According to this agreement, "German colonies" came under the authority of the Volksdeutsche Mittelstelle (Ethnic German Liaison Office). Thus recognized, the colonies were allowed to form their own SS police. The head of the Mittelstelle in Transnistria was SS Oberführer (Horst) Hoffmeyer, who nominated the heads of the administration of the German settlements pending formal approval by the Romanian prefect.[60]

Mostovoi was the major center of extermination of the Berezovka District Jews. According to the estimates of survivors and Romanian gendarmes, at least thirty thousand were murdered there. Other mass executions took place in Balaiciuc (two thousand victims), Cihrin (two thousand), Zaharovca (fifteen hundred), and Rastadt (six hundred).[61] In May 1942, Romanian gendarmes and German policemen killed forty Jews in Vasilinovo (Berezovka).[62] About 31,000 Jews in Berezovka District were transferred to the Germans by a gendarme commander, Adam Popescu. As far as is known, none survived.[63]

> Berezovka was the arrival point of almost twenty thousand Odessa Jews who had survived the Romanian army massacres of October 1941. The railroad station of the town of Berezovka, some sixty miles northeast of Odessa, was situated in the middle of a cluster of Ukrainian and ethnic German settlements. The Jews, brought there by train, were marched to the countryside and shot by ethnic German *Selbstschutz* [members of the "self-defense" corps]. . . . The death toll . . . was swelled by victims from smaller towns and villages. A cumulative figure was indicated by a

member of the German Foreign Office in May. "About 28,000 Jews had been brought to German villages in Transnistria," he [Popescu] wrote. *"Inzwischen wurden sie liquidiert"* (Meanwhile they have been liquidated).[64]

The same figure of 28,000 Jews liquidated by the German "colonists" in Transnistria has been given by Alexander Dallin.[65] According to the testimony of the gendarme Ilie Bădoiu, thirty thousand Jews, transferred by the Romanian gendarmes to the Mostovoi Volksdeutsche SS, perished there over several months.[66] Further details are available concerning some of those murders perpetrated by German troops, by Ukrainian-born Germans incorporated into the SS, and by other residents of German settlements in Transnistria: on February 12, 1942, the Jews of Ieroșinca were massacred by SS troops; on February 13, German policemen from Rastadt executed 130 in the village of Nova Umani;[67] on March 9, German police at Mostovoi and Zavadovca executed 372 Jews from the Khrincihrin camp;[68] also on March 9, German policemen from Mostovoi and Zavadovca killed 722 Jews from the camp at Cihrini-Berezovka; on the following day fifteen German policemen from the same villages executed 875 Jews at Balaiciuc. Three days later, on March 13, seventeen SS officers from the village of Carteica executed 650 Jews from the village of Hulievca; their corpses were burned later. On March 16, 1942, sixteen SS members of the village of Nova Candeli executed 120 Jews from the Catovska camp. On March 18, German policemen under a German officer executed 483 Jews from Odessa in the village of Bernadovka. On March 22, German police from Carteica executed 180 Jews at Staraia Balca and 370 at Zaharovca;[69] on March 24, in Neu-Fredental-Berezovka thirty Jews from Balaiciuc were executed by nineteen German policemen.[70]

A report from the Romanian Berezovka gendarmerie stated in April 1942 that 85 percent of the Jews of Berezovka District had been liquidated by SS formations.[71] A similar report of May 1942 indicated that all Odessa Jews who had been held in the Mostovoi castle had been executed in a field by the SS, which then burned the corpses.[72] In early June the SS troops of Lichtenfeld executed 1,200 Jews in Suha Verba; the Transnistria Gendarme Inspectorate reported that mass murder to the government of Transnistria.[73] On July 3, 1942, Romanian officials handed over 247 Jews at Brailov (Bratslav), ten kilometers northeast of Smerinka, after they had sought refuge on Romanian territory; the Germans killed them.[74] Romanian gendarmes executed three hundred Jews moved from Vapniarka to Berezovka during the spring of 1942.[75]

On August 19, 1942, at the request of the Todt Organization and with the consent of the Tulcin District prefect, Colonel Loghin, three thousand Jews who had been deported in June from Cernăuţi and taken beyond the Bug now were handed over to the Germans. "Of those three thousand Jews almost no one returned. The elderly, [as well as] some of the women, some of the children, and the weakest, were executed in the first days. The others were gradually killed once they could no longer work."[76] Then, on June 6, 1943, again at the request of the Todt Organization, another transport of 829 Jews was sent from Moghilev to Trihati for the construction of a bridge over the Bug.[77] The fate of these Jews is unknown.

The year 1942 also saw indigenous Jews in Olgopol and Jews from Odessa being handed over by Lieutenant Grigorescu to the Germans, who executed most of them right away. When eighteen young Jews escaped, Grigorescu sent them back to the Germans, who murdered them.[78] Matatias Carp discovered that on or about September 15, 1942, Romanian "gendarmes from Mostovoi supported SS troops in their looting and killing operations aimed at a group of six hundred Jews from Regat and Transylvania, [Jews who had been] deported two weeks earlier on orders of the Ministry of the Interior."[79] On September 22, 1942, SS troops carried out another massacre: 598 Jews from Moldavia and Walachia were deported for having petitioned to go to the USSR in 1940; they were removed from Mostovoi and taken to Rastadt upon request of the local German police, and they were joined by 423 indigenous Jews there. All were executed and their clothes confiscated. Only sixteen Jews survived that massacre.[80]

On October 16, 1942, the commander of the Pecioara camp handed over 150 young girls aged fourteen to twenty to Oberfeldwebel Hans Rucker, these to be shot in the woods between Bar and Vijniţa. One of those youngsters survived.[81] On October 20, north of Transnistria, twelve thousand Jews, including many children, were murdered in Bar, under German jurisdiction. Romanian officials in Balki saved several dozen Jews, doctors or other specialists, as well as several of those who were only wounded during the massacre and had managed to escape.[82]

On November 1, 1942, the Mostovoi station gendarmes handed ninety refugee Polish Jews to the Rastadt SS; these captives were executed on the spot.[83] On November 9, a major extermination sweep got under way on the German side of the Bug. This enveloped many of those who had been deported from the Romanian bank of the river. About one thousand Jews were killed at Garisin. Another large-scale massacre took place at Brailov, but 250 Jews escaped; the 40 Jewish specialists and doctors who had been saved by Romanian officials in Balki on October 20, however, had only been reprieved: they were killed at Bar.[84] On November 20, five hundred Jews from the Pecioara camp were handed over to the Germans, who transported them to the other side of the Bug and executed them.[85]

On December 5, 1942, the 250 Brailov massacre survivors who had sought refuge in Şmerinka were slain by the Germans.[86] Weeks later, on December 24, a German officer murdered three children in Krasnopolsk.[87] On January 15, 1943, two hundred Jews were slaughtered in that same town by the Germans, and three days later SS Lieutenant Robert Stolzmann executed fifteen more at Bratslav.[88] On March 29, 1943, again at Bratslav, the Germans killed another six Jews.[89] Romanian gendarmes had arrested them under the pretense that they were being sent to work. Those destined for extermination were taken to the nearby towns of Mostovoi and especially Vasilinovo, where, after having been tortured in a most atrocious manner, they were executed.[90]

Upon request of the German military authorities beyond the Bug, the new district prefect of Tulcin, Poiană Volbură, ordered the transfer of two hundred Jews to the other side of that river on August 2, 1943. Knowing what awaited them, they managed to organize, for a sum of money, the safeguarding of fifty-two children.[91] On October 28, 1943, the commander of the Nicolaev labor camp, Hans Schmidt, ordered Jews to hang the ten most exhausted of their number, who could no longer work. When the third victim was being hung, the rope snapped twice, so that those other Jews who had "mishandled" the hanging were also executed. The officer shot two of them himself. On November 15, 1943, the same German officer ordered the execution of twenty additional Jews in Nicolaev.[92] On December 10, the Germans massacred 438 Jews in Tarasivca, most of whom had come from Cernăuţi and Dorohoi.[93]

During the massive SS executions of the Jews who had been deported to the Berezovka District in the spring of 1942, Romanian gendarmes also wrought their own carnage. Among their many outrages, they killed one hundred Jews in early 1942 in Uleiovka, Berezovka.[94] Six Jews were executed on March 20 along the Șargorod-Moghilev road by a Romanian gendarme (the Jews who had been deported to Transnistria were not allowed to circulate from one town to another without approval); the executions took place in the cemetery of Șargorod on orders from the military prosecutor of the district, Dindelegan. On April 2, another Jew was killed by gendarmes nearby.[95] Two days later forty-eight Jews caught outside the ghetto of Râbnița were executed on orders from the gendarme legion commander, and on April 8, another Jew was executed in Șargorod, reportedly for having stolen four pounds of flour.[96] Several Jews were killed in the ghetto of Olgopol by Romanian gendarmes.[97]

During the spring of 1943, Iampol ghetto commander Dionisie Fotino and Gheorghe Popescu, a noncom, executed three Jews who had come to buy food from a neighboring ghetto.[98] In June 1943, four young Jews were executed in Trihati—one because he had left the "dormitory," the other three because they had received letters their parents had sent from other towns in Transnistria.[99] On June 18, two gendarmes who belonged to the guard detail of the Pecioara camp executed two Jews as they were buying cherries near the camp's fence. On July 11, a gendarme caught thirteen Jewish escapees from Tulcin in the town of Jurkovca (Tulcin District); he killed twelve, one escaped.[100]

Carp reports that on August 18, 1943, "in the woods of Sosnovca, near Șargorod, one Jew was executed on orders from [Major] Botoroagă. The corpse was burned. In the waters of the Dniester were floating corpses of Jews who had been riddled with bullets. Almost all of the victims belonged to the Nestervorka camp."[101] On August 25, in Sumovka, gendarmes executed two Jews who were begging and threw their bodies into the Bug; a day later sixty mental patients deported from Cernăuți were executed at the stone quarry of Ladijin.[102]

On September 9, a Jew was executed in the Trihati camp when the authorities determined that one hundred grams of oil were missing. On October 10, the Capusterna gendarme chief executed at Iaroșinca two brothers whom he had caught begging. On the same day the gendarme station chief at Lucineț executed a Crainic couple and their child, caught searching for kindling in the forest. They were buried at Grumovka.[103] On

November 15, 1943, a Jew caught outside the ghetto of Berşad was executed. Second Lieutenant Ghineraru terrorized the Jews in the ghetto, as he did the Ukrainians from that locality. Ghineraru killed a Jewish child, whom he dragged behind his motorcycle. Then, in January 1944, Ghineraru executed 320 Jews and several Ukrainians after torturing them for two weeks.[104] The local military command lodged a written protest against Ghineraru's atrocities.[105] On November 18, 1943, eighty-three Jews were executed in Balta; and on December 8, the gendarme station chief at Capusterna executed two Jewish children caught fleeing to the other side of the Bug.[106]

During the retreat of 1944, several Jews were executed by Romanian gendarmes and German troops in Balta.[107] On January 20, 1944, in the town of Derebcin, the Germans executed 11 Jews; and in Berşad, on January 25, Romanian gendarmes and the German police arrested 148 Jews, all of whom were executed after eight days of torture.[108] Romanian and German troops massacred eighty more Jews in Berşad on February 7, 1944.[109] On March 15, in the town of Slobodka, Balta District, Romanian gendarmes executed four Jews.[110] In the prison of Râbniţa Romanian and German soldiers executed fifty-two Jewish inmates; four survived.[111] Finally, between March 5 and 20, 1944, Soviet troops liberated Transnistria.

*   *   *

How many Jews perished in the massacres at Transnistria? At least 123,000 Romanian Jews had crossed the Dniester River in 1941 and 1942; only 50,741 remained alive as of 1943. About 25,000 Jews were killed in Odessa, at least 28,000 Jews were killed by the Germans in Berezovka, and 75,000 were killed in Golta, not to mention up to 19,000 Romanian Gypsies killed in Transnistria. Julius Fisher estimates that 87,000 Romanian Jews died in Transnistria along with 130,000 indigenous Jews.[112] The Germans bear direct responsibility for the deaths of about fifty thousand, mostly in the districts of Berezovka and Bar. The majority of them were handed over to the Nazis by the Romanians. The final result of all the efforts of the Romanians, the Germans, and their collaborators was the victimization of more than a quarter million innocent people.

Although, as we have seen, the murders continued after 1942, the zeal of Romanian officialdom began to abate in that year as the changing course of the war suggested to them to replace fanaticism with opportunism in Jewish matters. If outright mass murder occurred less frequently, however, soul-numbing persecution and grinding day-to-day oppression would continue, with widespread fatal results.

Ion Antonescu and Horia Sima take the oath following the establishment of the National Legionary State with General Antonescu as its leader and Sima, commander of the Legionary Movement, as vice-premier, September 1940. (MUSEUM OF THE JEWISH COMMUNITY, BUCHAREST)

A Jewish pharmacy destroyed during the Bucharest pogrom that took place when the
Iron Guard rebelled against General Antonescu, January 1941. (MUSEUM OF THE JEWISH
COMMUNITY, BUCHAREST)

Lying in the city morgue, the bodies of Jews killed by the Iron Guard during the January 1941 Bucharest pogrom. (MUSEUM OF THE JEWISH COMMUNITY, BUCHAREST)

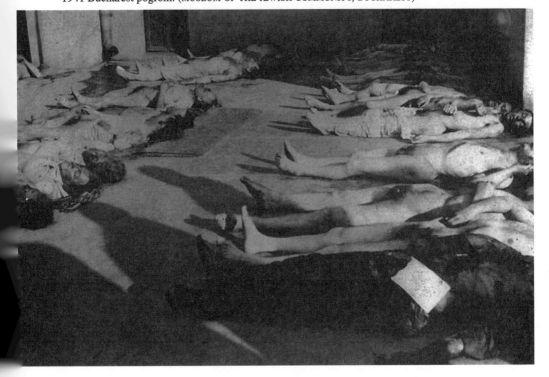

Leaders of the Jewish community, beaten and humiliated, during the Iaşi pogrom, June 1941. (YAD VASHEM)

Round-up of Jews at 157 I. C. Brătianu Street, during the Iaşi pogrom, June 1941. (MUSEUM OF THE JEWISH COMMUNITY, BUCHAREST)

Jews boarding the death train that journeyed from Iaşi to Călăraşi. Note the elderly man with the cap. Iaşi?, June 1941. (BILDERDIENST SÜDDEUTSCHER VERLAG)

Victims of the Iaşi-Călăraşi death train. Note the elderly man with the cap; he appears in the preceding photograph. Tîrgu-Frumos, July 1941. (YIVO INSTITUTE FOR JEWISH RESEARCH)

Gypsies forced to load onto a truck the bodies of Jews from the Iaşi-Călăraşi death train. Tîrgu-Frumos, July 1941. (NATIONAL ARCHIVES)

Jewish women under guard by Romanian soldiers. Kishenev, summer 1941. (YIVO INSTITUTE FOR JEWISH RESEARCH)

Severely beaten Jewish women in a village in Bessarabia, September 1941. (BILDARCHIV PREUSSISCHER KULTURBESITZ)

Jews from Bessarabia being deported at Iampol, one of the major crossing points over the Dniester. Note Italian troops in the background. October–November 1941.
(FONDAZIONE CENTRO DI DOCUMENTAZIONE EBRAICA CONTEMPORANEA, MILAN)

Jews from Bessarabia being deported over the Dniester at Iampol, October–November 1941. (FONDAZIONE CENTRO DI DOCUMENTAZIONE EBRAICA CONTEMPORANEA, MILAN)

Deportation of Jews from Dorohoi, Bukovina, over the Dniester. Atachi?, June 10, 1942.
(YAD VASHEM)

Execution of Jews in Odessa, Transnistria, October 22–24, 1941. (YAD VASHEM)

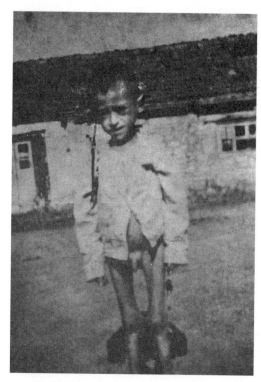

Jewish orphan in Mogilev-
Podolsk, 1942–1943. (YAD
VASHEM)

In Istanbul harbor, the refugee ship *Bellacita*, which transported Jewish orphans from
Transnistria to Palestine under the International Red Cross flag, spring 1944. (JEWISH
JOINT DISTRIBUTION COMMITTEE)

CHAPTER 6

Life in Transnistria

Having quantified the massacres in Transnistria throughout the war period in the previous chapter, this chapter now takes a step backward in an attempt to qualitatively represent the life of the Romanian Jewish deportees and the native Jews of the region of Transnistria during their internment there. Transport, housing (or lack thereof), hygienic conditions, labor, and interaction with the local population are the types of issues that appear on the following pages. In a number of episodes the Romanians deported Jews across the Bug River into the zone of German occupation, where their new masters shortly eliminated them. Yet in some of the ghettos the Romanians established between the Dniester and the Bug, the Jews were able to devise measures to make life survivable, especially for the children. With the passage of time and the Romanians' sense that victory was growing more remote, they themselves started to countenance Jewish efforts to organize for survival. In some cases the more fortunate Jewish community of Regat was permitted to extend aid to the Jews stranded in Transnistria, and even international organizations managed to contribute to the survival of a considerable portion.

*   *   *

As characterized by Raul Hilberg, "Transnistria was a prolonged disaster."[1] The government of the region was first based in Tiraspol, where a ghetto concentrated several hundred Jews working in a soap factory.[2] In October 1941, however, the government moved its seat to Odessa. From its occupation in 1941 to its abandonment in the winter of 1944, Gheorghe Alexianu served as Romania's governor of Transnistria. His portfolio was wide: Marshal Antonescu had told him during a December 16, 1941, meeting of the Council of Ministers:

> There you are king. . . . You proceed any way you see fit. All you have to do is to mobilize people to work, even with a whip if they do not co-operate. If things do not go well in Transnistria, you will be blamed. If it is necessary and you have no other choice, use bullets. You do not need my consent. . . . Govern there as if Romania had been in existence for two million years.[3]

Transnistria was divided into the following districts, many of which will figure in our account: Moghilev, Tulcin, Jugastru, Balta, Râbniţa, Golta, Duboşari, Ananiev, Tiraspol, Berezovka, Ovidopol, Oceakov, and Odessa.

Romanian officials had not initially selected Transnistria as the end of the line for the Jews. As you may recall, Antonescu actually once had talked about settling them beyond the Urals. But the basic idea was simply to drive the Jews as far away as possible. That was in the summer of 1941, when the deportations over the Dniester did not sit well with the Germans, who sent deportees back. Such events recurred throughout February 1942, though less frequently, now with the Romanians sending Jews across and the Germans sending them back from the Bug instead of from the Dniester. Hilberg succinctly described the new situation:

> At the beginning of February 1942, the [German] Ministry for Eastern Occupied Territories informed the German Foreign Office that the Romanians had suddenly deported ten thousand Jews across the Bug in the Voznesensk area and that another sixty thousand were expected to follow. The ministry asked the Foreign Office to urge the Romanian government to refrain from these deportations because of the danger of typhus epidemics. . . . [Adolf] Eichmann was ambivalent in his attitude toward the Romanians. He could not bring himself to condemn them for calling upon the Germans to kill some Jews, but he felt that they were doing so in a disorderly manner. The Romanian deportations, he wrote to the Foreign Office, "are approved as a matter of principle," but they were undesirable because of their "planless and premature" character.
>
> In Bucharest, Vice Premier Mihai Antonescu called in Governor Alexianu to report on the matter. By that time the crisis was beginning

to pass [i.e., because the Romanians had given in and were slowing the deportations]. The Generalkommissar in Nicolaev reported [to Berlin] that the [German] movement of Jews across the border had stopped.[4]

Gheorghe Davidescu, the general secretary of the Ministry of Foreign Affairs, and G. Steltzer, counselor of the German legation in Bucharest, discussed this topic in that capital city on March 13, 1942. Steltzer expressed concern that 14,500 Jews had been forced to cross the Bug and that another 60,000 were supposed to follow, asking the Romanian government to stop "these unorganized crossings" immediately.[5]

On October 4, 1941, the Second Section relayed to the Fourth Army Marshal Antonescu's order to deport all the Jews in Transnistria to camps close to the Bug River.[6] On November 26, 1941, the Transnistria Gendarme Inspectorate reported to the same field army headquarters:

1. The camps for the Jews were already established on the Bug in September 1941.
2. The camps are to function according to the following geographic conception:
   a. For Jews from the crossing point of Moghilev, there are ghettos in the towns of Lucineţ, Goroj, Koriskov, Copaigorod, and Kudievki-Kiotki.
   b. For those from Iampol, there are camps in the towns of Balanovka, Obodovka, Torkanovka, Zabocrita, Piatkovka, Berşad, Voitovka, Ustje, and Monkovka.
   c. For those to cross by way of the Râbniţa point, there are the towns of Krizkipine Slobodka, Kievilovka, Lukarovca, Godzovka, Sirovno, Voloschina, Agerevna, Ştefanovka, Bevrik, Zosenova, Gelinova, Liubasevka, Poznovska, and Gereoplova.
   d. For Jews to cross by way of the Iaska point, there is a camp at Bogdanovka.
   e. And for those from Tiraspol, there is the Tiraspol ghetto.
3. The numbers of Jews interned in the camps are as follows:
   a. Arrived through Moghilev: 47,545
   b. Arrived through Iampol: 30,891
   c. Arrived through Răbniţa: 163
   d. Arrived through Iasca: 2,200
   Total: 110,002[7]

Note that these and many of the figures that follow do not amount to an organized statistical analysis; the records left by the perpetrators and widely disparate postwar testimonies can hardly lend themselves to such treatment. But the majority of mutually confirming data corroborates the enormity of the crimes—and in astoundingly great detail, particularly given the circumstances. According to the November 19, 1943, report of General Vasiliu, general inspector of the gendarmerie and secretary of state at the Ministry of the Interior, 110,033 Jews had been deported to Transnistria from Bessarabia, Bukovina, and Dorohoi. The report mentioned that 50,741 Jews were still alive, most of them located in the districts of Moghilev, Golta, and Tulcin.[8] The "informational synthesis" produced by the General Inspectorate of the Gendarmerie of Transnistria for December 15, 1941, to January 15, 1942, claimed that "up until now, 118,847 Jews have crossed the Dniester to be placed along the Bug through the following border outposts: Iampol, 35,276; Moghilev, 55,913; Tiraspol, 872; Răbnița, 24,570; Iaska, 2,216."[9]

On December 9, 1941, General Vasiliu claimed 102,002 Jews deported to Transnistria: 47,545 in Tulcin; 30,981 in Balta; and 23,476 in Pervomaisk (Golta District).[10] The inspectorate's figure of 118,847 is very close to that of Dr. Costiner at the Central Office, who estimated on February 28, 1942, that during October 1941, 118,500 had been sent there, of whom 57,000 were from Bukovina and 56,000 from Bessarabia.[11] One postwar testimony claims that forty thousand Jews who had been evacuated from Bessarabia and parts of Bukovina had been executed[12] (this figure does not include the indigenous Ukrainian Jews). As of December 24, 1941, there were 70,000 Jews in Moghilev, 56,000 of these Romanian and the rest indigenous.[13] According to one undated statistic, probably from fall 1942, about 76,000 Jews lived in Transnistria, of whom 42,000 were in Moghilev, 20,000 in Balta, 8,060 in Iampol, and the remainder in five other districts. Few Jews survived in Odessa and in Golta District after the massacres there and the deportations from Odessa.[14]

A report signed by Governor Alexianu on April 1, 1942, counted Jews by ghetto, with a total of 88,187 internees.[15] His May 23 report, by which time the total figure had decreased to 83,699, broke the numbers down as follows:[16]

District	Men	Women	Children	Total
Ananiev	n.a.*	n.a.	n.a.	n.a.
Balta	6,288	6,474	3,741	16,503
Berezovka	n.a.	n.a.	n.a.	1,554
Duboşari	62	99	67	228
Golta	169	503	202	874
Jugastru	2,598	2,749	2,450	7,797
Moghilev	20,846	22,673	10,985	54,504
Oceakov	3	2	6	11
Odessa	172	220	195	587
Ovidopol	n.a.	n.a.	n.a.	n.a.
Răbniţa	254	548	569	1,371
Tiraspol	6	18	3	27
Tulcin	50	89	104	243
Total	30,448	33,375	18,322	83,699

*n.a. = data not available.

A table that contains the amount of aid sent by the Central Jewish Office to Jews in Transnistria from February 18, 1942, to December 12, 1942, shows figures that differ only slightly. According to this table, 47,278 Jews lived in Moghilev, 14,510 Jews in Balta, and 66,749 in Jugastru, Râbniţa, Ovidopol, and Golta.[17] A handwritten note from September 1942, found in the archives of the Romanian Ministry of Foreign Affairs, summarizes the numbers of Bessarabian and Bukovinan Jews sent to Transnistria and subsequently shifted toward the Bug:[18]

Region	Deported	Not Deported
Bessarabia	56,089	753
Bukovina	90,334	19,089
		(left in Cernăuţi)
Transnistria	65,252	6,759
Total	211,675	26,601

A source dated the following year, on March 22, 1943, distributed a still smaller number of 70,214 Jews in Transnistria as follows:[19]

District	No. of Jews
Balta	23,035
Berezovka	425

Golta	3,620
Jugastru	4,000
Moghilev	34,974
Odessa (city)	60
Răbnița	600
Tulcin	3,500
Total	70,214

Half a year earlier, on September 9, 1942, according to Report No. 9318 of the Transnistria Gendarme Inspectorate, there were 82,921 Jews in the region. The same report stated that 65,000 Jews had "disappeared" from Odessa, along with 4,000 from Moghilev and all the Jews of Berezovka, Ananiev, Ovidopol, and Oceakov.[20] A year later, on September 1, 1943, a report of the same inspectorate claimed that 50,741 of the Jews from Bessarabia and Bukovina sent to Transnistria were still alive and that 32,002 of these were then in Moghilev, and 12,477 in Balta. A report signed by General Vasiliu on March 1, 1944, stated that of the 43,519 Jews still surviving in Transnistria, 31,141 were from Bukovina, 11,683 from Bessarabia, and the remainder from Regat.[21] Finally, an enclosure sent with a note by the general inspectorate to the Central Office of Romanian Jews on February 10, 1944, stated that 43,065 of the Jews in Transnistria who had been deported from Bukovina, Bessarabia, Moldavia, and Walachia were still alive.[22]

In the district of Moghilev, close to the Dniester, more Jews survived than in the others. German involvement was less frequent here, so the Jewish community was better able to organize itself. Romanian officials did not manifest the same cruelty here as in Golta and Odessa. Although especially numerous in Moghilev and Balta, deported Jews found themselves in 120 localities throughout all the region's districts; some of these received one to six deportees while others ended up with thousands. Overall figures for deportation and survival appear in Alexander Dallin's study:

The total migration from Bukovina and Bessarabia began in October 1941 and involved more than 110,000 people. Inevitably, severe problems cropped up when it came time to organize them, shelter them, feed them in Transnistria. There were epidemics. The evacuees suffered from a harsh plight; some 28,000 Jews who stayed in villages inhabited by ethnic Germans were simply all liquidated. Of the more than 110,000 deportees, only 77,000 were still alive in March 1943; in September 1943, their numbers had dropped to 50,000.[23]

The following table suggests something of the evolution of the Jewish population in Transnistria:[24]

District	Nov. '41	Dec. '41	April '42	March '43	Nov. '43
Ananiev	n.a.*	n.a.	n.a.	n.a.	n.a.
Balta	30,981	n.a.	16,503	23,035	9,860
Berezovka	n.a.	n.a.	1,544	425	206
Duboşari	n.a.	228	n.a.	n.a.	17
Golta	23,476	n.a.	878	3,620	13
Iampol	n.a.	6,494	n.a.	n.a.	1,654
Jugastru	n.a.	n.a.	7,807	4,000	651
Moghilev	n.a.	70,000	54,504	34,974	35,826
Oceakov	n.a.	n.a.	11	n.a.	n.a.
Odessa	n.a.	44,417	676	60	n.a.
Ovidopol	n.a.	n.a.	n.a.	n.a.	n.a.
Răbniţa	n.a.	1,414	1,371	600	462
Tiraspol	n.a.	3,072	27	n.a.	363
Tulcin	47,575	n.a.	4,638	3,500	875
Total	102,032	125,625	87,959	70,214	49,927

*n.a. = data not available.

On October 10, 1941, convoys from Bessarabia and Bukovina crossed the Dniester at Moghilev, Răbniţa, and Iampol. "The first convoys from Vertujeni to Rezina crossed the Dniester at Râbniţa," a witness testified, "and were taken further to Birzula, where they stopped, rested in stables, and then were forced on toward Grozdovca. The ghetto that was organized there was commanded by a corporal. He greeted the first convoy by counting the people with iron bar blows on the back."[25]

On November 16, 1941,

a massive convoy of Jews from Dorohoi passed Şargorod and headed for a small town on the bank of the Bug. The people were in such pitiful shape that the Ukrainian peasant women who had arrived at the bazaar gave them food that they had brought to sell; the women knelt before the military prosecutor's office, crying and begging the military prosecutor, Dindelegan, to allow this convoy to remain. With much difficulty the heads of the local ghetto gained consent for them to remain until spring.[26]

On that same November 16, convoys of deportees from Mărculeşti and Vertujeni arrived in Obodovka (Balta District); those with valuables were permitted to stay in town. The rest stayed in dirty stables, where some got sick.[27] Israel Parikman from Secureni, deported to Transnistria by way of Vertujeni and Iampol, described his stay:

> Here they divided us among stables and pigsties. . . . What saved us was the hay that we found in almost every enclosure. We built fires with the hay in order to get a little heat [and boil water]. The water problem at that point was partially resolved because we had a lot of snow. I was sent several days later to Torkanovka [near Obodovka] with 550 other Jews. Only 117 to 118 came back from that lot. We also slept in pigsties there. When we had to bury our dead we first built a fire, because the ground was so frozen that it was almost impossible to dig. . . . That is where my mother died. I slept for seven days next to my mother's corpse, because the undertakers refused to bury her unless I gave them some clothing. After my mother's death I was sent back with my father and younger brother (seven years old then) to Obodovka. I remember that three days before the latter died he implored me to give him something to eat. I did not have anything, and that is how this child died, tortured by hunger.[28]

Parikman remained in Obodovka for three years, "working for bread" among the village peasants.

Another group of 780 Jewish deportees from Obodovka was sent to Lihova, on the banks of the Bug, where the mayor told them, "This is where you will find your grave." The deportees were piled into a windowless stable half occupied by livestock. On the mayor's order the doors were locked and the deportees allowed to come out only once every other day. Only then could they replenish their water supply from the streams.[29] In Ţibulovka (Balta District) two thousand deportees had to live in a building meant for only two hundred. Not allowed to use the well, the Jews were forced to drink unsafe water from a more distant pond; many became sick.[30]

Roundups in Moghilev on November 30 separated many children from their parents.[31] On December 1, typhus was discovered in Berşad and Şargorod, and typhoid fever appeared in Moghilev itself.[32] Fortunately, for some reason in this case Ion Antonescu allowed the Central Office of Romanian Jews to send medical supplies to Transnistria, albeit only on December 10.[33]

On the same day the government of Transnistria mandated the exchange of rubles for marks, but as peasants did not trust that currency, they agreed only to barter food for objects henceforth.[34] Officials were willing to accept new arrivals in Moghilev, Răbnița, and Iampol only if the deportees were in transit. On December 20, more than five hundred Jews recently sent to Moghilev were once again deported, this time deeper into Transnistria (five days later an epidemic of typhus broke out in Moghilev).[35]

M. Rudich later described the fate of the Jews who were deported in November and December 1941:

> The Jews were, as a rule, housed in stables or dilapidated buildings. From a convoy that left Iampol, two hundred people were allowed to remain in Crijopol [Jugastru District], and the rest went on foot to Tibulovka. In Crijopol the Jews lived in a former theater, [a building] without windows. In Țibulovka, of 1,900 Jews, only 400 people were still alive in spring 1942, the others having died of exposure, hunger, and typhus. In Molocina, near Obodovka, fifteen thousand Jews died from November 1941 to spring 1942; upon arrival they had been placed in five large stables. Among them were six hundred Ukrainian Jews from Savrani, all of whom had typhus.[36]

The Jews allowed to remain in Moghilev were those from Cernăuți and Dorohoi—individuals who had managed to cross the Dniester with money or other valuables. Of those deported from Moghilev some were able to purchase their transport inside German trucks to the ghettos of Șargorod, Copaigorod, Djurin, Murafa, and Smerinka.[37] A majority of the survivors remained in the district of Moghilev, a quarter in the district of Balta.[38] But even in the town of Moghilev conditions were terrible: severe bombardment at the beginning of the war "left much of the town in ruins, most of its buildings without doors or windows, many without roofs."[39]

Under the guidance of an engineer named Jagendorf, the community of thirteen thousand Jews now in Moghilev organized an asylum for the elderly, an orphanage, three hospitals, and communal kitchens by 1943. This infrastructure, the most efficient in Transnistria, enabled many to survive. But even there four thousand Jews perished during the winter of

1941–1942, as they reported to the Central Jewish Office on March 18, 1942.[40] According to a report of the International Committee of the Red Cross, 26 percent of these people died. In the district of Moghilev, about 50 percent of the deportees survived. There were also many smaller ghettos in the district, fifty-three of them in September 1943; of these, twenty-four housed fewer than one hundred deportees apiece, twenty-two under five hundred, but seven of the ghettos held more than one thousand. The largest were Şargorod, Djurin, and Murafa, with close to three thousand each, followed by Copaigorod, Lucineţ, Popoviţi, and Balki, with closer to one thousand each.[41]

The lot of the Jews in Moghilev was awful. M. Katz, former president of the Jewish Committee of the town, related the following:

> During my visit I discovered in the town of Conotcăuti, near Şargorod, a long and dark stable standing alone in a field. Seventy people were lying all over the place, men, women, children, half-naked and destitute. It was horrible to look at them. They all lived on begging. Their head was Mendel Aronevici, a former banker in Dărăbani, Dorohoi District. He too lived in abject misery.
>
> In the ghetto of Halcineţ people ate the carcass of a horse that had been buried. . . . The authorities poured carbonic acid on it, yet they continued eating it. I gave them some money, food, and clothing and took their promise not to touch the carcass. I placed them in a nearby village and paid the rent for three months in advance.
>
> The Jews in Grabvitz lived in a cave. I had to remove them to the village against their will. They couldn't part from the seven hundred graves of their loved ones. . . . I found similar scenes at Vinoi, Nemerci, Pasinca, Lucineţ, Lucincic, Ozarineţ, Vindiceni: everywhere men exhausted, worn out; some of them worked on farms, others in the tobacco factory, but the majority lived on begging.[42]

In Balta District deportees lived in twenty localities, most often in groups of several hundred; the towns with large concentrations of Jews were Berşad, Obodovka, Balta, and Berbca. A more important center, with more than one thousand people, was Nestervorka in the district of Tulcin. The other districts of Transnistria included smaller numbers of deportees: on September 1, 1943, for instance, the district of Ananiev included 31 Jews living in nine localities; the district of Berezovka, 66 Jews in seven; the district of Tiraspol, 170 in five localities; Golta, 874 in ten; Râbniţa, 499 Jews in two localities; and Jugastru, 1,625 Jews in eight.[43]

All these data on the deportees from Bessarabia, Bukovina, Moldavia, and Walachia do not include the indigenous Jewish population that had been concentrated especially in Odessa and in the district of Golta. Based on statistical data from the Romanian gendarmerie, it would appear that the numbers of Jews deported from Bessarabia and Bukovina to Transnistria were roughly equal: at least 55,687 from Bessarabia in 1941; at least 43,798 from Bukovina in 1941, plus another 4,000 in 1942. On September 1, 1943, the Romanian gendarmerie counted 50,741 Jews in Transnistria: 13,980 from Bessarabia and 36,761 from Bukovina; the survival rate among Jews from Bukovina appears to have been more than twice that of those from Bessarabia. The Jews from Bukovina were wealthier during and even after the deportation, and some of them had been deported in 1942, which meant one less winter spent in exile.

Thousands and thousands of Romanian Jews were deported to the other side of the Bug and handed over to the Germans, who then murdered them. The indigenous Jewish population underwent mass executions by the Romanians in Odessa and the district of Golta. But the Jews deported from Bessarabia and Bukovina died typically as a result of typhus, hunger, and cold. Food distribution was erratic. Many lived by begging or by selling their clothes for food, ending up virtually naked. They ate leaves, grasses, potato peels and often slept in stables or pigsties, sometimes not allowed even straw. Except for those in the Pecioara and Vapniarka camps and in the Răbniţa prison, the deported Jews lived in ghettos or in towns, where they were assigned a residence, forced to carry out hard labor, and subjected to the "natural" process of extermination through famine and disease. This "natural selection" ceased toward the end of 1943, when Romanian officials began changing their approach toward the deported Jews.

In January 1942, the typhus epidemic reached major proportions. On January 5, the Obodovka ghetto was declared contaminated, surrounded by barbed wire, and put under guard. The inmates were not allowed to leave even to get supplies, so that hunger killed even many of those with some means.[44] A January 15 memo from the Transnistria Gendarme Inspectorate reported 318 cases of typhus in Tulcin, Ovidopol, Ananiev, and Golta Districts, as well as cases of typhoid fever and diphtheria. The report also identified thirty-four cases of typhus among the convoy guards.[45]

According to Henriette Harnik's testimony, 1,140 out of 1,200 deportees in Tibulovka died during the winter of 1941–1942.[46] On January 20, 1942, of the twelve hundred Jews interned in November 1941, only one hundred men, seventy-four women, and four children survived, most of these suffering frozen extremities. Money or clothes purchased some of them permission to live in the village. The same situation prevailed in Budi, where there were initially twelve hundred Jews, including more than six hundred from Storojineţ; after having lived for some time in stables, most had died, among them Rabbi Sulim Ginsberg of Storojineţ and his entire family of ten.[47]

A monograph prepared by the leadership of the Şargorod ghetto described the conditions under which typhus appeared and spread:

> At our arrival in Şargorod we found about 1,800 local Jews. The number of deportees was about seven thousand souls. . . . All told, there were about 337 houses with an average of two to three incompletely furnished rooms in each [842 rooms], which usually held as many as two to three people each. . . . Most of the people were impoverished and could not obtain the minimum amount of food. Hence, from the outset . . . the people were undernourished. There was no way of earning a living; the only method of obtaining food was by trading one's clothes.[48]

Of the 9,000 Jews in Şargorod, 2,414 caught typhus and 1,449 died of it. In June 1942, the epidemic ended, but it broke out again in October; however, the community was then ready for it, taking efficient measures to delouse the area. As a result of those measures, there were only twenty-six recorded cases, and only four people died between October 1942 and February 1943.[49] Ninety-two cases of typhoid fever appeared, though with a negligible mortality rate, as well as 1,250 cases of severe malnutrition, of which 50 proved irreversible.[50]

Hygienic conditions in Moghilev were similar: as of April 25, 1942, there were 4,491 recorded cases of typhus, 1,254 of them deadly. The estimates of the health department of that area cited seven thousand cases throughout the city. The energetic activity of two Romanian army medical officers, Chirilă and Stuparu, who were concerned with the possible spread of the epidemic, as well as that of Jewish health agents, stopped the epidemic.[51]

In the meantime, hard labor continued for the Jews. On January 25, 1942, twelve hundred were forced to remove snow from the streets under threat of execution or deportation beyond the Bug. A day later all men served at hard labor ten kilometers from town; several returned with severe frostbite.[52] It was often difficult to bury the corpses.

> To the cemetery of Şargorod we brought 165 corpses that could not be buried because the ground was frozen. In temperatures of forty degrees below zero we kept a fire going for twenty-four hours, the only way we were able to dig. . . . Corpses in Berşad lay outside for three to four weeks . . . because of the frost and the lack of manpower. . . . Sometimes as many as two hundred corpses were piled up each day.[53]

The same thing occurred in Obodovka, where there was a hilltop cemetery that included three mausoleums for victims of the 1919 pogroms under the Ukrainian leader Symon Petlyura. Now thousands of new corpses joined them. As one eyewitness recalled, there were

> men, women, children, old people, lifeless corpses, frozen, almost glued to one another, because of the frost. The ground was hard, frozen deep down. The shovel could not break it, the hoe could not stir the earth. And there the corpses lay . . . for the entire winter. Here and there a dog ran through the streets . . . holding between its fangs a head or an arm. . . . Officials sent only orders . . . that required that the corpses be buried [and] gendarmes to beat people up. However, the ground would not yield. The ground was frozen down to its entrails, the corpses were now stiff and glued to one another. . . . People were divided into two groups: the sick, mostly due to typhus, and the healthy ones. These sold their belongings, or worked wherever and whenever, to get enough to eat and tend to the sick. When spring came the ground began to soften, and eight mass graves were dug. . . . One on top of the other, children and old people lay next to men and women, mutilated bodies, corpses, thousands of corpses.[54]

According to the testimony of Leopold Litman, one of the former deportees, during the first four to five months of 1942, 90 percent of the deportees in Obodovka died from the cold and contagious diseases.[55] In much the same vein the Second Section reported to the Third Romanian Army on the camps of Golta and Balta:

> In the Dumanovka camp we had just found fifty to sixty Jews, guarded by two Ukrainians who brought them [there]. In a dilapidated house four to five corpses had been devoured by dogs while several sick and mori-

bund Jews watched. . . . In a field near the camp several corpses were
not buried properly, and you could see their feet. In the camps of
Obodovka and Berşad the situation was about the same. We did not carry
out executions there; however, up to now, five thousand Jews have died
because of diseases and from the cold.[56]

The fate of Jewish doctors doing their best to contain the disease was
not favorable. In February 1942, twenty or twenty-five caught typhus in
Moghilev.[57] In Şargorod a Dr. Herman died of the disease on February 10,
1942, as did Drs. Reicher and Hart on March 7.[58] Of the twenty-seven
Jewish doctors of Şargorod, twenty-three became ill, and of those twelve
died.[59] Nor were Jewish doctors spared abuse and humiliation. According
to M. Rudich, "one day, in 1942, the gendarmes in Obodovka caught five
Jewish doctors in the narrow streets of the village. Five doctors who were
going to the houses of the sick to ease their suffering. . . . The gendarmes . . . harnessed them to a sleigh carrying a [huge] barrel of . . .
water."[60]

After the execution of at least 22,000 Jews in Odessa by Romanian
army units in October 1941, the tragedy of the survivors intensified in
January 1942. At that time they still numbered some forty thousand, but
they were living under close surveillance: they could be sent before martial courts for "spreading rumors" or concealing their ethnicity.[61] On January 2, Governor Alexianu signed Order No. 35, outlining details for
deportations to the northern part of Oceakov District and the southern part
of Berezovka District: property of the deported Jews would be sold to the
local population, the Jews would serve at hard labor, and the deportations
must commence on January 10.[62] That same day, acting on Ion Antonescu's personal instructions of December 16, Alexianu issued Order
No. 7, requiring all Jews from Odessa to turn in all gold, jewels, and valuables.[63] Central and district offices were formed to handle the Jews and
their assets. The central office was comprised of prefects from Odessa and
its environs, the chief prosecutor, the mayor, and a high-ranking officer
representing the army; the district offices were staffed by a military mag-
istrate, the chief of the police district, a high-ranking officer, and two residents of the district. The Jews were each allowed twenty kilograms of
luggage, carried by hand to the train station.[64] Order No. 7 mandated concentration of all Jews in Odessa in the ghetto of Slobodka before deportation.[65]

That deportation got under way on January 11, 1942, when the Odessa Jews began their departure for the Berezovka-Vasilievo region. Carp's research reveals that "on the first day 856 [probably an underestimate] Jews were deported, old people, women, and children for the most part."[66] The following day 986 were deported, again mostly the elderly, women, and children.[67] On January 14 and 15, 2,291 Jews were deported; on the sixteenth, another 1,746.[68] At least 20,792 Jews were thus deported from Odessa-Slobodka to Berezovka-Vasilievo by February 22, 1942, as shown in the following table:[69]

Date (1942)	No. of Deportees
January 11	1,000
January 12	856
January 13	986
January 14	1,201
January 15	1,090
January 16	1,746
January 17	1,104
January 18	1,293
January 19	1,010
January 20	926
January 22	1,807
January 23	1,396
January 24	2,000
January 31	1,200
February 1	2,256
February 12	711
February 22	210

The first transport reached Victorovka on January 12, 1942,[70] initiating an expeditious operation that by January 21—well under two weeks later—had removed 10,427 Jews to Berezovka; by January 24, the figure had reached 15,630 and by January 30, 16,800.[71] A report from the Transnistria gendarmerie estimated that up to January 22, 12,234 Jews had been evacuated out of the total of 40,000 in Odessa.[72] Aside from the ghetto of Slobodka, according to Izu Landau and a memo from the General Inspectorate of the Gendarmerie to Colonel Gheorghe Barozzi (then general gendarmerie inspector and military prosecutor of the Third Army), another temporary camp was in operation in Dalnic, the very place where the Jews of Odessa had been massacred the previous year.[73]

The mayor of Odessa, Gherman Pintea, tried to save three categories of Jews (artisans, Karaites, and teachers) by appealing to Governor Alexianu on January 20, but nothing came of it.[74] With respect to the Karaites, a people of Turkish ancestry but practicing Mosaic law, Romanian officials hesitated in the first weeks of 1942 before deciding not to lock them up in the ghetto.[75] A report of the Office of the Military Prosecutor of the Third Army described the evacuation of fifty-three Jews on February 16 from Odessa to Berezovka. On that day seventy-nine other Jews were confined in the ghetto of Slobodka, and on February 26, 1942, another release from the same prosecutor's office reported the internment of thirty-two Jews there after they had been arrested during sweeps of the city.[76] On February 22, there were approximately 1,200 Jews in the Odessa jail and over 200 in the ghetto;[77] on the next day 210 of the latter, including 59 men, most of them old, 113 women, and 38 children, were evacuated to Berezovka.[78] Some Jews chose suicide rather than allowing themselves to be transported to Berezovka.

On March 8, 1942, 1,207 Jewish inmates from the Odessa prison were deported to the camp of Vapniarka.[79] Dozens more were arrested in March and April 1942.[80] Totals vary here, just as statistics vary elsewhere in this study. According to a 1950 statement by Colonel Matei Velcescu, former prefect of Odessa, 23,000 Jews were ultimately deported from Odessa. Constantin Vidrascu, former head of one of the city departments, declared after the war that due to temperatures as low as thirty-five degrees below zero, 20 to 25 percent of the deportees died during transport.[81] A contemporary report from the Romanian gendarmerie (signed by Colonel Broșteanu on February 15, 1942) accounts for the deportation of 28,574 Jews from Odessa to Berezovka.[82] A slightly later report of the army (March 20, 1942) gave a figure of 33,000.[83]

A report drafted by a Romanian General Staff intelligence officer who had inspected the operation in the Slobodka ghetto described the deportation of one contingent:

> After having gathered about one hundred Jews who were screened by the committees, [they were formed] into columns and transported on foot to the train station of Sortirovocinaia, ten kilometers from the ghetto. Because the [gentile] residents of the area [near the] ghetto

did not want to shelter Jews, some [of the Jews] had to remain in the streets. For that reason, and because they were forced to walk to the train station under very unfavorable weather conditions, on the thirteenth of January thirteen Jews died in a column of 1,600, and on the fourteenth six died in a column of 1,201.... The Jews left without food. At the train station of Sortirovocinaia I found two corpses ... that the families had carried with them.... In the train station the Jews boarded German freight cars, which [then] were sealed. They were transported to Berezovka and from there on foot to the towns where the camps were located in the northern part of Oceakov District and the southern part of Berezovka District. Because of the cold, some Jews died on the train. In the first transport of about one thousand people ten Jews died.... In the second transport thirty were found dead. In the same transport thirty more died on the road [from the train station of Berezovka to the camp]. The Jews who had been interned in the [Odessa] ghetto were old men, not one under the age of forty-one [and] very few between forty-one and fifty years of age; children below the age of sixteen; and women. They were all so miserable that it was obvious they were the poorest Jews of Odessa.[84]

Another memorandum from the Transnistria Gendarme Inspectorate (No. 76, also signed by Broșteanu) described the deportations through January 17:

I am pleased to inform you that as of January 12, the evacuation of the Odessa Jews has begun. According to the order issued by the government of Transnistria, the Jews to be evacuated are interned in ghettos, after having appeared before the Asset Appraisal Committee [and] having exchanged [jewelry] and currency for German reichsmarks. The people in the ghetto will form convoys comprised of 1,500–2,000 Jews each, which will board German trains and will be transported to the region of Mostovoi-Vasilievo, in the district of Berezovka. From the train station of Berezovka they will be escorted to the [places] where they will be located. Up to now six thousand [Jews] have been evacuated in daily transports. In the towns where they will be located there are practically no housing opportunities, because the Ukrainian population does not welcome them, so that many of them are sheltered for one day in the stables of the *kolkhozes* [former Soviet collective farms]. As a result of temperatures dropping to minus twenty degrees [centigrade], and because of a lack of food, their age, and their frail nature, many of them fall on the way and freeze. For this deportation we used the Berezovka [gendarmerie] legion, but because of the major frost we had to change escorts continually. Along the way we bury the corpses in the area's antitank ditches; . . . we have a very difficult time finding people for this operation because they try . . . to evade [us].[85]

Upon arrival the Jews found themselves under the jurisdiction of the Germans, who began to orchestrate their extermination in March 1942.[86] The deportations ended early the same month, but the killings took longer. By December, however, "the suffering of the Jews of Odessa and . . . southern Transnistria [had] ended completely. Total extermination had been accomplished. Statistics from the Central Jewish Office of Romanian Jews indicated that as of March 1943, the only Jews remaining in southern Transnistria were 60 in Odessa and 425 in the district of Berezovka, a few local, the rest from Romania."[87]

On February 11, 1942, the Transnistria Gendarme Inspectorate asked the government of the region to approve the deportation of Jews from the district of Moghilev to that of Balta, east of the Smerinka-Odessa railroad, in order "to settle the Jewish question in [Moghilev] and cut off all communication between Jews from the Moghilev region and those who remained on Romanian territory."[88] On February 16, the prefect of Moghilev ordered the evacuation of four thousand Jews to the town of Scazineț, requiring the Jewish Committee of Moghilev to draw up the plan.[89] On March 12, forty-four Jews who had evaded labor were deported to the ghettos of Balki and Smerinka.[90] But on March 26, engineer Jaegendorf, president of the Jewish Committee of Moghilev and a man with certain connections among the local Romanian authorities, informed the gendarme commander that Scazineț could receive only two thousand Jews and only after buildings were repaired, envisioning a minimum of two square meters of living space per person.[91] Whether or not as a direct result of Jaegendorf's action, the order to evacuate four thousand Jews from Moghilev was canceled.[92] On April 25, the Jewish Committee was again informed by the same local authorities that, except for three thousand, the Jews of Moghilev would be deported to Smerinka. However, for unknown reasons the Moghilev prefecture again canceled the execution of that measure on April 29.[93] Finally, on May 19, the government of Transnistria ordered the deportation of four thousand Jews from Moghilev to Scazineț.

The order was repeated by the Transnistria Gendarme Inspectorate on May 22.

The deportation plan was initiated on May 25 by the general administrative inspector, Dimitre Ştefanescu, and the prefect, Năsturaş.[94] The Jewish Committee of Moghilev tried to get the commander of the gendarme legion to cancel the order,[95] but on June 14, 1942, the Jewish Committee was disbanded.[96] On May 29, May 30, and June 2, three thousand Jews from Moghilev and others from Kindiceni, Jaruga, Ozarineţ, and Crasna were sent on foot in four groups to Scazineţ. Here a closed camp had been set up in two damaged buildings that once had belonged to a military school.

> The camp of Scazineţ had been surrounded by barbed wire, and the Jews were not allowed to leave it to get supplies. The peasants were authorized periodically to bring food that was exchanged for valuables, so that after a while the Jews had nothing left to exchange and began to eat grass and leaves; eventually, this diet made their bodies bloat and they died. The same thing happened to the deportees of Pecioara, where horrible scenes took place.[97]

Another survivor of Scazineţ later testified:

> The inmates were divided by social background: on one side of the road the poor surrounded by barbed wire, on the other side the wing for people with means. The two rows of buildings were in the middle of a field twelve kilometers from Moghilev. The buildings were falling apart, without doors or windows, without floors. It was forbidden to go from one row to another, the penalty being death.
>
> By aiding in the burial of the first Jew executed for that reason, I was able to see the valley where [one year earlier] twenty thousand Jews from Bessarabia had been murdered; . . . human skulls and skeletons, remnants of documents and trunks, could be seen at the surface of the soil. You could even see the rusted bands of the machine guns at the execution site.[98]

This is more of the testimony of the aforementioned Israel Parikman, who remained in Scazineţ for several days in July 1941:

> About thirty thousand people were soon jammed into those barracks. There was nothing to eat. I saw with my own eyes people picking up

potato and onion peels, green plants, grass that they ate. I saw human beings turning into beasts, grabbing something to eat from other people's
hands. Aside from that, we received some sort of triangular pea that gave
us diarrhea. The water presented one of the worst problems. It was several hundred yards from us, but the soldiers made up a game, shooting
from time to time at those who went to get some water; dozens of victims fell for that reason.[99]

M. Katz, also mentioned earlier and also an inmate in Scazineţ, testified
that during the summer of 1942,

> on certain days of the week, the cheap pea soup was brought on carts
> pulled by Jews; this meal was designed, in effect, to exterminate the in-
> mates as rapidly as possible. They topped off their daily diet with grass
> and leaves. Potato peels were one of the camp's delicacies. I saw the en-
> gineer Oxman from Cernăuţi consume these meals. Bloated from
> hunger, like so many others, he eventually died. The latrines at the camp,
> even in the wings for the so-called people with means, were the same for
> men and women, and all relieved themselves in front of each other. The
> windows of the camp wings were bricked and barely let in air and light.
> Nine Jews were killed when they tried to go beyond the barbed wire;
> hundreds of others died of hunger. The drinking water became a real
> problem; a single uncovered well supplied dirty water . . . and was filled
> with mud. Diarrhea, scabies, hunger, and misery snuffed out the lives of
> the inmates. At one point Major Orăşanu eliminated the market, and the
> inmates were unable to obtain supplies. In the fall of 1942, when Alexi-
> anu decided to close the Scazineţ camp, the Jews who were still alive
> were brought on foot to the Bug (except for "specialists" returned to Mo-
> ghilev) to the villages of Voroşilovka, Tivriv, and Crasna. More than half
> died in Vorosilovka as a result of hunger and disease.[100]

Those who still remained in Scazineţ at the time the camp was closed on
September 12, 1942, were so bloated from hunger that they died soon
thereafter.

On May 20, 1942, Radu Lecca agreed, with the approval of Antonescu's office, to allow the Central Jewish Office to send money and
food to the Jews in Transnistria.[101] Actually, the first transport of medicine
sent by the Jews of Romania proper for the deportees arrived in Moghilev
on March 22, so there must have been an earlier approval.[102]

Meanwhile, Jews continued to be transported farther into the interior of Transnistria. On June 14 and 20, 1942, hundreds of deportees from Cernăuți and Dorohoi reached Serebria near Moghilev, only to be sent still farther up the Bug. On June 28, another five hundred were evacuated to Scazineț.[103] Three thousand more from Moghilev were deported from the city shortly after July 3, 1942.[104] The 450 Jews deported from Dorohoi reached Serebria on June 20, joining their families there and bringing their convoy to 950 people, then arrived in Oleanița (Tulcin District) on July 3; from Oleanița they were taken to the stone quarry of Ladijin. No food was supplied there, so they had to purchase it from the local peasants with their clothing.[105] A third convoy arrived in Ladijin from Cernăuți on July 6. At Ladijin the Jews from Dorohoi and Cernăuți were divided into four groups: 1,800 went to the stone quarry, 1,800 to Cetvertinovka, 600 to the town of Ladijin, and 600 to Oleanita.[106] Here is Matatias Carp's description of the stone quarry:

a deteriorating facility, several rusted carriages on partially disassembled rails, several collapsing barracks without doors or windows, and a gigantic stone protrusion jutting out of the hilltop. First of all, the Jews headed for the barracks for some rest. But . . . Second Lieutenant Vasilescu (a former pharmacist) did not allow it. He required that they undergo quarantine and delousing. He hit them and repeated the same thing: "Here you are not doctors, engineers, or lawyers. You are simply *Jidani,* numbers, and you must obey orders without uttering a word. Here hunger awaits you and then death."

[Vasilescu] set up an area along the banks of the Bug where everyone would have to spend days until the quarantine was organized and they were deloused. In order to aggravate their suffering Vasilescu selected a brute among the Jews in his own image, Lederman, a former guard at the old people's asylum in Cernăuți, to whom he assigned wide powers over his brethren. He was the one who enforced the delousing of the inmates. Carrying a large truncheon, he hit whomever he felt like, he stole as much as he could from rich and poor alike. . . . He ordered that women have their hair shorn, but he made an exception for those who paid a fee. Of course, the demeaning actions of Lederman in no way replaced the torments that the Second Lieutenants Vasilescu and Enăchiță orchestrated. They ordered beatings . . . they looted, and they raped . . . women.[107]

On July 7, 1942, ninety Jews who had been detained in Tiraspol were deported to Berezovka.[108] Four hundred were sent from Berşad to Tulcin in August 1943; another 1,387 were sent from Balta to Nicolaev to build a bridge in the summer of 1943.[109] On August 19, 1942, three thousand Cernăuţi Jews in the Ladijin area were handed over to the Todt Organization by Colonel Loghin, prefect of Tulcin District; nearly all were done to death, directly or through hard labor. Four hundred remained at the stone quarry, 140 in the town of Ladijin, 78 in Oleaniţa, and 1,000 in Cetvertinovka.[110] On August 22, several Jews managed to bribe Enăchiţă to allow them to leave the quarry for Ladijin. While on their way he changed his mind and ordered them back. But soon all the Jews were transferred from the Ladijin quarry, half to Cetvertinovka, the others to Ladijin. Only sixty mental patients (originally from Cernăuţi) remained, all executed on that same day.[111] Two days later the Jews who had been sent to Ladijin were back at the stone quarry, and on September 13, those sent to Cetvertinovka joined them.[112] On August 25, 550 Jews, 250 of them locals, were sent from Ladijin to the Krasnopolsk camp on the other bank of the Bug, where the Germans killed them. On November 30, six hundred local Jews deported from Iampol were brought to work in the stone quarry.[113]

Jews tried to escape from the camps along the Bug, especially alarmed by the executions being carried out by the Germans just on the other side. A January 4, 1942, report from the Second Army Corps to the Second Romanian Army emphasized that Article 8 of Order No. 23 of the government of Transnistria required the execution of any Jew attempting escape from the camps located on the Bug.[114] A similar gendarmerie report of March 15 states that such breakouts were quite frequent, not only from the camps but also from other localities to which the Jews had been assigned.[115]

In the meantime, the number of orphans mounted. In Moghilev, where it was possible to keep statistics, 450 orphaned Jewish children inhabited a town orphanage in the summer of 1942. On August 20, a second orphanage was established to house two hundred other children; as of November 28, three orphanages sheltered eight hundred. From April 1942 to May 1943, 356 children died there, mortality increasing especially during the last three months of 1942. Dr. Emanuel Faendrich depicted an apocalyptic situation on November 28, 1942:

The children live in large rooms that are not heated and that are badly ventilated, with fetid smells in some instances; during the day the children remain in dirty beds—they have no underwear, no bedding, nor the necessary clothing to leave their bed and walk around. . . . I found in one room 109 children. . . . I saw many children who suffered from boils, scabies, and other skin diseases.[116]

In September 1942, almost two thousand Jews ("Communist sympathizers" or people who had applied to emigrate to the USSR under the population transfer in 1940) were deported to Transnistria. Some of them were killed upon arrival, but about one thousand went to the camp of Vapniarka. Here the commander, Lieutenant Colonel Ion C. Murgescu, told them that they had arrived at "the death camp, from which they would leave on all fours or on crutches."[117] Fed on a variety of pea unfit for humans, 611 inmates became seriously ill and some of them were partially paralyzed.[118] Hilberg provides more details on the diet and its effect: "the inmates were regularly fed four hundred grams of a kind of chickpea (*Tathyrus savitus*), which Soviet agriculturists had been giving to hogs, cooked in water and salt and mixed with two hundred grams of barley, to which was added a 20 percent filler of straw. . . . The result manifested itself in muscular cramps, uncertain gait, arterial spasms in the legs, paralysis, and incapacitation."[119] But that was not all; the "political" inmates concentrated in Vapniarka suffered ill treatment not only from the guards but also from the common criminals.

The other Transnistrian camp, Pecioara, actually displayed the words "death camp" on its signpost above the entrance.[120] On October 12, 1942, the evacuation of Jews, eventually a total of three thousand of them, from Moghilev to the Pecioara camp began. General Iliescu, inspector of the Transnistria gendarmerie, had recommended that the poorest be sent there, since they were going to die anyway, and it was not intended that anyone survive Pecioara.[121] By November 8, five convoys of 1,500 Jews in all had been sent to Pecioara from Moghilev.[122] Pecioara was the most horrific site of the Jewish internment in all of Transnistria, as Carp's research has shown:

Those who managed to escape told incredible stories. On the banks of the Bug, the camp was surrounded by three rows of barbed wire and watched by a powerful military guard. German trucks arrived from the

German side of the Bug, on several occasions; camp inmates were packed into them to be exterminated on the other side. During that period Captain Fetecău was the commander of the Tulcin legion, and Colonel Loghin was prefect of that district. Unable to get supplies, camp inmates ate human waste and later [fed] on human corpses. Eighty percent died, and only the 20 percent who fled [when the guard became more lax] survived.[123]

Hilberg too records that in Pecioara "hunger raged to such an extent that inmates ate bark, leaves, grass, and dead human flesh."[124]

In September 1942, 196 Jews from Moldavia and Walachia were taken to Sârbca, near Odessa, for having violated rules governing compulsory labor. They were housed in stables and worked for six weeks at the Vigoda farm.[125] On November 10, they were brought to Alexandrovka, where they were forced to toil in a vineyard belonging to Governor Alexianu.[126] That job lasted until December 26, during which time the Jews lived in an abandoned barracks.[127] As Carp describes their plight, on that day the deportees from Alexandrovka were placed in freight cars in which they spent nineteen days without food or water in temperatures dropping to forty degrees below zero on the way to Bogdanovka. Here they were housed in a pigsty but forbidden to use the straw for cover: "The straw here is for swine, not for the *Jidani*," the farm administrator told them. Along the way hunger and hypothermia had already carried off eleven victims. The first four corpses were left in railroad stations, the others buried in Bogdanovka.[128] The survivors remained in the pigsty until February 5, 1943, when they were taken to Golta, where they also lived in stables. During this entire period they could obtain food only by selling clothing to other Jews residing in those areas.[129]

An overall picture of the lot of ghettoized deportees in Transnistria as of January 1943 emerges from the notes of Fred Șaraga, a member of the Aid Committee of the Central Jewish Office; numbers of these deportees would soon benefit from funds collected in Romania or received from the American Joint Distribution Committee. Previous attempts of the Aid Committee to enter Transnistria had been scuttled by Alexianu, who told them that "in Moghilev, the Jews live better than in Bucharest."[130] But an inspection of Transnistria by a delegation of the Aid Committee, including Șaraga and three others, was approved by the Office of the President of the Council of Ministers. Iuliu Mumuianu, who had been a secretary of state in the Goga-Cuza government and was now advisor to the Office of the President of the Council of Ministers, was appointed to "supervise" that delegation. The delegation left Bucharest on December 31, 1942, crossed the Dniester at Tiraspol on January 1, 1943, and arrived in Odessa that same evening. On January 2, the delegation was received by Alexianu, who made a speech that, in Şaraga's opinion, reflected a catalog of hatreds and bottomless cruelty: "It was hard to obtain your arrival here. It will perhaps be difficult to return. That depends on how you behave. You may go only where I allow you, you can speak only to those whom I allow, and you can talk about only what I allow."[131]

The delegation members met with Mayor Pintea, who greeted them in a civilized and "cordial" manner; they also met with General Iliescu, who displayed a hostile attitude. However, the latter did make it possible for the delegation to visit more towns than had been initially discussed, including Moghilev, Şmerinka, Balta, and Berşad.[132] Before leaving Odessa, the delegation visited the remnants of the ghetto there, now consisting of a single building at 8 Adolf Hitler Street, where thirty-one men, nineteen women (all skilled workers), and four children assembled furniture, sewed clothing, and baked bread. Most came from Cernăuți, but some were from Bucharest, Roman, and Dorohoi.[133] The visitors noted in particular the captives' "penitentiary" regimes and "desperate" shortage of clothing.[134]

During his travels Şaraga was escorted by Commander Ion Mihail from the general staff of the Transnistria gendarmerie and by a group of noncommissioned officers in civilian clothes. On the evening of January 4, the delegation arrived in Smerinka, where they found 3,274 Jews (1,200 of them natives, the others from Bukovina, Bessarabia, Moldavia, and Walachia), including 200 orphans "who had learned how to sing patriotic Romanian songs."[135] The situation seemed quite acceptable: the deportees were given reasonable work, and Şaraga believed there was a "more understanding public administration" there. Şmerinka was "one of those unusual camps [in fact, ghettos] where misery and starvation did not reign as absolute masters."[136] But while he was in Şmerinka Şaraga received reports regarding Jews in the localities of Cazaciovka, Stanilovici, Zatica, Catmazov, and Crasna. In Crasna the deported Jews lived in highly crowded conditions, eight to fifteen people per room in houses belonging to the local Jews.[137]

On the evening of January 6, the Aid Committee reached Moghilev, where it discovered nine hundred children in three orphanages (at a moment when twelve thousand Jewish deportees and three thousand original resident Jews lived in Moghilev). Most of the children were naked, four to six of them shivering in a single bed. Commander Orăşanu hit the director of one of the orphanages with a horsewhip for suggesting that the committee visit the upper level of the building. The reason became apparent when the visitors discovered an overcrowded room housing fifty or sixty children; the windows were broken and the children lay in so-called beds, freezing in the Siberian-like cold. "The children had not left their room for a month," the visitors learned. "Their food was served almost frozen, and they relieved themselves there as well."[138]

Since Şaraga was not able to visit all the ghettos in Transnistria, the Romanian authorities approved the assembling in Moghilev on January 8 and 9 of representatives of the Jewish Committees from Şargorod, Murafa, Djurin, Copaigorod, Crasna, Jaruga, Lucineţ, Vindiceni, Tropova, Nemerici, Derebcin, and Ozovineţ.[139] The delegates' reports helped Şaraga confirm the impressions he had gathered from the places he himself had visited.

On the evening of January 10, the delegation reached Balta. Here they found three hundred orphaned children. In the farms around the city there lived another hundred. Their sanitary conditions were good, according to the report drafted by Şaraga upon his return to Bucharest, though the Jews of Balta lived crowded, forty to fifty per room.[140] Reports flowed into Balta from the Jewish communities of Obodovka, Olgopol, and Berşad. According to Şaraga's winter 1943 report, 2,723 Jews lived in Balta (70 percent of them local, 18 percent from Bessarabia, 11 percent from Bukovina, and 1 percent from Moldavia and Walachia). There were 1,610 Jews in Obodovka, 724 in Olgopol, and 9,200 in Berşad (including 2,250 from Transnistria, 3,200 from Bessarabia, 3,500 from Bukovina, and 50 to 60 from Moldavia and Walachia).[141] Şaraga's report emphasized the extreme shortage of clothing and the insurmountable obstacles to communication with relatives in Romania. The table on page 221 presents the data from Şaraga's report. The ghettos with which Şaraga was in contact housed 61,144 Jews as of January 31, 1943, according to his best estimates and, among these inmates, 2,477 orphans whom the indigenous population had been forbidden to adopt. Şaraga was allowed to provide monetary aid from the Central Jewish Office to most of those ghettos.[142]

In February 1943, in the camp of Vapniarka and in the ghetto of

Ghetto	Total No. of Jews	No. of Romanian Jews	No. of Local Jews	No. of Orphans
Balta	2,723	1,906	817	75
Berşad	9,200	6,950	2,250	257
Catmazov	1,200	n.a.*	n.a.	n.a.
Cazaciovka	300	n.a.	n.a.	n.a.
Copaigorod	2,200	n.a.	n.a.	98
Crasna	995	665	300	n.a.
Cuşamite	400	n.a.	n.a.	n.a.
Derebcin	200	n.a.	n.a.	n.a.
Djurin	4,050	3,053	997	249
Gariscov	400	n.a.	n.a.	n.a.
Jaruga	785	416	365	15
Lucineţ	2,897	n.a.	n.a.	116
Moghilev	15,000	12,000	3,000	900
Murafa	4,500	3,700	800	n.a.
Nazarineţ	850	550	300	n.a.
Nemerici	402	n.a.	n.a.	n.a.
Ninoy	200	n.a.	n.a.	n.a.
Obodovka	1,460	n.a.	n.a.	17
Odessa	54	54	n.a.	n.a.
Olgopol	724	n.a.	n.a.	50
Popioti	1,200	n.a.	n.a.	n.a.
Şargorod	5,300	3,500	1,800	500
Smerinka	3,274	2,074	1,200	200
Stanislavcic	200	n.a.	n.a.	n.a.
Tropova	650	n.a.	150	n.a.
Tulcin	250	n.a.	n.a.	n.a.
Verhovca	980	n.a.	n.a.	n.a.
Vindiceni	750	n.a.	n.a.	n.a.
Total	61,144	34,868	11,979	2,477

---

*n.a. = data not available.

Berşad the military commands were replaced and the regime became stricter still.[143] In March, April, and May 1943, the Jewish population continued to be moved toward the interior of Transnistria. On March 15, 220 Jews from the Pecioara camp were sent to a farm in Rahni, and in April

100 more from the Tulcin ghetto were sent to other district farms. In May another thousand Jews were sent to Trihati, on the other side of the Bug, to build a bridge. Here they were constantly tormented by German supervisors who shot Jews for the slightest infraction.[144] In the spring of 1943, Captain Buradescu, now commander of Vapniarka, provoked a fight between the Christian inmates (Romanian and Ukrainian criminals) and the Jews, after which many Jewish deportees were punished.[145] In June 1943, 1,560 Jewish deportees were transported by Germans from Obodovka to Nicolaev, beyond the Bug, for forced labor. They walked the eighty kilometers to Balta and then continued by train. Along the way they had nothing to eat.

During this time the condition of the orphaned children in Moghilev improved.[146] Conversely, as of July 27, 1943, Tulcin District reported its 2,696 Jews from Moghilev at forced labor; 280 more were unable to work, and 259 were under punishment by the regime for attempted escape. According to Prefect Năsturaș, "90 percent of the Jews were almost naked, dressed only in pants from rags."[147]

On September 9, 220 Jews were brought to Trihati from Golta District and 70 from Vapniarka. Their state was even more wretched. Their clothes were in tatters, and "many used newspapers to cover themselves." Help that they were supposed to receive never materialized; one shipment of clothes from the Central Office was diverted by Germans, who sold them at the market.[148] In the fall of 1943, many Jews deported from the Transnistria ghettos sought to survive by begging, but they ran the risk of being caught and executed.

On November 16, 1943, a committee headed by Colonel Rădulescu, secretary of the Office of the President of the Council of Ministers, traveled through the Transnistria ghettos in preparation for a visit by the International Committee of the Red Cross.[149] Indeed, in December a delegation of the International Committee, under the leadership of Charles Kolb and accompanied by a representative of the Romanian Red Cross, a certain Mrs. Ioan, and one from the Romanian government as well, visited Jewish "colonies" in Transnistria. The visitors were shown only buildings where the deportees had clean laundry; statistical records were removed from the offices; and photography was barred. But individual Jews tried to inform the delegation of their actual situation,[150] which Kolb evidently gathered:

I saw horrible sites, filthy houses filled with malnourished residents, with practically no heat [in December], whose morale was very low, and several others whose will to live stimulated the other deportees, who had set up a hospital, a school, and an orphanage. But under what conditions? Where the prefect or the chief supervisor had been won over by anti-Semitic ideas life was harsher, but where skilled personnel had sought to maintain a minimum of humanitarian feelings, life was bearable, aside from the complete and total lack of freedom.[151]

On December 17, sweeps by the Romanian gendarmerie in Moghilev resulted in the arrest of hundreds of Jews, who were subsequently sent by train to Şmerinka for hard labor.[152] The chaotic deportation of the Jewish population to the hinterland of Transnistria continued sporadically even in January 1944. On January 20, some of the deportees in Nicolaev were sent to Dumbrava Verde. Carp has described this transport accordingly: "while it was snowing and freezing, men were in two cars, sixty per car. Disease, misery, starvation ate away at them."[153]

Transnistria finally ceased to exist on March 20, 1944, when the Red Army reached the Dniester. The last weeks saw less of the suffering to which the surviving deportees had grown accustomed. A witness recalled about that time, "No one was abusive, not the officers, not the soldiers, not the military prosecutors, not the pharmacists, not the agricultural engineers. The '*Jidani*' had now become 'the Jewish gentlemen.' "[154] But liberation by the Red Army brought new tribulations for the Jews, who were forced into work battalions and who now would experience enormous difficulties trying to return to Romania. But that is another story.

According to Carp's data, aside from the 30,000 or so Jews deported from Odessa, more than 25,000 had been deported farther into the interior of Transnistria. A report from Governor Alexianu dated March 9, 1942, indicated that 65,252 Jews had been deported from one place to another in Transnistria, including 32,819 from Odessa, 25,436 from Răbniţa, and 5,479 from Tulcin, with the remainder from other districts of Transnistria. Complete data for 1943 are lacking.[155]

Transnistria was, along with Bessarabia and Bukovina, Romania's primary killing field. When they were not executed outright, Jews and Gypsies were left to die in atrocious conditions. Epidemics, cold, and hunger took a huge toll on the survivors of the massacres. Nevertheless, the rate of survival of Jewish deportees was higher in Transnistria than in German-occupied Ukraine.

*   *   *

The survival of fifty thousand Romanian Jews (not to mention tens of thousands of indigenous Jews) in Transnistria reflected the indecision of both the Romanian government and the military, neither of which ever formally decided upon the outright and total extermination of all Jews. Not only traditional Romanian inefficiency but also (during the second half of the war) a growing sense that the war was lost and that people would be held accountable for the crimes committed in Transnistria opened windows of opportunity for the Jews mired in the region; these moved hesitantly to ensure the repatriation of some categories of surviving deportees (especially orphaned children and the Jews from Southern Bukovina). The Jewish community of Regat and even international organizations managed to make occasional contributions to their effort. The Germans had been more eager than the Romanians to exterminate the Jews all along, but the Romanians jealously guarded their own prerogatives: collaboration with the Germans evolved toward resistance to them until, with the growing collapse of the eastern front, the Germans eventually lost all influence over events in Transnistria. The death of a huge number of victims in that region constitutes a major segment in the history of the Holocaust, but the survival of approximately half of the Romanian Jewry there also constitutes an experience not paralleled in most other European countries under the rule of or allied to Nazi Germany.

CHAPTER 7

The Deportation, Persecution, and Extermination of the Gypsies

THE GYPSIES were another group of Romanian citizens deported to Transnistria during World War II, mostly from Regat, the Old Kingdom. Even before the war Legionnaire ideologues such as Constantin Papanace and Traian Herseni agitated for the elimination not only of the Jews but also of Gypsies and even Greeks.[1] (During the eighteenth century the Ottomans had imposed Greek princes over Romania; right-wing intellectuals continued to perceive ethnic Greeks as vestiges of Turkish domination.) In any event, the Romanian fascists never undertook any serious anti-Greek actions. The Gypsies were another matter, however, and Nazi Germany paid great attention to Romania's handling of "the Gypsy problem." Professor Burgdöfer, president of the Bavarian Statistical Office, even went to Romania as an official "expert" to study the matter.[2] Romanian experts, on the other hand, went further, coming up with concrete "solutions." A book by a certain Professor Ion Chelcea, for example, demanded that certain categories of Gypsies should be locked up in "reservations" and sterilized.[3] Nevertheless, only a small portion of Romania's Gypsies—approximately 2.5 percent—were deported under the accusation of being "nomads" or "asocials"; yet those who were deported experienced sufferings identical to those of the Jews.

*   *   *

The fate of the Romanian Gypsies was all the more tragic because some of them had been fighting as members of the Romanian army on the eastern front even as the deportations got under way. Gypsy invalids of World War I were deported; indeed, even Romanians mistaken for Gypsies were swept up in the deportations.[4] Some Gypsies still wearing Romanian military uniforms were seized and deported.[5] The "legal" basis for the deportations was a May 1942 measure, Order No. 70S/1942 of the president of the Council of Ministers. This was supplemented a few days later by another measure, Order No. 33911, attributed to C. Z. Vasiliu of the Ministry of the Interior and distributed to the police prefectures: the police were to conduct a census of both the nomadic and the sedentary Gypsies and then deport the former and certain categories of the latter.[6] The plan was rapidly implemented in actions such as the May 25 sweep of Gypsies in Bacău, an operation in which forty-five policemen blocked the town exits, drew up lists of all Gypsies, and deported them forthwith.[7] Ultimately, approximately 25,000 Gypsies in all were deported.[8]

Looking further into the details of this matter, we find that the General Inspectorate of the Gendarmerie followed up on the order to deport all nomadic Gypsies in Romania plus those nonnomads "dangerous to public order" (as per Report No. 43249/1942). The deportation of the nomads ended on August 15, 1942; that of the others paused on September 16, but it resumed shortly thereafter:[9] on September 22, 1,002 sedentary Gypsies were deported from Pitești on train E4, which left at 9:20 A.M. in the direction of Tighina. Another eight cars bearing 570 Gypsies from Turnu Măgurele were soon added to this transport.[10] Twelve thousand additional sedentary Gypsies were deported in five other trains; the property they had to leave behind, as well as other personal belongings, was sold at auction.[11]

During his trial General Vasiliu acknowledged his role in these deportations:

> STOICAN (the public prosecutor): After receiving basic instructions for the deportation of Gypsies, did you organize these deportations in detail?
>
> VASILIU: Sending 24,000 people from all over the country without organizing anything would have meant sending them to their death. I

took all the necessary measures [i.e., to ensure their well-being]; I provided five complete trains on which the Gypsies were to board.

PRESIDENT [of the War Crimes Tribunal]: Why were you the one who organized the deportations?

VASILIU: If I received the order, what could I do?

STOICAN: Did you draw up instructions for each Gypsy to bring with him only a bundle for the trip to Transnistria?

VASILIU: If we had allowed every deportee to bring the contents of his house with him, the five trains at my disposal would not have sufficed.

STOICAN: Did you draw up instructions to deport them in the shortest possible time to prevent unrest?

VASILIU: The Gypsies traveled for more than forty days from Timișoara to Bucharest until they reached Transnistria. It was a difficult operation, and measures had to be taken to forestall any incident. [Vasiliu was probably referring in this last answer to the considerable number of nomadic Gypsies deported village by village in horse carts; he apparently wanted to emphasize that the operation was carried out slowly and under humane conditions.][12]

Questioned after the war, Marshal Ion Antonescu confessed that the original decision to deport the Gypsies had been his. He sought to justify himself by citing "popular" demand for protection from armed robbers who entered people's homes at night: "After much investigation we concluded that these were armed Gypsies, many with military weapons, organizing these attacks. All the Gypsies were moved out. Since Mr. Alexianu needed manpower in Transnistria, I said, 'Let's move them to Transnistria, that is my decision.'"[13]

The deportation of 25,000 Gypsies placed a considerable strain on rail transport, causing, among other things, serious problems for the Romanian military bureaucracy in particular. Most disturbing to the authorities, armed Gypsy soldiers on leave arrived in Transnistria to free their relatives. Some discharged Gypsy soldiers were allowed to go to Transnistria to rejoin their families. Other Gypsy soldiers from nomadic families were actually discharged and deported to Transnistria themselves. Eventually, the Supreme General Staff asked officers to explain to Gypsy soldiers that their families no longer would be deported. This course was in part the result of a September 29, 1942, meeting in which the matter came up for discussion by the Council of Ministers, which backed off from its earlier radical position:

> MIHAI ANTONESCU (vice president of the Council): I would like to ask General Vasiliu to discuss this matter with Colonel Davidescu [chief of Ion Antonescu's military cabinet] because we have problems at the national level. Please communicate and transmit a memorandum for [immediate] enforcement: "All [Gypsies] eligible for military service, their families, and [those] who hold a manual trade, smiths, skilled workers, and others [?], do not qualify as evacuees."
>
> VASILIU (secretary of state at the Ministry of the Interior): We brought 26,000. There were also some burglars.
>
> ALEXIANU (governor of Transnistria): Please give me your approval [for repatriation] in case I find Gypsies [serving in the army], orphans, and invalids from the last war. . . .
>
> VASILIU: They all have a police file. Are you sending me back all the thieves?
>
> MIHAI ANTONESCU: The ones you arrested, may God protect them; we are not bringing them back.[14]

A month later (on October 31), as a result of the decision reached at this meeting, the Ministry of the Interior formally ended the deportation of Romanian Gypsies.[15]

Despite such examples of flexibility, one cannot help but note that nearly the entire Romanian political class—fascist and nonfascist alike—seems to have remained indifferent to the tragedy of the Gypsies. The only known exception among prominent political figures was Constantin I. C. Brătianu, head of the Liberal party. In the following letter of September 16, 1942, Brătianu begged Marshal Antonescu to show mercy:

> Marshal:
>
> Following the persecutions and expulsions of the Jews as reprisals against their coreligionists in Bukovina and Bessarabia, and influenced by German practice [in Jewish matters], we are now adopting very strict measures against the Gypsies, who are being forcibly removed and sent to Transnistria in sealed railroad cars, as in Pitești.
>
> No one understands the purpose underlying these expulsions.
>
> As you know full well, these Romanian citizens were not subject to

any special treatment in our state until now. They are Orthodox, just like Romanians, and they play an important economic role in our country because they are skilled artisans: blacksmiths, coppersmiths, masons, agricultural workers, construction workers. Many of them are small shopkeepers, small business owners, milkmen, and the like. Almost all the violinists in our country are Gypsies, and there is not one festival that can go on without their assistance.

In one fell swoop, the authorities are telling them to leave the country in which they were born and where their ancestors lived; the country where, as good Romanians, they shed their blood when fighting for our nation. On the eve of winter they are asked to liquidate in a matter of hours their homes, from which they can carry no more than twenty kilograms of belongings and clothing.

Old people, women, and children are thrown out of the country into regions that they do not know, where they are completely disoriented.

Why such cruelty?

What are these unfortunate people guilty of?

What will this expulsion accomplish?

Is our country, especially after the current war, overpopulated, and does it enjoy such an abundance of artisans and workers that it can sacrifice such a large number of its citizens?

I dare not imagine that such measures have been adopted upon the initiative or with the knowledge of the head of state, and that is why I am addressing myself to you to put an end to this persecution that will make us regress several centuries.[16]

The Gypsies were initially sent to the areas of Alexandrovka (Oceakov District), Karanika, Covaleovka (Berezovka District), Mancovca, Voitovka, and Stunovka (Balta District).[17] Some of the Gypsies reached Transnistria with their horses and their carts, according to the statement of the prosecutor at one of the postwar trials, O. A. Bunaciu. One of the witnesses, Alexandru Blumenfeld, stated that "aside from the Jews, Gypsies also came to the district of Golta, where their belongings were looted. They were not given lodgings, and they died like flies."[18] A witness of events in neighboring Acmecetka wrote that "Antonescu's" Gypsies, who had arrived in 1942, died there just as the Jews had:

They were told: "Since you are not Jews, you can bring your horses, your carts, and your belongings because there you will be colonists and we will give you land." They were also brought into [Prefect] Isopescu's empire [i.e., Golta Transnistria]. First, their carts and horses were taken away, and since Gypsies always carried their valuables with them, [such as] gold, they could therefore be completely despoiled. They lived in pigsties; they were not given any opportunity to work and earn a living. That is why thousands died. . . . The Gypsies suffered the same fate as the Jews; they died either by execution or because of the cold or hunger.[19]

Another witness, Virgil Nemeş, corroborated that the Romanian gendarmerie confiscated all horses and carts from the nomadic Gypsies,[20] and indeed, we know that on July 29, 1942, Alexianu ordered this.[21]

It is also known that the number of Gypsies in Transnistria diminished rapidly due to executions, starvation, and epidemics. Though the information is incomplete, it is clear that as of March 21, 1943, 3,423 Gypsies remained alive in Covaleovka, spread out among four labor colonies,[22] and that on November 28 of that same year 9,567 Gypsies still survived in the following important areas of resettlement: Golta, Crivoi Ozero, Vradievka, Liubaşevka, and Dumanovka.[23] According to Mihail Hausner, a Jewish survivor of Transnistria, after 11,500 Gypsies had been killed by the SS at Triháti, the survivors were imprisoned in the ghetto of Covaleovka, where their carts and horses were expropriated. Behind the barbed wire, without food, they were forced to sell their clothes to survive. Typhus and hunger destroyed them. The hardiest were transferred from Covaleovka to Suha Balca and Mostovoi, where they were given clothes because they were totally naked.[24] Indeed, on September 24, the prefect of Berezovka District, Colonel Leonida Pop, informed the labor administration of Transnistria that the Gypsies of Suha Balca and all the rest in his district were "without clothes, without shirts, barefoot." Pop enclosed the request by the head of the Gypsies of Suha Balca, Ion Natale Stan, for clothes for the 499 Gypsies who had been deported from Țăndărei (Ialomiţa District). Stan also asked that the Gypsies' shelter for the winter be improved, stressing that some had sons at the front. On October 2, 1943, two freight cars of lumber were sent to the Gypsies of Suha Balca so that they could build huts for the winter. On October 3, fifty-one suits arrived at a cost of 150 reichsmarks each. On October 4, the labor administration gave its consent for 150 pairs of shoes to be sold to the "good workers." But on October 29, Pop, who apparently had received fewer pairs than expected, complained that the number of shoes did not suffice since there were 2,620 Gypsies in Berezovka. Pop also reported that many were naked: the winter would mean certain death for them.

As of February 10, 1944, about 3,700 Gypsies survived in the Berezovka region; we have no exact figures for the other places at that time. Though the numbers had declined, the new year saw improvements for the surviving Gypsies, as for the surviving Jews. In late February changing times were signaled when the Gypsies of Suha Balca gained permission to correspond with their relatives in Romania by way of the Red Cross. Despite such concessions, we do not know whether Stan received official endorsement of his earlier request to establish a workshop to enable his community to survive by manufacturing and selling combs.[25]

On April 15, 1945, Lieutenant Colonel Vasile Gorsky, the former prefect of Oceakov, wrote at length of the Gypsy deportees in his district:

> At a conference of prefects from Transnistria in the summer of 1942, Governor Alexianu told me that on orders of Marshal Antonescu, several thousand nomadic Gypsies who had had run-ins with the law would be transported to the district of Oceakov and that I must use them for agricultural projects and in those crafts with which they were familiar. . . . I replied that there were no buildings or sheds in which they might shelter [on the farms to which I planned to send them] and that no firewood was available to prepare their food and provide them with heat. I was told that wood would be shipped. . . . In late August 1942, the Gypsies began to arrive in Triháti. They were greeted by the commander of the gendarme legion, who strictly ordered them not to leave the designated areas. The Gypsies were distributed among state farms. . . . Fifteen thousand Gypsies arrived over the course of one week. The commander . . . told me after the first trains had arrived that they were in an unbelievably miserable condition. I went by car and met them heading for the farms on foot or by cart.
>
> There were many old people, women, and lots of children. The carts bore cripples, people over seventy, the blind, and the grievously ill. Most were [almost] naked, wearing tatters. I spoke to them. They were incensed; they cried, they screamed, they cursed: why had they been arrested and sent to Transnistria? Many proved to me that they had sons at the front, husbands at the front, sons or husbands who had died at the

front. Others had relatives lying wounded in [military] hospitals. In these cases I reported in writing and by telephone to the governor, who [demanded] information as to the motives for which they had been sent to Transnistria. . . . After a few weeks approvals for their return began to arrive, and we sent them to Odessa in trucks and carts. I also sent a telegram to the Office of the President of the Council of Ministers wherein I showed that in violation of the orders of the marshal to send nomadic Gypsies with judicial problems, many families had been sent whose heads or children were at the front, or had died at the front, or lay wounded in hospitals, or were honest people in good standing, business owners and artisans. Following that telegram a committee chaired by Colonels Sandu Moldoveanu, C. Moldoveanu, and Ivascu arrived on December 3 for an eight- to ten-day stay, checked each family's situation, and compiled tables that broke down the population by category. (Because the Gypsies were infected with typhus, Colonel Ivascu was stricken, returned to Bucharest, and died in early January. . . . He had been appointed prefect of Oceakov, . . . but as a result of his death, I was forced to remain . . . even though my resignation had been accepted on October 1, 1942.)

After the selection in February [1943,] other approvals for return kept arriving. Meanwhile, many Gypsies in uniform came to Oceakov from Romania, from the front, or from hospitals—disabled veterans and even soldiers injured during the current war, missing a leg or a hand, in search of their wives, children, and parents. Their justifiable anger was terrible. During the winter they came from places as far away as Oltenia and Transylvania to Oceakov and other places to pick up their families. Some had arrived with permits from the Ministry of the Interior and the government [of Transnistria] for their safe return; others had come only with [military] papers, proof [considered insufficient], and had to go again to Odessa and Bucharest to obtain permits. I remember one of them who told me that he had to go three times to Bucharest to obtain such a permit: they kept asking him for [different] papers.[26]

The conditions of life for the Gypsies in Transnistria were all the more unbearable because of the humiliating circumstances under which deportation had been carried out. As Gorsky wrote, the Gypsies had been treated as convicts and felt themselves the victims of conscienceless robbers:

The Gypsies had been arrested in rural Romania by the gendarmes and by the policemen in the towns. Most of them were arrested [as they went about their affairs] and loaded directly onto trains without being allowed to retrieve from their house a winter coat, bedding, [or eating utensils]. Decent people were deported, people who owned houses, farms, or shops, well-to-do men: the owner of a hotel in Iași (near the train station); the owner of two clothing and shoe stores in Galați. . . . One Gypsy had three million in his possession, so the government [of Transnistria] forced him to deposit one and a half million at the National Bank of Tighina, the remainder to be exchanged for marks. . . . I allowed him to open a shop. A woman from Craiova showed me a postcard that she had received from the commander of a company belonging to the Thirty-fifth Infantry Regiment, in which he informed her that her son had died a hero's death at the front and had done honor to his regiment and his country. Another woman told me that a gendarme had forced her to sell a cow worth forty thousand lei for ten thousand in return for not being sent to Transnistria but that several days later she had been arrested and deported anyway. Another very kind woman with three young girls in Craiova showed me a postcard from her sister, who had written, "You were stupid; I gave the [police] commissioner five thousand lei and I escaped." A Gypsy woman from Transylvania was brought in with two Romanian children. She had been married to a Romanian, a widower with two children; he died, but since the woman was a Gypsy, she was deported with her two children (ten and twelve years old), whose mother was Romanian. I drafted a report [asking] the government [of Transnistria] to investigate this matter. The older child was placed in a windmill at Oceakov because the child said that he had worked in other mills, and the youngest was taken in by Deputy Prefect Dragomir. I believed that it was important to conduct research throughout the country, to know what orders the police and gendarmerie were acting on, how these orders were enforced, and the abuses that they perpetrated, because many Gypsy men and women told me that many acquaintances with police records had been left alone because they had paid money.[27]

Though treated as convicts, the Gypsies nevertheless officially remained exiles: despite the fact that this status was on the surface less humiliating, the Gypsies' living conditions were infinitely worse than those of incarcerated criminals:

Difficulties related to housing and food for fifteen thousand Gypsies were very significant. They arrived . . . starved and in true poverty. They were sent to farms, by foot or cart, forty to fifty kilometers away. I [Gorsky] took measures to feed them along the way, [but] there was food just enough for the indigenous population. . . . The Gypsies . . . stole what they could, [and] it was easy to spot the places they had been by the poultry feathers covering the ground. . . . Several Gypsies were executed by the inhabitants of German villages and then burned (Schonfeld, for instance). Armed civilian sentinels did not allow anyone to get close or to cross through until the corpses had been thoroughly cremated. . . . [On] the farms the Gypsies stayed in the fields for several weeks without shelter. [Neighboring farmers were required to feed them.] They . . . did not want to work at all; they requested to be sent to Romania. Because I did not receive any lumber with which to build huts, I was ordered to settle them in the barracks at Alexandrodar and Balşaia Carinika, which had no doors or windows. They stayed there until early November. Because it was so cold at night, they burned the wood from the rooftops, the floors, the outhouses, trees, telegraph poles, and so on. . . . I requested that the Gypsies in the district of Oceakov be taken into custody and sent to a district where there were forests. But I was ordered to evacuate some local residents from several villages and settle the Gypsies there. The wood issue did not go away. I chose four villages close to the Bug; I personally conveyed to the local residents the order from the government [of Transnistria]. The obedient and submissive [Ukrainian] residents moved out in a week to neighboring villages. . . . The Gypsies were [under orders] not to leave the villages. Food was guaranteed by the military prosecutor of Varvarovca, Dan Anton, a man of initiative [and a former attorney from Galaţi]. It was very difficult to feed the Gypsies because the district had to feed Romanian troops heading for the front. . . . The most serious problem remained firewood. They gathered grass from the fields, far away from the villages; then they began to cut down fruit trees, fences, outhouses, even rooftops. They destroyed windows, doors, and floors and gradually moved into fewer rooms. By the spring of 1943, the villages were unrecognizable; everything lay in ruins. I photographed them and sent the collection to the government. . . . I kept copies for myself, but they were burned last year during the bombing raids. I got the government to supply wood to rebuild the villages and heard after my departure from the prefecture (on

April 1, 1943) that part had been delivered and that the residents had been able to rebuild their homes.[28]

The Gypsies perished as victims of outright violence and also in consequence of their unbearable material circumstances. Cold and hunger so weakened them that they fell victim to disease—above all others, as Gorsky explained, typhus:

> The Gypsies were infested with lice. A first attempt at disinfection took place upon their arrival in Tribak, but it was not thorough. . . . They began to die shortly after arrival. Doctors noted too late that the culprit was typhus. Since the Gypsies' skin is darker, one could not detect the red spots. . . . Disinfection equipment was sent by the government, as well as lamp oil, soap, firewood, and doctors. . . . During the winter of 1942–1943, three to four thousand Gypsies died. Even though precise orders had been given to issue death certificates, no exact numbers could be determined; because of a shortage of gendarmes, some Gypsies were able to flee toward Odessa or Romania. These were arrested along the way, locked up in other towns, or died without identification papers. My resignation from the prefecture of Oceakov was dated September 1, 1942, and was not approved until April 1, 1943. After that date I do not know what happened to the Gypsies. The [deportations] were a colossal fiasco, both materially and morally. . . . The material outcome in Romania was immediately noticeable owing to the shortage of labor power. In Oceakov entire villages were destroyed, fruit groves were burned down, and four thousand Gypsies died, along with several hundred local civilians, gendarmes, and soldiers [swept away by typhus], not to mention the difficulties [for] the railroad system and the burden of policing [the deportees].[29]

Information about the numbers and locations of the survivors is sadly fragmentary. At the beginning of October 1942, 24,686 Gypsy deportees were in Transnistria. Of these, 11,441 were nomadic Gypsies, 13,176 non-nomads, and the other 69 former prison inmates.[30] According to the prosecutor's statement in the Antonescu trial, six to eight thousand Gypsies had been murdered in Golta on orders from the district prefect, Modest Isopescu.[31] A handwritten postwar testimony stated that 11,500 Gypsies had been removed by the SS and executed in the train station of Triháti.[32] Also according to that document, only 1,500 of the Gypsies who had been

deported to Transnistria survived. In his testimony the Jewish deportee
Mihail Hausner said that these Gypsies were sent to Trihăti, where the
Germans liquidated them. Hausner stated that initially there had been
twenty thousand confined in Kovaleovka but that only a small fraction
had survived.[33] It is not really clear how many Gypsies perished in Transnistria. In any case, in May 1944, when the Romanian gendarmerie nom-
inally registered all Gypsies who returned from Transnistria, the lists that
were compiled did not contain more than six thousand names.[34]

The deportation of Romanian Gypsies to Transnistria was a much
smaller operation than that of the Jews. Not only was the absolute number lower but so was the percentage of the Gypsies actually sent away.
There had been no anti-Gypsy legislation (i.e., besides administrative orders), and this made the deportations even more arbitrary than those of the
Jews. Finally, the fact that the deported Gypsies had relatives in the Romanian army created a very serious bureaucratic problem for the military
authorities. It became clear after a few months that it was easier to stop
the deportations than to face the problems triggered by their continuation.

Antonescu ordered the deportation of other minority groups too.
Ukrainians were initially a target, but there were simply too many of them
in Bukovina. However, Romanian officials did want to "solve" "the
Ukrainian question" there, based on Antonescu's advocacy of "forced migration of the entire Ukrainian element."[35] This intention was opposed by
German officials, who wished to utilize Ukrainian nationalists for their
own purposes, something that irked Romanian officials. After the Berlin
encounter between Hitler and Mihai Antonescu on November 27, 1941,
the Romanian dignitary complained: "I asked the Führer to clarify his
stance on the Ukrainian question, because in Bukovina elements in the
German army favored the Ukrainians, and the Romanian government
would soon have to develop a position . . . opposed to the Ukrainian element. . . . The numerous, primitive mass of Slavs is . . . a serious biological problem with regard to European birthrates."[36] Though Hitler did
agree to let the Romanians handle the Ukrainian issue on their own territory, anti-Ukrainian plans never got off the ground. Toward the end of the
war the Romanian military authorities faced increasing problems with
Ukrainian partisans, both nationalist (Bandera) and Soviet, as their German allies did.

Religious dissidents, particularly the Innocentists and others who
refused to serve in the armed forces, were also targeted. As a result, two

thousand Innocentists were imprisoned in camps during the summer of 1942, a measure later applied to Baptists and other sects.[37]

*   *   *

Though the persecution of Gypsies had barely gathered a full head of steam by the time Romanian policy makers began to worry about the possibility of postwar answerability for their crimes, the case of the Gypsies demonstrates that the Jews constituted an insufficient field of action for Romanian racists. If the Third Reich had prevailed in Europe, would fascist Romania have liquidated the rest of its Jews? And having thus solved "the Jewish question," would the country have done the same to the Gypsies? The Greeks? The Ukrainians? Hungarians? Religious minorities? Others? We shall never know. But the horrors of the Holocaust in Romania suggest that the malice of its fascists would not easily have been spent. The fact that the Gypsy Holocaust gave every sign of repeating that of the Jews indicates that, given the opportunity, Romania's fascists would indeed have continued to pursue their racist utopia. And if this had taken place, there is every reason to believe that continued "elimination" of other "elements" of discord would have proceeded not only on the grounds of race but also on those of religion, ideology, and politics.

[CHAPTER 8]

The Survival of the Romanian Jews

Two FACTORS played especially important roles in the fact that half of Romanian Jewry survived the war: the fact that Romania never carried out plans to deport the Jews of Regat, and the fact that a considerable portion of those deported to or native to Transnistria managed to hold out until the German defeat at Stalingrad forced Antonescu and his government to consider minimizing the culpability they might have to bear after the war. In regard to the experience of the Jewish community of Regat, one thing was clear during the Holocaust: not having come into contact with the Soviets in 1940, the Jews were not held accountable for the loss of Bessarabia and Northern Bukovina and therefore not singled out for prompt punishment at the beginning of the war. This is not to say that they would not have been deported, for some plans discussed at the highest levels of power involved deportation not to Transnistria, but directly to the German extermination camps in Poland. Nazi Germany sought to influence Romania in this direction, but that very pressure may have backfired: even Romanian fascists did not want to be told what to do with "their" Jews.

Secondly, in regard to the Jews languishing in Transnistria, there was enough need for their labor for the administration to allow them to live; their own exertions, those of their coreligionists in Regat, and the aid that eventually reached them from international organizations and the diplomatic community spelled the difference between death and life, at least for

[238]

those not too old, too young, or too feeble. None of this, however, would have been possible had the war not turned against Germany and its allies.

ABORTIVE PLANS TO DEPORT THE JEWS FROM MOLDAVIA, WALACHIA, AND SOUTHERN TRANSYLVANIA TO NAZI EXTERMINATION CAMPS

Despite the pogrom at Iași, the deportations from Bessarabia and Bukovina, the repeated massacres in those provinces, and the Transnistria disaster, a large segment of the Jewish population of Romania was still alive in 1942. The Jewish population of Moldavia, Walachia, and Transylvania (the portion not occupied by Hungary) was not subjected to deportation or extermination (except for the pogrom at Iași and the deportations from Dorohoi, Suceava, and Rădăuți). This did not go by unnoticed by Nazi Germany, which continued to pressure Romania and its other allies to solve "the Jewish question" within the framework of the "Final Solution." Situation reports on the campaign in the east compiled at the Reich Security Main Office (RSHA) reflected the same thing.[1]

The bureaucratic details of the Final Solution were drawn up on January 20, 1942, at the Wannsee Conference, which took place under the leadership of RSHA head Reinhard Heydrich and brought together fifteen high-level officials representing major German state agencies. At this meeting Martin Luther of the Foreign Office expressed confidence that neither southeastern nor Western Europe would present obstacles.[2] Though this prognosis proved largely correct, Romania and Bulgaria constituted partial exceptions. Even before 1942, German-Romanian relations, viewed through the prism of the Jewish question, were far from harmonious. The SS, along with regular German military units, had protested in the summer of 1941 the disorganized manner in which Romanian military units were killing Jews. In the eyes of the SS in particular the Romanian "technique" was inadequate; the Wermacht (armed forces) worried that it would affect the prestige of the German army.

As we have seen, in August 1941, the Germans had resisted Romanian deportations to the other side of the Dniester River, and a similar situation occurred on the Bug River in the spring of 1942. Nevertheless, in August 1941, despite "problems in the field," German-Romanian collaboration at the government-to-government level appeared to be total. On

August 7, Mihai Antonescu wrote to Heinrich Himmler to request that
Gustav Richter, Adolf Eichmann's envoy, be reposted to Bucharest:

> During the short period of time that [Richter] worked in Bucharest [he]
> provided us . . . immense assistance. Dr. Richter studied with great care
> and a high level of competence the anti-Semitic reforms of Romania
> and . . . based on a collaboration that lasted several months, provided me
> with a draft reorganization of the National Center for Romanization. . . .
> The Jewish question carries with it international solutions and has to be
> settled in an in-depth and definitive fashion, drawing upon German ex-
> perience. . . . [Richter's was] a contribution that I have always been
> grateful for and that, Excellency, I thank you for as well. I would be ex-
> tremely happy if Dr. Richter could return to Romania and pursue his
> fruitful activities.[3]

But on October 26, 1941, German-Romanian relations with regard to the
Jewish question were not as amiable as they were before, as becomes clear
from such evidence as Mihai Antonescu's discussion with top German
diplomats Richter, Hermann von Ritgen, and Willi Roedel, who were
posted to Bucharest at that time:

> Mssrs. von Ritgen, Richter, and Roedel discussed the possibility of
> German-Romanian collaboration in . . . the Jewish question. We pon-
> dered the possibilities of an international solution and the ways in which
> Germany had resolved the Jewish question. I drew the attention of the
> special counselors to the fact that the Jewish question in Romania was
> quite different from that in Germany, both in terms of the numbers of
> Jews and their economic status. . . . Mr. Richter related to me some of
> the German interpretations of Romania's anti-Semitic reforms, stating
> that it was being said in Germany that we had a tendency to protect
> wealthy Jews and that only Jewish proletarians would be subjected to
> harsh treatment. . . . I told Mr. Richter that this was not the first time that
> I had heard such rubbish and [news about German] interference in the
> activities of the Romanian government. But, fortunately, [this informa-
> tion] had not come from official or qualified agencies, in which case I
> would have had to take a stand on those arguments. However, I learned
> recently that this topic had been discussed between the [German] lega-
> tion in Bucharest and the SS, . . . and I deemed it my duty to send a writ-
> ten protest to Berlin, demanding that whoever meddled in Romanian

internal affairs . . . should be recalled for having transmitted false information and hatching unacceptable intrigues.[4]

No wonder the Germans were irritated with Mihai Antonescu after such a sudden change of attitude. On November 19, 1941, during a press conference with German reporters in Bucharest, Ambassador Manfred von Killinger declared:

> Problems associated with the war are mounting. . . . We need many things [from Romania], including oil. The significant interests of the Reich require us to make important concessions to Romania and to Marshal Antonescu. The marshal has shown bravery and loyalty in his behavior. . . . We must take into account the special status of the marshal with regard to the Führer. . . . It has been said that [Mihai] Antonescu is playing a double game [i.e., secretly making overtures to the Allies]. I think that that would be foolish. He is too compromised by the policies he enacts on behalf of our side to play a double game. . . . The Führer trusts the marshal, and Mihai Antonescu is the marshal's trusted aide. He has the right to choose the aides that he deems most reliable. He knows that the ruling strata and the bourgeoisie of Romania are against us. If it were up to me, I would douse the entire Romanian bourgeoisie with gasoline. But it is in our interest to see that the marshal is supported.[5]

Killinger's statement illustrates the latent hostility of the German authorities toward the Romanian ruling class. However, the need for Romanian oil, and particularly the special relationship between Hitler and Antonescu, moderated German behavior.

Throughout the summer and fall of 1942, relations between Romania and Germany deteriorated. Cooperation on the Jewish question displayed a seesaw pattern of fluctuations. As Hilberg wrote,

> On July 26, 1942, the Eichmann Referat of the RSHA reported that its representative in Bucharest, Hauptsturmführer Richter, had scored a complete breakthrough. "Political and technical preparations for a solution of the Jewish question in Romania," reported Eichmann, "have been completed by the representative of the Reich Security Main Office to such an extent that the evacuation transports be able to roll in a short time. It is planned to remove the Jews of Romania in a series of transports beginning approximately September 10, 1942, to the district of

Lublin, where the employable segment will be allocated for labor uti-
lization, while the remainder will be subjected to special treatment."

Provision had been made to insure that the Romanian Jews would
lose their nationality upon crossing the border. Negotiations with the
Reichsbahn with respect to train schedules were already far advanced.[6]

During his interrogation in Jerusalem Eichmann confirmed that Richter
had been in possession of Mihai Antonescu's written agreement for the
deportation of the Jews from Moldavia, Walachia, and southern Transylvania.[7] In any case, according to German diplomatic documents, several
days earlier Ion Antonescu had given von Killinger a verbal agreement to
the same effect.[8]

According to a census of the Jewish population in the spring of 1942,
about 300,000 Jews still lived in Romania. On August 8, 1942, *Bukarester
Tageblatt,* a paper that reflected the viewpoint of the German embassy,
published an article entitled "Rumanien wird judenrein" ("Romania Will
Be Free of Jews"). On the same day *Donauzeitung* in Belgrade published
an article entitled "Judenaussiedlung in Rumanien" ("Jewish Resettlement in Romania"), and two days later a similar article appeared in *Völkisher Beobachter* in Berlin.[9] The *Bukarester Tageblatt* article lauded
Romania's "energetic steps" toward a Final Solution in Romania under
the guidance of Marshal Antonescu. Also lauded was the "exemplary" activity of Radu Lecca, who "supervised" the Central Office of Romanian
Jews as part of his "mission" to purge Romania of its Jews.[10] The *Tageblatt* announced a planned deportation of 25,000 Jews from Moldavia and
Walachia during the autumn of 1942 and the deportation of other Romanian Jews, including those from Transylvania, by fall 1943, though without mentioning the destination.[11]

Censorship prevented Romanian newspapers from making similar
announcements.[12] But after August 15, 1942, rumors of a deportation
from Transylvania and Banat (encompassing Timişoara, Arad, Beiuş,
Turda, Sighişoara, and Braşov) toward Hungary grew more frequent.[13]
Matatias Carp recalled that "Dr. Ligheti and Dr. Tener from Timişoara
came to see me and stated that an order had been given to the Sixth Territorial Command to set up train cars [for deportations]."[14] By various
means the heads of the Jewish communities tried to avert deportation. It
would seem that the first to intervene at their request was one Dr.
Stroescu, Antonescu's personal physician and the director of the so-called

Palace of the Handicapped, who had received from the Jews of Transylvania and Banat a donation of 100 million lei for his establishment.[15] It could be that the visit of Baron Neumann (a very wealthy converted Jew) to Bucharest on or about August 20, 1941, was connected with that donation.[16] The outcome remains unclear. In a statement after the war Baron Mocsoni-Styrcea, who had had close ties to the Romanian royal house, stated that Neumann and Max Auschnitt (a wealthy Jewish industrialist) donated in a three-day period to Maria Antonescu's Patronage Society four billion lei (fifty million Swiss francs).[17] In any event, we know that the Germans were informed because one of Richter's reports mentions Neumann and ties him to the sum of 400 million lei and because the November 11, 1942, issue of *Bukarester Tageblatt* violently attacked Neumann for stopping the deportations.[18]

These people were not alone in attempting to halt deportations. Chief Rabbi Alexandru Şafran also intervened before Metropolitan Bălan of Transylvania (whose anti-Semitic views were well known), begging him to intercede with Antonescu.[19] The metropolitan met with Şafran in Bucharest, and the former did intercede, most likely supported by Queen Mother Elena.[20] The apostolic nuncio Andrea Cassulo interceded with Antonescu too, as did Swiss diplomat René de Weck.[21] Whether or not such entreaties had an effect, Antonescu decided to temporarily postpone enactment of the deportation orders.

Meanwhile, German-Romanian negotiations regarding the dispatch of Romanian Jews to Nazi camps continued:

> On August 17, 1942, Luther informed Ernst von Weizsäcker [secretary of state at the German Ministry of Foreign Affairs], Ernst Woermann [the ministry's undersecretary for political affairs], and Foreign Minister Joachim von Ribbentrop that Mihai Antonescu and Marshal Antonescu had given their consent to the deportation . . . and had agreed that transports would begin . . . from the districts of Arad, Timişoara, and Turda. . . . Lecca wished to come to Berlin to discuss the details with the Foreign Office and the RSHA. A few days later Luther wrote to the legation in Bucharest that Lecca was definitely coming to the German capital.
>
> Lecca visited Berlin sometime during the week of August 20–27. It seems that in Abteilung Deutschland [the Germany section of the RSHA] his visit was regarded as a mere formality. The two Antonescus

had, after all, already voiced their agreement, and Lecca was not considered an important Romanian personage. In Berlin Lecca therefore received the brush-off treatment. That was a mistake. When he returned to
Romania on or about August 27, the German diplomats were already
aware that things had gone wrong.[22]

But, as Hilberg has pointed out, the Romanians were no longer enthusiastic.[23] This was compounded by the German-Romanian differences over
economic and ethnic problems emerging from meetings on Transnistria
between Mihai Antonescu and General Rotkirchen on August 28, 1942,
and between Mihai Antonescu and G. Steltzer, the German legation counselor, in September 1942.[24] During the same period leading economic circles in Germany fretted over the high volume of trade between Romania
and the neutral countries, which lowered Germany's ability to export.[25]

On September 11, Lecca submitted to Mihai Antonescu a plan for the
"evacuation" of Jews from Banat and Transylvania,[26] with the exception
of those "who had demonstrated . . . that they fit into the spirit of the
Romanian nation and those useful to the economy and trade."[27] Lecca "re-
spectfully suggested" that certain other Jews be exempted from deportation: Jews married to Christians; Jews who had converted before August
9, 1940; foreign-born Jews with valid passports; Jews who were older
than sixty-five; Jews who had received certain decorations; invalids, orphans, and widows of soldiers who had died during World War I; and
some officials of the Central Office. "During the evacuation," Lecca proposed, "special efforts should be made to keep children under sixteen with
their parents."[28] This plan also envisioned that "a group of three thousand
Jews among those slated for deportation to Poland might be allowed to
emigrate to Palestine in exchange for two million lei."[29] These exceptions
made Lecca's plan slightly more lenient than that for the deportations
from Bessarabia and Bukovina the previous year, when (aside from
twenty thousand Jews in Cernăuți) there had been no permission to emigrate.

Richter's plan resembled the Romanian version, but there were differences: the German plan called for the deportation of all Romanian
Jews; the age up to which children might stay with their parents was set
at fourteen; and some categories were still exempted ("for now"). But of
course the German plan did not mention any emigration to Palestine. The
plan did, however, provide details about transports to Poland, their secu-

rity, and transfer to the Germans at the border post of Sniatin. The Central Jewish Office would be made to finance the deportations.[30]

On September 13, 1942, the Jewish New Year, U.S. Secretary of State Cordell Hull may have issued a message of solidarity to the European Jews over the radio.[31] According to a subsequent memorandum from Richter to von Killinger, the Swiss legation in Bucharest had forwarded a message from Hull (U.S. interests were represented by the Swiss legation) that condemned the deportations and threatened the Romanian government with reprisals against Romanians in the United States. All of this was apparently discussed at the September 18 meeting of the Council of Ministers, where Mihai Antonescu decided not to submit to these pressures.[32]

Nevertheless, Hull's alleged message definitely had an impact in Romania. On September 15, the vehemently anti-Semitic newspaper *Porunca Vremii* published a commentary calling for the elimination of derogatory adjectives when referring to Jews and expressing admiration for their tenacity. On September 20, Nicolae Mareş, a former minister of agriculture, refused an invitation to participate in the government again, declaring this no time "to get in trouble with the Jews." On September 21 and 22, Deputy Minister of the Interior Ion ("Jack") Popescu met with Wilhelm Filderman, the de facto leader of the Romanian Jewish community, and told him that he regretted the actions taken against the Jews of Romania and that he had had nothing to do with them, the decisions having come from General Vasiliu.[33]

However, in spite of all this, the general feeling in the Romanian bureaucracy was that deportation of the Jews from Walachia and Moldavia would begin soon. On September 23, the General Administration of the Romanian Railroads (CFR, or Căile Ferate Romane) informed Radu Lecca that it had been invited to take part in a conference to be held in Berlin on September 26 and 27 concerning the transport by train of Jews from Romania to Poland. Lecca's response, drafted on the following day, stated that, pursuant to an order from Ion Antonescu, the deportation plan must be drawn up in detail by the Ministry of the Interior (i.e., not by the CFR) and must reflect the guidelines set up by Mihai Antonescu.[34] On the day of the conference, therefore, the CFR cabled Berlin that it could not attend, asking for a postponement.[35] The conference took place anyway, without the Romanians and with the participants discussing "the transfer of 280,000 Romanian Jews to Belzec."[36] On September 27, the CFR complained to Lecca that it had indeed already written to the Interior Ministry and that the ministry had responded that it had no information and that the CFR should talk to Lecca himself about this matter.[37]

On October 10, the Office of the President of the Council of Ministers ordered the Ministry of the Interior to begin deporting all Jews from Transylvania and Banat, slating forty thousand people for transfer over the next few days. However, it was probably on the next day that Ion Antonescu canceled the order, citing concerns about the weather and indicating that the operation would have to be postponed until spring. Antonescu's decision came on the heels of a report by General Vasiliu, who offered the same reasoning. Vasiliu's report may have been influenced by the repeated interventions of Filderman and Dr. Stefan Antal, one of the leaders of the Jewish community of Banat.[38] According to the then chief rabbi of Romania, Rabbi Şafran, the pivotal reason for the delay may have been the interventions of Metropolitan Bălan and Nuncio Cassulo discussed earlier (allegedly supported by the Swiss and Swedish ambassadors); representatives of the International Committee of the Red Cross may have helped too.[39] Much later, on January 24, 1944, the Council of Ministers linked the decision to cancel the deportations to Cassulo.[40] Perhaps it was actually the intervention of all these parties that influenced Antonescu's decision.

Beyond the German-Romanian disagreements, there were definite signs of serious dissent between Lecca on the one hand and those like Popescu and Vasiliu in the Ministry of the Interior on the other. This does not mean that the bureaucracy was riven by factions supporting and opposing deportation of the Jews to the German extermination camps but only that the personal rivalries among the above-mentioned functionaries slowed down action on the planned deportations. Lecca, an opportunist who navigated between masters in Bucharest and Berlin while also pursuing his own interests, gave a strange version of the ultimate failure of the deportation: in jail after the war Lecca claimed that he had helped persuade Himmler to abandon the plan. According to Lecca, Mihai Antonescu had already given his verbal consent for the deportation but then regretted it and asked Lecca to help find a way out; Lecca went with Richter to Berlin, where they met with Himmler at an SS villa in Wannsee (after talking to RSHA officials Ernst Kaltenbrunner and Friedrich Suhr) and convinced him of the unacceptable disorganization of wartime economic life in southern Transylvania and Banat that would ensue from the deportation, thus winning him over to a six-month postponement.[41] Although Lecca's version is not completely improbable, there are some strange elements in his testimony. Lecca stated that he took his trip in the winter of 1943–1944, but as we have seen, it actually occurred in August 1942. His behavior during the trip did not resemble that of an opponent to the deportation plan. Furthermore, there is no known documentation of any meeting between him and Himmler.

The Germans were unhappy with the Romanians' lack of enthusiasm. But on October 22, 1942, Mihai Antonescu charged that "it was Germany that had been inconsistent: on the one hand the Germans had insisted on a 'resettlement' from Old Romania [Regat], while on the other hand they had opposed the deportations across the Bug."[42] Mihai Antonescu and Richter again discussed the topic on November 11. Antonescu's changed stance on the Jewish question was clear. He described in a diplomatic report what he told the Nazi official:

> I prefer to strike at the economic activity of the rich, rather than carry out massacres and engage in hostile acts against the poor. . . . The Hungarians are watching, photographing, and producing propaganda abroad against us about our so-called barbarism against the Jews. The abuses are not the work of the government, and I have already intervened three times to ensure that the Jews are treated in an orderly fashion. Some peripheral agencies have made mistakes and carried out abuses that must come to an end. In this regard I have ordered that clothes be sent to the Jews in Transnistria. . . . With regard to the treatment of the Jews I am not backing down, but I am not escalating either. I intend to adopt measures that will strengthen the good situation of the Romanian people, rather than undertake savage steps to fight against physical persons through useless barbaric acts. . . . I used this opportunity to talk to Mr. Richter about the problem of the Jews who have suffered severe circumstances . . . along the Bug.[43]

Sixteen months now separated Mihai Antonescu from his anti-Semitic statements and the orders of summer 1941. In his response Richter boasted about the system of "physical preservation" of the Jews deported to Poland and minimized the crimes of German units on the Bug. According to him, the murder of thousands was merely a security measure by those "defending the rear front."[44]

Now others started coming to the defense of the Jews: aside from the interventions already mentioned, several Romanian politicians spoke out, among them the leader of the National Peasant party, Nicolae Lupu, who had petitioned Antonescu the previous year and who was the politician who fought hardest on behalf of the Jews. Another National Peasant party leader, Iuliu Maniu, and the leader of the Liberal party, Constantin I. C. Brătianu, also sent memoranda to Antonescu seeking an end to the deportations. Both of these men, just like Ion Mihalache, another National Peasant leader, felt that the deportations had been carried out to please the Germans against "the humanitarian traditions" of the Romanian people.[45] Intellectuals protested too. According to an SSI report dated September 18, 1942, some of them sent King Michael a letter of protest. On October 7, another SSI note reported several intellectuals petitioning to free the Jewish poet Magnus Sperber: the poets Ion Pilat and Vasile Voiculescu, the critic Eugen Lovinescu, and the novelist Oskar Walter Cisek.[46]

As Aureliu Weiss, one of Maniu's assistants, wrote:

> The opposition of Marshal [Antonescu] to German demands [to deport the Jews of Regat] to which he had [earlier] consented . . . is explained less as an act of will and reflection than as one of proud independence and autocratic character. He did not like receiving orders; he liked giving them. He especially did not like . . . orders from abroad. Deep inside, he was offended, irritated, by German demands regarding "his" Jews. They had grown like weeds in the great garden of Romania. To uproot them from Romanian soil required local measures. . . . But why were the Germans meddling with the question of the Jews of Romania, which remained an internal matter?[47]

Thus Antonescu's pride, the fact that Hitler respected him and was willing to make certain concessions to him, the hesitating nature of the Romanian bureaucracy, internal and external interventions, and the unfavorable turn of the war were all factors that contributed to the cancellation of plans to deport the Jews from Moldavia and Walachia, and thus to the saving of nearly 300,000 lives. The path to moderation was soon confirmed by other developments, and now, as Carp observed, "the interministerial committee created as an organ of execution for deporting all the Jews from Romania began to involve itself in the repatriation of Jewish deportees."[48]

THE RETURN FROM TRANSNISTRIA

The selective repatriation of the Jews deported to Transnistria began only at the end of 1943. But individuals in the highest ranks of the Romanian bureaucracy had begun expressing signs of goodwill toward a few Jewish deportees as early as spring 1942. On May 22, the governors of Bessarabia, Bukovina, and Transnistria received a secret note from the Office of the President of the Council of Ministers specifying categories of Jews who could be released from the ghettos (but would have to remain in Transnistria), conditional only upon the consent of the concerned administrators and the ministers of the interior and justice. This list included:

- war invalids, their parents, and their children;
- war widows and orphans;
- parents of those killed in battle;
- those who fought in Romania's wars and were wounded or decorated for acts of bravery;
- former military personnel previously on active duty in the Romanian army;
- retired civil servants who had contributed actively to the state;
- Jews married to Christian women or men;
- Jews baptized before 1920;
- senior citizens older than seventy who could not take care of themselves and who had relatives in Romania; and
- special cases of meritorious men not included in any of the above categories, to be submitted for gubernatorial consideration.[49]

In May and June 1942, seven Jews from the camps of Moghilev and Djurin received permission to return to Bucharest, Vatra Dornei, and Rădăuți;[50] forty-eight were allowed to leave various ghettos of Transnistria.[51] It remains unclear whether such Jews were allowed to return to Walachia or Moldavia, however. And these selective reprieves were followed several days later by the deportation of thousands of Jews from Cernăuți and Dorohoi to Transnistria, despite pleas to Antonescu from Lupu and Antonescu's personal architect, Herman Clejan.[52]

The idea of a temporary repatriation from Transnistria of Walachian and Moldavian Jews appeared in a memorandum of Nandor Ghingold, president of the Central Jewish Office, that was sent to Ion Antonescu on

November 19, 1942,[53] suggesting that Romanian Jews be officially authorized to emigrate and that permission be granted to Jews from Transnistria to pass through Romania en route to another country in exchange for payment of taxes, to be funded in part by foreign Jewish organizations. At a meeting attended by various leaders of the Central Office and Wilhelm Filderman on November 22, Lecca seemed to approve of such a plan. On December 29, Lecca answered a request of the Ministries of Justice and Defense and of the Supreme General Staff for the deportation to Transnistria of eleven Jews who had avoided forced labor: "I consider that the Jews should be interned in labor camps in Romania rather than in Transnistria, because the Jews are going to be evacuated from that province."[54]

Discussions based on the idea that certain categories of Jews should be repatriated then started. These discussions especially affected the case of some five thousand orphaned children who had been living in Transnistria. On January 2, 1943, Filderman asked Ion and Mihai Antonescu to permit repatriation of these orphans, as well as that of widows, invalids, and war heroes. Filderman also asked that deportees from Dorohoi be repatriated, along with those who had applied in 1940 to go to the USSR.[55] On January 6 and 9, 1943, in the house of a certain Dr. A. Tester (according to Carp, a Gestapo agent) in Bucharest, Filderman and Lecca held a series of meetings. The main topic was permission for the orphans to emigrate to Palestine (by way of Romania, Bulgaria, and Turkey). Tester, a friend of Ambassador von Killinger, promised support if large "Jewish contributions" could be extorted.[56] Since the Jewish community proved unable to finance the orphans' emigration, however, Filderman next appealed to the British and American governments by way of Switzerland's Jewish community. An attorney, Constantin Bursan, was thus sent to Istanbul to get the approval of the Jewish Agency for Palestine (headquartered in Jerusalem).[57] We shall return to the fate of these children.

On January 19, 1943, Order No. 55347 and No. 21955 of the Ministry of the Interior established a committee to sort out the Jews deported to Transnistria's Vapniarka camp (the only one then functioning) and repatriate those who had been sent for "unjustifiable" reasons;[58] those Jews sent there as Communists were excepted.[59] At the same time officials began preparing to repatriate other categories of deportees: those who had petitioned to move to the Soviet Union in 1940, those whose names were found in the Soviet legation of Bucharest, and those deported by the army for avoiding forced labor.[60]

On March 16, the Vapniarka committee identified 554 inmates, 427 of whom were approved for release because "most of the files [on them] ... contained only extremely summary data, without material proof, and vaguely articulated suspicions."[61] Release did not mean repatriation, however, since the committee recommended that the Jews should remain in various ghettos in Transnistria.[62] On March 30, 1943, another sorting committee recommended that "218 inmates return to Romania; 29 inmates be released from the camp but remain in Transnistria; 116 remain in the camp [indefinitely]; and 11 inmates remain in the camp pending further review."[63]

Even though General Vasiliu proposed to repatriate 218 Jews from Vapniarka (among them decorated veterans),[64] the Transnistria Gendarmerie Inspectorate ordered on April 17 that those released must settle in Transnistria.[65] On May 1, Governor Alexianu ordered 427 Jews sent to Olgopol (100), Savrani (127), Trihǎti (200); they were transported under guard, and their new existence was often even harder than that at Vapniarka.[66]

The hesitation of various law enforcement agencies to enact such orders was confirmed on April 22, 1943, when Ion Antonescu proclaimed that Jews released from the camps "should no longer be allowed to return to Romania but, rather, are required to settle where they will in Transnistria."[67] Petitions by families for repatriation of relatives were refused by the Office of the President of the Council of Ministers.[68] However, Mihai Antonescu set a significant precedent when he attached the following resolution to one such petition on July 10: "In my opinion, the right thing to do is to repatriate him [the prisoner in question], since he is the son of a war invalid."[69]

Meanwhile, Tester and Filderman's talks about repatriating the orphans continued, focusing on how much to pay in taxes per child.[70] During a meeting with Filderman on April 7, Mihai Antonescu declared that the Romanian government would support the emigration of the Transnistrian orphans. He confirmed this in a statement to Chapuissat, vice president of the International Red Cross, on May 19.[71] Similarly, during another meeting of Filderman's, this one on August 4 with Vasiliu, the general reacted "cordially" to all of Filderman's requests, signing papers right there and giving orders by telephone. Filderman complained about the harsh food situation in the ghetto of Moghilev and about the situation of the Jews, mostly women and children, deported from Dorohoi, Dărăbani, and Herța, asserting that minors who had run away from forced labor had been executed.[72] The small bureaucratic steps the Ministry of the Interior took to repatriate certain categories of deportees stretched into the summer of 1943.

On August 11, the Ministry of the Interior asked for situation reports relating to the Jews deported to Transnistria from the General Inspectorate of the Gendarmerie, from the Odessa Gendarme Inspectorate, and from the Supreme General Staff of the Romanian army. The ministry was especially concerned about the 578 Jews deported in September 1942 for having requested repatriation to the USSR in 1940, but the search proved futile because all of them had been slaughtered upon arrival in Transnistria (the Odessa gendarmerie told the ministry it was "unable to find" them).[73] But also on August 11, Vasiliu refused to release from Transnistria the Jews of Arad, rhetorically asking his subordinates if they had been working improperly in 1941, when they approved the deportation of "innocent Jews," and in 1943, when they recommended their return[74]— Vasiliu spoke as if he himself was unaware that the Arad police had only been following orders from Bucharest over the years. On August 24, Vasiliu told Minister of Justice Ioan C. Marinescu that the categories of Jews eligible for repatriation included those born in Moldavia and Walachia, those who had requested repatriation to the USSR, and those deported for violation of the forced labor regime. Repatriation was not for deportees suspected of being Communists.[75]

On September 7, the Central Jewish Office drew up a request for repatriation of the following categories of Jews, which Ghingold conveyed to Lecca:

- orphans, widows, invalids, and medal recipients of the 1916–1918 war;
- Jews born in Dorohoi (deported as "collaborators" even though they had not been under the Soviet occupation, as had the Jews of Northern Bukovina and Bessarabia);
- Jews born in Moldavia and Walachia present in regions under deportation orders and unfairly swept up in them;

- retired or former civil servants;
- Jews deported in September 1942 (for "banned" political activity or for violating the forced labor laws); and
- orphaned children.[76]

In a report to Mihai Antonescu on September 23, Lecca further asked for the repatriation of the Jews born in Walachia and Moldavia and of those deported in September 1942. Subsequently, Mihai Antonescu approved the repatriation of orphans, widows, invalids, medal recipients, and retired or former state employees. Mihai Antonescu also demanded statistics pertaining to the Jews who had been deported in the fall of 1942 and decided that the Transnistria orphans should be brought to an orphanage in Odessa, from which they would emigrate with help from the Red Cross.[77] On September 16, the General Inspectorate of the Gendarmerie presented numerical data to the Ministry of the Interior on the Jews deported from Bessarabia and Bukovina, as well as the names of those evacuated from Moldavia and Walachia for having allegedly requested repatriation to the USSR or for other political reasons.[78]

On September 23, Vasiliu received Filderman again, boasting that mail service between the Jews in Romania and those in Transnistria was improving. Filderman was not satisfied and reiterated emphatically that the Jews of Dorohoi had to be repatriated, reminding Vasiliu that he had promised to support their cause.[79] On the same day Lecca suggested to the prime minister that Jews from Moldavia and Walachia be repatriated, those who had been deported in September 1942 selectively. Lecca proposed to concentrate the orphaned children so that they might benefit more quickly from aid by the Central Office,[80] and on October 3, Vasiliu expressed willingness to allow back all the Jews who had evaded forced labor, a crime once punishable by deportation with the perpetrator's entire family.[81]

On October 12, Filderman urged the government to go much further, demanding no less than repatriation of all Jews deported to Transnistria.[82] In his memorandum Filderman estimated that two-thirds of the deportees were dead and that others were on the verge of dying. Anticipating that many of the Jews would soon be brought back to Bessarabia and Bukovina to work for the war effort, Vasiliu recommended repatriation for the vast majority on November 10.[83] But the following categories of Jews were denied repatriation:

- those deported from the camp of Tîrgu Jiu (407);
- Jews active in the Communist movement and free at the time of deportation (554);
- Jews accused of communism and deported from Romanian penitentiaries (85); and
- Polish Jews who entered Bukovina clandestinely and were subsequently evacuated (unknown number).[84]

This response confirmed that as of September 1, only 50,741 of the 110,033 Jews (in actual fact, at least 123,000, possibly as many as 140,000) deported to Transnistria remained alive.[85] On the same day Ghingold and Filderman were called in to Ion Antonescu's office, where in the presence of General Vasiliu and Colonel Davidescu, they were told that Antonescu had decided to repatriate all deportees from Transnistria.[86] The Council of Order, the new state organ dealing with repatriation, shortly confirmed the decision. On November 13, Vasiliu told Filderman, "We have decided to repatriate all the Jews from Transnistria: those from Dorohoi to Dorohoi; those from Bukovina to the localities whence they had left; and those from Bessarabia and all orphans to Romania."[87] The Council of Order refused to repatriate only Polish Jews, Communists, and those deported on special orders.[88]

The plan was to begin with those who had made the mistake of being in Bessarabia or Bukovina at the time of the deportation, government retirees, invalids, war widows and orphans, Jews needed as professionals in particular regions, and all orphans less than twelve years old. The plan also included the repatriation of all the Jews of Dorohoi.[89]

General Vasiliu, Governor Dragalina of Bukovina, and Marshal Antonescu had a long discussion about the issue of repatriation on November 17. Their only decision, however, was that repatriation should not be hurried. While voicing his fear of new German massacres, Antonescu authorized only the return of Jews from Dorohoi and the gathering of most Jews of Transnistria at Vijniţa.[90] In spite of his own order of November 16 requiring the General Inspectorate of the Gendarmerie to repatriate all categories of Jews listed in his November 12 memorandum,[91] Vasiliu admitted to Filderman on November 30 that "we have not yet taken any definitive measures concerning the repatriation of the deportees. For now [Antonescu] proposes to repatriate [only] about 220 from the camp of Vapniarka and about 6,000 from the district of Dorohoi."[92] According to

Vasiliu, moreover, "the Vijniţa solution" was infeasible because there were only 220 dwellings there, many without doors or windows, which could shelter only 1,800, and that only after repairs.[93] However, two weeks earlier General Tobescu had outlined to Filderman a repatriation plan based on Vasiliu's report of November 12. The orphan category had been expanded to include all children under eighteen. Specific crossing points had also been established: Moghilev (for 45,000 people from the districts of Moghilev, Tulcin, and Jugastru), Rezina-Orhei (for about 18,000 people from Răbniţa, Balta, and Golta Districts), and Tiraspol-Tighina (for 5,000 from Ananiev, Berezovka, Duboşari, Oceakov, and Tiraspol).[94] Despite the fact that these plans had been radically trimmed back, the same crossing points were also mentioned in Lecca's November 20 report to Ion Antonescu. At this time Lecca estimated that 54,000 Romanian Jews deported from Bessarabia, Bukovina, Moldavia, and Walachia were still alive, as were another 20,000 native to the area:

- Jews from Dorohoi (approx. 5,600);
- Jews from Moldavia, Walachia, Transylvania, and Banat visiting Bessarabia or Bukovina during (or who had recently settled there before) the deportations (approx. 2,000);
- Jews from Moldavia, Walachia, Transylvania, and Banat deported in 1942 for suspicion of banned political activities (approx. 1,000);
- Jews from Northern Bukovina deported after the Soviets had been driven out (approx. 1,000);
- Jews from Southern Bukovina who had never been under Soviet occupation, but who were nevertheless evacuated with those from Northern Bukovina (approx. 12,000);
- deportees from Bessarabia (approx. 7,000 to 8,000); and
- orphaned and single-parent children (approx. 5,000).[95]

On December 8, 1943, the repatriation of the Dorohoi Jews (6,430 survivors), the 218 who had been interned at Vapniarka, and the 16 survivors of the group of 586 deported in fall 1942 for having requested immigration to the USSR was ordered.[96] From December 20 to 25, 6,107 Jews, mostly from Dorohoi, were transferred to Moldavia from Transnistria; 72 of them crossed the Dniester at Tiraspol-Tighina.[97] Among the repatriates 163 came from the Vapniarka camp, where successive review committees had ruled them innocent of any crime.[98] Also in December 5,263 crossed the Dniester at Atachi-Soroca.[99] Before reaching the crossing points, however, the deportees had to endure the last blows and surrender the last bribes.[100] Once at the river they were again deloused, struck with a horsewhip on their naked bodies (especially the women), and only then fed and loaded onto train cars.[101] According to a report of the Aid Committee of the Central Office of Romanian Jews, when the former deportees arrived at Dorohoi on December 26, 1943, two-thirds were "quite literally naked or dressed in rags,"[102] including the 130 orphaned children who were "almost completely naked and not fed."[103] After the former inmates of Vapniarka were sorted one more time, a new lot of 192 was repatriated on January 11, 1944.[104]

Despite this beginning, on January 27, 1944, Ion Antonescu called off further repatriation, arguing that one million Romanians in Transnistria, Bessarabia, and Bukovina should enjoy priority. "Welcoming Jews," he said, "would provoke a lot of resentment."[105] On February 6, Antonescu resuscitated his old policy of refusal to repatriate the Jews.[106] The following day Vasiliu limited the repatriation of orphans to those under fifteen. Despite Filderman's repeated requests to the Ministry of the Interior, children who had lost only one parent were not repatriated. On March 6, 1,846 orphaned children were repatriated, 1,400 crossing the Dniester at Moghilev-Atachi, another 446 at Tiraspol-Tighina. Both groups reunited in Iași, whence they were apportioned to Jewish communities in Moldavia and Walachia.[107]

On March 14, Antonescu reversed his decision to deny a general repatriation.[108] Interestingly, on that same day Mihai Antonescu sent a long telegram to Alexandru Cretzianu, the Romanian minister in Ankara, the best contact for talking to the Americans. While asserting that he had always supported emigration, Mihai Antonescu stressed that the Romanian government "stands against any physical solution or measure that implies severe individual constraints" and that "the Romanian people are tolerant and do not approve of crime as a political method."[109] In early March 1944, Ira Hirschmann, President Roosevelt's special representative and a member of the War Refugee Board, urged Cretzianu to persuade the Romanian government to return the Jewish deportees from Transnistria and permit Jewish orphans to emigrate to Palestine. Noting that the Romanian leaders might soon be killed by the Russians, Hirschmann underscored that his government should not have to reward Romanian leaders to get them to stop killing their own citizens; but he did promise Cretzianu and three members of his family U.S. passports if he could obtain a positive answer from Bucharest.[110] Cretzianu brought such an answer from Ion and Mihai Antonescu, and soon five ships were carrying about three thousand Jewish orphans to Palestine. According to Carp,

> Following Ion Antonescu's decision on March 14, 1944, to allow the return of all Jews from Transnistria, two repatriation committees belonging to the Centrala Evreilor [Central Office] left for Moghilev and Tiraspol. The first committee reached Atachi but could not organize any repatriation because of the Soviet offensive. The second committee, which went through Tiraspol, managed to reach Balta and brought back to the south of the province 2,518 deportees. . . . Most of them were allowed to go to their homes, but 563 of the former inmates at Vapniarka [suspected of communism] who transited through the Grosolovo ghetto were led under escort to Tîrgu Jiu [a camp in Walachia from which they would be liberated only in late August 1944].[111]

Officials repatriated 10,744 Romanian Jews from Transnistria at this time, including 1,846 orphaned children, approximately one-fifth of those surviving as of fall 1943. Amid the chaos following the German-Romanian retreat and the advance of the Red Army, some deportees managed to reach Romania on their own. According to the memorandum submitted by the Romanian delegation to the Paris Peace Conference in 1946, 22,300 deportees from Transnistria returned to Romania in the fall of 1944;[112] however, we know that the memorandum contained serious statistical errors. It asserted, for example, that in Romania, with few exceptions, compulsory labor had occurred under "tolerable conditions"; that only 1,528 Jews had died in Transnistria, to whom were added 3,750 from the remainder of the country (except northern Transylvania);[113] and that "it was never the intention of the Romanian government to give up protecting Romanian Jews living abroad."[114]

At that conference Gheorghe Tătărescu, the head of the Romanian delegation and also now the vice president of the Council of Ministers and the minister of foreign affairs, reminded—threatened, actually—Chief Rabbi Şafran, who could have contradicted the official version, that he remained a Romanian citizen and that they would meet again in Romania.[115] Lucreţiu Pătrăşcanu, the Communist minister of justice who organized the trial of Romanian war criminals, as well as a sophisticated intellectual who felt more affinity toward London and Washington than Moscow, admitted about the restitution of Jewish real estate confiscated by the Antonescu administration, "a period of four years has produced situations that cannot simply go away; for instance, with respect to Jewish tenants I admit that I am still unable to render justice."[116]

*   *   *

Doubts about when, whether, and how to deport the Jews of Regat delayed action on the question until late in the war. Complex considerations were entailed in this delay, though ideally for the Romanian fascists the entirety of Romanian Jewry should have been eliminated and though serious discussions of plans did take place. By the time the regime might have settled accounts with the Jews of Walachia, Moldavia, and the rest of Regat the growing probability of an Allied victory in the war stayed the hand of Antonescu's government. Similarly, multiple and complex considerations motivated the Romanian authorities in Transnistria to hold back from systematic and total mass murder. While numerous outright massacres punctuated the story of their sway over that land, they nonetheless kept a considerable portion of the Jews alive. When changing military circumstances forced a reconsideration of the previous anti-Semitic policies, the government (both in Transnistria and Bucharest) began to back down from its earlier posture. Nonetheless, this didn't happen all at one time but, rather, as a result of a series of dubious and contradictory half measures that brought hope to the Jewish population there only gradually. In neither place—Regat nor Transnistria—was the shape of things to come foreordained: it took the courage, resourcefulness, and ingenuity of the Jewish leadership, the Red Cross, the War Refugee Board, and of course the refugees themselves. A particularly crucial role in both stories was played by the most important wartime leader of Romanian Jewry, Wilhelm Filderman, though many others, such as Ira Hirschmann and René de Weck played crucial roles.

CHAPTER 9

The Fate of Romanian Jews Living Abroad

ROMANIAN FOREIGN POLICY reflected the fluctuating policies of the Romanian fascist leaders toward citizens of Jewish ancestry living abroad. In 1938–1939, the Goga-Cuza government and the royal dictatorship responded to international protests against their anti-Semitic policies with a diplomatic offensive, proposing emigration as the only solution to "the Jewish question." But the Legionnaire regime established on September 6, 1940, intensified anti-Semitic policy, including that toward Romanian Jews abroad. Passport renewals were denied for a wide range of reasons (not having paid military taxes, for instance), and return to Romania became more difficult. Sometimes Jews were flatly told not to come back, even when they had been expelled from other states, which led to protests by several governments.[1] On March 7, 1941, the Ministry of Foreign Affairs ordered Romanian consulates to stamp the word "Jew" on passports held by Romanian Jews.[2] At the urging of the Romanian consul general in Berlin, Constantin Karadja (who cited the need to assuage public opinion and "Jewish interests" in Great Britain and the United States), Marshal Antonescu rescinded this order but had the word "Jew" replaced with a special notation Romanian officials would recognize.

To simplify the situation somewhat, one could generalize that Romanian fascist policy on the issue went through two phases: during the first year of Romania's involvement in the war Romanian diplomats were to refuse to intervene on behalf of Romanian Jewish citizens abroad, including those threatened with being sent to Nazi concentration camps from Germany or countries occupied by or allied with Germany; after it became clear that the Axis countries would not prevail in the war Romanian diplomats were then told to protect Romanian Jews abroad from persecution. The motivations for the move toward extending diplomatic protection to Romanian Jewish citizens in other countries were knowledge that the leaders might be held accountable for their actions after the war was over and the fact that Hungary, Romania's traditional rival, did protect its Jews living in other countries. From the point of view of Romanian nationalists (and the fascists were in some ways traditional nationalists), why should Romania's Jews be considered any worse than Hungary's?

*   *   *

The Foreign Ministry suffered from the legal chaos emerging from the contradictory instructions of Romania's fascist governments. According to international convention, Romanian consulates were expected to protect Romanian citizens abroad, regardless of their "nationality." In May 1941, this protection was withdrawn from those Jews whose citizenship had been "revised," as well as from Jews born in Bessarabia and Northern Bukovina (then held by the USSR); in the summer of 1942, Romania backtracked and once again treated Jews born in Bessarabia and Bukovina as its citizens.[3] The expropriation of Jewish rural holdings, the expropriation of vessels belonging to Jews, and other related matters naturally led to a flurry of diplomatic protests. (A 1941 law stipulating that "foreigners could not dispose of any assets, rights, or interests they own in Romania, except with the prior approval of the Ministry of the Economy" also caused protests.[4] On August 29, 1941, this clause also had to be abrogated.)[5]

On August 31, 1941, the Foreign Ministry complained that while some states (e.g., France and Hungary) had introduced their own anti-Semitic measures, they had demanded that Romanian anti-Semitic measures not be applied to their Jewish citizens residing in Romania.[6] On September 23, Mihai Antonescu complained of this to the minister of the interior, writing:

In the course of the last year the minister of foreign affairs received repeated protests concerning the application to Jewish foreign nationals of the laws suspending the civil and political rights of Jews or expropriating some of their property.

After submitting this problem to discussion the Council of Ministers has decided that in applying the laws in question, the status of the foreign nationals should be respected without discrimination, on the basis of the conventions in force and of reciprocity.

Therefore, we ask you to please annul all measures against foreign Jews with respect to their property or their right to settle and exercise their profession—measures that derive from the laws applying to the Jews as such. . . . Please be so kind as not to undertake such measures in the future without prior notification of the Ministry of Foreign Affairs.[7]

Romanian diplomatic offices were soon instructed (in Circular No. 81/557 dated November 11, 1941) to protect "all Romanian citizens abroad without distinction and to report cases in which individuals or their property are subjected to discriminatory measures."[8]

Romanian diplomatic problems stemmed not only from "Romanization" of assets belonging to Jews of foreign citizenship but also from cases such as the disappearance of several American citizens during the pogrom of Iași and the deportation of other American citizens to Transnistria. In October 1942, the French legation intervened on behalf of Madeleine Wolloch, an eight-year-old French citizen deported to Transnistria while visiting relatives in Bukovina.[9]

Romania was also in violation of international agreements governing refugee issues. Thus in April 1942, (former) German, Czechoslovakian, or Austrian citizens in the city of Roman were expelled to Transnistria.[10] In certain instances Polish Jews who had sought refuge in Romania, as well as the Jews who held *Nansen* (refugee) or Chilean passports, were forced by local police to cross the border of Bukovina into Transnistria, there to be killed by the Germans.[11]

On November 30, Wilhelm Filderman interceded with General Vasiliu on behalf of such Polish refugees:

I told him that there were some foreigners who had been deported by mistake: Argentines and Poles, and so forth. He stopped—when I mentioned the Poles—and emphasized that the Jews often crossed the border illegally. I talked to him about the surgeon at Moghilev Hospital who had sought refuge after the collapse of Poland and who had been solicited by our officials to work . . . in a military hospital in Bessarabia, whence he had been deported. He replied that they [the Polish Jews] could be brought back, but they have to be sent across the borders, because Romania can't take all of them. Let each one meet his own destiny in his own country. . . . Concerning the matter of bringing around seven hundred Romanian Jews from France, he told me that he was opposed to it. I said that they were Romanian citizens with valid passports and that if the Germans wanted to deport them, Romania [had] to welcome them. He replied that he did not agree, because they had left [more than] ten years ago.[12]

In any event, as of November 14, 1943, there were more than five hundred Jewish refugees in Romania, most of them Polish but some German, Austrian, or Czech.[13] Thousands of Jews from Hungary and occupied Transylvania also sought refuge in Romania, especially in 1944. A December 1944 report from the Consular Section of the (postwar) Ministry of Foreign Affairs states that in 1944 the Romanian consulate in Budapest granted 51,537 transit visas (the author of that report could not say how many had actually been used).[14]

In January 1942, Romanian Jews in Amsterdam had had to declare their assets before the upcoming deportations. The Romanian consulate requested instructions on February 12 and learned that General Vasiliu opposed their repatriation.[15] In March Romanian citizens of Jewish ancestry in Germany and Austria were forced to wear the yellow star on orders of the Gestapo. This discriminatory measure applied to Croatian and Slovak (not to mention German and Austrian) Jews but not to Hungarian, Bulgarian, Turkish, Italian, or Swiss Jews. Furthermore, Romanian Jews in Berlin had to hand over furs, wool items, typewriters, bicycles, and cameras. The Romanian consulates in Berlin and Vienna, assured by German officials of the existence of an "agreement" between the Romanian and German governments, requested clarification from the Ministry of Foreign Affairs, which in turn requested the same from the German legation in Bucharest.[16] While this bureaucratic exchange continued, in occupied Bohemia and Moravia the first Jewish families with Romanian passports were interned at Theresienstadt.[17]

All these discriminatory measures offended the national pride of Romanian officials, especially since Hungarian Jews in occupied Europe enjoyed a privileged status compared to their Romanian counterparts. This convinced General Secretary Davidescu to telegram the Romanian consulate in Prague: "The Romanian government has never agreed to the adoption of discriminatory measures aimed at Romanian Jews. Please insist that they should be treated as the equals of Jews from Hungary, Switzerland, and so forth.... Please require the release of [those] interned or deported, with the exception of common criminals. Demand that sequestered assets be returned."[18] In Berlin legation counselor Văleanu made this point very clearly in a discussion with a German Foreign Office official, Kligenfuss, in July 1942,[19] as did Davidescu in a meeting with German legation counselor Steltzer in Bucharest on August 8, when the latter asserted that Ion Antonescu "had agreed with Ambassador von Killinger that Romanian citizens of Jewish ancestry in Germany and the occupied territories should be treated in the same fashion as German Jews."[20] However, as early as November 1941, von Killinger had told the Auswärtiges Amt (the Ministry of Foreign Affairs) that Antonescu approved of the Reich's intention to deport Romanian Jews under German jurisdiction to eastern ghettos together with German Jews; the Romanian government "had stated no interest in bringing Romanian Jews back to Romania."[21]

In the course of a discussion held on August 10, 1942, among Mihai Antonescu, Radu Lecca (the commissar for Jewish affairs), and Gustav Richter (Eichmann's representative in the German embassy) in Bucharest, the SS officer alluded to the approval Ion Antonescu had originally given to von Killinger. Mihai Antonescu's concluding remark was that

> we have to realize that Romania has no interest in seeing Romanian Jews who have settled abroad returning. Henceforth, the following instructions should be followed:
>
> 1. As regards German Jews living among us, the expired German passports should be canceled and replaced with provisional certificates. It should be made obligatory for real property to be declared and [the documents] kept strictly up to date.
> 2. With regard to Romanian Jews in Germany, in the Protectorate, and in the general government, as well as those in the occupied territories, word will be sent to the Berlin legation and the concerned consular offices that the measures to be undertaken have been agreed

upon with the Romanian government. The issue that interests us is
the real estate of Romanian nationals abroad, the administration of
this property, and the various means of liquidating it. The Berlin
legation and its subordinate consulate is asked to draw up a register.[22]

Romanian diplomatic interest had thus shifted to the assets of Romanian
Jews living abroad. One week later, on August 17, an internal memorandum from German Deputy Minister of Foreign Affairs Martin Luther cited
both Mihai Antonescu's agreement to the deportation of Jews from Moldavia and Walachia to concentration camps in Poland and the approval of
other Romanian officials for inclusion of Romanian Jews abroad in Germany's anti-Jewish measures.[23] Accordingly, on August 21, 1942, Davidescu telegrammed (No. 5120) the Romanian legation in Berlin that as
a consequence of the consensus between Marshal Antonescu and Ambassador von Killinger, earlier orders concerning protection of Romanian
Jews abroad were being revoked. Romanian diplomats were henceforth
forbidden to protest German measures against Romanian citizens of Jewish ancestry, their only concern being recovery of their assets.[24] The
Antonescu-Killinger conversation during which Antonescu agreed to
hand over to the Germans Romanian Jews living in Nazi-occupied Europe
had actually taken place sometime before July 23, 1942, when a ciphered
telegram from the Romanian Ministry of Foreign Affairs mentioned it for
the first time, without, however, making it the basis of policy.[25] Kligenfuss
had also sent Eichmann a communication (on August 20) containing the
gist of the discussion before the new policy formally went into effect.[26]

    The direct impact of the agreement, and of Mihai Antonescu's ex-
changes with Richter on August 10, 1941, was the deportation of nearly
1,600 Romanian citizens of Jewish ancestry living in Germany and Austria (the last statistics, for 1939, indicated 1,760, of whom 618 were in the
former Austria);[27] of an unknown number from occupied Bohemia and
Moravia, Poland, and Holland; and of 3,000 more from France. Most perished in concentration camps.[28] According to the September 1942 estimates of the Romanian chargé d'affaires in Berlin, M. Stănescu, most
Romanian-Jewish residents of Germany had already been deported.[29] On
October 15, 1942, all Romanian Jews in Prague were arrested.[30] The massive deportation of Romanian Jews from France began in late September
1942. (Deportations of Romanian Jews had taken place before that time
as well.)

As mentioned elsewhere, decrees in spring 1941 and again in summer 1942 (we do not know why the bureaucracy had to adopt the same policy twice) deprived Jews from Bessarabia and Northern Bukovina who were living abroad of their Romanian citizenship. This perhaps explains why some of the Romanian Jews born in Bessarabia and Bukovina appear as "Russian citizens" in the lists of Jews deported from Drancy, France. Without taking the latter into account and leaving aside "stateless" people born in Romania, more than three thousand Romanian citizens of Jewish ancestry were deported between March 27, 1942, when the first convoy with a Romanian Jew left France, and September 25, 1942, when the thirty-seventh convoy left, this time filled mostly with Romanian Jews.

"On September 24, at 10:50 in the morning, the Parisian police arrested 959 Romanian Jews; at 6:45 P.M. it detained 562 men, 829 women, and 183 children, or a total of 1,574 people."[31] Convoy number 37 of 1,000 people included 729 of them. At Kassel 175 of the men were selected for work details, another 40 at Auschwitz upon arrival on September 27 (and given numbers 66,030 through 66,069). Ninety-one women were also selected for work (numbers 20,914 through 21,003), but all the others were gassed. In 1945, only fifteen Jews from convoy number 37 were alive.[32] Ninety-eight children—63 bearing French and 35 bearing Romanian nationality—accompanied the 729 Romanian adults from convoy 37, all of the youngsters to be gassed along with most of the adults.[33]

On September 28, 1942, convoy number 38 carried nine hundred deportees, two-thirds of which left Paris. Among them, 594 were Romanian Jews. "The convoy arrived at Auschwitz on the night of September 29. One hundred twenty-three men were selected for work and received numbers 66,515 to 66,637. Forty-eight women were assigned numbers 21,373 through 21,420. Other men between the ages of seventeen and forty-five who were able to work were selected to do so before reaching Auschwitz. The remainder of the convoy was immediately gassed,[34] including sixty-seven children."[35] In 1945, only 18 people had survived from convoy 38.[36] The table on page 266 provides summary data pertaining to such deportations.

Serge Klarsfeld has estimated that about 3,300 Romanian Jews were deported from France to the Nazi extermination camps, 2,958 of whom were still Romanian citizens and the remaining 320 "stateless" Romanian Jews or individuals whose status was "unclear."[37] In 1943, the number of Romanian Jews being deported from France dropped sharply when the

Date	Convoy No.	No. of Romanian Jews Deported
June 2, 1942	2	90
June 22, 1942	3	56
July 19, 1942	7	28
July 20, 1942	8	34
July 22–August 21, 1942	9–22	17
August 24–September 11, 1942	23–31	33
September 14, 1942	32	40
September 18, 1942	34	18
September 24, 1942	37	729
September 28, 1942	38	594
November 4, 1942	40	76
November 6, 1942	42	72
November 11, 1942	45	59
February 9–11, 1942	46–47	109
March 2–25, 1943	49–53	71

Romanian government began extending diplomatic protection to them; by March it was almost nil. An RSHA order dated April 23, 1943, required the German police in Paris, one week later, to put an end to all deportations of Romanian Jews.[38] Indeed, in late 1942 (i.e., when Stalingrad made it increasingly clear to Romania's leaders that Germany could not win the war), German-Romanian relations underwent a cooling period. This frost came at a time, however, when Hitler continued to see in Antonescu a privileged interlocutor and ally, for both military and personal reasons. Hitler's stance, to a certain extent, inhibited the German Foreign Ministry from strongly expressing disagreements with the Romanians.

During a November 11, 1942, discussion with Richter, Mihai Antonescu (while stressing only his *economic* anti-Semitism) surprised the German official when he objected to the fact that along the Bug River Jews were being subjected to cruelties at the hands of the Germans. The Romanian said that he opposed these "acts of terror against defenseless people."[39] What worried him most, however, was Romania's image abroad, for the Hungarians were distributing propaganda about Romanian brutality against the Jews.[40] In spite of Lecca's refusal to allow repatriation of Romanian Jews stranded under German occupation, Romanian diplomats in Berlin, Vienna, and Vichy continued to protest. On April 6, 1943, Mihai Antonescu approved a request from Davidescu and Karadja at the Ministry of Foreign Affairs for permission to repatriate Romanian Jews from Germany, France, and other occupied countries, promising to agree to their subsequent deportation to Transnistria. They warned explicitly that, failing this, these Romanian citizens would die: "it is obvious that we are practicing a discriminatory treatment toward our non-Aryan citizens, in contrast with the treatment applied to Hungarian, Swedish, Swiss, and other Jews."[41] This report had been preceded by another, one Karadja signed on March 27, 1943, in which he insisted that in Germany, Hungarian Jews enjoyed preferential status by comparison with Romanian Jews:

> In view of this clearly discriminatory treatment of . . . "Romanian Jews" in comparison with Hungarian Jews, I have the honor to ask you if it would be proper to instruct our legation in Berlin to insist that our citizens of the Israelite race be given treatment identical to that of Jews from other countries and, in the first instance, to those of Hungary. If this matter is in our interest, we propose respectfully that it is treated with greatest urgency, promptly; otherwise, it will be too late.[42]

On March 25, 1943, a sweep of Romanian Jews in Vienna got under way,[43] and on April 6, a roundup of Croatian, Slovakian, and Romanian Jews began in Berlin; Hungarian, Bulgarian, and Swedish Jews went untouched.[44] With Mihai Antonescu's approval, the Romanian legation in Berlin began granting entry visas and requesting the German authorities to provide Romanian Jews the same treatment given to Hungarian Jews.[45] Moreover, on April 12, the Romanian legation requested that "the concerned German agencies, and especially the Geheime Staatspolizei [the Gestapo]," begin considering the release of non-Aryan Romanians arrested after March 31 and the departure of these individuals for Romania. Political considerations moved the Auswärtiges Amt to comply. On April 15, Lecca finally agreed to the return of Romanian Jews from all territories occupied by Germany, stipulating only that they must be transferred subsequently to Transnistria.[46] And on April 30, the Sicherheitsdienst (security service) asked all subordinate units to cease arresting Romanian Jews, though it did not order the release of those already detained.[47] Despite all of this, however, a number of Romanian Jews found themselves among two thousand of their coreligionists deported from Mechelen, Belgium.[48]

But the new approach of the Bucharest regime explains why, at the end of spring 1943, the German occupation authorities in France and Belgium stopped arresting Romanian Jews, twelve of whom were actually repatriated from Belgium.[49] In November 1943, the arrests of Romanian Jews in France did resume but only briefly; on November 8, the Romanian ambassador in Vichy affirmed that all arrests had ended, requiring all Romanian Jews to return to Romania by December 31.[50] On December 3, the same representative interceded with the German police chief in Lyon to cease interfering with repatriation.[51] Jean Ancel estimates that more than four thousand Romanian Jews in France survived as a result of such diplomatic interventions, several hundred being repatriated on a train that crossed Reich territory.[52] In fact, even though the repatriated Jews were supposed to be deported to Transnistria, Ion Antonescu consented to their remaining in Romania,[53] committing himself formally on July 20.[54] However, on November 15, 1943, General Vasiliu informed the Ministry of Foreign Affairs that the Council of Order (in charge of repatriation) had decided not to allow Romanian Jews from Germany and France to return to Romania.[55] In a memorandum sent to Mihai Antonescu on November 18, 1943, Karadja (apparently ignoring Ion Antonescu's decision not to interfere with the Germans' treatment of Romanian Jews) protested the Council's "interference in the affairs of the Ministry of Foreign Affairs."[56] Thus Mihai Antonescu, on December 17, 1943, and on behalf of the Ministry of Foreign Affairs, instructed the Ministry of the Interior to accept repatriated Romanian Jews from France, Greece, and Italy otherwise threatened with extermination.[57] Karadja subsequently gained Mihai Antonescu's acceptance for his new formulation of policy toward Romanian Jews living abroad:

1. The Jewish problem, one of the most difficult to resolve in Romania, to which the Jews have immigrated, especially after the union of Moldavia and Walachia, coming in compact masses from Poland and Ukraine, has undergone meticulous study by the royal government and will continue to be studied in the future.
2. Our traditional policy has always been tolerant. Over the course of the centuries generations of refugees, whether members of the Ro-

manian minority in Hungary and Bulgaria [or] Bulgarian, Greek, Armenian, Turkish, Ukrainian, and Jewish foreigners, have found asylum . . . in Moldavia and Walachia.

3. Having ascertained that Romanian citizens of the Israelite race settled or residing in Central Europe under German occupation are today threatened with the loss of property, freedom, and life in defiance of conventional rights, the royal government considers it only proper to bring them back to our country, whenever necessary and whenever the persons concerned desire it. . . .

4. These unfortunate people will thus find themselves forced, by non-Romanians, to leave their homes where they have long been settled. Having no emotional bonds with our people, and not even knowing the Romanian language, they will find, it is true, only a temporary asylum in Romania, where they will be treated well. Soon they themselves will realize that current conditions in Romania—independent of the wishes of the Romanian government—are hardly favorable for a long stay. [Therefore,] it may be safely predicted that the majority of these Jews will not be capable of making a livelihood and of leading worthy and honest lives in Romania.

5. That said, it would be in the interest of Romania and of those directly concerned that the Romanian Jews who arrive under these conditions be able to find, as soon as possible, a country for their final destination—that is, as far removed from Europe as possible—where they can live in peace by contributing through the qualities peculiar to them to the general progress of humanity.

6. The permanent duty of all Romanian diplomatic and consular agencies is to cooperate in reaching this goal, henceforth exploiting every opportunity to facilitate the emigration of Romanian Jews. . . .

7. The royal government, on the other hand, is entitled to receive more documentation about the Jewish problem than in the past. Diplomatic agents must report not only the cases where Romanian citizens have been injured in their rights or persecuted but also all legislative and administrative measures undertaken by foreign authorities at the expense of the Jews in general—or in their favor, especially when these measures could facilitate the immigration of "Romanian" Jews to the countries concerned.

8. The principles expounded here could also be applied just as they are by the Romanian propaganda abroad, in the event that the vice pres-

ident of the Council [of Ministers] would agree with this decision
and the theme could be developed in accordance with local conditions required by each country.[58]

Romanian consular initiatives aimed at the release of Romanian Jews
already in concentration camps ran up against the unequivocal refusal of
German officials. Releases from German concentration camps were extremely rare; in any case, most of the deportees had died a long time ago.
The German argument, as the Romanian ambassador in Berlin, General
Ion Gheorghe, learned, was that "internment of those specific individuals
by German officials took place with the consent of the Romanian government; on that basis, the internment of Jews was considered final."[59] Romanian bureaucrats, not all of whom were diplomats, nevertheless
continued to seek the release of Romanian Jews interned in Nazi concentration camps. On April 27, 1944, for instance, even Lecca sent a request
to the German Ministry of Foreign Affairs asking that Romanian Jews interned at Bleichauer and Auschwitz be repatriated.[60] Needless to say, such
attempts were fruitless.

*   *   *

The policy of the Antonescu regime toward the Romanian Jews in occupied Europe was determined by the personal involvement of both Ion and
Mihai Antonescu in changing Romanian foreign policy, in particular with
regard to the Western powers. Ion and Mihai Antonescu, first and foremost, are directly responsible for the deportation of the Romanian Jews
from Nazi-occupied Europe to concentration camps. Mihai Antonescu attempted to use the Romanian Jews as a bargaining chip. Later, especially
in 1943 and 1944, this resulted in Romanian consular offices extending
protection to surviving Romanian Jews abroad. Reports generated in the
Romanian Ministry of Foreign Affairs emphasizing that Hungarian Jews
in Central and Western Europe were being treated better than Romanian
Jews had an almost strangely powerful impact on the decisions of both
Antonescus in this regard. In any case, Romanian interventions in favor of
Romanian Jews in the Reich and in Nazi-occupied Europe were not motivated by humanitarian concerns but, rather, by opportunistic reasons or
considerations of national pride.

[CHAPTER 10]

Antonescu and the Jews

On MAY 6, 1946, during his postwar trial Ion Antonescu stated, "If the Jews of Romania are still alive, it is on account of Ion Antonescu."[1] This statement bears a grain of truth. The survival of the Jews from Walachia, Moldavia, and southern Transylvania stemmed from Antonescu's decision in the fall of 1942 to postpone indefinitely the deportation of Romanian Jews to Poland. However, Antonescu's responsibility is overwhelming with respect to the death of the Jews of Bessarabia, Bukovina, and Transnistria. The Jews of Romania and Transnistria thus owe both life and death to Antonescu.

* * *

Ion Antonescu's anti-Semitism did not prevent him from maintaining contacts with Jews, either before rising to power or after. Aureliu Weiss, a Jew who was an assistant to Iuliu Maniu (the National Peasant party leader), wrote after the war:

> I was personally acquainted with Antonescu in Predeal, where he had a villa on the mount of Cioplea. He was a general at that time. In 1935 and 1936, he used to come to the villa . . . that a friend of his, Mrs. Catargief, rented to me. The general had learned how to play bridge and played rounds with my wife and visitors at the villa. His irascible and impetuous temper forced me to be continually reserved. I avoided his presence. . . . An anti-Semite to the core, . . . he did nurture, however,

relationships with Jews. . . . One day in my absence, on the veranda of the villa where I stayed in Predeal, forgetting my wife's presence, he launched into an anti-Semitic diatribe against a humble [town] official who came to collect local taxes. At one point, realizing that my wife was present, he told him, as if he were making an excuse: "not all Jews are alike."[2]

Although Antonescu believed that "the *Jidani* are . . . the cause of all the misfortunes that have descended upon our country,"[3] this "not all Jews are alike" would be echoed in his anti-Semitic policies, especially with regard to exceptions for Jews who had acquired citizenship after the War of Independence of 1877, those who had been wounded and decorated in World War I, and their families.

But Ion Antonescu was dominated by his hatred of Jews and Judaism. On April 15, 1941, at a session of the Council of Ministers, Antonescu revealed his true feelings about the Jews: "I give the mob complete license to slaughter them. I withdraw to my fortress, and after the slaughter I restore order."[4] This was a fairly accurate vision of what took place in Iaşi shortly thereafter. In numerous instances Antonescu personally inspired specific anti-Semitic steps adopted by the Romanian fascist state. On June 19, 1941, for instance, Antonescu ordered the closure of all Jewish "Communist cafés" and the completion of regional lists of all "*Jidani*, Communist agents, and [Communist] sympathizers." The Ministry of the Interior was to prevent such elements from "circulating" and be prepared to "deal with them" when Antonescu ordered the ministry to do so.[5] On July 4, Antonescu asserted that "the Jewish people had embezzled and impoverished, speculated on and impeded the development of the Romanian people for several centuries; the need to free us from this plague is self-evident."[6] In spite of his innate sympathy toward pogroms, Ion Antonescu condemned such undisciplined acts, and on July 12, 1941, after the Iaşi pogrom, he condemned the soldiers who had taken part.[7] But this did not inhibit him from asserting that the Jews were "the open wound of Romanism," a people who "had robbed the bread from the poor." On September 6, he wrote in a letter to Mihai Antonescu that "everybody should understand that this is not a struggle with the Slavs but one with the Jews. It is a fight to the death. Either we will win and the world will purify itself, or they will win and we will become their slaves. . . . The war in general and the fight for Odessa especially have proven that Satan is the

Jew."[8] This was perhaps the justification for less ideologically and more materialistically motivated steps such as the October 3, 1941, Order No. 8507 (formally promulgated by Colonel Davidescu), in which the Romanian dictator ordered the National Bank of Romania to "exchange"—that is, confiscate—money and jewelry belonging to Jews about to be deported.[9]

In early October 1941, Colonel Gheorghe Petrescu of the Supreme General Staff and General Ion Topor of the gendarmerie initiated the deportation of the Jews from Bukovina at Antonescu's order. Petrescu declared in 1945 that they had received their orders from Colonel Radu Dinulescu in the Second Section of the Supreme General Staff;[10] this order, No. 6651 of October 4, 1941, also cited the decision of Marshal Antonescu that all Jews in Bukovina would have to be deported to Transnistria within ten days.[11] The governor of Bukovina, General Corneliu Calotescu, also confirmed that Petrescu and Topor had only been fulfilling Antonescu's instructions.[12]

On October 6, Antonescu explicitly told the Council of Ministers that he intended to permanently deport the Jews from Bessarabia and Bukovina.[13] On November 14, in another address to the Council of Ministers, Antonescu stated: "I have enough difficulties with those *Jidani* that I sent to the Bug. It is only me who knows how many died on the way."[14] Participants at the same meeting heard the following situation reports from General Voiculescu, governor of Bessarabia: "The *Jidani* don't exist anymore. There are one hundred sick Jews in the ghetto at the crossing point for the deportees from Bukovina."[15]

At the November 13, 1941, session of the Council of Ministers, Antonescu expressed interest in the repression of the Jews of Odessa then under way:

ANTONESCU: Has the repression been sufficiently severe?

ALEXIANU (governor of Transnistria): It has been, Marshal.

ANTONESCU: What do you mean by "sufficiently severe"? . . .

ALEXIANU: It was very severe, Marshal.

ANTONESCU: I said that for every dead Romanian, two hundred Jews [should die] and that for every Romanian wounded, one hundred Jews [should die]. Did you see to that?

ALEXIANU: The Jews of Odessa were executed and hung in the streets. . . .

> ANTONESCU: Do that, because I am the one who answers for the country
> and before history. [If the Jews of America don't like this,] let them
> come and settle the score with me.[16]

Nor did the Conducator overlook pettier cruelties. At that same session
Antonescu ordered that state pensioners among the deportees be deprived
of their pensions.

At the December 4, 1941, meeting of the Council of Ministers, Antonescu indicated his frustration that the Jews of Chişinău had been deported before they could be plundered. To correct this oversight, the Jews
were robbed by their escorts at the crossing points on the Dniester River
rather than by the state bank in the ghetto. In fact, Antonescu's demand for
a commission of inquiry on the matter was motivated by this very frustration, certainly not by any outrage at the abuses the Jews suffered. "Instead
of eating the bread of the Romanian country," he declared, "it is better that
they eat the bread of that region."[17] Observing at a Council of Ministers
meeting on December 16, 1941, that even Nazi Germany was slow in re-
solving "the Jewish question," Antonescu urged his lieutenants to hasten
Romania's solution to its side of the question: "Put them in the catacombs,
put them in the Black Sea. I don't want to hear anything. It does not matter if one hundred or one thousand die; [for all I care] they can all die."[18]

One of the most revealing indications of Antonescu's anti-Semitic
convictions is the letter he sent on October 20, 1942, to Liberal party
leader Constantin I. C. Brătianu shortly after canceling his decision to deport the Jews from southern Transylvania, Moldavia, and Walachia to occupied Poland. The letter is especially noteworthy because though it does
not deal directly with the Jewish question, it nonetheless conveys powerful xenophobic undercurrents in its frequent anti-Semitic discourse. Similar to prefascist Romanian anti-Semites of the nineteenth and twentieth
centuries, and much like Legionnaire and Nazi theoreticians, Antonescu
was obsessed with the interference of foreign powers in the defense of minorities in Romania and boasted about having put such interference to an
end: "The Romanian people are no longer subject to the servitude imposed by the Congress of Berlin in 1878, by the amendment of Article 7
of the constitution [granting Jews citizenship], nor to the humiliation imposed after the last war as concerns the minorities."[19] In particular Antonescu felt that as a result of the amendment of Article 7, "the country
has been Judaized, the Romanian economy compromised, just like our

country's purity."[20] Like Legionnaire ideologues, Antonescu believed the general corruption of Romanian political life resulted from "Pharisaic, Judaic, and Masonic" influence.[21] He cast himself as the savior of the Romanian nation after the proclamation of the "National Legionnaire State."[22]

By contrast, Antonescu accused Maniu of the National Peasant party of having been supported by Jewish newspapers.[23] He further accused his predecessors of having been brought to power by "the occult, Masonic, and Judaic lobby."[24] Antonescu faulted Brătianu for wavering in his nationalism: "You are a nationalist—at least it would seem so—and yet you side with the Jews you protest, like Mr. Maniu, against the Romanization measures I have just introduced."[25] According to Antonescu's vision, Germany had always been Romania's ally, and its external enemies were "the Jew from London"[26] and "the British, the Americans, and the Jews who dictated their terms for peace after the previous war."[27] The internal enemies, on the other hand, were "*Jidani,* Hungarians, and Reds,"[28] all of whom waited for the first signs of anarchy "to ignite trouble . . . to strike the final blow at our nation."[29]

Ion Antonescu's attitude toward the Jews alternated between violent hatred and pangs of patriarchal generosity. During the fall of 1941, for example, Antonescu claimed before the Council of Ministers that he was "fighting to cleanse Bessarabia and Bukovina of *Jidani* and Slavs";[30] but on September 8, 1941, in the presence of Nicolae Lupu and Mihai Antonescu, Wilhelm Filderman obtained Antonescu's promise to rescind the order for Jews to wear the Star of David throughout all of Romania, the permission for Jews to emigrate to Spain or Portugal, and a commitment to exempt from deportation the Jews of Moldavia and Walachia.[31] The next day Antonescu also asked the government to differentiate between "useful" and "useless" Jews, presumably to halt the persecution of at least some.[32] And yet one month later, in response to Filderman's appeal for clemency toward the Jews of Bessarabia and Bukovina, Antonescu issued a violent reply accusing the Jews in those two regions of having been the enemies of the Romanian people and justifying their deportation to Transnistria.[33] Published in the press, Antonescu's reply provided fodder for a savage anti-Semitic campaign, which cited Antonescu's "arguments" about "acts of barbarism" by the Jews in 1940 and 1941. The Ministry of Justice even launched an investigation into Antonescu's erstwhile guest!

On December 3, 1941, Lupu, who was sympathetic to the Jews, gave

Antonescu three memoranda concerning the judicial inquiry into Filderman, the repatriation of the Dorohoi deportees, and the repatriation of the deportees from Bessarabia and Bukovina. Antonescu refused to intervene on behalf of Filderman, claiming that he could not stop the course of justice. But he promised to issue instructions to repatriate the deportees from Bessarabia and Bukovina, provided that the UER guarantee (!) that the peasants would not kill them.[34] None of this, of course, prevented Antonescu's statement of December 16 quoted earlier—that he was not going to wait for the example to come from Germany but was going to proceed swiftly against the Jews, even if they should all die.[35]

Antonescu was directly responsible for, or complicit in, even the pettiest decisions on the persecution of the Jews. It was he who signed the April 1942 order (No. 462/CBBT) to deport the remaining 425 Jews of Bessarabia to Transnistria.[36] It was his decision to carry out the second deportation of Jews from Bukovina, formally enacted on May 28, 1942.[37] On August 31, 1942, Antonescu went over some late 1941 statistics indicating the presence in Romania of 375,422 Jews, 2.2 percent of the population; on his copy he wrote "a very large number." Where the text reported a remnant in Bessarabia of 6,900 Jews (3.4 percent of the 1930 number), Antonescu wrote: "Impossible! My order was to have all the Jews deported." When he saw the figure of 60,708 Jews in Bukovina at the time (1941), Antonescu noted again: "Impossible. Please verify. My order stated that only ten thousand Jews should remain in Bukovina. Please check. This is fantastic! Judaized cities, simply, purely Judaized."[38] (The figures for Cernăuți, Dorohoi, Botoșani, Iași, and Bacău had indeed risen by anywhere from 26 to 58 percent, but this was because of Antonescu's decision to move the Jews from rural areas to the towns.) Antonescu also resolved to publicize information "to show Romania to what extent its economic life has been compromised, threatened . . . owing to felonious Judaic and Masonic politicking." The Conducator swore that "if my legacy to the heirs of this regime reflects the same situation, I will have made this regime into an accomplice of a crime," and he promised that "in order to purify the nation . . . I will flatten all those who [attempt to] prevent me from carrying out the wish of the absolute majority."[39]

On October 12, 1942, Antonescu reassured the Central Office of Romanian Jews of his openness to moderation: "the better the Jews behave, the better they will be treated." He was even big enough to acknowledge that some good Jews "have paid dearly for the mistakes of some of their own" and that "these bastards [are] comparable only to some of our own bastards." Fully aware of the corruption of the Romanian bureaucracy in charge of the Jewish question, Antonescu even promised that if the Jews helped him identify Romanians who had blackmailed them, "they can rest assured, I will not spare them [the corrupt officials]." But Jews who were reprehensible, he warned, would not be spared either.[40]

In 1943, Antonescu's mood swings continued. On the one hand he still declared that he tolerated those Jews who might deserve partial protection by the Romanian state; on the other he demanded his subordinates to display stern behavior toward the Jews. In a letter written to his architect, Herman Clejan, on February 6, Antonescu stated that the Jews "only display hostility and bad faith toward the Romanian state" and that the state in turn was "only defending and continuing to defend itself against the Jews' perfidy."[41] Antonescu nevertheless decided that those Jews who had been settled in Romania before 1914 and those who had "participated sincerely . . . in the interests of the Romanian state" should enjoy the possibility of living in Romania, though "based on the criteria of proportionality."[42] Antonescu also promised to protect Jews who had "served the country on the battlefield or in other areas of public life."[43] But, according to him, those who had come after 1914 (i.e., those from Bessarabia, Northern Bukovina, and beyond the Dniester) had

> accumulated wealth in dishonest ways, through corruption, looting of the public treasury, exploitation, and [taking advantage of] the poverty of Romanians; through fueling disorder and encouraging activities that were noxious to the interests of the Romanian people. [These Jews] from Bessarabia, Northern Bukovina, and beyond the Dniester will be struck without pity and kicked out of the country. They do not have the right to seek humanitarian sympathy because humanitarianism should not mean weakness [on our part]. After having repaid with hostility and crimes the limitless tolerance they have enjoyed in Romania, where their prosperity defied even their own dreams, these Jews no longer have any right to human understanding. They [should] only receive their just deserts for their ill deeds. . . . All those who support them will suffer the same fate.[44]

On April 30, 1943, Filderman argued again on behalf of Jews in Romania, contrasting the tolerance those in Finland enjoyed. This seems to have made an impression on Antonescu, who told General Vasiliu, "If that is the case in Finland, let's leave [the Jews of Regat] alone here."[45] Six months later, on October 30, Antonescu declared that he was "happy" with the results obtained from Romanizing trade in Moldavia: "all trade in Moldavia, Dorohoi, [and] right up to Focşani must be Romanized in a civilized fashion."[46] On November 17, Antonescu betrayed anxiety over the fate of the Jews in Transnistria—but only once it appeared that he might end up bearing responsibility for the murders committed by the Germans there. He no longer spoke of sending the Jews "beyond the Urals," but he did speak of a reservation for them in Vijniţa:

> We want to establish a large sanatorium in Vijniţa. There is [also] a major Jewish center there that was dissolved long ago. There too we will bring many Jews. Regarding the Jews who are in danger of being murdered by the Germans, you have to take measures and warn the Germans that I will not tolerate this, because in the last analysis I will gain a bad reputation for these terrible murders. Instead of letting this happen, we will take them away and bring them into [Vijniţa]. There they will be organized securely in a camp, so that we can fill up Bukovina again. They should be organized for labor service there. We will pay them. Until they are organized, however, they will be supplied by the Jewish community. I have just talked with Mr. Lecca, and I told him he should call those from the Jewish community—he says he has already collected 160 million lei [over 2.5 million reichsmarks, or slightly over $1 million]—in order that clothing and foodstuffs become available. At the same time the foreign countries should be informed, so that foodstuffs may be sent from there too—just like the shipments to the American prisoners of war—and from Switzerland, and clothing, because I will not take anything from supplies allocated for the Romanian soldier, worker, and civil servant to clothe the Jews.[47]

The reluctance of Antonescu and the Romanians to be blamed for the behavior of their allies is reflected in the following dialogue on the issue of German atrocities, which took place between Marshal Antonescu and General Vasiliu during a cabinet meeting of November 17, 1943:

> ANTONESCU: I was told that Jews in Golta had been murdered [by the Germans].
> VASILIU: That is not true, Marshal.

ANTONESCU: Regardless, the Germans must be warned that I will not tolerate these murders.

VASILIU: The Germans have only taken several columns of Jews and led them across the Bug.

ANTONESCU: Please notify the German intelligence services that I will not tolerate these murders.

VASILIU: You want to send those sixty thousand Jews to Vijniţa?

ANTONESCU: That is impossible because there is not enough room for all of them there. The ones in the villages will have to remain where they are until the front stabilizes.

VASILIU: We have to clear up Moghilev District, where there are 39,000 Jews, then Balta, which has 10,000. Tulcin and Iampol contain just as many.

ANTONESCU: Clear up Moghilev and place the Jews in Vijniţa.

VASILIU: We will return to Dorohoi the ones who came from there.

ANTONESCU: The ones from Regat who were mistakenly expelled will be brought back home.[48]

Documents originating from the military office of Ion Antonescu show that during 1943 he was often informed by high-ranking members of his administration about the fate of Jewish and Gypsy deportees in Transnistria. For example, a report dated May 20 emphasized the terrible conditions of the Jews interned in Mostovoi ("dirty, without clothes, very thin") and the fact that the Gypsies from Berezovka kept their dead in their houses in order to receive their food allowance.[49] Several additional reports moved Antonescu to decide on June 3, 1943, to decrease the number of inmates in the Berşad ghetto (8,061 internees); to reorganize the Vapniarka concentration camp; to relocate the Gypsies outside the villages, where they could cultivate land; and in general to improve sanitary conditions in the camps and ghettos.[50]

In a speech to Romanian soldiers on January 1, 1944, Antonescu struck a new tone:

Your deeds in the occupied lands and wherever you have been have been marked by humanity. . . . Man to us is a human being, regardless of the nation he belongs to and the evil that he may have caused. All those whom we have encountered on our journey we have helped and protected as no one else would. The children have been cared for like our own; the old people as if they were our own. . . . We have deported no one, and you have never driven the dagger into the chest of anyone. In our jails there are no innocent people. The religious beliefs of all and everyone's political creeds have been respected. We have not uprooted their communities . . . or families for our own political or national interests.[51]

But in a private letter to Clejan dated February 4, 1944, Antonescu demonstrated again how virulent his anti-Semitic tendencies still were. He justified anew the deportations, regretting only that they had not removed all the Jews from the affected regions. He acknowledged that he had refused to repatriate the surviving Jews—"the enemies" of the Romanian nation—but at the same time he claimed that he would not tolerate their abuse:

> Mr. Clejan,
>
> Concerning your letter about the fate of the Jews in Transnistria and those of the Bug, and about the compulsory labor exemption fees, allow me to broach anew some issues that relate to the Jewish question in Romania in terms of reality, results of war, and the events that preceded it.
>
> As I have told you in person, I was forced to plan the evacuation of the Jews from Bessarabia and Bukovina because of their terrible behavior during the occupation . . . by the Russians; the population was so angry toward them that otherwise the most horrible pogroms would have occurred. Even though I decided to evacuate all the Jews, . . . various intercessions and initiatives prevented it. I regret today that I did not do it because . . . the largest number of enemies of this country is recruited among the Jews who remained there. There is no terrorist or Communist organization that does not have Jews in it, and often they are exclusively made up of Jews. . . .
>
> Under these circumstances, it is morally and politically inconceivable . . . to return the Jews from Transnistria. . . . But I will give the order to allow them to stay away from the front line and to settle them in southern Transnistria, where the Jewish community, with help from abroad, can assist them in leaving the country. Among those [already] repatriated are those who had been mistakenly deported— 7,000 Jews from Dorohoi and 4,500 orphaned children. . . . As a man with a European outlook, I have never tolerated . . . crimes against persons and will continue to take measures so that they will not happen to the Jews.[52]

As he did in 1941, Antonescu here argued that the Jews from Bessarabia and Bukovina had been deported to protect them from pogroms, an idea that he reiterated at his postwar trial. True, on April 22, 1944, during a Council of Ministers session Antonescu did reconsider repatriation from Transnistria, but only if returnees would be confined to specific towns; he actually toyed with the idea of ghettos, but he rejected any full repatriation to Romania.

> It would be a solution to transfer them . . . to certain towns, if they return in large numbers—to settle them as in Buhuşi, in one or two towns, to resettle all the Romanians and allow the Jews to live together. All we would have to do is to send them supplies. . . . They will work for one another, sew, do carpentry, and so forth. That is one solution. Another solution is to bring them together into ghettos inside each city. We would tell them: "This is where you will live; do not leave. We will bring you food, do what you wish; we will not kill you, we will not harm you." The third solution is to bring them back to Romania. This is the most dangerous one . . . for the Romanian people. I cannot order their return; . . . people would stone me to death.[53]

Whatever his idealized goals of allowing the deportees to move away from the front or of concentrating them in places from which the Anglo-American Jewish community might evacuate them after the war, Ion Antonescu was soon mobilizing the young Jewish men into labor detachments for work on roads and rail lines among prisoners and new conscripts. This was not simple necessity, and Antonescu insisted that doctors, engineers, and professors not be left out. He urged the Council of Ministers to take action lest the Jews "spread throughout the country."[54]

*   *   *

At his trial Ion Antonescu assumed responsibility for all the mistakes and distortions of orders by his subordinates, though not for the outright crimes and plundering some had perpetrated.[55] At the beginning of the war Antonescu had believed that he would be able to resolve "the Jewish question" once and for all, as well as that of the other minorities (Ukrainians in particular). He was a harsh, even violent anti-Semite. But a comparison to Adolf Hitler, whom he admired and who admired him, shows him in a different light. A direct or indirect dialogue between the German dictator and the leader of the Jewish community in Germany would have been in-conceivable. In spite of his apparent inflexibility, though, Antonescu tol-erated, even encouraged, contact with minority leaders in his own country and with the Allies (in Cairo and Stockholm), which suggests that he had a more realistic assessment of the overall chances of winning the war. After the end of 1942, he had imagined, like many other Romanian politi-cians, that the Romanian Jews could be used as capital to improve Roma-nia's position with regard to the United States and England. But this does not mean that the decision not to deport the Jews from southern Transyl-vania, Moldavia, and Walachia to Nazi camps in occupied Poland was strictly opportunistic. In all likelihood, numerous appeals, including Met-ropolitan Bălan's, the ones from the royal family, and others from various diplomatic corps, played a significant role. While acknowledging that "bloody repression"[56] had occurred under Romanian aegis during the war, Antonescu nevertheless declared that under his authority, there had been no massacres: "I passed a lot of repressive laws, [but] we did not execute a single Jew. . . . I gave orders for reprisals, not for perpetrating mas-sacres."[57]

More than any appeal, however, Antonescu's national pride counted heavily in his restraint. It was not up to the Germans to decide what to do with "his" Jews. Antonescu was concerned about Romania's image abroad. Reports from the Ministry of Foreign Affairs indicating that Ro-manian Jews under Nazi occupation were treated worse than Hungarian Jews annoyed Antonescu. His position of relative equality with Hitler had commanded the respect of Nazi dignitaries and the German embassy. At a certain point even Himmler gave up and intended in 1943 to order the withdrawal of his murdering bureaucrats from Romania, having lost all hope of collaboration in the destruction of Romania's Jews (we don't know if he recalled Richter, but Richter ended up in Moscow's Lubianka Prison in 1945, suggesting that he failed to clear out before the Romani-ans changed sides).

Even though he shared many ideas with the Legionnaires, Antonescu was not an adventurer in the economic arena. Politically, he placed him-self between Goga and Codreanu. He nurtured an obsession with a Ro-mania purged of minorities, who represented a "danger" to the state, especially in territories that had been reallocated to Romania after World War I. Antonescu's anti-Semitism was economic, political, and social, but it did not bear the mystical and religious aspects of Legionnaire anti-Semitism. His hatred was not that of the middle-class man, armed with a truncheon; rather, it was that of the bureaucrat, pretending to resolve a problem in a fundamental, reasonable, and nuanced fashion, by law. The fate of the Jews might have been different had the Legionnaire government lasted longer; the Legionnaires would certainly have been more closely aligned with Germany.

*   *   *

In contrast with Ion Antonescu, his distant relative Mihai Antonescu was an opportunist in the most concrete meaning of the word. During a 1928 student congress, which the Legionnaires dominated, members of the Legion of the Archangel Michael (later renamed the Iron Guard) ravaged synagogues and stores in Oradea, beating Jews in the streets: in *Cuvîntul Nostru* Mihai Antonescu criticized them for presenting a negative image of Romania to the world. A true Christian movement, he argued, would not behave in this manner.[58] In 1937, Mihai Antonescu told the Jewish National Peasant party member Aureliu Weiss that he was writing an anti-Nazi booklet. But by the summer of 1938, when victory on the side of fascism and anti-Semitism seemed more certain, "the pamphlet had turned into an apology for the Führer." The turn in the course of the war and the Allies' capture of the initiative moved an opportunist Antonescu to attempt to attenuate Romanian anti-Semitic policy.[59] Indeed, as early as the fall of 1941, German intelligence had come to suspect Mihai Antonescu of duplicity. Ambassador von Killinger noted at a press conference that Mihai "once wrote a book against us" (perhaps the 1937 booklet?), although he reasoned that "the Führer trusts the marshal, and Mihai Antonescu has the marshal's confidence. He has the right to choose those collaborators he feels are best suited."[60]

None of this means that Mihai Antonescu ever hesitated to carry out the violent anti-Semitic policies of his regime in 1941. He ordered the military and civilian administrations of Bessarabia and Bukovina to be merciless toward the Jews, asking Himmler to send an aide to Bucharest to coordinate Romanian anti-Jewish policies with Germany's. But in the fall of 1942, Mihai Antonescu was explaining to Richter that he preferred "economic measures" to "useless acts of barbarism"; he also demanded an end to "the severe regime" the Germans had imposed on Romanian Jews across the Bug. Later he declared that he intended to allow Romanian Jews to emigrate to Palestine.[61]

As head of the Ministry of Foreign Affairs Mihai Antonescu did generate administrative precedents for improving the Romanian Jews' chances of survival abroad. The closer the end of the war came, the more moderate Mihai Antonescu's anti-Semitism sounded. By the time he met with Chief Rabbi Alexandru Şafran, according to the rabbi, "Mihai Antonescu received me with great honor and shook my hand, saying that he was truly happy to see me."[62] On June 9, 1944, a committee that included Mihai Antonescu, Radu Lecca, and Generals Popescu, Vasiliu (Interior Ministry), and Şova (navy) assembled on Ion Antonescu's orders to consider easing Jewish emigration from Romania. The committee stressed that the Romanian government would resist German pressure to place the Jews in Romania under German control, that emigration had not thus far been possible because of the lack of international cooperation, and that Romania could not spare the ships necessary for emigration due to the war.[63] Thus did the committee exculpate Romania for its own anti-Semitism by blaming the rest of the world and the war itself.

On June 27, the prime minister received through the Romanian legation in Switzerland a note from the American government placing direct responsibility on the governments of Bulgaria, Hungary, and Romania for persecution of the Jews—both citizens and refugees—committed within their borders.[64] On July 20, a worried Mihai Antonescu telegrammed Bern, outlining "specific measures recently taken by the Romanian government . . . such as granting permission to four thousand Jews to practice their professions, assistance to Jews previously deported to Transnistria, repatriations from Transnistria with the help of the Romanian Red Cross, the release of Jews in trouble with the law like the Zionist leaders Josef Fisher and Mişu Benvenisti, and the emigration of thousands of Jews in 1944, among them escapees from Hungary."[65] During his trial Mihai Antonescu contended that the deportations of the Jewish population from Bessarabia and Bukovina had not borne a "racial" character and that the massacres there and in Transnistria "should be viewed as individual acts" carried out by the gendarmes.[66]

The same stance was adopted by the former undersecretary of state for Romanization, Titus Dragoş, at his postwar trial, where he declared that "I did not conceive, I could not have conceived, such a racially motivated law, and all laws that I recommended were aimed at softening the Jews' situation following the suggestion made by the regime and the approach that Marshal Antonescu intended to pursue."[67] This approach was shared by other high-ranking civil servants in the Romanian state charged with crimes against the Jews and Gypsies, though there were exceptions. One of them was General Vasiliu, who, in spite of his desire to evade responsibility, admitted his complicity in the deportation of the Gypsies.[68] (This deportation had been ordered by Ion Antonescu, who assumed full responsibility for it.)[69]

Radu Lecca, director of the wartime Office for Jewish Problems, had coordinated contacts with the Central Office of Romanian Jews. Former correspondent for *Völkisher Beobachter,* this onetime diplomat was certainly a German agent. In his capacity as director, Lecca met Eichmann at least once in Berlin.[70] According to a member of the Jewish community in Iaşi who knew him well, Lecca "was an anti-Semite, but he had a thirst for money; he was ready to do anything for money, for a nice drink and a beautiful woman. Whatever he did, he did out of greed, not out of conviction."[71] Various sources confirm the fact that Lecca did not hesitate to demand from Jewish interlocutors large sums of money or other favors. At the time of his arrest on November 15, 1944, according to his indictment, two thousand gold pieces and sixty gold watches were discovered in his apartment. Lecca denied owning so many watches but did concede owning both a gold ingot weighing twelve and one-half kilograms and forty thousand francs in gold.[72]

Lecca's chief of staff was Vasile Isăceanu, former member of the Christian National Defense League, a group that behaved extremely brutally against the Jews. Isăceanu's behavior certainly reflected the spirit that Lecca fostered in his office. One day after having sent away Chief Rabbi Şafran, who had come to request a meeting with Lecca, Isăceanu reported: "a bearded *Jidan* wearing a large hat came to me and asked to speak to the minister, Mr. Lecca. I sent him to hell telling him that no piece-of-shit *Jidan* could even dare bother the minister. I took him by the collar and threw him out."[73] Lecca himself had no compunction about victimizing the Jews: he requested and received millions of lei from the Jewish community of Iaşi, for example, at least part of which he kept for himself. The following account of an encounter between him and Avram Haham, president of the Departmental Office of the Jewish Committee of Iaşi, suggests the gist of his attitude:

He [Lecca] told me [Haham] that he was having a meal with von
Killinger and three German generals and would need an exceptional
wine. He led me to his cellar and showed me a collection of about two
thousand wine bottles.

LECCA: I want something really special. I heard that in Stefan cel Mare
   Street there is a Jewish bar owner who has an amazing wine from
   Cotnari.
HAHAM: I know what you are talking about, Minister, but he was killed
   during the pogrom.
LECCA: What a pity, he sold such good wines.

Later on, when Haham returned from Iași with some wine, a similar conversation further illustrating Lecca's greed ensued:

LECCA: This is truly a rare wine. How many bottles did you bring?
HAHAM: Only ten.
LECCA: What a pity! Bring me some more.[74]

Haham further recalled that in April 1944, when he requested a military
permit to transport nine hundred children from Transnistria in twenty
trucks from Iași to Constanța, Lecca told him: "I grant you this permit, but
in two of those [trucks] you must bring from Iași my brother-in-law's furniture."[75]

Always in exchange for something, then, Lecca granted other favors
such as the cancellation of plans to establish a ghetto in Iași. This particular decision was reached during a meeting with the first lady, Maria Antonescu, at her office (she was the president of Comisia de Patronaj
[Patronage Society], an official philanthropic association). Having received the sum of five million lei from Iași's Jewish community via
Haham, Lecca handed it over to the first lady's society for cessation of the
ghetto. (Lecca certainly received some cash award himself for his part in
the transaction.) Maria Antonescu did not always reveal herself to be so
compassionate, however: "on a hot day in August, men, women, and children destined for expulsion were assembled in Macabi Square in
Cernăuți," Rabbi Șafran recalled. "That same day I went to see her—for
she directed the state's charitable institutions—to implore her to telephone
instructions to the charitable Christian women of the capital of Bukovina
for water and milk for the children until their fate should be settled. . . .
She refused to respond."[76]

* * *

The trials of the Romanian war criminals began in 1945 and ended in 1952. On January 21, 1945, Law 50 pertaining to the punishment of war criminals was drafted by Lucrețiu Pătrășcanu, Communist minister of justice, and was signed by King Michael. Four of the accused were executed in Romania: Ion Antonescu, Mihai Antonescu, C. Z. Vasiliu, and Gheorghe Alexianu. In dozens of cases civil servants and high-ranking officers had death sentences commuted. For instance, on June 1, 1945, Pătrășcanu successfully requested that the king commute the capital punishment for twenty-nine of the accused in the first trial of war criminals.[77] Hundreds of officers and high-ranking officials were sentenced to life or lengthy prison terms. Hundreds of noncommissioned officers, gendarmes, and enlisted men were also sentenced to prison terms or hard labor. All who did not die in prison were released between 1958 and 1962. The publicity surrounding the first trials permitted the Communist party to propagandize against its political enemies. But as the Romanian Communist party tightened its grip on power, this publicity diminished and eventually vanished completely.

In actuality, the postwar regime went easy on the mass of genocidal anti-Semites, condemning them to relatively minor sentences and often granting early amnesties. In the future the regime tacitly tolerated anti-Semitism, thereby indicating that it didn't regard it as a major sin, as long as people didn't make it an open rallying principle. And by quietly allowing the culpability of leading politicians and intellectuals of the prewar and wartime generation to be forgotten, the Communist regime in effect buried the crimes of its predecessor. Indeed, under Nicolae Ceausescu the regime openly and aggressively fostered a revival of Romanian nationalism, a nationalism that has continued to flourish since his regime's overthrow.

In extreme nationalist circles today an attempt is under way to restore to Ion Antonescu a place of honor in Romanian history as a great patriot. But whether the marshal loved his country is not the point: the point is that he was a war criminal in the purest definition of the term. His leadership involved the country's government in crimes against humanity unrivaled in Romania's sometimes glorious, sometimes cruel, history; perhaps more ironically, this leadership's war against a defenseless and innocent civilian population was only part of a broader folly involving the country in a conflict promising only illusory gains but actually bringing very definite, catastrophic consequences. A modern Romanian patriotism must not only reject the legacy of five decades of Communist misrule but also years of fascist tyranny if it is to be able to recount and take an honest pride in Romania's history.

[CHAPTER 11]

A Summing Up

In 1930, Romania had been home to 756,000 Jews. At the end of World War II about 375,000 of them had survived. As a consequence of the wartime changes in borders, 150,000 of the original population ended up under Hungarian sovereignty in northern Transylvania, deported in 1944 to concentration camps and extermination centers in the Greater Reich; nearly all of these—130,000—perished before the war's end.

We may never have a full statistical picture of the human carnage caused by the Holocaust in Romania. More than 45,000 Jews—probably closer to 60,000—were killed in Bessarabia and Bukovina by Romanian and German troops in 1941. At least 75,000 of the deported Romanian Jews died as a result of the expulsions to Transnistria. During the postwar trial of Romanian war criminals, Wilhelm Filderman declared that at least 150,000 Bessarabian and Bukovinan Jews, both those deported and those who remained, died under the Antonescu regime; Mişu Benvenisti estimated 270,000,[1] a number also reached by Raul Hilberg.[2] In Transnistria at least 130,000 indigenous Jews were liquidated (especially in Odessa and in the districts of Golta and Berezovka). In all, at least 250,000 Jews under Romanian jurisdiction died, either on the explicit orders of Romanian officials or as a result of their criminal barbarity. As shown throughout, sometimes Romanian officials worked with German help, but more often they required no outside guidance. Those Gypsies who were deported seem to have suffered a higher proportion of deaths than did the deported Jews: of 25,000 sent to Transnistria, only 6,000 ever returned; but these 25,000 were indeed a tiny portion of the original population of 1,000,000 Gypsies living in Romania.

The story of Romanian Jewry's near destruction during World War II is filled with paradoxes. The victims of the Legionnaire pogroms of January 1941 amounted to a numerically small portion of those against whom crimes were committed by the Romanian army and gendarmerie later. But mass murder represented an ideological victory for the Legionnaires and resulted in considerable part from long years of Legionnaire propaganda, the realization of Iron Guard dreams. The irony was that the Guard had been banned by the time most of the killing took place. It would nonetheless have rejoiced to learn that a nonpareil historian like Hilberg would one day write that "no country, besides Germany, was involved in massacres of Jews on such a scale."[3]

As in Hungary in 1941 and Bulgaria in 1942, so in Romania was anti-Jewish discrimination compounded by geography. Jews were killed first and foremost in territories over which neighbors fought. In Hungary Jews who were viewed as non-Hungarian were killed (e.g., in occupied Yugoslavian territory and in Ukraine); and in Bulgaria Jews from Thrace and Macedonia were deported to German camps. In Romania deported and murdered Jews were from Bukovina and Bessarabia, territories once lost to, and then regained from, the USSR. Paradoxically, in Bucharest, even at moments of near utter despair, a strange dialogue between Romanian officials and leaders of the Jewish community went forward. Branded enemies of the Romanian nation along with the rest of their kinsmen by an ugly official propaganda, those leaders nevertheless proved able to maintain channels of communication with Romanian officials. The Romanian bureaucracy, theoretically united with Germany's in the desire to liquidate the Jews, coordinated its efforts with the latter only in spite of serious difficulties and only for brief periods: irreconcilable differences over matters of style, timing, and methodology triggered negative reactions from the Germans, too often ired by the Romanians' inefficient pogrom "techniques," by the improvised nature of the "death marches," by the haste of Romanian officials in pressing huge groups of deportees across the Dniester River in 1941 and the Bug River in 1942, and by the fact that the Romanians did this so often with little clear plan as to what to do with the Jews once they were there. Perhaps they even expected the Germans to handle the problem for them.

In the fall of 1942, those very same Romanian officials refused German pressure to deport their country's Jews to camps in Poland, where certain death clearly awaited them. Romania had indeed initially approved the Germans' deportation of Romanian Jews from Germany and the territories Germany occupied; about 4,500 Romanian citizens had died as a result. But when the shifting tides of war changed minds in Bucharest, thousands of Romanian Jews living abroad gained the chance to survive thanks to renewed Romanian diplomatic protection. Romanian Jews may have been deported en masse to Transnistria, but thousands were subsequently (if selectively) repatriated. And as the vast German camp system actualized its horrific potential, the number of murders committed by the Romanians decreased, as did the determination with which they enforced their country's anti-Semitic laws. Such contradictions go a long way toward explaining the survival of at least half of Romania's Jews.

Historians and journalists writing under Ceausescu sometimes maintained that the country's humanitarianism thwarted the very undertaking of the Holocaust in Romania. Disciples of the official version often tried to dilute or completely deny the responsibility of Romanians in the slaughter of the Jews, placing all blame on the Germans. The documents do record numerous instances of Romanians—both civilian and military—rescuing Jewish co-citizens. During the Iași pogrom, for instance, the owner of the Dacia windmill saved dozens. Lieutenant Colonel Alexandru Constantinescu, the first commander of the Vertujeni camp, refused to be involved in systematic cruelty, successfully requesting transfer to other duties. Romanian civilian and military officials were condemned by wartime courts-martial for attempting to bring into Romania letters on behalf of Jews deported to Transnistria. Traian Popovici, the mayor of Cernăuți, resisted the deportations and saved thousands. Romanian military doctors struggled selflessly against the typhus epidemic in Moghilev. Colonel Sabin Motora, the last commander of Vapniarka, arranged under difficult circumstances to repatriate Jews sent there under accusations of communism. Innumerable other instances of civilian or military assistance and rescue were lost to history amid the chaos of war and revolution. But these initiatives were isolated cases—in the final analysis exceptions to the general rule. And the rule was terror, plunder, rape, deportation, and murder. The survival of more Jews resulted from the inefficient and corrupt nature of the Romanian administrative system or from Ion Antonescu's decision to postpone and then abandon plans to deport the Jews from Regat, rather than from the kindness and courage of the few.

The treatment meted the Jews from Bessarabia, Bukovina, and Transnistria triggered a series of external and internal appeals that influenced Ion Antonescu's decision to cancel deportations from Moldavia, Walachia, and southern Transylvania. Clergymen, diplomats from Switzerland and Sweden, representatives of American agencies (especially the War Refugee Board in Istanbul), the International Committee of the Red Cross, and the Vatican itself all helped. Indeed, German pressure to hand over the Jews of Regat produced a countereffect: no foreign power was going to tell Romanian nationalists what to do with *their* Jews. And indeed, various liberal, or simply decent, Romanian politicians and public figures intervened on behalf of the Jews; those who would not simply stand by included Iuliu Maniu, Constantin I. C. Brătianu, Nicolae Lupu, and the Queen Mother herself.

Iuliu Maniu, head of the National Peasant party, interceded; in his meeting with James Webb Benton, first secretary of the American legation, Maniu ascribed the license originally granted for anti-Semitic atrocities in Romania to the fact that "the marshal did not have total control of his mental faculties." Maniu felt that "the Germans, and especially the German army, were responsible" for manipulating the Conducator.[4] Maniu of course was attempting to foster a positive image of Romania abroad by blaming Germany, but he himself harbored resentments toward the Jews of Transylvania, whom he viewed as pro-Hungarian. Nevertheless, Maniu remained committed to the idea that moral limits should restrain ethnic resentments.[5] As late as 1946, Maniu (whose party had been in a de facto alliance with the Legionnaires in 1937) told a group of Jewish interlocutors: "for now the state has more important problems than the Jewish question. . . . Remember that generals are working in the government, and they work slowly. And anyway, how serious are your problems? You have been able to manage [so far] with your money and your brains."[6] Not really an anti-Semite, Maniu nonetheless reflected the prejudices of his society and generation.

One must also remember that not only voices of moderation clamored for Ion Antonescu's intervention: the Conducator also received numerous pleas to proceed still more vigorously against Romanian Jewry. In a memorandum of October 1943, the so-called 1922 Generation (former

Legionnaires and Cuzists) demanded that "all the assets" of the Jews be "transferred to the state" in order that they might "be placed in the hands of pure-blooded Romanians." These diehards continued to demand "the mandatory wearing of a distinctive insignia by all Jews" and their prohibition from numerous professions. "The radical and final solution of the Jewish question," they wrote, as if the recent course of the war had been completely lost on them, "must be carried out in conjunction with [the plan for] the future Europe."[7] When the repatriation of Jews from Transnistria began, Gheorghe Cuza, son of Alexandru C. Cuza of the National Christian party, and Colonel Barcan, prefect of Dorohoi, publicly protested.[8]

Romania under Antonescu was a fascist dictatorship and a totalitarian state. The dictator's orders could seal the fate of the Jews from Bessarabia and Bukovina, just as they might decide the survival of most Jews from Moldavia and Walachia. The courageous but isolated behavior of some Romanians unfortunately weighed too little on the scale of life and death. The entire repressive military, police, and judicial apparatus became the instrument with which Antonescu carried out his anti-Semitic fantasies during the first half of the war. And under a militaristic dictatorship protests on behalf of the Jews would have been difficult to organize. In any case, official propaganda successfully continued to present the Jews as the most important domestic enemy, as Moscow's or London's agents, and as the main cause of Romania's economic difficulties; widespread belief weighed more heavily than fear as the explanation for the lack of protest.

The Antonescu regime mixed the ideology of the fascist Iron Guard and that of the profascist National Christian party. Basic propaganda by both parties found its way into Antonescu's stances. Many civil servants in midlevel positions were former members of the National Christian party, and the regime's anti-Semitic legislation was typically fascist, sometimes overtly inspired by Nazi racial laws.[9] The idea of forced emigration had found widespread support among fascists and nonfascist anti-Semites in many European countries during the interwar period. The Nazis had seriously promoted such a solution before 1939. In Romania the Legion of the Archangel Michael and the National Christian party had propounded this doctrine, which Antonescu wholeheartedly assimilated. Many Romanian historians have sought to absolve the Antonescu regime of responsibility for the abuses the Jews suffered at the hands of this government; these scholars argue that emigration had been the intent of its program, a goal that was basically humane.[10] And indeed, sometimes emigration was permitted (more for financial considerations, it would seem, than anything else), but the main tools employed by Antonescu and his regime in their plan to eliminate the Jews from Romania were executions, deportations, forced labor, and starvation.

If the anti-Semitic policies and practices of the Antonescu regime were inspired by hatred, the behavior of its bureaucrats was guided for the most part by petty, pragmatic criteria; this sometimes lent its practice a distinct, opportunistic flavor. The result was tragedy for innumerable Romanian Jews, but it also left open the door to salvation for many. When it became evident, for example, that "Romanization" was having a negative effect on the economy, Antonescu put a halt to this extraeconomic process. To take one other instance, as long as developments in the war seemed to favor Romania, official anti-Semitism went unchallenged, and it was anticipated that any survivors of mass slaughter, pogroms, and other measures would be deported beyond the Urals; but the opposite side of the equation was that such plans were dropped after Stalingrad. Bureaucracy helped: the haste to destroy the Jews from Bessarabia and Bukovina was equaled only by the chaos and the improvisation that this process revealed, translating into delays that could spell opportunities for Jews to improvise means of surviving the process. It seemed as if it was only a matter of time before the government would deport the Jews of Walachia and Moldavia, these deemed less "treasonous" according to the official line than those from Bessarabia and Bukovina but nevertheless deserving only of dispatch to the German camps in occupied Poland; by that time, however, the opportunists had begun deserting a sinking ship.

However, internal and external appeals; misunderstandings in relations with Germany; Mihai Antonescu's early realization—even before the outcome of Stalingrad had become fully clear—that the situation on the eastern front was not what had been envisioned; and perhaps Antonescu's pride (dictators do not like to be dictated to) all impeded overall plans for extermination. In the fall of 1942, a second phase, one offering meaningful chances for Jewish survival, arrived. Ion Antonescu remained a violent anti-Semite, but as the war dragged on, ideological criteria ceased to inspire policy.

Three factors, then, weighed heaviest in the death and the survival of

Romanian Jews: malice, greed, and opportunism. Raul Hilberg captured the essence perhaps better than anyone when he wrote:

> Opportunism was practiced in Romania not only on a national basis but also in personal relations. Romania was a corrupt country. It was the only Axis state in which officials as high as minister and mayor of the capital city had to be dismissed for "dark" transactions with expropriated Jewish property.
>
> The search for personal gain in Romania was so intensive that it must have enabled many Jews to buy relief from persecution. . . .
>
> In examining the Romanian bureaucratic apparatus, one is therefore left with the impression of an unreliable machine that did not properly respond to command and that acted in unpredictable ways, sometimes balking, sometimes running away with itself. That spurting action, unplanned and uneven, sporadic and erratic, was the outcome of an opportunism that was mixed with destructiveness, a lethargy periodically interrupted by outbursts of violence. The product of this mixture was a record of anti-Jewish actions that is decidedly unique.[11]

Documentary Sources

THIS TEXT relies primarily on previously unpublished Romanian documents located in the archives of the United States Holocaust Memorial Museum (USHMM) in Washington, D.C., in a collection that exceeds 800,000 pages. The documents cited herein come from the archives of the Mareles Stat Major (MSM, or the Supreme General Staff of the Romanian army), the Romanian Intelligence Service (SRI), the Romanian Ministry of Foreign Affairs (RMFA), the Romanian State Archives (RSA), the Central Archives of the Republic of Moldavia, and the local archives of the Republic of Ukraine (Cernăuţi, Odessa, Nicolaev, and Vinnytsya).

The files from the MSM (RG 25.003M) derive from the office responsible for Jewish hard labor (the Tenth Office) and surveillance of the Jews (Second Section); they also include reports on anti-Jewish operations by major military units and reports on Jews and Gypsies by the military gendarmerie. Military documents provide a complete picture of the Romanian system of forced labor camps for Jews.

The archives of the SRI (RG 004M) contain the trials of the Romanian war criminals. In addition to the indictments, testimonies, and court decisions therein, the SRI files contain many original documents used as evidence in the trials.

Most of the documents in the RMFA's files (RG 25.006M) belong to diplomatic records that reflect German-Romanian relations and the fate of Romanian Jews living abroad. This collection also contains part of the reports from the Civilian-Military Cabinet of the Administration of Bessarabia, Bukovina, and Transnistria (CBBT) and, most important, the statistics on the deportations from Bessarabia and Bukovina to Transnistria.

The RSA files (RG 002M and RG 25.005M) yield reports from central and local administrative units concerning the persecution of Jews, the files of Ion Antonescu's military office, anti-Jewish administrative decisions from 1940 to 1944, and surveillance reports of the Romanian secret police.

The Central Archives of the Republic of Moldavia (RG 54.001M) contain the orders and reports on the formation of ghettos and transit camps in Bessarabia and on deportations from Bessarabia and Bukovina.

The local archives of the Republic of Ukraine from Cernăuți (RG 31006M) include the files on the history of the Cernăuți ghetto and documents on the deportation of the Jews from Bukovina in 1941 and 1942. Those from Odessa (RG 31004M) and Nicolaev (RG 31008M) contain administrative reports on the situation of the Jews and Gypsies in Transnistria.

Also used were documents from the National Archives in Washington, D.C.; records from the Yad Vashem in Jerusalem; and published sources, among them the most important being Matatias Carp's *Cartea neagră* and Jean Ancel's edited collection *Documents Concerning the Fate of Romanian Jewry During the Holocaust.*

Notes

Preface

1. Carol Iancu, *Bleichröder et Crémiaux: Le combat pour l'émancipation des juifs de Roumanie devant le Congrès de Berlin: Correspondence inédite, 1878–1880* (Montpellier, 1987), p. 6.

2. Lucretiu Patrascanu, *Sub trei dictaturi* (Bucharest, 1970), p. 221.

3. Sabin Manuila and Wilhelm Filderman, *Regional Development of the Jewish Population in Romania* (Rome, 1957), p. 13.

4. Matei Dogan, *Analiza statistica a democratiei parlamentare din Romania* (Bucharest, 1946); "*Federatia Comunităţilor Evreiesti: Monografie*" (Bucharest, unpublished), vol. 2; and Manuila and Filderman, *Regional Development*.

5. Jean Ancel, ed., *Documents Concerning the Fate of Romanian Jewry During the Holocaust* [hereafter *DCFRJDH*] (New York, 1986), vol. 8, p. 497.

6. Raul Hilberg, *The Destruction of the European Jews* (New York, 1985), vol. 3, p. 1220.

7. George Voicu, "Reactia de Prestigiu," *Sfera politicii* 63 (October 1998).

Chapter 1: The Legal Status of the Jews in Romania

1. Iancu, *Bleichröder,* p. 19.

2. I. C. Butnaru, *Holocaustul uitat* (Tel Aviv, 1985), p. 485; available in English as *The Silent Holocaust: Romania and Its Jews* (New York, 1992).

3. Iancu, *Bleichröder,* p. 25.

4. Ibid., p. 29.

5. Ibid., p. 58.

6. Carol Iancu, *Les Juifs de Roumanie, 1866–1919: De l'exclusion à l'émancipation* (Aix-en-Provence, 1978), pp. 186–87.

7. Emanuel Turczynski, "The Background of Romanian Fascism," in Peter F. Sugar, ed., *Native Fascism in the Successor States* (Santa Barbara, 1971), p. 106.

8. Iancu, *Les Juifs de Roumainie*, p. 203.

9. Iancu, *Bleichröder*, p. 27.

10. Ibid., p. 30.

11. Carol Iancu, *L'émancipation des Juifs de la Roumanie* (Montpellier, 1992), p. 32.

12. *DCFRJDH*, vol. 1, p. 52.

13. Ibid., vol. 1, pp. 24–25.

14. Ibid., p. 93.

15. Iancu, *L'émancipation*, p. 115.

16. Ibid., p. 95.

17. Gheorghe Dumitras-Bitoaica, *Statutul juridic al evreilor si legislatia romanizarii* (Bucharest, 1942), p. 28.

18. *La Situation de Juifs en Roumanie: Petition du Comité Executif du Congres Mondial Juif au Conseil de la Societé des Nations* (Geneva, 1938), p. 6.

19. Ibid., p. 7.

20. Carol Iancu, *Les Juifs en Roumaine, 1919–1938: De l'émancipation à la marginalisation* (Paris-Louvain, 1996), p. 51.

21. Ezra Mendelsohn, *The Jews of East Central Europe Between the World Wars* (Bloomington, Ind., 1983), p. 174.

22. Ibid.

23. Ibid., p. 176.

24. Ibid., p. 177.

25. Mendelsohn, *The Jews of East Central Europe*, p. 189.

26. *United States Holocaust Memorial Museum/Romanian Ministry of Foreign Affairs Archives* [hereafter *USHMM/RMFA*], RG 25.006M, roll 4, Chronology of Anti-Semitism in Romania, 1926–1927, p. 1.

27. Ibid., p. 6.

28. Ibid., p. 16.

29. Ibid., p. 18.

30. Ibid.

31. Ibid.

32. Ibid., p. 22.

33. Dumitraş-Biţoaica, *Statutul juridic*, p. 391.

34. *DCFRJDH*, vol. 1, p. 209.

35. Ibid., pp. 211–12.

36. Ibid., p. 214.

37. Bela Vago, *The Shadow of the Swastika: The Rise of Fascism and Anti-Semitism on the Danube Basin, 1936–1939* (Farnborough, U.K., 1975), p. 39.

38. Dumitraş-Biţoaica, *Statutul juridic*, p. 42.

39. *DCFRJDH*, vol. 1, p. 214.

40. Hilberg, *The Destruction,* p. 72.

41. Ibid., p. 68.

42. Dumitraş-Biţoaica's book *Statutul juridic,* published in 1942, cites about one hundred anti-Semitic laws, decrees, and other administrative regulations. Immediately after its publication, this book was sent to the German legation in Bucharest with a request to have it distributed to those Nazi German institutions that might be interested (*National Archives and Records Administration* [hereafter *NARA*], T175M, roll 663).

43. Dumitraş-Biţoaica, *Statutul juridic,* p. 33.

44. Ibid., p. 47.

45. Ibid., p. 55.

46. *DCFRJDH,* vol. 3, p. 58.

47. Dumitraş-Biţoaica, *Statutul juridic,* p. 59.

48. *DCFRJDH,* vol. 3, p. 59.

49. Dumitraş-Biţoaica, *Statutul juridic,* p. 59.

50. *Monitorul Oficial* [Official Monitor] (Bucharest, 1942), Decree No. 1257, April 30, 1942.

51. *NARA,* T175, roll 662; *Monitorul Oficial* 156 (August 1943) and 171 (July 1943).

52. *DCFRJDH,* vol. 1, p. 536.

53. Mihail Manoilescu, *Sensul si destinul burgheziei naţionale* (Bucharest, 1942), p. 260.

54. Ibid.

55. Ibid., p. 267.

56. Dumitraş-Biţoaica, *Statutul juridic,* p. 109.

57. Ibid., p. 121.

58. Aurică Simion, *Preliminarii politico-diplomatice ale insurecţiei române din august 1944* (Cluj, 1979), p. 125.

59. Dumitraş-Biţoaica, *Statutul juridic,* pp. 127–28.

60. Ibid., p. 128.

61. Matatias Carp, *Cartea neagră* (Bucharest, 1946–1948), vol. 1, pp. 43–44.

62. *DCFRJDH,* vol. 3, p. 484.

63. Carp, *Cartea neagră,* vol. 1, pp. 43–44.

64. Dumitraş-Biţoaica, *Statutul juridic,* p. 127.

65. Ibid., p. 99.

66. Ibid.

67. Ibid., pp. 81–82.

68. Carp, *Cartea neagră,* vol. 1, p. 144.

69. Dumitraş-Biţoaica, *Statutul juridic,* p. 71.

70. *Procesul marii trădări naţionale* [Juridical Status of the Jews and the Roumanization Legislation] (Bucharest, 1946), p. 43.

71. Dumitraş-Biţoaica, *Statutul juridic,* p. 75.

72. *DCFRJDH,* vol. 3, p. 79.

73. Dumitraş-Biţoaica, *Statutul juridic,* p. 380.

74. Ibid., p. 389.
75. Ibid., pp. 155–56.
76. Ibid., pp. 160–61.
77. *DCFRJDH,* vol. 3, p. 310.
78. Ibid., p. 572.
79. Ibid., vol. 4, p. 219.
80. Ibid., p. 701.
81. Dumitraş-Biţoaica, *Statutul juridic,* pp. 59, 389.
82. *DCFRJDH,* vol. 2, p. 441.
83. Ibid., p. 502.
84. Ibid., vol. 3, p. 1.
85. Ibid., p. 22.
86. Ibid., p. 27.
87. Ibid., p. 28.
88. Ibid., p. 75.
89. Ibid., p. 85.
90. Ibid., p. 105.
91. Ibid., p. 120.
92. Ibid., pp. 116–17, 123–25.
93. Ibid., p. 126.
94. Ibid., p. 131.
95. Ibid., p. 137.
96. Ibid., p. 136.
97. Ibid., vol. 2, p. 172, and vol. 3, p. 404.
98. Ibid, vol. 4, p. 489.
99. Ibid., p. 503.
100. Ibid., p. 648.
101. Ibid., vol. 3, p. 532.
102. Ibid., vol. 10, p. 706.
103. Ephraim Nathanson, "Romanian Governments and the Legal Status of the Jews," *Romanian Jewish Studies* (Jerusalem) 1:1 (1987): 56.

Chapter 2: The Massacres Before the War

1. Jean Ancel, "The Jassy Syndrome," *Romanian Jewish Studies* 1:1 (1987): 43.
2. *DCFRJDH,* vol. 3, p. 376.
3. Ibid., vol. 10, p. 30.
4. Ibid., vol. 8, pp. 575–77.
5. Carp, *Cartea neagră,* vol. 3, pp. 25–26.
6. Ibid., p. 26.
7. Marius Mircu, *Pogromurile din Bucovina si Dorohoi* (Bucharest, 1945), p. 23.
8. Carp, *Cartea neagră,* vol. 3, p. 26.
9. Ibid., p. 27.

10. Ibid.

11. Ibid., p. 28.

12. Mircu, *Pogromurile din Bucovina*, p. 53.

13. This was taken from Report No. 59, dated July 29, 1940, cited in ibid., p. 140.

14. *United States Holocaust Memorial Museum/Romanian Intelligence Service Archives* [hereafter *USHMM/SRI*], RG 25.004M, reel 7, vol. 4087.

15. *DCFRJDH*, vol. 10, p. 495.

16. Mircu, *Pogromurile din Bucovina*, pp. 139–40.

17. Carp, *Cartea neagră*, vol. 3, pp. 26–27, 43–45; Mircu, *Pogromurile din Bucovina*, pp. 119–39; Ancel, "The Jassy Syndrome," pp. 43–46; *DCFRJDH*, vol. 8, p. 539.

18. *DCFRJDH*, vol. 10, p. 495.

19. Ibid., vol. 3, pp. 172–73.

20. Ibid., vol. 1, p. 436.

21. Carp, *Cartea neagră*, vol. 1, p. 54.

22. Ibid., p. 55.

23. Ibid., p. 109.

24. Ibid., p. 116.

25. Ibid., p. 117.

26. *DCFRJDH*, vol. 1, pp. 538–88.

27. Ibid., p. 585.

28. Carp. *Cartea neagră*, vol. 1, p. 119.

29. Ibid., p. 141.

30. Ibid., p. 145.

31. Ibid., pp. 125, 127, 150; *DCFRJDH*, vol. 2, pp. 34, 55.

32. *Asasinatele de la Jilava: Strejnicul si Snagov* (Bucharest, 1941), p. 259.

33. *Procesul marii trădări*, p. 10.

34. *Asasinatele de la Jilava*, pp. 123–43, 164–65.

35. *Procesul marii trădări*, p. 132.

36. Carp, *Cartea neagră*, vol. 1, p. 132.

37. Ibid., p. 143.

38. Ibid.

39. Ibid., p. 173.

40. Ibid., p. 193.

41. *DCFRJDH*, vol. 2, p. 74.

42. Carp, *Cartea neagră*, vol. 1, p. 195.

43. Ibid., p. 121.

44. Aurica Simion, *Regimul politic in România in perioada septembrie 1940–ianuarie 1941* (Cluj, 1976), p. 117.

45. Carp, *Cartea neagră*, vol. 1, p. 160.

46. *DCFRJDH*, vol. 2, p. 47.

47. Ibid., pp. 115–16.

48. Ibid., p. 168.

49. Ibid., p. 111.

50. Philippe Marguerat, *Le Ille Reich et le pétrole roumain, 1938–1940* (Geneva, 1977), p. 75.

51. *DCFRJDH,* vol. 9, pp. 112–13.

52. Marguerat, *Le Ille Reich,* p. 90.

53. *DCFRJDH,* vol. 9, p. 112–13.

54. Ibid., p. 141.

55. Ibid., p. 150.

56. *Mémorial Antonescu: Le troisième homme de l'Axe* (Paris, 1950), pp. 72–76.

57. *DCFRJDH,* vol. 2, p. 259.

58. Walter Schellenberg, *Hitler's Secret Service* (New York, 1971), pp. 205–6.

59. *Memorial Antonescu,* p. 104.

60. Ibid., vol. 2, p. 259.

61. Simion, *Regimul politic,* p. 265.

62. Ibid.

63. *Timpul* (Bucharest), July 30, 1941.

64. *Asasinatele de la Jilava,* p. 524.

65. Ibid., pp. 281–82.

66. Ibid., pp. 294–95.

67. *DCFRJDH,* vol. 9, p. 161.

68. Ibid., p. 327.

69. *Procesul marii trădări,* pp. 157, 171.

70. Schellenberg, *Hitler's Secret Service,* p. 320.

71. *NARA,* roll 626/1; *DCFRJDH,* vol. 9, p. 669; Simion, *Preliminarii,* pp. 256–63.

72. Simion, *Regimul politic,* pp. 226–27.

73. *DCFRJDH,* vol. 2, p. 155.

74. Ibid., p. 163.

75. Ibid., p. 156.

76. Ibid., p. 159.

77. Carp, *Cartea neagră,* vol. 1, pp. 228, 370–73.

78. *DCFRJDH,* vol. 3, p. 170.

79. Simion, *Regimul politic,* p. 84.

80. *Foreign Relations of United States: Diplomatic Papers, 1941* (Washington, D.C., 1959), vol. 2, p. 861.

81. Hilberg, *The Destruction,* vol. 2, p. 764.

82. Carp, *Cartea neagră,* vol. 1, pp. 223–24, 228–29.

83. Ibid., pp. 229–30.

84. *DCFRJDH,* vol. 3, pp. 174–75.

85. Carp, *Cartea neagră,* vol. 1, pp. 231–32; *DCFRJDH,* vol. 3, p. 196.

86. *DCFRJDH,* vol. 3, p. 175.

87. Carp, *Cartea neagră,* vol. 1, pp. 233–34.

88. Ibid., p. 235.

89. Ibid., pp. 221–22.

90. Ibid., pp. 239–40.

91. Ibid., pp. 246–323.

92. *DCFRJDH*, vol. 2, pp. 335–36.

93. Ibid., vol. 9, p. 666.

94. Carp, *Cartea neagră*, vol. 3, pp. 28–29; *DCFRJDH*, vol. 2, pp. 268–69.

Chapter 3: The Massacres at the Beginning of the War

1. Carp, *Cartea neagră*, vol. 2, p. 11.

2. Ibid., p. 39.

3. *DCFRJDH*, vol. 2, p. 468.

4. Ibid., vol. 6, p. 445.

5. *Procesul marii trădări*, p. 53.

6. Ibid., p. 64.

7. Carp, *Cartea neagră*, vol. 2, p. 48.

8. Ibid., p. 50.

9. *USHMM/SRI*, RG 25.004M, roll 44, fond 108233, vol. 54.

10. Carp, *Cartea neagră*, vol. 2, p. 41; *Procesul marii trădări*, p. 170.

11. Carp, *Cartea neagră*, vol. 2, p. 19.

12. Ibid., pp. 51–52.

13. Aurel Karețki and Maria Covaci, *Zile însingerate la Iasi* (Bucharest, 1978), p. 50.

14. Carp, *Cartea neagră*, vol. 2, p. 61; *DCFRJDH*, vol. 6, p. 35.

15. Carp, *Cartea neagră*, vol. 2, pp. 22, 95; Karețki and Covaci, *Zile însingerate*, p. 53.

16. Karețki and Covaci, *Zile însingerate*, p. 45.

17. Ibid., pp. 45–46.

18. Marius Mircu, *Pogromul de la Iasi* (Bucharest, 1945), p. 5; *USHMM/SRI*, RG 25.004M, roll 43, fond 108233, vol. 38.

19. *DCFRJDH*, vol. 6, p. 43.

20. Carp, *Cartea neagră*, vol. 2, p. 58; *DCFRJDH*, vol. 6, pp. 376–77.

21. Carp, *Cartea neagră*, vol. 2, p. 53; *DCFRJDH*, vol. 6, p. 377. See also the testimony of Beno Beer, *USHMM/SRI*, roll 44, RG 25.004M, vol. 36.

22. Carp, *Cartea neagră*, vol. 2, pp. 22–23; *DCFRJDH*, vol. 6, p. 368.

23. *DCFRJDH*, vol. 6, p. 369.

24. Carp, *Cartea neagră*, vol. 2, p. 66.

25. Ibid., pp. 25, 61; *DCFRJDH*, vol. 6, p. 369.

26. Karețki and Covaci, *Zile însingerate*, p. 57.

27. Carp, *Cartea neagră*, vol. 2, p. 25; *DCFRJDH*, vol. 6, p. 369.

28. *USHMM/SRI*, RG 25.004M, roll 46, fond 108233, vol. 109.

29. Ibid., roll 43, fond 108233, vol. 36; Mircu, *Pogromul de la Iași*, p. 9.

30. Carp, *Cartea neagră*, vol. 2, p. 25.

31. Ibid., p. 26; *DCFRJDH*, vol. 2, p. 433, and vol. 6, pp. 369–70.

32. Carp, *Cartea neagră,* vol. 2, p. 89; *DCFRJDH,* vol. 6, p. 370.

33. Carp, *Cartea neagră,* vol. 2, pp. 26–27.

34. Ibid., p. 26.

35. Ibid., p. 116.

36. *DCFRJDH,* vol. 6, p. 35.

37. Carp, *Cartea neagră,* vol. 2, p. 83.

38. Ibid., pp. 70, 108.

39. Ibid., pp. 27–28; *DCFRJDH,* vol. 6, p. 371.

40. Mircu, *Pogromul de la Iaşi,* pp. 30–31; *DCFRJDH,* vol. 5, p. 38, and vol. 6, p. 37.

41. Mircu, *Pogromul de la Iaşi,* p. 15.

42. *DCFRJDH,* vol. 6, pp. 40–41.

43. Ibid., p. 20.

44. Ibid.

45. Ibid., pp. 364–419.

46. *USHMM/SRI,* RG 25.004M, roll 44, fond 108233, vol. 45, part 2.

47. *DCFRJDH,* vol. 6, pp. 394–95, 397.

48. Ibid., p. 20.

49. Ibid., pp. 384–85, 388, 390, 392, 398.

50. Ibid., pp. 387, 392–93, 395–97.

51. Ibid., pp. 20–22.

52. Ibid., p. 24.

53. Ibid., pp. 28–29.

54. Ibid., p. 34.

55. Ibid., p. 19.

56. Ibid., pp. 29–30.

57. *Minimum* (Tel Aviv) 18 (1988).

58. *Revista Cultului Mozaic* (Bucharest, 1986), p. 4.

59. Carp, *Cartea neagră,* vol. 2, p. 66; Kareţki and Covaci, *Zile însingerate,* p. 80.

60. *DCFRJDH,* vol. 6, p. 41.

61. Carp, *Cartea neagră,* vol. 2, p. 83.

62. Ibid., p. 85.

63. Ibid., pp. 102, 112.

64. Ibid., p. 109.

65. Mircu, *Pogromul de la Iaşi,* p. 38; *DCFRJDH,* vol. 6, pp. 388–96.

66. Mircu, *Pogromul de la Iaşi,* p. 38; *DCFRJDH,* vol. 6, p. 39.

67. *DCFRJDH,* vol. 6, p. 387.

68. Ibid., p. 44.

69. Carp, *Cartea neagră,* vol. 2, p. 112.

70. Mircu, *Pogromul de la Iaşi,* p. 43.

71. *USHMM/SRI,* RG 25.004M, roll 44, fond 108233, vol. 36.

72. Ibid., roll 48, fond 108233, vol. 20.

73. Carp, *Cartea neagră*, vol. 2, pp. 143–46; *USHMM/SRI*, RG 25.004M, roll 47, fond 108233, vol. 20.

74. *USHMM/SRI*, RG 25.004M, roll 43, fond 108233, vol. 38.

75. Carp, *Cartea neagră*, vol. 2, p. 109.

76. Ibid., p. 76.

77. Ibid., pp. 118–19.

78. Ibid., pp. 143–46; *DCFRJDH*, vol. 2, p. 434.

79. *USHMM/SRI*, RG 25.004M, roll 13, fond 2983, vol. 323.

80. Mircu, *Pogromul de la Iași*, p. 83.

81. Ibid., pp. 82–83; *USHMM/SRI*, RG 25.004M, roll 43, fond 108233, vol. 38.

82. Mircu, *Pogromul de la Iași*, p. 80.

83. Ibid.; Carp, *Cartea neagră*, vol. 2, pp. 97–98.

84. Carp, *Cartea neagră*, vol. 2, pp. 97–98, 147.

85. Ibid., p. 197.

86. Ibid., p. 34.

87. *DCFRJDH*, vol. 8, p. 574.

88. Ibid.

89. Carp, *Cartea neagră*, vol. 2, p. 92.

90. Ibid.

91. Ibid., pp. 31, 123.

92. *DCFRJDH*, vol. 6, p. 401.

93. Carp, *Cartea neagră*, vol. 2, pp. 122, 129.

94. *DCFRJDH*, vol. 6, p. 401.

95. Carp, *Cartea neagră*, vol. 22, p. 401.

96. Ibid., p. 134.

97. *DCFRJDH*, vol. 6, p. 402.

98. Carp, *Cartea neagră*, vol. 2, p. 92.

99. Ibid., p. 125.

100. Ibid., p. 129.

101. *DCFRJDH*, vol. 3, p. 448, and vol. 6, p. 402.

102. Ibid., vol. 6, p. 397.

103. *USHMM/SRI*, RG 25.004M, roll 17, fond 39912, vol. 1.

104. Carp, *Cartea neagră*, vol. 2, p. 131.

105. Ibid., p. 125.

106. Ibid., pp. 127, 136; *DCFRJDH*, vol. 6, pp. 40, 403; Mircu, *Pogromul de la Iași*, p. 63.

107. Carp, *Cartea neagră*, vol. 2, p. 35.

108. Ibid.; *DCFRJDH*, vol. 6, pp. 40, 403; Mircu, *Pogromul de la Iași*, p. 65.

109. Carp, *Cartea neagră*, vol. 2, pp. 36, 197.

110. Ibid., pp. 137–38.

111. *USHMM/SRI*, RG 25.004M, roll 48, fond 108233, vol. 30; Carp, *Cartea neagră*, vol. 2, p. 94; Mircu, *Pogromul de la Iași*, pp. 88–90.

112. *USHMM/SRI*, RG 25.004M, roll 48, fond 108233, vol. 30.

113. Carp, *Cartea neagră,* vol. 2, p. 94; Mircu, *Pogromul de la Iași,* pp. 97–99.

114. *USHMM/SRI,* RG 25.004M, roll 44, fond 108233, vol. 55.

115. Carp, *Cartea neagră,* vol. 2, p. 36; *DCFRJDH,* vol. 6, p. 39.

116. Carp, *Cartea neagră,* vol. 2, p. 33; *DCFRJDH,* vol. 2, p. 408, and vol. 6, pp. 406–7; Mircu, *Pogromul de la Iași,* pp. 76–79.

117. Karețki and Covaci, *Zile însingerate,* p. 105.

118. Hilberg, *The Destruction,* vol. 2, p. 767.

119. Curzio Malaparte, *Kaputt* (New York, 1946), p. 144.

120. Gheorghe Zaharia, *Pages de la résistance antifasciste en Roumanie* (Bucharest, 1974), p. 45.

121. Cristian Troncotă, *Eugen Cristescu, asul serviciilor secrete românești* (Bucharest, 1996), pp. 118–19; archival source quoted by the author: *USHMM/SRI,* folder 11314, p. 28.

122. Ibid., pp. 54–55.

123. Carp, *Cartea neagră,* vol. 2, p. 51.

124. *DCFRJDH,* vol. 6, p. 378.

125. *USHMM/SRI,* RG 25.004M, roll 35, fond 40010, vol. 89.

126. Ibid., fond 108233, vol. 63.

127. Ibid.

128. Ibid., roll 48, fond 108233, vol. 29.

129. Ibid., vol. 30.

130. *United States Holocaust Memorial Museum/Mareles Stat Major* [Supreme General Command] *Archives* [hereafter *USHMM/MSM*], RG 25.003M, roll 305, fond Marele Cartier General, vol. 3828; *Martiriul evreilor din Romania, 1940–1944* (Bucharest, 1991), p. 96.

131. *Universul* (Bucharest), July 2, 1941.

132. *USHMM/SRI,* RG 25.004M, roll 48, fond 108233, vol. 28.

133. *Procesul marii trădări,* p. 64.

134. *USHMM/SRI,* RG 25.004M, roll 48, fond 108233, vol. 28.

135. *DCFRJDH,* vol. 2, p. 434.

136. Carp, *Cartea neagră,* vol. 2, p. 102.

137. *DCFRJDH,* vol. 3, p. 178.

138. Ibid., p. 372.

139. Ibid., pp. 99–100.

140. Ibid., p. 37.

141. Ibid.

142. Ibid., p. 44.

143. *Foreign Relations of the United States: Diplomatic Papers, 1941,* vol. 2, pp. 868–69, 878–79.

144. *USHMM/MSM,* RG 25.003M, roll 11(781), fond Armata aIVa.

145. *USHMM/SRI,* RG 25.004M, roll 16, fond 22539, vol. 32; *DCFRJDH,* vol. 5, pp. 2–7, and vol. 6, p. 445.

146. *USHMM/SRI,* RG 25.004M, roll 18, fond 22539, vol. 1, and roll 24, fond 20725, vol. 5.

147. Ibid., roll 24, fond 20725, vol. 5.

148. Carp, *Cartea neagră*, vol. 3, p. 91.

149. *DCFRJDH*, vol. 5, p. 4.

150. *Procesul marii trădări*, p. 302; *DCFRJDH*, vol. 5, p. 4.

151. *USHMM/MSM*, RG 25.003M, roll 125(655), fond Guvernamîntul Basarabiei, Cabinet Militar, vol. 25.

152. *DCFRJDH*, vol. 5, p. 5.

153. Carp, *Cartea neagră*, vol. 3, p. 92.

154. *USHMM/MSM*, RG 25.003M, roll 125(655), fond Guvernamîntul Basarabiei, Cabinet Militar, dosar 25.

155. Ibid., roll 26, roll 11(781), fond Armata aIVa.

156. *USHMM/SRI*, RG 25.004M, roll 26, fond 20725, vol. 11.

157. Carp, *Cartea neagră*, vol. 2, plate 11.

158. *DCFRJDH*, vol. 2, p. 430.

159. Ibid., vol. 6, p. 204.

160. Carp, *Cartea neagră*, vol. 2, p. 23.

161. Ibid., p. 24.

162. Ibid., p. 73.

163. Ibid., p. 74; emphasis added.

164. Ibid.

165. Ibid., p. 77.

166. Ibid., p. 78; *DCFRJDH*, vol. 6, pp. 195–98.

167. *USHMM/SRI*, RG 25.004M, roll 44, fond 108233, vol. 46; Carp, *Cartea neagră*, vol. 2, p. 78; *DCFRJDH*, vol. 6, p. 80.

168. Ibid.

169. Ibid.

170. Carp, *Cartea neagră*, vol. 3, p. 30; Mircu, *Pogromurile din Bucovina*, p. 24.

171. Mircu, *Pogromurile din Bucovina*, p. 26; *DCFRJDH*, vol. 6, p. 147.

172. Mircu, *Pogromurile din Bucovina*, p. 28.

173. Carp, *Cartea neagră*, vol. 3, p. 30.

174. Mircu, *Pogromurile din Bucovina*, p. 29.

175. Ibid., pp. 29–30.

176. Carp, *Cartea neagră*, vol. 3, p. 30.

177. Mircu, *Pogromurile din Bucovina*, p. 30.

178. Ibid., pp. 30–32.

179. Carp, *Cartea neagră*, vol. 3, p. 30.

180. Ibid., p. 31; *DCFRJDH*, vol. 6, p. 147.

181. *DCFRJDH*, vol. 6, p. 147.

182. Ibid., p. 146.

183. *USHMM/SRI*, RG 25.004M, roll 28, fond 37818, vol. 1.

184. Mircu, *Pogromurile din Bucovina*, pp. 37–44.

185. Ibid., p. 43.

186. Carp, *Cartea neagră*, vol. 3, p. 31.

187. Ibid.; Mircu, *Pogromurile din Bucovina*, pp. 37–44.

188. Carp, *Cartea neagră*, vol. 3, p. 31; Bucharest Office of War Criminals, file no. 5260/1947.

189. Mircu, *Pogromurile din Bucovina*, pp. 36–37.

190. Carp, *Cartea neagră*, vol. 3, p. 31.

191. Ibid.; *DCFRJDH*, vol. 8, p. 617; Mircu, *Pogromurile din Bucovina*, p. 46.

192. Carp, *Cartea neagră*, vol. 3, p. 31; Mircu, *Pogromurile din Bucovina*, p. 44.

193. Carp, *Cartea neagră*, vol. 3, p. 32; Mircu, *Pogromurile din Bucovina*, p. 49.

194. Carp, *Cartea neagră*, vol. 3, p. 32; Mircu, *Pogromurile din Bucovina*, pp. 44–46.

195. Mircu, *Pogromurile din Bucovina*, p. 33.

196. Ibid., pp. 51–52; *DCFRJDH*, vol. 6, pp. 425–26.

197. *USHMM/SRI*, RG 25.004M, roll 47, fond 108233, vol. 7; Mircu, *Pogromurile din Bucovina*, p. 55.

198. Mircu, *Pogromurile din Bucovina*, p. 49.

199. Ibid., pp. 104–6; Carp, *Cartea neagră*, vol. 3, p. 31; *DCFRJDH*, vol. 6, pp. 426–27.

200. *USHMM/SRI*, RG 25.004M, roll 23, fond 20521, vol. 4, p. 7; Mircu, *Pogromurile din Bucovina*, pp. 104–5.

201. *USHMM/SRI*, RG 25.004M, roll 23, fond 20521, vol. 2.

202. Mircu, *Pogromurile din Bucovina*, pp. 61–64; *DCFRJDH*, vol. 6, pp. 304–7.

203. Mircu, *Pogromurile din Bucovina*, pp. 64–65.

204. Carp, *Cartea neagră*, vol. 3, p. 32; Mircu, *Pogromurile din Bucovina*, p. 73.

205. Mircu, *Pogromurile din Bucovina*, p. 68; Carp, *Cartea neagră*, vol. 3, p. 32; *USHMM/SRI*, RG 25.004M, roll 15, fond 1241, vol. 1.

206. Carp, *Cartea neagră*, vol. 3, p. 33.

207. Ibid., p. 35.

208. Ibid.

209. *DCFRJDH*, vol. 6, pp. 411–12.

210. Carp, *Cartea neagră*, vol. 2, p. 72, and vol. 3, p. 58.

211. Ibid., vol. 3, p. 55.

212. Ibid., pp. 34, 54–58.

213. *USHMM/SRI*, RG 25.004M, roll 23, fond 20521, vol. 2.

214. Ibid., vol. 7; Carp, *Cartea neagră*, vol. 3, p. 35.

215. *DCFRJDH*, vol. 6, p. 205.

216. Carp, *Cartea neagră*, vol. 3, pp. 35, 59.

217. *USHMM/SRI*, RG 25.004M, roll 15, fond 582, vol. 1.

218. Carp, *Cartea neagră*, vol. 3, pp. 32–33.

219. Ibid., p. 32.

220. *USHMM/SRI*, RG 25.004M, roll 23, fond 20521, vol. 11.

221. Ibid., roll 47, fond 108233, vol. 7, and fond 20521, vol. 5; *DCFRJDH*, vol. 6, p. 429.

222. *USHMM/SRI*, RG 25.004M, roll 23, fond 20521, vol. 7.

223. Ibid., vol. 2.

224. Carp, *Cartea neagră,* vol. 2, p. 75.

225. Ibid., vol. 3, p. 60.

226. Ibid., p. 75.

227. Ibid., p. 60

228. *USHMM/SRI,* RG 25.004M, roll 15, fond 18209, vols. 1–2; *DCFRJDH,* vol. 6, pp. 269–70.

229. *DCFRJDH,* vol. 6, p. 272.

230. *United States Holocaust Memorial Museum/Serviciul de Stat de Arhiva al Republicii Moldova* [Central Archives of the Republic of Moldova; hereafter *USHMM/SSARM*], RG 54.001M, roll 5, fond 192 (Direcţia Generala a Politiei), opis 3, vol. 142.

231. Carp, *Cartea neagră,* vol. 3, p. 60; Julius Fisher, *Transnistria: The Forgotten Cemetery* (South Brunswick, N.J., 1969), p. 40.

232. *DCFRJDH,* vol. 6, pp. 445–46.

233. *USHMM/SRI,* RG 25.004M, roll 17, fond 22539, vol. 45; *DCFRJDH,* vol. 6, pp. 460–65.

234. *DCFRJDH,* vol. 6, p. 462.

235. Ibid., pp. 489–90.

236. *USHMM/SRI,* RG 25.004M, roll 17, fond 22539, vol. 45.

237. *DCFRJDH,* vol. 6, pp. 447–48.

238. *USHMM/SRI,* RG 25.004M, roll 17, fond 22539, vol. 45.

239. *DCFRJDH,* vol. 6, pp. 447–48.

240. Ibid., p. 448.

241. *USHMM/SRI,* RG 25.004M, roll 17, fond 22539, vol. 45.

242. *DCFRJDH,* vol. 6, p. 449.

243. *USHMM/SRI,* RG 25.004M, roll 17, fond 22539, vol. 45.

244. Ibid.; *DCFRJDH,* vol. 6, p. 450.

245. *USHMM/SRI,* RG 25.004M, roll 17, fond 22539, vol. 45; *DCFRJDH,* vol. 6, p. 453.

246. *DCFRJDH,* vol. 6, p. 453.

247. Ibid., p. 464.

248. Ibid., p. 209.

249. Ibid., p. 458.

250. Ibid., pp. 463–64.

251. Ibid., p. 464.

252. Ibid., p. 465.

253. Ibid., p. 466.

254. Ibid.

255. Ibid., pp. 470–71.

256. *USHMM/SRI,* RG 25.004M, roll 17, fond 20725, vols. 25–26; *DCFRJDH,* vol. 6, pp. 216, 238–300.

257. *DCFRJDH,* vol. 6, pp. 494–98.

258. Ibid., pp. 516–18.

259. *USHMM/SRI*, RG 25.004M, rolls 25–26, fond 20725, vols. 25–26; *DCFRJDH*, vol. 6, pp. 216, 238–300.

260. *USHMM/SRI*, RG 25.004M, roll 26, fond 20725, vol. 11.

261. *DCFRJDH*, vol. 6, p. 294.

262. *USHMM/SRI*, RG 25.004M, roll 17, fond 18424, vol. 1.

263. *DCFRJDH*, vol. 6, p. 288.

264. *USHMM/SRI*, RG 25.004M, roll 24, fond 20521, vol. 21.

265. Hilberg, *The Destruction*, vol. 2, p. 768.

266. Carp, *Cartea neagră*, vol. 3, p. 55.

267. Henry Monneray, *La Persécution des Juifs dans les Pays de l'Est* (Paris, 1949), p. 291.

268. Hilberg, *The Destruction*, vol. 2, p. 771.

Chapter 4: Transit Camps and Ghettos, Deportations, and Other Mass Murders

1. *DCFRJDH*, vol. 2, pp. 414–15.

2. Carp, *Cartea neagră*, vol. 2, p. 22.

3. Ibid., pp. 21, 22, 40; *Procesul marii trădări*, p. 100.

4. *DCFRJDH*, vol. 3, p. 65.

5. Ibid., vol. 10, p. 77; Carp, *Cartea neagră*, vol. 3, p. 80.

6. *DCFRJDH*, vol. 10, p. 131.

7. Ibid., vol. 4, p. 303.

8. Ibid., vol. 7, p. 327.

9. Ibid., vol. 4, p. 274.

10. Ibid., vol. 10, p. 699.

11. Ibid., p. 599.

12. Ibid., vol. 6, pp. 315–18.

13. Ibid., pp. 234, 426.

14. Ibid., p. 238.

15. Ibid., p. 239.

16. Carp, *Cartea neagră*, vol. 3, pp. 234, 245–46.

17. Ibid., p. 241.

18. Ibid., pp. 241–42.

19. *DCFRJDH*, vol. 6, p. 165.

20. Ibid.

21. Ibid., pp. 101–2.

22. Zaharia, *Pages de la résistance*, pp. 46–47.

23. *DCFRJDH*, vol. 7, p. 531.

24. Carp, *Cartea neagră*, vol. 3, p. 36.

25. Ibid., p. 37.

26. Ibid., p. 38.

27. Mirjam Korber, *Deportiert* (Konstanz, 1993), p. 217.

28. Carp, *Cartea neagră*, vol. 3, pp. 36–63.

29. *USHMM/MSM*, RG 25.003M, roll 653, fond Guvernamîntul Basarabiei, Cabinet Militar, folder 5.

30. *USHMM/SRI*, RG 25.004M, roll 24, fond 20725, vol. 5; Carp, *Cartea neagră*, vol. 3, pp. 37, 65–67.

31. Carp, *Cartea neagră*, vol. 3, pp. 37, 70; *DCFRJDH*, vol. 5, p. 42; *USHMM/SRI*, RG 25.004M, roll 17, fond 22539, vol. 45.

32. *USHMM/SRI*, RG 25.004M, roll 46, fond 108233, vol. 99; Carp, *Cartea neagră*, vol. 3, plate 4; *DCFRJDH*, vol. 5, p. 39.

33. *USHMM/SRI*, RG 25.004M, roll 24, fond 20725, vol. 5.

34. Ibid.

35. Ibid., roll 20, fond 3981, vol. 10.

36. *DCFRJDH*, vol. 10, pp. 351–52.

37. Ibid., p. 79.

38. Carp, *Cartea neagră*, vol. 3, p. 92.

39. Ibid., p. 91.

40. Ibid., p. 92.

41. *USHMM/SSARM*, RG 54.001M, roll 2, fond Direcţia Generala a Poliţiei, opis 2, vol. 299.

42. *USHMM/SRI*, RG 25.004M, roll 35, fond 40010, vol. 89.

43. *DCFRJDH*, vol. 10, p. 84.

44. Hilberg, *The Destruction*, vol. 2, pp. 768–69.

45. Carp, *Cartea neagră*, vol. 3, pp. 81, 96.

46. Ibid., p. 82.

47. Ibid., pp. 82, 98.

48. *USHMM/SRI*, RG 25.004M, roll 35, fond 40010, vol. 89.

49. *USHMM/MSM*, RG 25.003M, roll 781, fond Armata aIVa.

50. Hilberg, *The Destruction*, vol. 2, p. 769.

51. Carp, *Cartea neagră*, vol. 3, pp. 82, 99.

52. Hilberg, *The Destruction*, vol. 2, p. 770.

53. Carp, *Cartea neagră*, vol. 3, pp. 82, 103–4.

54. *USHMM/MSM*, RG 25.003M, roll 656, fond 3467 Guvernamîntul Basarabiei, Cabinet Militar, folder 29.

55. Carp, *Cartea neagră*, vol. 3, p. 36.

56. *USHMM/SRI*, RG 25.004M, roll 24, fond 20725.

57. *USHMM/MSM*, RG 25.003M, roll 656, fond 3467 Guvernamîntul Basarabiei, Cabinet Militar, folder 29.

58. Korber, *Deportiert*, p. 217.

59. Carp, *Cartea neagră*, vol. 3, pp. 37–38.

60. *USHMM/MSM*, RG 25.003M, roll 203, fond Armata aIVa, vol. 870.

61. Carp, *Cartea neagră*, vol. 3, p. 117.

62. *Procesul marii trădări*, p. 247.

63. *DCFRJDH*, vol. 5, p. 129. Ironically, the anti-Semitic newspaper editor seems to conflate the Jews with the non-Jewish king, Ahasverus, who played a role in the Book of Esther.

64. Hilberg, *The Destruction*, vol. 2, p. 771.

65. *USHMM/SRI*, RG 25.004M, roll 28, fond 37818, vol. 1.

66. *DCFRJDH*, vol. 6, p. 145.

67. Ibid.

68. Ibid., pp. 144, 149.

69. Ibid., p. 147.

70. Ibid., p. 148.

71. Ibid.

72. Ibid., p. 153.

73. Carp, *Cartea neagră*, vol. 3, p. 78.

74. *DCFRJDH*, vol. 8, p. 579.

75. Carp, *Cartea neagră*, vol. 3, p. 78.

76. *USHMM/SRI*, RG 25.004M, roll 35, fond 40010, vol. 107; Carp, *Cartea neagră*, vol. 3, p. 93, plate 4; *DCFRJDH*, vol. 5, p. 17.

77. *USHMM/MSM*, RG 23.003M, roll 653, fond Guvernamîntul Basarabiei, Cabinet Militar, vol. 5.

78. Carp, *Cartea neagră*, vol. 3, plate 4; *DCFRJDH*, vol. 5, p. 18.

79. Carp, *Cartea neagră*, vol. 3, p. 94.

80. *USHMM/SSARM*, RG 54.001M, roll 5, fond 192 (Direcția Generala a Poliției), opis 3, vol. 142.

81. *USHMM/SRI*, RG 25.004M, roll 24, fond 20725, vol. 4.

82. Ibid., roll 15, fond 18209, vol. 2; *USHMM/SSARM*, RG 54.001M, roll 5, fond 192 (Direcția Generala a Poliției), opis 3, vol. 142.

83. *USHMM/MSM*, RG 25.003M, roll 352, fond Armata aIIIa, vol. 413.

84. *USHMM/SSARM*, RG 54.001M, roll 5, fond 192 (Direcția Generala a Poliției), opis 3, vol. 142.

85. Ibid.

86. Carp, *Cartea neagră*, vol. 3, p. 97.

87. *DCFRJDH*, vol. 5, p. 38.

88. Carp, *Cartea neagră*, vol. 3, pp. 98–99; *DCFRJDH*, vol. 5, p. 37.

89. *DCFRJDH*, vol. 5, p. 37.

90. Carp, *Cartea neagră*, vol. 3, p. 101.

91. *USHMM/SRI*, RG 25.004M, roll 35, fond 40010, vol. 107; Carp, *Cartea neagră*, vol. 3, pp. 98–99; *DCFRJDH*, vol. 5, p. 40.

92. *DCFRJDH*, vol. 5, p. 41.

93. Carp, *Cartea neagră*, vol. 3, p. 102; *DCFRJDH*, vol. 5, p. 47.

94. Carp, *Cartea neagră*, vol. 3, p. 10; *DCFRJDH*, vol. 5, p. 47.

95. *USHMM/SRI*, RG 25.004M, roll 15, fond 9614, vol. 1.

96. Carp, *Cartea neagră*, vol. 2, p. 47.

97. *USHMM/MSM*, RG 25.003M, roll 657, fond Guvernamîntul Basarabiei, Cabinet Militar, vol. 35.

98. Carp, *Cartea neagră*, vol. 3, p. 83; *DCFRJDH*, vol. 5, p. 56.

99. Carp, *Cartea neagră*, vol. 3, p. 107.

100. Ibid., *DCFRJDH*, vol. 5, p. 56.

101. Ibid.

102. *USHMM/SRI*, RG 25.004M, roll 35, fond 40010, vol. 107.

103. *USHMM/MSM*, RG 25.003M, roll 657, fond Guvernamîntul Basarabiei, Cabinet Militar, vol. 35.

104. Carp, *Cartea neagră*, vol. 3, p. 107; *DCFRJDH*, vol. 5, p. 57.

105. *USHMM/MSM*, RG 25.003M, roll 657, fond Guvernamîntul Basarabiei, Cabinet Militar, vol. 35.

106. Carp, *Cartea neagră*, vol. 3, p. 85.

107. Ibid., vol. 1, p. 40; *NARA*, T165, roll 662.

108. Carp, *Cartea neagră*, vol. 1, pp. 40–41.

109. *USHMM/SRI*, RG 25.004M, roll 10, fond 2694, vol. 17.

110. *USHMM/MSM*, RG 25.003M, roll 657, fond Guvernamîntul Basarabiei, Cabinet Militar, vol. 32.

111. *DCFRJDH*, vol. 5, pp. 70–71.

112. Ibid., p. 82.

113. Carp, *Cartea neagră*, vol. 1, p. 41; *DCFRJDH*, vol. 5, p. 74.

114. *USHMM/MSM*, RG 25.003M, roll 657, fond Guvernamîntul Basarabiei, Cabinet Militar, vol. 32.

115. Hilberg, *The Destruction*, vol. 2, p. 771.

116. *DCFRJDH*, vol. 10, p. 487.

117. Carp, *Cartea neagră*, vol. 3, pp. 60–61, 78.

118. *DCFRJDH*, vol. 6, p. 274.

119. Ibid., p. 275.

120. *USHMM/SRI*, RG 25.004M, roll 15, fond 9614, vol. 1.

121. *Encyclopedia of the Holocaust* (New York, 1990), p. 418.

122. M. Rudich, *La braţ cu moartea* (Bucharest, 1945), pp. 25–27.

123. *Encyclopedia of the Holocaust*, p. 1339.

124. *DCFRJDH*, vol. 5, p. 83.

125. Carp, *Cartea neagră*, vol. 3, p. 119; *DCFRJDH*, vol. 5, p. 82.

126. *DCFRJDH*, vol. 5, p. 83.

127. Ibid., vol. 6, p. 157.

128. *USHMM/MSM*, RG 25.003M, roll 657, fond Guvernamîntul Basarabiei, Cabinet Militar, vol. 35.

129. *USHMM/MSM*, RG 25.003M, roll 352, fond Armata aIIa, vol. 413.

130. *DCFRJDH*, vol. 8, pp. 579–80.

131. *USHMM/SRI*, RG 25.004M, roll 28, fond 40013, vol. 1; *DCFRJDH*, vol. 6, p. 116.

132. Ibid.

133. *USHMM/SRI*, RG 25.004M, roll 28, fond 40013, vol. 1.

134. *DCFRJDH*, vol. 6, p. 119.

135. *USHMM/SRI*, RG 25.004M, roll 28, fond 40013, vol. 1.

136. *DCFRJDH,* vol. 6, pp. 123–24.

137. *USHMM/SRI,* RG 25.004M, roll 29, fond 40013, vol. 6; *DCFRJDH,* vol. 6, pp. 123–24.

138. *DCFRJDH,* vol. 6, p. 118.

139. Ibid.

140. *USHMM/SRI,* RG 25.004M, roll 29, fond 40013, vol. 6; Carp, *Cartea neagră,* vol. 3, pp. 120–23; *DCFRJDH,* vol. 6, pp. 124–25.

141. *USHMM/MSM,* RG 25.003M, roll 656, fond Guvernamîntul Basarabiei, Cabinet Militar, vol. 29.

142. *Encyclopedia of the Holocaust,* p. 943.

143. *USHMM/SRI,* RG 25.004M, roll 28, fond 40013, vol. 1.

144. Ibid., roll 24, fond 40013, vol. 1.

145. Ibid.

146. Ibid., roll 29, fond 40013, vol. 5.

147. Ibid.

148. Ibid.

149. Ibid.

150. *DCFRJDH,* vol. 6, p. 131.

151. Ibid., p. 133.

152. *USHMM/SRI,* RG 25.004M, roll 28, fond 40013, vol. 1.

153. Ibid.

154. Ibid.

155. *DCFRJDH,* vol. 6, p. 133.

156. Ibid., p. 127.

157. Carp, *Cartea neagră,* vol. 3, p. 90.

158. Ibid., vol. 6, p. 131.

159. Ibid., vol. 5, pp. 243–44.

160. *USHMM/MSM,* RG 25.003M, roll 656, fond Guvernamîntul Basarabiei, Cabinet Militar, vol. 29.

161. Ibid., roll 657, fond Guvernamîntul Basarabiei, Cabinet Militar, vol. 35; *USHMM/SSARM,* RG 54.001M, roll 6.

162. *DCFRJDH,* vol. 10, p. 92.

163. *USHMM/SRI,* RG 25.004M, roll 25.

164. *USHMM/MSM,* RG 25.003M, roll 29, fond Guvernamîntul Basarabiei, Cabinet Militar, vol. 29.

165. Ibid., roll 657, fond Guvernamîntul Basarabiei, Cabinet Militar, vol. 32.

166. Ibid., RG 25.004M, roll 656, fond Guvernamîntul Basarabiei, Cabinet Militar, vol. 29.

167. *USHMM/SRI,* RG 25.004M, roll 25.

168. *USHMM/SSARM,* RG 54.001M, roll 3, fond 204, opis 1, vol. 23.

169. *USHMM/MSM,* RG 25.003M, roll 657, fond Guvernamîntul Basarabiei, Cabinet Militar, vols. 32, 35; *USHMM/SRI,* RG 25.004M, roll 25.

170. Carp, *Cartea neagră,* vol. 3, p. 139.

171. *USHMM/SRI,* RG 25.004M, roll 19, fond 40011, vol. 1.

172. Ibid., vol. 5.

173. Ibid.

174. Ibid.

175. Carp, *Cartea neagră,* vol. 3, pp. 155–56.

176. Ibid.

177. Ibid.

178. Ibid., p. 143.

179. *USHMM/SRI,* RG 25.004M, roll 25, fond 20725, vol. 9.

180. Ibid., roll 34, fond 40010, vol. 4; *Procesul marii trădări,* p. 144.

181. *USHMM/SRI,* RG 25.004M, roll 34, fond 40010, vol. 45.

182. Carp, *Cartea neagră,* vol. 3, pp. 85, 116–17; *DCFRJDH,* vol. 5, p. 73.

183. Ibid.

184. Carp, *Cartea neagră,* vol. 3, p. 85.

185. *USHMM/MSM,* RG 25.003M, roll 656, fond Guvernamîntul Basarabiei, Cabinet Militar, vol. 29; *USHMM/SSARM,* RG 54.001M, fond 706 (Preşedenţia Consiliului de Ministrii), opis 1, vol. 22; author's emphasis on point 11.

186. *USHMM/SRI,* RG 25.004M, roll 25, fond 20725, vol. 9; emphasis added.

187. Ibid.

188. *DCFRJDH,* vol. 5, p. 84.

189. *USHMM/MSM,* RG 25.003M, roll 656, fond Guvernamîntul Basarabiei, Cabinet Militar, vol. 29; *DCFRJDH,* vol. 5, pp. 85–86; emphasis added.

190. *USHMM/MSM,* RG 25.003M, roll 656, fond Guvernamîntul Basarabiei, Cabinet Militar, vol. 29.

191. Ibid.

192. Ibid.

193. *USHMM/SRI,* RG 25.004M, roll 28, fond 40013, vol. 1.

194. *USHMM/MSM,* RG 25.003M, roll 656, fond Guvernamîntul Basarabiei, Cabinet Militar, vol. 29.

195. Ibid.

196. *USHMM/SRI,* RG 25.004M, roll 28, fond 40013, vol. 1.

197. *USHMM/MSM,* roll 657, fond Guvernamîntul Basarabiei, Cabinet Militar, vol. 32.

198. Carp, *Cartea neagră,* vol. 3, p. 40.

199. *USHMM/SRI,* RG 25.004M, roll 15, fond 9614, vol. 1; Carp, *Cartea neagră,* vol. 3, p. 65.

200. Carp, *Cartea neagră,* vol. 3, p. 88.

201. *USHMM/SRI,* RG 25.004M, roll 23, fond 20521, vol. 2.

202. Ibid., vol. 5.

203. Carp, *Cartea neagră,* vol. 3, p. 40.

204. *DCFRJDH,* vol. 6, p. 158.

205. Carp, *Cartea neagră,* vol. 3, pp. 88, 90, 128; *DCFRJDH,* vol. 6, p. 158.

206. Carp, *Cartea neagră,* vol. 3, p. 40.

207. Ibid., p. 88.

208. *USHMM/SRI,* RG 25.004M, roll 20, fond 20725, vol. 10.

209. *USHMM/MSM,* roll 656, fond Guvernamîntul Basarabiei, Cabinet Militar, vol. 29.

210. Carp, *Cartea neagră,* vol. 3, p. 87.

211. *DCFRJDH,* vol. 6, p. 122.

212. Rudich, *La braţ cu moartea,* p. 51.

213. *DCFRJDH,* vol. 10, pp. 101, 102.

214. *USHMM/SRI,* RG 25.004M, roll 25, fond 20725, vol. 10.

215. *USHMM/MSM,* RG 25.003M, roll 656, fond Guvernamîntul Basarabiei, Cabinet Militar, vol. 29; *USHMM/SRI,* RG 25.004M, roll 18, fond 22539, vol. 1, and roll 17, fond 22539, vol. 41.

216. *USHMM/SRI,* RG 25.004M, roll 25, fond 20725, vol. 10.

217. Ibid., roll 18, fond 22539, vol. 1.

218. Ibid., vol. 32.

219. Ibid., roll 25, fond 20725, vol. 10.

220. *USHMM/MSM,* RG 25.003M, roll 656, fond Guvernamîntul Basarabiei, Cabinet Militar, vol. 29; *USHMM/SRI,* RG 25.004M, roll 16(2), fond 18844, vol. 3.

221. Ibid.

222. Carp, *Cartea neagră,* vol. 3, p. 88.

223. Ibid., p. 90.

224. *DCFRJDH,* vol. 6, p. 134.

225. *USHMM/MSM,* RG 25.004M, fond 20725, vol. 10.

226. *USHMM/MSM,* RG 25.003M, roll 656, fond Guvernamîntul Basarabiei, Cabinet Militar, vol. 29.

227. *USHMM/SRI,* RG 25.004M, roll 25, fond 20725, vol. 10.

228. *USHMM/MSM,* RG 25.003M, roll 656, fond Guvernamîntul Basarabiei, Cabinet Militar, vol. 29.

229. Ibid., roll 657.

230. Ibid., roll 658.

231. *USHMM/SRI,* RG 25.004M, roll 25, fond 20725, vol. 10.

232. Ibid., roll 15, fond 582, vol. 2.

233. Carp, *Cartea neagră,* vol. 3, pp. 90, 128; *USHMM/SRI,* RG 25.004M, roll 16(2), fond 18844, vol. 3; *DCFRJDH,* vol. 5, pp. 131–33.

234. *USHMM/SRI,* RG 25.004M, roll 25, fond 20725, vol. 10.

235. *USHMM/MSM,* RG 25.003M, roll 656, fond Guvernamîntul Basarabiei, Cabinet Militar, vol. 29.

236. Ibid.

237. *USHMM/SRI,* RG 25.004M, roll 25, fond 20725.

238. *USHMM/MSM,* RG 25.003M, roll 657, fond Guvernamîntul Basarabiei, Cabinet Militar, vol. 32.

239. *USHMM/SRI,* RG 25.004M, roll 25, fond 20725, vol. 10.

240. Ibid.

241. *USHMM/MSM,* RG 25.003M, roll 658, fond Guvernamîntul Basarabiei, Cabinet Militar.

242. Ibid., roll 657, fond Guvernamîntul Basarabiei, Cabinet Militar, vol. 96.

243. Ibid., roll 658, fond Guvernamîntul Basarabiei, Cabinet Militar.

244. Ibid., roll 657, fond Guvernamîntul Basarabiei, Cabinet Militar, vol. 96.

245. *USHMM/SRI*, RG 25.004M, roll 34, fond 20725, vol. 10.

246. *USHMM/MSM*, RG 25.003M, roll 353, fond Armata aIIa, vol. 1122, and roll 658, fond Guvernamîntul Basarabiei, Cabinet Militar, vol. 96.

247. *USHMM/SRI*, RG 25.004M, roll 34, fond 40010, vol. 75.

248. *USHMM/MSM*, RG 25.003M, roll 658, fond Guvernamîntul Basarabiei, Cabinet Militar, vol. 96.

249. *USHMM/SRI*, RG 25.004M, roll 25, fond 20725, vol. 10.

250. *USHMM/MSM*, RG 25.003M, roll 658, Guvernamîntul Basarabiei, Cabinet Militar, vol. 120.

251. Carp, *Cartea neagră*, vol. 2, pp. 48–50.

252. *USHMM/SRI*, RG 25.004M, roll 19, fond 40011, vol. 5.

253. Ibid., roll 25, fond 20725, vol. 9; Carp, *Cartea neagră*, vol. 3, p. 143.

254. Carp, *Cartea neagră*, vol. 3, pp. 135, 152.

255. Ibid., p. 139.

256. Ibid., p. 171.

257. *USHMM/SRI*, RG 25.004M, roll 19, fond 40011, vol. 5; Carp, *Cartea neagră*, vol. 3, p. 153; *DCFRJDH*, vol. 5, p. 96.

258. *USHMM/SRI*, RG 25.004M, roll 19, fond 40011, vol. 5; Carp, *Cartea neagră*, vol. 3, p. 155; *DCFRJDH*, vol. 5, p. 99.

259. *USHMM/SRI*, RG 25.004M, roll 19, fond 40011, vol. 1.

260. Carp, *Cartea neagră*, vol. 3, p. 137.

261. *USHMM/SRI*, RG 25.004M, roll 19, fond 40011, vol. 5.

262. Ibid.

263. Ibid.

264. Carp, *Cartea neagră*, vol. 3, p. 137.

265. Ibid., p. 138.

266. *DCFRJDH*, vol. 5, p. 104.

267. *USHMM/SRI*, RG 25.004M, roll 19, fond 40011, vol. 5; *United States Holocaust Memorial Museum/Czernowitz Oblast Archives* [hereafter *USHMM/COA*], RG 54.001M, fond 307, opis 3, vol. 10.

268. Carp, *Cartea neagră*, vol. 3, p. 173.

269. Ibid., p. 180.

270. Ibid., p. 139.

271. *USHMM/SRI*, RG 25.004M, roll 14, fond 2868, vol. 207; Carp, *Cartea neagră*, vol. 3, p. 141.

272. Carp, *Cartea neagră*, vol. 3, p. 176.

273. Ibid., pp. 75, 134.

274. Ibid., pp. 133–34.

275. *USHMM/COA*, RG 31.006M, roll 5, fond 307, opis 3, vol. 10.

276. Carp, *Cartea neagră*, vol. 3, pp. 137–38.

277. Ibid., pp. 148–51.

278. *DCFRJDH*, vol. 6, p. 257.

279. Carp, *Cartea neagră,* vol. 3, p. 139.

280. *USHMM/SRI,* RG 25.004M, roll 35, fond 40010, vol. 17; *DCFRJDH,* vol. 5, pp. 134–35, 170–73.

281. *USHMM/MSM,* RG 25.003M, roll 452, fond Corpul 4 Armata, vol. 6262.

282. *DCFRJDH,* vol. 3, p. 413.

283. Ibid.

284. Ibid., pp. 413–14.

285. *USHMM/SRI,* RG 25.004M, roll 34, fond 40010, vol. 75.

286. Carp, *Cartea neagră,* vol. 3, p. 239.

287. *USHMM/SRI,* RG 25.004M, roll 19, fond 40011, vol. 5; Carp, *Cartea neagră,* vol. 3, p. 232.

288. *USHMM/RMFA,* RG 25.006M, roll 10, fond Preşedenţia Consiliului de Miniştrii, vol. 20.

289. *USHMM/COA,* RG 25.006M, fond 307, opis 1, vol. 244; *USHMM/RMFA,* RG 25.006M, roll 10, fond Preşedenţia Consiliului de Miniştrii, vol. 20.

290. Carp, *Cartea neagră,* vol. 3, p. 232.

291. *USHMM/COA,* RG 31.006M, roll 9; *USHMM/RMFA,* RG 006M, roll 10, fond Preşedenţia Consiliului de Miniştrii, vol. 20.

292. *USHMM/SRI,* RG 25.004M, roll 15, fond 7197, vol. 2; *DCFRJDH,* vol. 6, p. 265.

293. Carp, *Cartea neagră,* vol. 3, p. 245.

294. Ibid.

295. *DCFRJDH,* vol. 6, p. 266.

296. Ibid., p. 254.

297. Ibid., p. 255.

298. *USHMM/COA,* RG 31.005M, fond 307, opis 1, vol. 1254.

299. *DCFRJDH,* vol. 5, p. 280.

300. Ibid., p. 281.

301. Ibid., p. 283.

302. *Foreign Relations of the United States: Diplomatic Papers, 1941,* vol. 2, p. 871.

303. Ibid., p. 874.

304. *Martiriul evreilor din Romania* (Bucharest, 1991), p. 171.

305. Ibid.; *DCFRJDH,* vol. 3, pp. 370–77.

306. *DCFRJDH,* vol. 10, p. 50.

307. Carp, *Cartea neagră,* vol. 3, p. 39.

308. Ibid., vol. 1, p. 19, and vol. 3, p. 39; Jean Ancel, "The Romanian Way of Solving the Jewish Problem in Bessarabia and Bukovina, June–July 1941," *Yad Vashem Studies* (Jerusalem) 29 (1988).

309. Carp, *Cartea neagră,* vol. 1, p. 20.

310. Ibid.

311. *DCFRJDH,* vol. 8, p. 617.

312. Ibid., vol. 10, p. 586, and vol. 8, p. 576.

313. Ancel, "The Romanian Way," p. 230.

314. Hilberg, *The Destruction,* vol. 2, p. 768.

315. Ibid., p. 771.

316. *NARA,* Document No. 29958, PB 226, 16 Box 270, Encl. No. 2, Dispatch No. 1302, January 11, 1943, American legation in Stockholm.

317. *American Jewish Archives* (AJA) (Cincinnati), IJA 15/OSS (Office of Strategic Services); the Canadian source mentioned is Eugen Kulisher's *The Displacement of Population in Europe* (Montreal, 1943).

318. *USHMM/MSM,* RG 25.003M, fond Guvernamîntul Basarabiei, roll 654, folder 13.

319. Carp, *Cartea neagră,* vol. 3, p. 61.

320. Ibid.

321. Ibid.

322. *USHMM/RMFA,* RG 25.006M, roll 10, fond Preşedenţia Consiliului de Miniştrii, vol. 20.

323. Ibid.

324. *USHMM/COA,* RG 31.006M, roll 9, fond 807, opis 1, vol. 292.

325. *USHMM/MSM,* RG 25.003M, roll 658, fond Guvernamîntul Basarabiei, Cabinet Militar.

326. Carp, *Cartea neagră,* vol. 3, pp. 444–45.

327. *USHMM/SRI,* RG 25.004M, roll 31, fond 40010, vol. 1.

328. Ibid., roll 169(2), fond 18844, vol. 3.

329. *DCFRJDH,* vol. 5, pp. 510–13.

330. Carp, *Cartea neagră,* vol. 1, p. 40.

331. *American Jewish Archives,* OSS-Labor Supply Section, Economics Subdivision, Europe-Africa Division, IJA 8A/2/OSS.

332. Alexander Dallin, *Odessa, 1941–1944: A Case Study of Soviet Territory Under Foreign Rule,* Rand Corporation Memorandum No. 1875 (Santa Monica, 1957), p. 317.

333. Fisher, *Transnistria,* p. 135.

334. *USHMM/MSM,* RG 25.003M, roll 353, fond Armata aIIa, vol. 421.

335. Carp, *Cartea neagră,* vol. 3, p. 320.

336. *USHMM/RMFA,* RG 25.006M, roll 10, fond Preşedenţia Consiliului de Miniştrii, vol. 20.

337. *USHMM/SRI,* RG 25.004M, roll 25, fond 20725, vol. 9.

338. *USHMM/RMFA,* RG 25.006M, roll 10, fond Preşedenţia Consiliului de Miniştrii.

Chapter 5: The Massacres in Transnistria

1. Dallin, *Odessa,* p. 306.

2. Hilberg, *The Destruction,* vol. 2, p. 776.

3. Dallin, *Odessa,* p. 308.

4. Hilberg, *The Destruction,* vol. 2, p. 759.

5. *USHMM/SRI,* RG 25.004M, roll 28, fond 40013, vol. 1.

6. Carp, *Cartea neagră,* vol. 3, p. 184, plate 7; *DCFRJDH,* vol. 3, p. 286.

7. Dora Litani, "The Destruction of the Jews of Odessa in the Light of Romanian Documents," *Yad Vashem Studies* 6 (1967): 137.

8. Dallin, *Odessa,* p. 308.

9. Cited in Litani, "The Destruction," p. 137; Carp, *Cartea neagră,* vol. 3, p. 95.

10. *Procesul marii trădări,* pp. 55, 285.

11. Ibid., p. 54.

12. *USHMM/MSM,* RG 25.003M, roll 12(203), fond Armata aIVa, vol. 870.

13. Carp, *Cartea neagră,* vol. 3, p. 209; *Procesul marii trădări,* p. 286.

14. *USHMM/MSM,* RG 25.003M, roll 12(203), fond Armata aIVa, vol. 870.

15. Carp, *Cartea neagră,* vol. 3, pp. 199, 208.

16. *USHMM/MSM,* RG 25.003M, roll 12(203), fond Armata aIVa, vol. 870.

17. Carp, *Cartea neagră,* vol. 3, pp. 199, 208; Litani, "The Destruction," p. 139; *DCFRJDH,* vol. 6, p. 59.

18. Carp, *Cartea neagră,* vol. 3, p. 199; *DCFRJDH,* vol. 6, p. 65.

19. *USHMM/MSM,* RG 25.003M, roll 12(203), fond Armata aIVa, vol. 870.

20. Ibid.

21. *NARA,* T501M, roll 2T8; Hilberg, *The Destruction,* vol. 1, p. 306.

22. *Martiriul evreilor din Romania,* p. 175.

23. Carp, *Cartea neagră,* vol. 3, p. 200; *USHMM/SRI,* RG 25.004M, roll 19, fond 40011, vol. 1.

24. Carp, *Cartea neagră,* vol. 3, p. 200; *USHMM/SRI,* RG 25.004M, roll 19, fond 40011, vol. 6.

25. Carp, *Cartea neagră,* vol. 3, pp. 210–11; *USHMM/SRI,* RG 25.004M, roll 19, fond 40011, vol. 6.

26. Carp, *Cartea neagră,* vol. 3, p. 200; *USHMM/SRI,* RG 25.004M, rolls 19, 20, 26, fonds 40011, 39181.

27. *USHMM/SRI,* RG 25.004M, roll 20, fond 39181, vol. 10; *DCFRJDH,* vol. 6, p. 82.

28. Carp, *Cartea neagră,* vol. 2, pp. 51–52.

29. *USHMM/SRI,* RG 25.004M, roll 20, fond 40011, vol. 6.

30. *DCFRJDH,* vol. 6, p. 282; Litani, "The Destruction," p. 139.

31. *USHMM/SRI,* RG 25.004M, roll 20, fond 40011, vol. 7.

32. Ibid., roll 19, fond 40011, vol. 7.

33. Ibid., roll 30, fond 20401, vol. 2.

34. Litani, "The Destruction," p. 139.

35. *NARA,* T501, roll 278.

36. Carp, *Cartea neagră,* vol. 3, p. 200.

37. *USHMM/SRI,* RG 25.004M, rolls 19, 20, 26, fond 40011.

38. Ibid., roll 32, fond 40010, vol. 9.

39. *DCFRJDH,* vol. 5, p. 541.

40. *USHMM/SRI,* RG 25.004M, roll 19, fond 40011, vol. 7.

41. Ibid., vol. 1, and roll 21, fond 40011, vol. 17; Carp, *Cartea neagră*, vol. 3, pp. 215–16.

42. *USHMM/SRI*, RG 25.004M, roll 19, fond 40011, vols. 1, 6, and roll 21, fond 40011, vol. 17; *DCFRJDH*, vol. 6, p. 93.

43. *USHMM/SRI*, RG 25.004M, roll 19, fond 40011, vol. 1; *DCFRJDH*, vol. 6, p. 90.

44. *DCFRJDH*, vol. 5, p. 541.

45. Ibid., vol. 6, p. 93.

46. Litani, "The Destruction," p. 141.

47. *USHMM/SRI*, RG 25.004M, roll 36, fond 40010, vol. 127.

48. Ibid., roll 31, fond 40010, vol. 1.

49. Sonia Palty, *Evrei treceti Nistrul* (Bucharest, 1992), pp. 187–88, 195–96.

50. *DCFRJDH*, vol. 6, p. 93.

51. *USHMM/SRI*, RG 25.004M, roll 20, fond 40011, vol. 6.

52. Ibid., roll 21, fond 40011, vol. 17.

53. *USHMM/MSM*, RG 25.003M, roll 20(354), fond Armata aIIIa, vol. 1128.

54. Monneray, *La Persecution*, p. 263.

55. Ibid., pp. 263, 267.

56. *DCFRJDH*, vol. 10, p. 193.

57. Ibid.

58. Carp, *Cartea neagră*, vol. 3, p. 206.

59. *DCFRJDH*, vol. 5, p. 541.

60. *United States Holocaust Museum/Nikolaev Oblast Archives*, RG 31.008M, fond P2178, opis 1, folder 58.

61. *USHMM/SRI*, RG 25.004M, roll 26, fond 38891, vol. 1.

62. Ibid.

63. Ibid.

64. Hilberg, *The Destruction*, vol. 1, p. 374.

65. Dallin, *Odessa*, p. 317.

66. *USHMM/SRI*, RG 25.004M, roll 26, fond 39181, vol. 4.

67. Ibid., roll 20, fond 40011, vol. 8; Rudich, *La brat cu moartea*, p. 77.

68. *United States Holocaust Memorial Museum/Romanian State Archives* [hereafter *USHMM/RSA*], RG 25.002M, roll 5.

69. *USHMM/SRI*, RG 25.004M, roll 20, fond 40011, vol. 8; Carp, *Cartea neagră*, vol. 3, pp. 205, 226, 227; *DCFRJDH*, vol. 5, pp. 261, 263–64.

70. *USHMM/RSA*, RG 25.002M, roll 5.

71. *USHMM/SRI*, RG 25.004M, roll 36(2), fond 23004, vol. 13.

72. Ibid., roll 28, fond 38891, vol. 23.

73. Ibid., roll 36(2), fond 23004, vol. 13; Carp, *Cartea neagră*, vol. 3, pp. 205–6, 227; *DCFRJDH*, vol. 5, p. 274.

74. *USHMM/MSM*, RG 25.003M, roll 11(202), fond Armata aIVa, vol. 779.

75. Ibid., fond 39181, vol. 5.

76. Carp, *Cartea neagră*, vol. 3, p. 282.

77. *United States Holocaust Memorial Museum/Odessa Oblast Archives* [hereafter *USHMM/OOA*], RG 31.004M, opis 1, folder 40.

78. *USHMM/SRI*, RG 25.004M, roll 20, fond 40011, vol. 15.

79. Carp, *Cartea neagră*, vol. 3, p. 240.

80. *USHMM/SRI*, RG 25.004M, roll 36(2), fond 23004, vol. 13; Carp, *Cartea neagră*, vol. 3, pp. 283–84.

81. Carp, *Cartea neagră*, vol. 3, pp. 285–86.

82. Ibid., p. 286.

83. Ibid.

84. Ibid.

85. Ibid., p. 288.

86. Ibid.

87. Ibid., p. 289.

88. Ibid.

89. Ibid., p. 293; *United States Holocaust Memorial Museum Archives,* testimony of David Wasserman.

90. Carp, *Cartea neagră*, vol. 3, p. 295.

91. Ibid., p. 300.

92. Ibid., p. 302.

93. Ibid., p. 304.

94. *USHMM/SRI*, RG 25.004M, roll 26, fond 38891, vol. 1.

95. Carp, *Cartea neagră*, vol. 3, pp. 269, 271, 338–39.

96. Ibid., p. 271.

97. *USHMM/SRI*, RG 25.004M, roll 29, fond 40013, vol. 5.

98. Ibid., vol. 6.

99. Carp, *Cartea neagră*, vol. 3, p. 295.

100. Ibid., pp. 298–99, 385–86.

101. Ibid., p. 301.

102. *USHMM/COA*, RG 31.006M, roll 9, name lists; *USHMM/SRI*, RG 25.004M, roll 19, fond 40011, vol. 5; Carp, *Cartea neagră*, vol. 3, p. 282.

103. Carp, *Cartea neagră*, vol. 3, p. 301.

104. *USHMM/RIS*, RG 25.004M, roll 19, fond 40011, vol. 1, and roll 20, fond 40011, vol. 15.

105. Ibid., roll 20, fond 40011, vol. 6, and roll 29, fond 40013, vol. 5.

106. Carp, *Cartea neagră*, vol. 3, pp. 301–2.

107. *USHMM/SRI*, RG 25.004M, roll 28, fond 22981, vol. 1.

108. Carp, *Cartea neagră*, vol. 3, p. 305.

109. Ibid., p. 306.

110. *DCFRJDH*, vol. 6, pp. 310–14.

111. *USHMM/SRI*, RG 25.004M, roll 30, fond 40013, vol. 6; Carp, *Cartea neagră*, vol. 3, pp. 307–8.

112. Julius Fisher, "How Many Jews Perished in Transnistria?" in *American Jewish Archives/World Jewish Congress Records* [hereafter *AJA/WJCR*].

Chapter 6: Life in Transnistria

1. Hilberg, *The Destruction*, vol. 2, p. 776; see also Fisher, *Transnistria*, p. 9.
2. *USHMM/SRI*, RG 25.004M, roll 39, fond 40030, vol. 11.
3. *Procesul marii trădări*, pp. 148–49.
4. Hilberg, *The Destruction*, vol. 2, p. 777; see also Dallin, *Odessa*, p. 313.
5. *USHMM/RMFA*, RG 25.006M, roll 6, vol. 15, p. 58.
6. *USHMM/MSM*, RG 25.003M, roll 12(202), fond Armata aIVa, vol. 781.
7. Ibid., roll 18(352), fond Armata aIIIa, vol. 421.
8. Carp, *Cartea neagră*, vol. 1, p. 19.
9. *USHMM/MSM*, RG 23.003M, roll 17(351), fond Armata aIIIa, vol. 410; Carp, *Cartea neagră*, vol. 1, p. 19; *DCFRJDH*, vol. 5, p. 220.
10. *USHMM/SRI*, RG 25.004M, roll 16(2), fond 18844, vol. 3.
11. *NARA*, XL 13166, roll 6226, Encl. No. 19, Box 0179, and T175, roll 658.
12. *DCFRJDH*, vol. 5, p. 541.
13. *USHMM/SRI*, RG 25.004M, roll 14, fond 2869, vol. 208.
14. *DCFRJDH*, vol. 5, p. 541.
15. *USHMM/RMFA*, RG 25.006M, roll 10, fond Preşedenţia Consiliului de Miniştrii, vol. 20.
16. Ibid.
17. *DCFRJDH*, vol. 5, pp. 306–13.
18. *USHMM/RMFA*, RG 25.006M, roll 10, vol. 20.
19. *DCFRJDH*, vol. 7, p. 348.
20. *USHMM/RMFA*, RG 25.006M, roll 10, fond Preşedenţia Consiliului de Miniştrii, vol. 20.
21. *USHMM/SRI*, RG 25.004M, roll 34, fond 40010, vol. 59.
22. *DCFRJDH*, vol. 7, p. 681.
23. Dallin, *Odessa*, p. 317.
24. *USHMM/SRI*, RG 25.004M, roll 17, fond 18844, vol. 3; *USHMM/RSA*, RG 25.002M, fond Preşedenţia Consiliului de Miniştrii, vol. 86; *USHMM/RMFA*, RG 25.006M, roll 10, vol. 20.
25. Carp, *Cartea neagră*, vol. 3, p. 88.
26. Ibid., p. 262.
27. Ibid.
28. *DCFRJDH*, vol. 8, p. 580.
29. Carp, *Cartea neagră*, vol. 3, p. 262.
30. Ibid., p. 263.
31. Ibid.
32. Ibid., p. 264.
33. Ibid., pp. 264, 326.
34. Ibid., p. 265.
35. Ibid., pp. 265–66.
36. Rudich, *La braţ cu moartea*, pp. 63–65.

37. Carp, *Cartea neagră*, vol. 3, p. 261.

38. Dallin, *Odessa*, p. 317.

39. Fisher, *Transnistria*, p. 100.

40. *USHMM/MSM*, RG 25.003M, roll 354, fond Armata aIIIa, vol. 1127.

41. Fisher, *Transnistria*, p. 104.

42. Ibid., p. 105.

43. Carp, *Cartea neagră*, vol. 3, pp. 439–42.

44. Ibid., p. 266.

45. *DCFRJDH*, vol. 5, p. 228.

46. *USHMM/SRI*, RG 25.004M, roll 28, fond 40013, vol. 1.

47. Carp, *Cartea neagră*, vol. 3, p. 267.

48. Ibid., p. 322.

49. Ibid., p. 323.

50. Ibid., p. 325.

51. Ibid., p. 331.

52. Ibid., pp. 267–68.

53. Ibid., p. 268.

54. Rudich, *La braţ cu moartea*, p. 70.

55. *USHMM/SRI*, RG 25.004M, roll 35, fond 40010, vol. 89.

56. *USHMM/MSM*, RG 25.003M, roll 20(352), fond Armata aIIIa, vol. 410.

57. Carp, *Cartea neagră*, vol. 3, p. 329.

58. Ibid., pp. 268–69.

59. Ibid., p. 270.

60. Rudich, *La braţ cu moartea*, pp. 71–72.

61. *DCFRJDH*, vol. 10, p. 171.

62. *USHMM/MSM*, RG 25.003M, roll 17(351), fond Armata aIIIa, vol. 410.

63. Carp, *Cartea neagră*, vol. 3, p. 202; Litani, "The Destruction," p. 135; *USHMM/SRI*, RG 25.004M, roll 31, fond 40010, vol. 8.

64. *USHMM/SRI*, RG 25.004M, roll 18(352), fond Armata aIIIa, vol. 410.

65. Ibid.

66. Carp, *Cartea neagră*, vol. 3, pp. 202, 220; *DCFRJDH*, vol. 5, p. 202.

67. Ibid.

68. Carp, *Cartea neagră*, vol. 3, p. 203; *DCFRJDH*, vol. 5, pp. 203–5.

69. *USHMM/MSM*, RG 25.003M, roll 18(352), fond Armata aIIIa, vol. 421; *Yad Vashem/Odessa Oblast Archives* [hereafter *YV/OOA*], M.39, rolls 1, 4; Carp, *Cartea neagră*, vol. 3, pp. 203–5; *DCFRJDH*, vol. 5, p. 241.

70. *YV/OOA*, M.39, roll 4.

71. Ibid., roll 1.

72. *DCFRJDH*, vol. 5, p. 214.

73. *USHMM/SRI*, RG 25.004M, roll 20, fond 40011, vol. 7; *DCFRJDH*, vol. 5, p. 217.

74. *USHMM/SRI*, RG 25.004M, roll 30, fond 21401, vol. 2.

75. *YV/OOA*, M.39, roll 1; Dallin, *Odessa*, p. 308.

76. *DCFRJDH,* vol. 5, pp. 232–35.

77. *USHMM/MSM,* RG 25.003M, roll 352, fond Armata aIIIa, vol. 421.

78. *DCFRJDH,* vol. 5, p. 231.

79. *USHMM/MSM,* RG 25.003M, roll 20(354), fond Armata aIIIa, vol. 1196.

80. Ibid., roll 353, fond Armata aIIIa, vol. 1122.

81. *USHMM/SRI,* RG 25.004M, roll 30, fond 21401, vol. 2.

82. *USHMM/RSA,* RG 25.002M, roll 5.

83. *USHMM/MSM,* RG 25.003M, roll 20(354), fond Armata aIIIa, vol. 1127.

84. Ibid., roll 18(352), fond Armata aIIIa, vol. 421.

85. Carp, *Cartea neagră,* vol. 3, p. 205; *DCFRJDH,* vol. 5, p. 222.

86. Carp, *Cartea neagră,* vol. 3, p. 205.

87. Ibid., p. 206.

88. Ibid., pp. 286, 336–37; *DCFRJDH,* vol. 5, p. 241.

89. Carp, *Cartea neagră,* vol. 3, p. 269.

90. Ibid.

91. Ibid., pp. 270, 347–49.

92. Ibid., p. 271.

93. Ibid., p. 272.

94. Ibid., pp. 272–73; *DCFRJDH,* vol. 5, pp. 269.

95. Carp, *Cartea neagră,* vol. 3, pp. 273, 353–56; *DCFRJDH,* vol. 5, pp. 270–71.

96. Carp, *Cartea neagră,* vol. 3, p. 275.

97. *DCFRJDH,* vol. 10, p. 665.

98. Carp, *Cartea neagră,* vol. 3, pp. 357–58.

99. *DCFRJDH,* vol. 8, p. 579.

100. Carp, *Cartea neagră,* vol. 3, pp. 274–75, 283, 357–58.

101. Ibid., pp. 273, 356.

102. Ibid., p. 270.

103. Ibid., pp. 275–76.

104. Ibid., pp. 276, 278.

105. Ibid.

106. Ibid., p. 280.

107. Ibid., pp. 279–80.

108. *YV/OOA,* M.39, roll 1.

109. Ibid., roll 3.

110. Carp, *Cartea neagră,* vol. 3, p. 282.

111. Ibid.

112. Ibid., pp. 282–83.

113. Ibid., pp. 283, 288.

114. *USHMM/MSM,* RG 25.003M, roll 19(353), fond Armata aIIa, vol. 421.

115. *USHMM/RSA,* RG 25.002M, roll 5.

116. Carp, *Cartea neagră,* vol. 3, pp. 369–72.

117. Ibid., p. 367.

118. Ibid., pp. 201, 376–77.
119. Hilberg, *The Destruction*, vol. 2, p. 779.
120. Carp, *Cartea neagră*, vol. 3, p. 285.
121. Ibid.
122. Ibid., p. 287.
123. Ibid., p. 368.
124. Hilberg, *The Destruction*, vol. 2, p. 779.
125. Carp, *Cartea neagră*, vol. 3, p. 284.
126. Ibid., p. 287.
127. Ibid., p. 289.
128. Ibid., p. 290.
129. Ibid., p. 291.
130. *DCFRJDH*, vol. 8, p. 545.
131. Ibid., p. 548.
132. Ibid., p. 550.
133. Litani, "The Destruction," p. 152.
134. *DCFRJDH*, vol. 8, p. 550; *NARA*, T175, roll 663.
135. Ibid.
136. *DCFRJDH*, vol. 8, p. 550.
137. *NARA*, T175, roll 663.
138. *DCFRJFH*, vol. 8, p. 550.
139. *NARA*, T175, roll 663.
140. Ibid.
141. Ibid.
142. *USHMM/SRI*, RG 25.004M, roll 9, fond 2710, vol. 33.
143. Carp, *Cartea neagră*, vol. 3, p. 292.
144. Ibid., pp. 293–96.
145. Ibid., p. 293.
146. Ibid., p. 296.
147. *USHMM/OOA*, RG 1.006M, fond 2364, opis 1, folder 23.
148. Carp, *Cartea neagră*, vol. 3, p. 301.
149. Ibid., p. 302.
150. Ibid., p. 304.
151. *DCFRJDH*, vol. 8, p. 615.
152. Carp, *Cartea neagră*, vol. 3, p. 304.
153. Ibid., p. 305.
154. Ibid., p. 308.
155. *USHMM/RMFA*, RG 25.006M, roll 10, fond Preşedenţia Consiliului de Miniştrii, vol. 20.

Chapter 7: The Deportation, Persecution, and Extermination of the Gypsies

1. Traian Herseni, "Rasa si destin national," *Cuvîntul Nostru* [Our Word], January 16, 1941.

2. *DCFRJDH*, vol. 4, p. 53.

3. Ion Chelcea, *Ţiganii in Romania* (Bucharest, 1944).

4. *USHMM/SRI*, RG 25.004M, roll 34, fond 40010, vol. 59.

5. *USHMM/MSM*, RG 25.004M, roll 14, vol. 2695.

6. *USHMM/SRI*, RG 25.004M, roll 14, fond 9721, vol. 2.

7. Ibid.

8. *YV/OOA*, roll 14, fond 9721, vol. 2.

9. *USHMM/MSM*, RG 25.003M, roll 148(14), vol. 2695.

10. *USHMM/SRI*, RG 25.004M, roll 64, fond 18844, vol. 4.

11. Ibid., roll 34, fond 40010, vol. 59.

12. *Procesul marii trădări*, p. 108.

13. Ibid.

14. *USHMM/SRI*, RG 25.004M, roll 34, fond 40010, vol. 74.

15. *USHMM/MSM*, RG 25.004M, roll 14, vol. 2695.

16. *DCFRJDH*, vol. 6, p. 225.

17. *USHMM/SRI*, RG 25.004M, roll 34, fond 40010, vol. 59; *YV/OOA*, roll 4, M.39.

18. *DCFRJDH*, vol. 6, p. 94.

19. *USHMM/SRI*, RG 25.004M, roll 19, fond 40011, vol. 1; *DCFRJDH*, vol. 6, p. 90.

20. *DCFRJDH*, vol. 6, p. 94.

21. Ibid.

22. *YV/OOA*, roll 2, M.39.

23. Ibid., roll 4, M.39.

24. *USHMM/SRI*, RG 25.004M, roll 26, fond 38891, vol. 1.

25. *YV/OOA*, roll 2, M.39.

26. *USHMM/SRI*, RG 25.004M, fond 40010, roll 34, vol. 59, and roll 33, vol. 28.

27. Ibid.

28. Ibid.

29. Ibid.

30. Viorel Achim, *Ţiganii in istoria Romaniei* (Bucharest, 1998), p. 143.

31. *Procesul marii trădări*, p. 305.

32. *DCFRJDH*, vol. 5, p. 541.

33. *USHMM/SRI*, RG 25.004M, roll 26, fond 3891, vol. 1.

34. Achim, *Ţiganii in istoria Romaniei*, p. 147.

35. *Procesul marii trădări*, p. 302.

36. *DCFRJDH*, vol. 9, pp. 279–80.

37. Ibid., vol. 10, p. 473.

Chapter 8: The Survival of the Romanian Jews

1. Richard Breitman, "Himmler and the Origins of the Final Solution," paper presented at the Smithsonian Institution, December 3, 1987 (RSHA) document *Ereignismeldung USSR 52,* August 14, 1941, in *NARA,* 6 238, No. 4540, p. 13.

2. Arno Mayer, *Why Did the Heavens Not Darken?: The "Final Solution" in History* (New York, 1988), p. 305.

3. *DCFRJDH,* vol. 9, p. 185.

4. Ibid., pp. 240–41.

5. Ibid., p. 253.

6. Hilberg, *The Destruction,* vol. 2, p. 784.

7. Jean Ancel, "Plans for Deportation of the Romanian Jews and Their Discontinuation in the Light of Documentary Evidence," *Yad Vashem Studies* 16 (1984): 382.

8. *USHMM/RMFA,* RG 25.006M, roll 17, fond Preşedenţia Consiliului de Miniştrii, vol. 32.

9. Carp, *Cartea neagră,* vol. 3, p. 256.

10. Ibid., p. 247.

11. Ibid., pp. 248–49.

12. Ibid., p. 236; *DCFRJDH,* vol. 4, p. 299.

13. Carp, *Cartea neagră,* vol. 3, p. 237; *DCFRJDH,* vol. 4, p. 299.

14. *DCFRJDH,* vol. 4, p. 299.

15. Carp, *Cartea neagră,* vol. 3, p. 237.

16. *DCFRJDH,* vol. 10, p. 353.

17. *USHMM/SRI,* RG 25.004M, roll 36, fond 40010, vol. 35, p. 103.

18. Ancel, "Plans for Deportation," p. 390.

19. *DCFRJDH,* vol. 1, p. 127.

20. Ibid., vol. 8, p. 599.

21. Carp, *Cartea neagră,* vol. 3, p. 237.

22. Hilberg, *The Destruction,* vol. 2, p. 785.

23. Ibid., p. 787.

24. *DCFRJDH,* vol. 9, p. 422.

25. Ibid.

26. Ancel, "Plans for Deportation," p. 384.

27. Ibid., p. 396.

28. Ibid.

29. Ibid., p. 398.

30. *DCFRJDH,* vol. 4, pp. 239–40.

31. Carp, *Cartea neagră,* vol. 3, pp. 239–40.

32. Ancel, "Plans for Deportation," p. 399; *DCFRJDH,* vol. 4, p. 254.

33. Carp, *Cartea neagră,* vol. 3, p. 24; *DCFRJDH,* vol. 4, pp. 300–301.

34. Ancel, "Plans for Deportation," pp. 400, 418.

35. *DCFRJDH,* vol. 10, p. 237.

36. Ibid., pp. 237–38.

37. *DCFRJDH,* vol. 10, p. 236.

38. Carp, *Cartea neagră*, vol. 3, p. 242.

39. *DCFRJDH*, vol. 8, pp. 599–600.

40. Ibid., vol. 10, p. 357.

41. *USHMM/SRI*, RG 25.004M, roll 36, fond 40010, vol. 127.

42. Hilberg, *The Destruction*, vol. 2, p. 787.

43. *DCFRJDH*, vol. 10, pp. 241–42.

44. Ibid., p. 243.

45. Ibid., pp. 354–57.

46. *USHMM/SRI*, RG 25.004M, roll 14, fond 2869, vol. 208.

47. *DCFRJDH*, vol. 8, p. 608.

48. Carp, *Cartea neagră*, vol. 3, p. 243.

49. *DCFRJDH*, vol. 10, p. 203, and vol. 5, p. 376; Carp, *Cartea neagră*, vol. 3, pp. 407–8.

50. *DCFRJDH*, vol. 10, pp. 202, 204.

51. Ibid., p. 205.

52. Ibid., vol. 4, pp. 10–11.

53. Ibid., vol. 10, pp. 592–95.

54. Ibid., p. 605.

55. Carp, *Cartea neagră*, vol. 3, p. 414.

56. Ibid., pp. 414–15.

57. Ibid., pp. 418–19.

58. Ibid., p. 406.

59. Ibid.

60. Ibid., p. 619; *DCFRJDH*, vol. 5, p. 330.

61. *DCFRJDH*, vol. 5, p. 335.

62. Carp, *Cartea neagră*, vol. 3, p. 407.

63. Ibid., pp. 407, 424–25.

64. Ibid., p. 427.

65. Ibid., p. 428.

66. Ibid., pp. 407, 428–29.

67. Ibid., pp. 407, 430.

68. *DCFRJDH*, vol. 7, pp. 312, 321.

69. Ibid., p. 347.

70. Carp, *Cartea neagră*, vol. 3, pp. 407, 423–24.

71. Ibid., pp. 407–8.

72. *DCFRJDH*, vol. 4, p. 638.

73. Carp, *Cartea neagră*, vol. 3, pp. 408, 431–33; *DCFRJDH*, vol. 5, p. 380.

74. Carp, *Cartea neagră*, vol. 3, pp. 408, 434.

75. Ibid., pp. 408, 434–35; *DCFRJDH*, vol. 5, p. 381.

76. Carp, *Cartea neagră*, vol. 3, pp. 409, 435–37; *DCFRJDH*, vol. 5, pp. 438–40.

77. Carp, *Cartea neagră*, vol. 3, pp. 409, 437.

78. Ibid., pp. 409, 438–43; *DCFRJDH*, vol. 5, p. 440.

79. *DCFRJDH*, vol. 4, p. 654.

80. Ibid., vol. 5, pp. 458–59.

81. Carp, *Cartea neagră*, vol. 3, pp. 443–44.

82. Ibid., pp. 409, 444–47; *DCFRJDH*, vol. 5, pp. 511–12.

83. Carp, *Cartea neagră*, vol. 3, p. 410; *DCFRJDH*, vol. 5, p. 510.

84. Carp, *Cartea neagră*, vol. 3, pp. 447–50; *DCFRJDH*, vol. 5, pp. 511–12.

85. Carp, *Cartea neagră*, vol. 3, p. 450; *DCFRJDH*, vol. 5, p. 513.

86. *DCFRJDH*, vol. 4, p. 692.

87. Ibid.

88. *USHMM/RSA*, RG 25.002M, roll 6.

89. Carp, *Cartea neagră*, vol. 3, pp. 410, 451–52.

90. *USHMM/SRI*, RG 25.004M, roll 13, fond 2898, vol. 237; Hilberg, *The Destruction*, vol. 2, pp. 792–94.

91. *DCFRJDH*, vol. 5, pp. 515–16.

92. Carp, *Cartea neagră*, vol. 3, pp. 410, 452–53.

93. Ibid., p. 453.

94. *DCFRJDH*, vol. 4, pp. 694–699, and vol. 5, pp. 518–19.

95. Ibid., vol. 7, pp. 547–51.

96. Carp, *Cartea neagră*, vol. 3, p. 410.

97. Ibid., p. 411; *DCFRJDH*, vol. 5, pp. 539–40.

98. *DCFRJDH*, vol. 7, p. 610.

99. *USHMM/MSM*, RG 25.003M, roll 129(659), fond Guvernamîntul Basarabiei, vol. 177.

100. Carp, *Cartea neagră*, vol. 3, p. 411.

101. Ibid.; *DCFRJDH*, vol. 5, pp. 539–40, and vol. 7, pp. 610–11.

102. Ibid., vol. 7, p. 587.

103. Ibid.

104. Carp, *Cartea neagră*, vol. 3, pp. 411, 455–56.

105. Ibid., p. 411.

106. Ibid., p. 412.

107. Ibid.

108. Ibid.; *DCFRJDH*, vol. 8, p. 26.

109. Ion Calefeteanu, Nicolae Dinu, and Teodor Gheorghe, *Emigrarea populatiei evreieşti din Romania intre anii 1940–1944* (Bucharest, 1993), p. 136.

110. Ira Hirschmann, *Caution to the Winds* (New York, 1962), p. 157.

111. Carp, *Cartea neagră*, vol. 3, p. 412.

112. *DCFRJDH*, vol. 8, p. 497.

113. Ibid., pp. 487–97.

114. Ibid.

115. Alexandre Şafran, *Resisting the Storm: Romania, 1940–1947* (Jerusalem, 1987), p. 243.

116. *AJA/WJCR*, from a meeting between the reunited Jewish delegations and the Romanian delegation, August 29, 1946.

Chapter 9: The Fate of Romanian Jews Living Abroad

Somewhat changed here, this chapter first appeared under the title "The Fate of Romanian Jews in Nazi-Occupied Europe," in Randolph L. Braham, ed., *The Destruction of the Romanian and Ukrainian Jews During the Antonescu Era* (New York, 1997); reproduced with permission.

1. Ion Calefeteanu, "Regimul cetățenilor romani de origine evreiasca aflati in strainatate in anii dictaturii antonescience," *Anale de Istorie* [Annals of History] 5 (1986): 163.

2. Ibid.

3. Ibid., p. 131.

4. Ibid., p. 315.

5. Ibid., p. 328.

6. *DCFRJDH*, vol. 10, p. 88.

7. Ibid., p. 99.

8. Ibid., p. 182.

9. *Ukrainian Archival Administration/Odessa Regional Archives*, RG 31.006M, fond 2264, opis 1, folder 40A/1943.

10. Ibid., vol. 4, p. 550, and vol. 8, pp. 121, 139.

11. Ibid., vol. 4, p. 543.

12. Carp, *Cartea neagră*, vol. 3, pp. 452–53.

13. *DCFRJDH*, vol. 4, pp. 696–97.

14. Ibid., vol. 10, p. 416.

15. *USHMM/RMFA*, RG 25.006M, roll 18, fond Germania, vol. 33.

16. Ibid., roll 17, fond Germania, vol. 32; *DCFRJDH*, vol. 10, pp. 792–93; Calefeteanu, "Regimul," p. 130.

17. *DCFRJDH*, vol. 10, pp. 182–83; Calefeteanu, "Regimul," p. 130.

18. Calefeteanu, "Regimul," p. 130.

19. Ibid., p. 131.

20. Ibid., p. 132.

21. Ibid.

22. *USHMM/RMFA*, RG 25.006M, roll 16, fond Germania, vol. 32; *DCFRJDH*, vol. 9, p. 421.

23. *DCFRJDH*, vol. 4, pp. 110–12, and vol. 11, p. 209.

24. Calefeteanu, "Regimul," p. 312; *USHMM/RMFA*, RG 25.006M, roll 17, fond Germania, vol. 32.

25. *USHMM/RMFA*, RG 25.006M, roll 17, fond Germania, vol. 32.

26. *USHMM/SRI*, RG 25.004M, roll 16, fond 22539, vol. 32, Document No. NG 291/948.

27. *USHMM/RMFA*, RG 25.006M, roll 16, fond Germania.

28. Jean Ancel, "Simpozion stiintific Romano-Israelian, Jerusalem, 12–14 ianuarie 1986," *Anale de Istorie* 3 (1986): 139.

29. Calefeteanu, "Regimul," p. 133.

30. *USHMM/RMFA*, RG 25.006M, roll 17, fond Germania, vol. 32.

31. Serge Klarsfeld, *Vichy-Auschwitz* (Paris, 1983), p. 180.

32. Serge Klarsfeld, *Mémorial de la Déportation des juifs de France* (Paris, 1978), p. 312.

33. Klarsfeld, *Vichy-Auschwitz,* pp. 182, 454.

34. Klarsfeld, *Mémorial,* p. 319.

35. Klarsfeld, *Vichy-Auschwitz,* pp. 182, 454.

36. Klarsfeld, *Mémorial,* pp. 312, 319.

37. Ibid., p. xxxvii.

38. *DCFRJDH,* vol. 4, p. 547.

39. Ibid., vol. 10, p. 242.

40. Ibid.

41. Ibid., p. 316.

42. Ibid., p. 314.

43. *USHMM/RMFA,* RG 25.006M, roll 17, fond Germania, vol. 32.

44. Ibid., roll 16, fond Germania, vol. 32.

45. Ibid.

46. Ibid., roll 17, fond Germania, vol. 33.

47. Calefeteanu, "Regimul," p. 135.

48. *USHMM/RMFA,* RG 25.006M, roll 15, fond Belgia, vol. 28.

49. Ibid., p. 135.

50. Ibid., p. 136.

51. *DCFRJDH,* vol. 4, p. 702.

52. Ancel, "Simpozion," pp. 138–39.

53. Ibid.

54. *USHMM/RMFA,* RG 25.006M, roll 16, fond Germania, vol. 30.

55. Ibid.

56. Ibid.

57. *DCFRJDH,* vol. 10, p. 417.

58. Ibid.

59. Ibid., pp. 331, 372, 424–26.

60. *USHMM/RMFA,* RG 25.006M, roll 16, fond Germania, vol. 30.

Chapter 10: Antonescu and the Jews

1. *Procesul marii trădări,* p. 71.

2. *DCFRJDH,* vol. 8, p. 608.

3. Ibid., vol. 2, p. 47.

4. *USHMM/SRI,* RG 25.004M, roll 31, fond 40010, vol. 1; *Evreii dia Romania între Anii 1940–1944, vol. II, Problema evreiască în stenogramele Consiliului de Miniştrii,* (Bucharest, 1996), p. 229.

5. *USHMM/SRI,* RG 25.004M, roll 32, fond 40010, vol. 1; Carp, *Cartea neagră,* vol. 2, p. 39.

6. *USHMM/SRI,* RG 25.004M, roll 32, fond 40010, vol. 1.

7. *DCFRJDH,* vol. 10, p. 79.

8. *USHMM/RSA,* RG 25.002M, roll 18, fond Preşedenţia Consiliului de Miniştrii, Cabinet Dosar 167/1941.

9. *USHMM/SRI,* RG 25.004M, roll 35, fond 40010, vol. 89.

10. Ibid., roll 19, fond 40010, vol. 5.

11. Ibid., roll 31, fond 40010, vol. 1.

12. *USHMM/RMFA,* RG 25.006M, roll 10, fond Preşedenţia Consiliului de Miniştrii, vol. 20.

13. Carp, *Cartea neagră,* vol. 3, p. 143.

14. *USHMM/SRI,* RG 25.004M, roll 35, fond 40010, vol. 78.

15. Ibid.

16. Ibid., vol. 28, and roll 35, fond 40010, vol. 78.

17. *USHMM/SSARM,* RG 54.001M, roll 3, fond CBBT, Office 3.

18. *USHMM/SRI,* RG 25.004M, roll 31, fond 40010, vol. 1.

19. *23 August 1944, Documente* (Bucharest, 1984), vol. 1, p. 499.

20. Ibid., p. 437.

21. Ibid., p. 433.

22. Ibid., p. 436.

23. Ibid., p. 422.

24. Ibid., p. 424.

25. Ibid., p. 442.

26. Ibid., p. 426.

27. Ibid., p. 438.

28. Ibid., p. 444.

29. Ibid.

30. *USHMM/SRI,* RG 25.004M, fond 40010, vol. 77.

31. *DCFRJDH,* vol. 3, pp. 130–32.

32. *USHMM/SRI,* RG 25.004M, fond 40010, vol. 1.

33. *DCFRJDH,* vol. 3, pp. 258–62, 378–81.

34. Ibid., p. 425.

35. *USHMM/SRI,* RG 25.004M, roll 31, fond 40010, vol. 1.

36. Ibid., roll 25, fond 20725, vol. 10.

37. Ibid., roll 34, fond 40010, vol. 75.

38. *DCFRJDH,* vol. 10, pp. 214–15.

39. Ibid., p. 215.

40. Ibid., p. 233.

41. Ibid., vol. 3, p. 522.

42. Ibid.

43. Ibid., p. 523.

44. Ibid.

45. Ibid., vol. 4, p. 544.

46. Ibid., p. 667.

47. Ibid., vol. 7, p. 547; Hilberg, *The Destruction,* vol. 2, pp. 792–93.

48. Ibid.

49. *USHMM/RSA,* RG 25.002M, fond Preşedenţia Consiliului de Miniştrii, Cabinet Militar, folder 205.

50. Ibid.

51. *DCFRJDH,* vol. 4, p. 712.

52. Carp, *Cartea neagră,* vol. 3, pp. 458–59; *DCFRJDH,* vol. 8, p. 19; *NARA,* OSS Report No. 19533, May 22, 1944.

53. *DCFRJDH,* vol. 10, p. 422.

54. Ibid.

55. Ibid., vol. 8, p. 486.

56. *Procesul marii trădări,* p. 51.

57. Ibid., p. 54.

58. *DCFRJDH,* vol. 8, pp. 608–9.

59. Ibid.

60. Ibid., vol. 9, p. 253.

61. Ibid., vol. 10, pp. 241–43.

62. Alexandre Şafran, "The Rulers of Fascist Romania Whom I Had to Deal With," *Yad Vashem Studies* 6 (1967): 179.

63. *DCFRJDH,* vol. 8, pp. 68–73.

64. Ibid., pp. 97–98.

65. Ibid., vol. 10, pp. 413–15.

66. *Procesul marii trădări,* pp. 91–92.

67. Ibid., p. 109.

68. Ibid., pp. 97–109.

69. Ibid., p. 66.

70. Ibid., p. 153.

71. *DCFRJDH,* vol. 8, p. 623.

72. *Procesul marii trădări,* p. 153.

73. *DCFRJDH,* vol. 8, p. 620.

74. Ibid.

75. Ibid., p. 624.

76. Şafran, "The Rulers," pp. 175–76.

77. *AJA/WJCR,* OSS/Romania, June 9, 1945, p. 2.

Chapter 11: A Summing Up

1. *USHMM/SRI,* RG 25.004M, roll 31, fond 40010, vol. 1.

2. Hilberg, *The Destruction,* vol. 3, p. 1220.

3. Ibid., vol. 2, p. 759.

4. *Foreign Relations of the United States: Diplomatic Papers, 1941,* vol. 2, p. 877.

5. *DCFRJDH,* vol. 6, p. 606.

6. Ibid.

7. Ibid., vol. 4, p. 660.

8. Butnaru, *Holocaustul uitat,* p. 375.

9. Paul Shapiro, "Prelude to Dictatorship in Romania: The National Christian Party in Power, December 1937–February 1938," *Canadian-American Slavic Studies* 8 (January 1974).

10. Calefeteanu, Dinu, and Gheorghe, *Emigrarea.*

11. Hilberg, *The Destruction,* vol. 2, pp. 759–60.

Index

Acmecetka, 229–230; massacre of Jews in, 183, 185–186

Adîncata, massacres of Jews in, 41

Agapie, Vasile, 136–138, 152

Albu, Ioan, 166–167

Alexianu, Gheorghe, 19, 198–199, 214, 219, 223, 228, 251; execution of, 4, 287; relationship with Ion Antonescu, 176, 196–197, 208, 273–274; Transnistria policies, 142, 154, 166, 208, 210, 230, 231

Ancel, Jean, 170f, 268

Antal, Stefan, 246

Anti-Semitism, 4–5; of Carol II, xviii–xix, 18f, 22, 28, 259; in Communist Romania, 287; and economic problems, xviii–xix; during Goga-Cuza government, xix, xx, 17–19, 259; of Iron Guard, 13, 18–19, 24f, 49, 225, 283; in nineteenth-century Romania, xvii–xviii, 6–11, 13–14; in post-Communist Romania, xxiii–xxiv; in Romanian army, 10–11, 27, 37–38; in Romanian gendarmerie, 64, 91; in Romanian political parties, xviii, 12–13, 16–17; Romanization as expression of, 23–26, 278; in Russia, 13f. *See also* Antonescu, Ion, anti-Semitism of.

Antonescu, Ion, 62, 115, 238; anti-Semitism of, xx–xxi, 21–22, 23f, 26f, 30, 34–35, 43–44, 45, 47, 50–51, 87–88, 90–91, 118, 177, 271–283, 294; and Chișinău ghetto, 124, 139f, 143, 147; deportation of Jews from Regat considered/canceled by, 242, 243–244, 245f, 248, 264, 271, 274, 277–278, 292–293; deportations of Gypsies ordered by, 226–227, 228–229, 231, 285; deportations of Jews ordered by, 35, 64, 110f, 117–119, 121f, 141f, 152ff, 159, 168–170, 174, 271, 273, 275–276, 280–281; execution of, 3–4, 287; expropriation of Jewish property ordered by, 137, 208, 273f; forced labor by Jews ordered by, 34, 113, 119, 121, 196, 281; and Iași pogrom, 63–64,

Antonescu, Ion (*cont.*)
  87–88, 90; and Odessa massacre,
  177–180; overthrown, 35; policies on
  Jewish repatriation, 249–250, 251, 254,
  256–257, 279, 280–281; policies on
  Romanian Jews living abroad, 259–260,
  263, 268, 270; policies on Transnistria,
  176, 177–180, 187–188, 196–197, 203,
  208, 214, 226–227, 228–229, 236, 271;
  post-Communist rehabilitation of, xxii,
  xxiii–xxiv, 4, 287–288, 293–294;
  relationship with Alexianu, 176,
  196–197, 208, 273–274; relationship
  with Mihai Antonescu, 32, 43, 87, 91,
  118, 272, 283; relationship with Carol
  II, 19, 22, 43, 47; relationship with
  Filderman, 32f, 44f, 47, 51, 177,
  275–276, 277–278; relationship with
  Hitler, xxiv, 53f, 55–56, 236, 241, 248,
  281–282, 283; relationship with Iron
  Guard, 19, 23ff, 43, 47, 49, 50–57, 60,
  87, 275, 282–283, 292–293; trial of, 86,
  142, 174, 178–179, 186, 235, 271, 281.
  See also Antonescu, Mihai; Romanian
  government.
Antonescu, Maria, 243, 286
Antonescu, Mihai, 33f, 275, 294;
  deportation of Jews from Regat
  considered by, 240–248 passim; and
  deportations of Gypsies, 228; and
  deportations of Jews from
  Bessarabia/Bukovina, 91–92, 118–120,
  121f, 152, 168–169, 196–197, 283;
  execution, 4, 287; during Iaşi pogrom,
  78, 87, 88; and policies toward
  Romanian Jews living abroad, 260–270
  passim; relationship with Ion
  Antonescu, 32, 43, 87, 91, 118, 272,
  283; and repatriation policies, 250f,
  253, 256, 257, 284. *See also* Antonescu,
  Ion; Romanian government.
Antoniu, Lascăr, 11
Arad, 44, 252
Argeşeanu, Gheorghe, 46
Argetoianu, Constantin, 46
Arion, C. C., 11
Atachi, 148, 158, 163, 164
Auschnitt, Max, 243

Austro-Hungarian Empire: Jews in,
  14–15; relations with Romania, xviii, 14

Bacău District, 8, 9, 11, 32, 226
Bădescu, Gheorghe, 71
Baia District, 32
Balaiciuc, massacre of Jews in, 188f
Bălan, Metropolitan, 243, 246, 282
Balkan War, Second, 11, 21, 23
Balotescu, Gheorghe, 66, 69, 86
Balta/Balta District, 198–204 passim, 212,
  220, 229, 255, 257, 279; massacres of
  Jews in, 193
Bălţi District, 32, 124, 128, 131f, 137,
  142, 172; massacre of Jews in,
  103–104, 107
Banat, 12, 118; deportation plans for,
  242–243, 244, 246–247; Transnistria
  survivors from, 255
Banila, massacre of Jews in, 98
Bank of Romania. *See* National Bank of
  Romania.
Baptists, 155, 237
Bar District, massacres of Jews in, 190,
  193
Barozzi, Gheorghe, 71, 209–210
Becescu-Georgescu, Florin, 66, 87
Bechi, Filip, 104
Belgium, 268
Bengliu, Ion, 46
Benton, James W., 292
Benvenisti, Mişu, 284, 289
Berbca, 204
Berezovka District, 199ff, 204, 208,
  210–212, 216, 229, 230–231, 255, 279;
  massacres of Jews in, 187–190,
  191–193, 289
Berşad, 202, 204, 207, 220f, 279;
  massacre of Jews in, 193
Bessarabia, xxiii, 13, 260, 265; acquired
  by Romania after WWI, xviii, 12, 14;
  deportations of Jews from, 35, 39, 110f,
  116, 117–122, 141, 142–155, 169,
  170–175, 177, 198f, 200–201, 205, 271,
  273, 275f, 280–281, 284, 294; Jewish
  culture/politics in, xx, 14, 15; Jewish
  hostages in, 93, 104; Jewish population

of, 170; massacres of Jews in, 66, 94–96, 103–108, 116–117, 147–149, 172–173, 181–182, 289; non-Jewish religious sects persecuted in, 154–155; number of Jews killed in, xxi, 132, 170–174, 289; number of Jews residing in, xx, 14; number of Transnistria survivors from, 255; repatriation to, 248–258, 254, 284, 291, 293; Soviet occupation, 38–39, 60–61, 110, 114, 118, 238, 290; transit camps in, 122–138; Ukrainians in, 92; yellow star in, 31, 119. *See also* Chişinău.

Black Book, 178

Blumenfeld, Alexandru, 229

Bogdanovka, massacres of Jews in, 182, 183–185, 186f

Borcescu, Traian, 64–65, 66, 86, 181–182

Borobaru, Traian, 55

Botoşani District, 9, 11, 31, 32

Brăileanu, Traian, 43

Brailov, massacre of Jews in, 191

Brătianu, Constantin I. C., 49, 228–229, 248, 274f, 292

Brătianu, Ion, 6, 7

Bratslav, massacre of Jews in, 191

Bravicea, massacre of Jews in, 105, 106

Broşteanu, Emil, 174, 210, 211

Bucharest, 55; anti-Semitism in, 9, 10, 33, 44; expropriations of Jewish property in, 50; Jews residing in, xix, 13, 15, 68, 84, 118; massacres of Jews in, 45–46, 48, 57–60, 61

Budineţ, massacre of Jews in, 99

Bukovina, xxiii, 236, 260, 265; acquired by Romania after WWI, xviii, 12; deportations of Jews from, 35, 39, 98f, 117–122, 141–142, 155–175, 177, 198f, 200–201, 205, 271, 273, 275f, 280–281, 284, 294; Jewish culture/politics in, 15; Jewish hostages in, 93, 100, 102; Jewish population of, 170; massacres of Jews in, 39–41, 96–103, 107–108, 164, 172–173, 289; number of Jews killed in, xxi, 132, 170–174, 289; number of Jews residing in, xx, 14; number of Transnistria survivors from, 255; repatriation to, 248–258, 284, 291, 293;

Soviet occupation, 38–41, 60–61, 110, 114, 118, 238, 290; transit camps in, 130, 134–135, 142; Ukrainians in, 92; yellow star in, 31, 33–34, 119, 141. *See also* Cernăuţi.

Bund, 15

Buradescu, Sever, 136–137, 152, 222

Burdujeni, massacre of Jews in, 60–61

Buzău, 44

Cahul District, 131f

Călăraşi, 48, 84–85; massacre of Jews in, 102

Calfeteanu, Ion, 42, 132

Calotescu, Corneliu, 33–34, 141, 155–157, 159, 166, 173, 273

Camps. *See* Internment camps; Transit camps.

Captaru, Dumitru, 68, 77–78, 87, 112

Caracal camp, 66, 111

Carol I, xvii, 6

Carol II, 46, 141; anti-Semitism of, xviii–xix, 18f, 22, 28, 259; relationship with Antonescu, 19, 22, 43, 47; relationship with Iron Guard, 38

Carp, Matatias: on deportation plans for Regat, 242, 248; on deportations/massacres, 63, 98, 111–112, 120, 130, 159, 166, 170–171; on pre–WWII conditions, 41f, 49–50, 57, 60; on repatriation from Transnistria, 257; on Transnistria, 186, 190, 192, 215, 217–218, 223

Carp, Valeriu, 40, 96–97

Cartea neagră, 49–50, 60, 103

Cassulo, Andrea, 243, 246

Ceausescu, Nicolae, xxiii, 287–288, 291

Central Jewish Office. *See* Central Office of Romanian Jews.

Central Office of Romanian Jews, 22, 26, 198, 200, 204, 212, 276–277; provides aid to Transnistria, 199, 203, 214, 218–220; relationship with Lecca, 34–35, 242, 244, 285; and repatriation, 249–250, 252–253, 256f

Cernăuţi, 17, 170–171; deportation of Jews from, 125, 126–127, 133,

Cernăuți (*cont.*)
141–142, 155–158, 164–166, 169, 173, 249, 286, 291; ghetto in, 130, 141–142, 156–158, 173; Jewish population of, xix, 15, 172, 214; massacre of Jews in, 101, 107, 116; yellow star in, 141–142
Cernavodă, 45
Cetatea Albă District, 131, 132, 170; massacre of Jews in, 106–107
Chamberlain, Houston Stewart, xix
Chelcea, Ion, 225
Chilia Nouă District, 131f
Chirilovici, Constantin, 68f, 75, 77, 87
Chirova, massacre of Jews in, 105
Chișinău, 92, 124–125, 170, 274; ghetto in, 117, 124, 129ff, 136, 139–141, 142, 146f, 152–154, 173f; massacres of Jews in, 66, 104, 107, 116, 182
Christian National Defense League, 12–13, 16, 17, 63, 285
Cihrin, massacre of Jews in, 188
Cîmpulung District, 44, 159–160, 166
Cires, massacre of Jews in, 99–100
Cîrlan, Vasile, 102–103
Cisek, Oskar Walter, 248
Ciudei, massacres of Jews in, 40, 96–97
Clejan, Herman, 249, 277, 280
Climăuți, massacre of Jews in, 102
Codreanu, Corneliu Zelea, 16, 18–19, 46, 63, 282
Cojocaru, Romulus, 167
Comisia de Patronaj (Patronage Society), 243, 286
Communist party, xxii–xxiii, 86, 287–288, 291
Concentration camps. *See* Internment camps; Transit camps.
Congress of Berlin of 1878, xviii, 7, 10, 18, 36, 274
Constantinescu, Alexandru, 135–136, 291
Constantinescu, Emil, xxii
Cosăuți, 121, 148
Costești, massacre of Jews in, 99
Covaci, Maria, 132
Covaleovka, 229, 230
Covurlui District, 9
Crăciunescu, Nicolae, 114
Crăiniceni, massacres of Jews in, 41

Craiova camp, 66, 111, 159
Crețu, Gheorghe, 55
Cretzianu, Alexandru, 256–257
Crișana, 12
Cristescu, Eugen, 86, 182; and Iași pogrom, 65, 68, 87
Cristescu, Gică, 86
Cuza, Alexandru C., xix, xx, 16–17, 63, 293
Cuza, Alexandru Ioan, xvii, 6
Cuza, Gheorghe, 293

Dallin, Alexander, 176f, 189, 200–201
Dalnic, 210; massacres of Jews in, 182
Dărăbani District, 112, 165, 252
Davidescu, Gheorghe, 197, 263f, 267
Davidescu, Radu, 137, 179–180, 254, 273
Deleanu, Nicolae, 181
Densușianu, Ovid, 11
Deportations of Jews: from Bessarabia/Bukovina, 35, 98f, 110f, 116, 117–122, 141–175, 177, 198f, 200–201, 205, 271, 273, 275f, 280–281, 284, 294; from/within Transnistria, 195, 196–197, 199, 208–214, 215–218, 221–223
Derebcin, massacre of Jews in, 193
Dinulescu, Radu, 65, 119, 127–128, 155, 182, 273
Dobruja, percentage of Jews in, xx
Dorohoi District, 9, 11, 38, 112, 278; deportations of Jews from, 111, 126, 159, 165f, 173f, 177, 198, 201–202, 239, 249, 252; massacres of Jews in, 39, 41–43, 61, 170; number of Transnistria survivors from, 255; repatriation to, 250, 252ff, 255–256, 276, 279, 280, 293
Dragalina, C. I., 141–142, 167, 254
Dragoș, Titus, 284–285
Dranceni District, 43
Drumont, Edouard, xix
Dumanovka: camp at, 207–208; massacre of Jews in, 183, 185, 186–187
Dumitrescu, Eugen, 152, 153–154

Edineți transit camp, 123–135 passim,
143–144, 148–149, 163
Ehrenburg, Ilya, 178
Eichmann, Adolf, 196, 240, 241–242,
263f, 285
Elena, Queen Mother of Romania, 243,
292
Extraordinary Congress of Romanian
Jews, 10

Fabricius, Wilhelm, 54
Fălciu District, 9, 11
Falik, David, 17
Fascism, Romanian: German fascism
compared to, 33, 74, 175; origins of, 10,
16–19, 38, 259; and religion, 29–30,
236–237. *See also* Carol II; Goga-Cuza
government; Iron Guard.
Filderman, Wilhelm, xix, 15f, 186, 245,
261–262, 289; Regat deportation plans
protested by, 245f, 258, 277–278;
relationship with Antonescu, 32f, 44f,
47, 51, 177, 275–276, 277–278;
repatriation from Transnistria advocated
by, 250, 251–252, 253–255, 256; yellow
star protested by, 32–34, 275
Finland, 277–278
Fisher, Josef, xix, 284
Fisher, Julius, 174, 193
Fisher, Theodor, xix
Florescu, I. M., 8
Folkist movement, 15
Forced labor, Jewish, xxii, 26–27, 48–49,
67, 92f, 113–124 passim, 205–223
passim, 252f, 257, 281; ordered by Ion
Antonescu, 34, 113, 119, 121, 196, 281
France, 260–261, 265–266, 268
Frölich, Heinrich, 117

Galați, 118; massacres of Jews in, 41, 61
Garisin, massacre of Jews in, 191
Geheime Feldpolizei, 65
Geisler, Kurt, 56
Georgescu, Corneliu, 55
German army: Abwehr, 65–66, 180;
during Iași pogrom, 65–66, 67–68, 70,

72–73, 74, 76ff, 82–83, 87, 89;
massacres of Jews in Bessarabia/
Bukovina by, 101, 103, 107, 116, 170,
289; massacres of Jews in Transnistria
by, 104, 176ff, 182, 186, 187–191, 193,
205, 208; relations with Romanian
army, 65–66, 102, 107–108, 116–117,
119–122, 188, 239. *See also* Germany;
SS.
Germans, ethnic, in Romania, 12, 23–24,
28, 49
Germans, ethnic, in Ukraine: Gypsies
murdered by, 234; Jews massacred by,
176f, 186, 187–190, 200
Germany: relations with Iron Guard,
52–54, 55–56, 65, 283; relations with
Romania, xxi, xxiii, 33, 35, 38, 46–47,
49, 52–53, 55, 63f, 66, 109, 121, 127f,
135, 141, 175, 188, 196–197, 205, 224f,
236, 238, 239–242, 243–244, 245–248,
262, 263–264, 266, 268, 270, 278–279,
282, 283–284, 290–291, 292, 294;
relations with Soviet Union, 37, 55, 63,
66. *See also* German army; Romanian
government, German influence on.
Gestapo, 56, 65, 167, 250, 262, 267
Ghelmegeanu, Mihail, 46
Gheorghe, Ion, 270
Ghica-Dumbrăveni, Leon, 11
Ghidighici, massacre of Jews in, 181
Ghika, Alexandru, 54, 55
Ghingold, Nandor, 249–250, 252, 254
Gigurtu, Ion, 19, 22, 38, 46, 52, 90
Gîrneață, Ilie, 55
Goering, Hermann, 38, 52
Goga, Octavian, xix, xx, 13, 17–19, 259,
282
Goga-Cuza government, xix, xx, 13,
17–19, 259
Golta District, 199ff, 204–205, 222,
229–230, 235, 255; massacres of Jews
in, 182–187, 193, 198, 205, 278–279,
289
Gorsky, Vasile, 231–235
Great Britain, 282
Greeks, ethnic, in Romania, 225, 237
Grossman, Vasily, 178
Grozea, Dumitru, 55, 57

Gruia, Ion V., 19
Gunther, Franklin Mott, 89–90, 168–169
Gura Căinari, massacre of Jews in,
    101–102
Gypsies, 193, 225–237, 279, 285;
    massacres of, 230; number of deaths in
    Transnistria, 235–236, 289–290;
    number deported to Transnistria, 226;
    repatriation from Transnistria, 236;
    robbed during deportation, 226, 229,
    230, 232; in Romanian army, 226f,
    231–232, 233, 236

Haham, Avram, 285–286
Harnik, Henriette, 205–206
Hauffe-Tătăranu Convention for
    Transnistria, 122, 171
Hausner, Mihail, 230, 236
Herseni, Traian, 225
Herţa District, 126, 252; massacre of Jews
    in, 100–101, 170
Heydrich, Reinhard, 54, 239
Hilberg, Raul, xxi, 57, 86, 290, 295; on
    Bessarabia/Bukovina, 108, 119, 132,
    171, 173, 177, 289; on deportation
    plans for Regat, 241–242, 244; on
    Transnistria, 195, 196–197, 217
Himmler, Heinrich, 46, 56, 240, 246–247,
    282, 283
Hirschmann, Ira, 256–257, 258
Hîrsova, 47, 61
Hitler, Adolf, 16, 22, 43, 44, 161;
    relationship with Antonescu, xxiv, 53f,
    55–56, 236, 241, 248, 281–282, 283
Hotin: deportation of Jews from, 125f,
    133; massacre of Jews in, 102, 107
Hotin District, 126–127, 131, 133, 166;
    massacre of Jews in, 101–102
Hulievca, massacre of Jews in, 189
Hull, Cordell, 245
Hungary, xxi, xxiii, 5, 14, 263, 270, 284,
    289f; relations with Romania, 115,
    260–261, 262, 266f
Huși, 43
Huston, Cloyce K., 90

Iampol/Iampol District, 120f, 192, 197f,
    201, 203, 279; massacre of Jews in,
    107, 116
Iancu, Carol, 6, 7
Iași: anti-Semitism in, 10f, 32, 44, 50, 63;
    Jews residing in, xix, xx, 6, 285–286.
    See also Iași pogrom.
Iași pogrom, 31, 63–90, 239; German
    army during, 65–66, 67–68, 70, 72–73,
    74, 76ff, 82–83, 87, 89; Iron Guard
    during, 66–67, 68f, 73, 87, 89; Jews
    helped during, 74f, 82, 291; massacres
    of Jews during, 69–81; mob violence
    during, 63, 70, 73, 74–75, 76, 272;
    number killed in, 77, 85–86, 111;
    origins of, 63–68, 115–116; planning
    of, 67, 69, 77f, 82, 86–87; Romanian
    army during, 64–65, 67, 69–71, 75, 77,
    87; Romanian gendarmerie during, 64,
    68, 70, 71, 76, 78, 81–84, 89; Romanian
    police during, 68–78 passim, 81f, 85,
    87, 89; Secret Intelligence Service (SSI)
    during, 64–66, 69, 86–87; trains remove
    Jews during, 78, 80–85, 88
Iașinschi, Vasile, 43, 55
Iaska, 197, 198
Iliescu, General (inspector of Transnistria
    gendarmerie), 217, 219
Iliescu, Paul, 17
Innocentists, 236–237
International Red Cross, 222, 246, 251,
    258, 292
Internment camps, 27, 43, 197–198;
    Dumanovka, 207–208; Pecioara, 190f,
    217–218, 221–222; Tîrgu Jiu, 61, 64,
    66, 111, 115, 159, 254, 257; Vapniarka,
    210, 217, 220, 250–251, 254, 255–256,
    257, 279, 291. *See also* Transit camps.
Ionescu, Vasile, 155–156, 159
Ionescu-Micandru, Constantin, 66, 68
Iorga, Nicolae, 46, 47, 55
Iron Guard: anti-Semitism of, 13, 18–19,
    24f, 49, 225, 283; during Iași pogrom,
    66–67, 68, 69, 73, 87, 89; massacres of
    Jews by, 45–46, 47–48, 57–60, 61, 290;
    origins, 16, 17, 63; relations with
    Germany, 46–47, 52–54, 55–56, 65,
    283; relationship with Antonescu, 19,

23ff, 43, 47, 49, 50–57, 60, 87, 275, 282–283, 292–293; relationship with Carol II, 38
Isăceanu, Vasile, 285–286
Ismail District, 131, 132
Isopescu, Modest, 183–186, 230, 235
"Iţic Ştrul, Deserter," 11
Ivanoiu, Vasile, 93–94

Jadova Veche, massacre of Jews in, 99
Janca, Ion, 161
Jehovah's Witnesses, 155
Jewish party, xix–xx, 16
Jews, Hungarian, 260, 263, 267, 270, 282, 284
Jews, Polish, 167, 191, 254, 261–262
Jews, Romanian: considered capitalists, 23–24, 37; considered Communists/enemies of Romania, 30, 37ff, 63, 66–67, 70f, 79f, 82, 87f, 91–92, 110, 114–115, 118, 123, 128, 177, 217, 238, 250ff, 254, 257, 272, 275, 277, 280, 282–283, 291, 293; cultural diversity among, xix, 13, 14–16; economic conditions for, xvii, xx, 23–26; emigration of, 9, 12, 34, 244, 250f, 256, 284; excluded from National Association of Physicians, 27–28; expropriation/robbery of, 23–26, 44–45, 48, 49–50, 52, 72, 81, 94, 108–109, 110, 123f, 136, 137–138, 147ff, 150–151, 153, 157–158, 160–164, 165, 167–168, 208, 260–261, 264, 273f, 277, 281, 285; as hostages, 91, 93, 100, 102, 104, 112, 179; and legal definitions of "Jew," 19–23, 24–25, 31; legal restrictions on citizenship for, xvii, xviii, 7, 10ff, 14, 18–19, 260, 265; legal restrictions on economic activities of, 23–26; legal restrictions on education of, 10, 28–29; legal restrictions on practice of medicine by, 27–28; living abroad, 259–270; military status of, 27; nineteenth-century attitudes toward, xvii–xviii, 4f, 6–11; nineteenth-century laws discriminating against, 5–11;

number killed in Holocaust, xxi, xxii, 289; as percentage of population, xx, xxi; physical abuse of, 44, 48, 57–59; politics of, 15–16; pre-nineteenth-century repression, 4–5; and Romanian nationalism, xvii, 4, 37, 38; during Soviet occupation of Bessarabia/Bukovina, 38–41, 170, 171–172; survival factors for, xxi, 35, 175, 195, 238–239, 291–292, 294–295; taxes on, 27, 28–29, 30–31; yellow star worn by, 31–34, 119, 141–142, 262, 275; Zionism among, xix–xx, 15f. *See also* Deportations of Jews; Forced labor, Jewish; Massacres of Jews; Mob violence against Jews.
Jews, Ukrainian, xxii, 10, 122, 195, 198, 203, 205, 220; deaths of, 193, 289; massacres of, 176f, 190
Jugastru District, 199ff, 205, 255

Kaltenbrunner, Ernst, 246
Karadja, Constantin, 259, 267, 268–270
Katz, M., 204, 214
Keitel, Wilhelm, 53
Khazars, 5
Killinger, Manfred von, 54, 188, 241f, 245, 263f, 283
Klarsfeld, Serge, 265
Kogălniceanu, Mihail, 6, 7, 8–9
Kolb, Charles, 222–223
Kulisher, Eugen, 173

LANC. *See* Christian National Defense League.
Landau, Izu, 209–210
Lăpuşna District, 128–129, 131f
Lăpuşneanu, Alexandru, 5
Lecca, Junius, 65
Lecca, Radu, 113, 115, 214, 263, 278, 284, 285–286; and Jewish deportation, 242, 243–244, 245–247; and Jewish repatriation, 250, 253, 255, 266–267, 270; relationship with Central Office of Romanian Jews, 34–35, 242, 244, 285

Legion of the Archangel Michael. *See* Iron Guard.
Leoveanu, Emanoil, 88–89
Liberal party, 228–229, 248, 274
Liga Apararrii National Crestine (LANC). *See* Christian National Defense League.
Lihova, 202
Limbenii Noi transit camp, 128ff, 131, 137, 142, 152
Litani, Dora, 177, 186
Lovinescu, Eugen, 248
Lugoj camp, 111
Lupu, Constantin, 68f, 71, 87–88
Lupu, Nicolae, 33, 141, 248f, 275–276, 292
Luther, Martin, 264

Madgearu, Virgil, 46
Magyars, ethnic, in Romania, 12, 28, 115, 237
Malaparte, Curzio, 86
Mamuica, Constantin, 54f
Mănescu, Vasile, 183, 185
Maniu, Iuliu, 248, 271, 275, 292
Manoilescu, Mihail, 23–24, 38
Manoliu, T. R. Mircea, 68, 69–70, 88, 94
Maramureş, 12
Marcu, Octavian, 55
Mărculeşti, massacre of Jews in, 102
Mărculeşti transit camp, 123–138 passim, 142, 152, 158, 165, 202
Mareş, Nicolae, 43, 245
Marinescu, Gabriel, 46
Marinescu, Ioan C., 252
Marinescu, Nicolae, 46
Marinescu, Stere, 166f
Massacres of Jews: in Bessarabia/Bukovina, 39–42, 61, 66, 91, 92–108, 116–117, 147–149, 150–151, 164, 181–182, 289f; in Bucharest, 45–46, 48, 57–60, 61; during Iaşi pogrom, 69–81; in Transnistria, 66, 176, 177–193, 205, 208, 252, 258, 284
Matieş, Ermil, 94–96, 101–102
Maurras, Charles, xix

Meculescu, Colonel (commander of Bessarabian gendarmerie), 92, 121–122, 130, 139, 143, 144–147, 151, 154
Melinescu, Vasile, 185, 186–187
Mendelsohn, Ezra, 13, 14–15
Micescu, Istrate, 18
Michael I, 35, 43, 248, 287
Mihăiescu, Ion, 137–138
Mihăilescu, Eugen, 94–96, 103
Mihailiuc, Vasile, 164
Mihalache, Ion, 248
Milcoreni, massacres of Jews in, 39–40
Milenaristi, 154
Milie, massacre of Jews in, 100
Mircu, Marius, 67, 77, 99, 101
Mischlinge, 20, 22
Mob violence against Jews, 37–38, 39, 42, 44–45, 48, 62, 108–109; in Bukovina, 98, 101; during Iaşi pogrom, 63, 70, 73, 74–75, 76, 272
Mocsoni-Styrcea, Baron, 243
Moghilev/Moghilev District, 120f, 127, 163, 169–170, 197–208 passim, 219–220, 255, 279, 291; deportation of Jews from, 212–214, 215, 217, 223
Moldavia, 12, 41, 50, 93, 278; deportation/internment of Jews in, 35, 63–65, 66, 111–115, 118, 121, 155, 174, 190, 200, 218; deportation plans for, 239, 242, 245–248, 258, 264, 274, 282, 292, 294; Jewish culture in, xx, 5, 13; Jews expelled from rural areas of, 43; nineteenth- and early twentieth-century repression of Jews in, 6, 8–9, 11; number of Jews in, xx, 13, 18; number of Transnistria survivors from, 255; repatriation to, 249–250, 252–253; Revolution of 1848 in, 6; yellow star in, 31–33, 119, 275. *See also* Iaşi; Iaşi pogrom.
Molotov, Vyacheslav, 37, 38, 178
Molotov-Ribbentrop Pact, 37
Moore, Barrington, 52
Morusov, Mihail, 46
Mostovoi, 230, 279; massacres of Jews in, 188f, 191
Motora, Sabin, 291
Mumuianu, Iuliu, 218–219

Muntenia, percentage of Jews in, xx
Murgescu, Ion C., 217

National Agrarian party, 17
National Bank of Romania, 25, 43,
    137–138, 147, 153, 157, 161, 163,
    273
National Christian party, xix, 13, 17–18,
    293
National Liberal party, xviii, 16
National Peasant party, xviii, 16, 33, 46,
    141, 248, 271, 283, 292
National Socialist German Workers' Party
    (NSDAP), 52
Nationalism, Romanian. *See* Romania,
    nationalism in.
Neamţ District, 9
Neumann, Baron, 243
Nicodeme (Orthodox patriarch), 33
Nicolau, Pompiliu, 43
Niculescu-Coca, Mihail, 181
Noua Suliţă: deportation of Jews from,
    120, 125f, 133; massacre of Jews in,
    102–103
Nova Umani, massacre of Jews in, 189
Nuremberg Laws, xx, 19–20, 21, 293

Obodovka, 202, 204f, 207f, 220
Oceakov District, 208, 211, 229, 231–235,
    255
Odessa, 195–196, 198, 200, 219, 272–273;
    deportations of Jews from, 208–212,
    223; massacres of Jews in, 66, 177–182,
    193, 198, 205, 208, 273–274, 289
Office for Jewish Problems, 34, 285. *See
    also* Lecca, Radu.
Ohlendorf, Otto, 187
Oil, Romanian, 52, 241
Olgopol, 220
Oltenia, xx
Oradea, 283
Organization of Native Born Jews, 15
Orhei District, 128f, 131f; massacre of
    Jews in, 104–106
Ottoman Empire, Jews under, 4, 5
Ovidopol District, 19, 200, 205

Pădure, Aristide, 183, 185f
Palade, Lt. Col. (chief of Military
    Statistics Office in Iaşi), 127–128, 144
Palestine, Jewish emigration to, 244, 250f,
    256, 284
Papanace, Constantin, 225
Papon, Maurice, xxiv
Parikman, Israel, 202, 213–214
Paris Peace Conference of 1856, 36
Paris Peace Conference of 1923, 36
Paris Peace Conference of 1946, xxi,
    257–258
Party of the Nation, 38
Pătrăşcanu, Lucreţiu, 35, 257–258, 287
Pătraşcu, Nicolae, 55
Pecioara camp, 190f, 205, 217–218,
    221–222
People's party, 16
Pervomaisk, 198
Petrescu, Gheorghe, 64–65, 155–156, 158,
    273
Petrovicescu, Constantin, 43, 50, 54
Petrovici, Grigore, 86–87, 182
Pilat, Ion, 248
Pintea, Gherman, 182, 210, 219
Ploieşti, massacres of Jews in, 46, 48, 61
Podul Iloaei, 85, 88
Poland, 244–245
Pop, Constantin, 55
Pop, Leonida, 230–231
Popescu, Ion "Jack," 27, 32–33, 64, 93,
    119, 245f, 284
Popescu, Savin, 103
Popovici, Traian, 155–156, 159, 165–166,
    167–168, 172, 291
Porfir, Grigore, 75
Prahova District, 45
Progromurile din Bucovina si Dorohoi, 99
Protestants in Romania, 29–30, 155

Queen Mother of Romania, 243, 292

Răbniţa/Răbniţa District, 197–205 passim,
    223, 255
Rădăuţi/Rădăuţi District, 159–160;
    deportations of Jews from, 125, 127,

Rădăuți/Rădăuți District (*cont.*)
133, 164–165, 166, 239; massacres of
Jews in, 41
Răducăneni District, 43
Rădulescu-Motru, Constantin, 11
Rășcani transit camp, 128f, 130f, 137,
142, 152
Rastadt, massacre of Jews in, 188, 190f
Răuțel transit camp, 128–137 passim, 142,
152
Rebreanu, Liviu, 11
Regat (Old Kingdom of Romania), 14–15,
31; aid to Transnistria from Jews in,
195, 199, 203, 214, 218–220, 224, 238;
deportation plans for, 239, 242,
245–248, 247, 258, 294; Jewish culture
in, xix, xx; Jewish population of, 13,
18; number of Jews killed in, xxi;
treatment of Jews in, 110–115, 121,
169, 174. *See also* Moldavia; Walachia.
Ribbentrop, Joachim von, 37f, 53, 56, 243
Richter, Gustav, 263–264, 266; and plans
to deport Jews from Regat, 240–242,
243, 244–245, 246f, 283–284
Rioșanu, Alexandru, 43, 46, 141
Ritgen, Hermann von, 240
Rivera, Miguel A., 42, 58, 89
Roedel, Willi, 240
Roman District, 9, 32
Romania: Bessarabia/Bukovina acquired
after WWI, xviii, 12, 14; Communist
attitudes toward Holocaust in,
xxii–xxiii, 287; entrance into WWII,
62f, 66, 115–116; ethnic minorities in,
xx, xxi, 12f, 23–24, 28, 38f, 49, 115,
225, 236, 237, 281; Jewish population
of, xx, xxi, 13; nationalism in, xvii, 3–4,
37f, 63, 287–288, 292; post-Communist
attitudes toward Holocaust in, xxii,
xxiii–xxiv; relations with Austro-
Hungarian Empire, xviii, 14; relations
with France, 260–261, 265–266;
relations with Germany, xxi, xxiii, 33,
35, 38, 46–47, 49, 52–53, 55, 63f, 66,
109, 121, 127f, 135, 141, 175, 188,
196–197, 205, 224f, 236, 238, 239–242,
243–244, 245–248, 262, 263–264, 266,
268, 270, 278–279, 282, 283–284,

290–291, 292, 294; relations with
Hungary, 115, 260–261, 262, 266f;
relations with Ottoman Empire, 4, 5;
relations with Russia, xviii, 5–6, 8, 13f;
relations with Soviet Union, 31, 37f,
60–61, 62f, 66, 290; relations with
United States, 89–90, 168–169, 245,
256–257, 282, 284; relations with
Vatican, 243, 246, 292; and Second
Balkan War, 11, 21, 23; Transylvania
returned to, xviii; and Treaty of Berlin,
xviii, 7, 10, 18; and Treaty of St.
Germain, 12; and Treaty of Versailles,
xviii; War of Independence, 7, 21. *See
also* Romanian army; Romanian
gendarmerie; Romanian government;
Romanian police.
Romanian army: anti-Semitism in, 10–11,
27, 37–38; deportations of Jews from
Bessarabia/Bukovina by, 119–122,
127–128, 135–137, 155–156, 165;
Gypsies in, 226f, 231–232, 233, 236;
during Iași pogrom, 64–65, 67, 69–71,
75, 77, 87; internment camps managed
by, 135–137, 144–146; during Iron
Guard rebellion, 53f; massacres of Jews
in Bessarabia/Bukovina by, 39–42, 61,
94–98, 99, 100–102, 103f, 107–108,
117, 170, 181–182, 289; massacres of
Jews in Transnistria by, 176ff, 182, 186,
187–191, 193, 205, 208; relations with
German army, 65–66, 102, 107–108,
116–117, 119–122, 188, 239; Supreme
General Staff, 26, 64–65, 87, 119, 128,
142, 144, 155, 165, 179, 182, 187–188,
197, 273. *See also* Romanian
gendarmerie; Romanian government.
Romanian gendarmerie, 233, 290; anti-
Semitism in, 64, 91; deportations of
Gypsies by, 226–230; deportations of
Jews from Bessarabia/Bukovina by,
121–125, 127–129, 130, 134, 143–152,
154, 157, 273, 284; during Iași pogrom,
64, 68, 70f, 76, 78, 81–84, 89;
massacres of Jews in Bessarabia/
Bukovina by, 91, 92–94, 101ff,
104–106, 107, 117, 150–151, 164;
massacres of Jews in Transnistria by,

181, 182–187, 190, 192–193; during
Transnistria occupation, 174, 188–191,
197–198, 209–212, 217–218, 223, 230.
See also Romanian army; Romanian
government.
Romanian government: corruption/
opportunism in, 277, 281, 285–286,
295; German influence on, xx–xxi,
19–20, 23–24, 35, 64, 224, 248, 276,
293; legal definitions of "Jew" used by,
19–23, 24–25, 31; legal restrictions on
Jewish economic activity imposed by,
23–26; legal restrictions on Jewish
education imposed by, 28–29; legal
restrictions on practice of medicine by
Jews imposed by, 27–28; military
defeats change policies of, 35, 111, 116,
195, 205, 223f, 238–239, 248, 258, 260,
266, 291, 294; origins of fascism in, 10,
16–19, 38. *See also* Alexianu,
Gheorghe; Antonescu, Ion; Antonescu,
Mihai; Romania; Romanian army;
Romanian gendarmerie; Romanian
police; Vasiliu, C. Z.
Romanian police, 44, 48–49, 55, 62, 226,
233; during Bessarabia/Bukovina
deportations, 124–125, 126, 166–167;
during Iași pogrom, 68ff, 71, 75–76,
77–78, 81f, 85, 87, 89; massacres of
Jews by, 37–38, 40, 42, 45–46, 61, 102
Ropcea, massacre of Jews in, 98
Rosenberg, Alfred, xix
Rosetti, Radu, 30
Rostochi-Vijnita, massacre of Jews in,
100
Rubin, Moses Iosif, 44
Russia: anti-Semitism in, 13, 14; relations
with Romania, xviii, 5–6, 8, 13, 14
Russians, ethnic, in Romania, 39
Rusu, Cristea, 44

Sadagura, massacre of Jews in, 101
Șafran, Alexandru, 33, 243, 246, 257,
284ff
Saharna, massacre of Jews in, 105
Salazar, Antonio, 43
Șaraga, Fred, 218–220

Șargorod, 202, 206–207, 208
Satu Mare, 12, 15
Savu, Constantin, 55
Scazineț, 128, 212–214, 215; massacre of
Jews in, 121
Schellenberg, Walter, 54
Șchiopul, Petru, 5
Scriban, Nicolae, 70f
Sculeni, massacre of Jews from, 94–96
SD (Sicherheitsdienst), 52, 54f
Second Section of Supreme General Staff.
See Romanian army, Supreme General
Staff.
Secondary and Higher Education Law of
1893, 10
Secret Intelligence Service (SSI), 64–66,
69, 86–87, 107, 181–182, 248
Secureni transit camp, 120–134 passim,
143–144, 147–148, 202
Șefanescu, Dimitre, 213
Șerbăuți, massacres of Jews in, 40–41
Sicherheitsdienst (SD), 52, 54, 65, 267
Sima, Horia, 22, 56, 60; as leader of Iron
Guard, 38, 43, 46, 53, 55
Simion, Aurica, 42
Singer, Sami, xix–xx
Slobozia Doamnă, massacre of Jews in,
104
Șmerinka, 219, 223; massacre of Jews in,
191
Soroca District, 32, 128–129, 131f, 135,
142, 172; massacres of Jews in, 101,
102
Soviet Union: Bessarabia/Bukovina
occupied by, 38–41, 60–61, 110, 114,
118, 170–172; and Jews in
Bessarabia/Bukovina, 39, 170,
171–172; relations with Germany, 37,
55, 63; relations with Romania, 31, 37f,
60–61, 62f, 66, 290
Sperber, Magnus, 248
Spiegel, Alexandru, 47
SS, 239–240, 246–247, 282, 283–284;
Einsatzgruppen, 107f, 116, 120, 121f,
187; massacres of Gypsies by, 230,
235–236; massacres of Jews by, 67,
76, 117, 176f, 182, 186, 187–191;
relations with Iron Guard, 46–47, 52,

SS (*cont.*)
    54ff. *See also* Eichmann, Adolf;
        Himmler, Heinrich; Richter, Gustav.
SSI. *See* Secret Intelligence Service (SSI).
Stalingrad, 35, 111, 116, 238, 266, 294
Stan, Ion Natale, 230, 231
Staraia Balca, massacre of Jews in, 189
Stavrescu, Gheorghe, 75, 77
Ştefăniţă, 5
Stihi, Ion, 94–96, 101
Stînca Roznovanu, massacre of Jews in,
    94–96, 101, 103
Storojineţ/Storojineţ District: deportations
    of Jews from, 120, 123ff, 127, 133, 158,
    166, 206; massacre of Jews in, 97–100,
    117
Stransky, Hermann von, 65–66, 67–68
Sturdza, D. A., 8
Sturdza, Mihail, 43, 53, 55
Sturdza, Vlad, 50
Suceava District, 9, 19; deportations of
    Jews from, 159–164, 166, 239;
    massacres of Jews in, 40–41
Suha Balca, 230f
Suhr, Friedrich, 246

Tănăsescu, Ioan, 55
Tarasivca, massacre of Jews in, 191
Tătăranu, General (Supreme General
    Staff), 120, 122, 147, 179
Tătăraşi-Chilia camp, massacre of Jews at,
    117
Tătăreşcu, Gheorghe, 46, 257
Tecuci District, 9
Teich, Meyer, 160–164
Teişani, 45
Teleneşti, massacre of Jews at, 104
Teodorescu, Paul, 82
Ţepeş, Vlad (the Impaler), 5
Tester, A., 250f
Tibirica, massacre of Jews in, 105
Tighina/Tighina District, 129, 131f;
    massacre of Jews in, 107
Tiraspol/Tiraspol District, 195, 197f, 204,
    255
Tîrgu Frumos, 80f, 82–83, 88

Tîrgu Jiu camp, 61, 64, 66, 111, 115, 159,
    254, 257
Todt Organization, 67, 76, 190, 216
Topor, Ion, 92f, 124–142 passim,
    155–156, 273
Totu, Nicolae, 17
Transit camps, 35, 99, 117–118, 122–132;
    conditions in, 133–138; deaths of Jews
    in, 132, 171, 173; Edineţi, 123–135
    passim, 143–144, 148–149, 163;
    evacuation of, 142–152, 163; Limbenii
    Noi, 128ff, 137, 142, 152; Mărculeşti,
    123–138 passim, 142, 152, 158, 165,
    202; Răşcani, 128f, 130f, 137, 142, 152;
    Răuţel, 128–137 passim, 142, 152;
    Secureni, 120–134 passim, 143–144,
    147–148, 202; Vertujeni, 121–134
    passim, 135–137, 142f, 144–146,
    149–150, 152, 201–202, 291. *See also*
    Internment camps.
Transnistria: camps in, 197–198, 207, 210,
    212–214, 217–218, 221–222; conditions
    in, xxii, 110f, 202–208, 213–218,
    219–224, 229–230, 234–235; creation
    of, 122, 171, 176; deportations of
    Gypsies to, 225–230; deportations of
    Jews from/within, 195, 196–197, 199,
    208–214, 215–218, 221–223;
    deportations of Jews to, 26, 35, 98f,
    111, 114–115, 142–175, 177, 198,
    200–201, 249, 289; Jews in Regat
    provide aid to, 195, 199, 203, 214,
    218–220, 224, 238; massacres of Jews
    in, 66, 176, 177–193, 205, 208, 252,
    258, 284; number of Gypsies deported
    to, 226; number of Gypsy deaths in,
    193, 235–236, 289–290; number of
    Jewish deaths in, xxi, xxii, 132, 173f,
    176–177, 193, 198–201, 205, 254f, 289;
    number of Jews deported to, 174, 177,
    198–199, 200–201, 205, 254; orphaned
    children in, 250f, 253ff, 256–257, 280;
    repatriation of Jews from, 248–258,
    284, 291, 293; yellow star in, 31. *See
    also* Alexianu, Gheorghe; Odessa.
Transylvania, 50, 111, 262, 289;
    deportation of Jews from, 35, 118, 169;

deportation plans for, 239, 242, 244, 246, 247, 274, 282, 292; Jewish culture/politics in, xx, 14–15; number of Jews in, xx, 14; number of Jews killed in, xxi; returned to Romania, xviii, 12, 14; Transnistria survivors from, 255
Treaty of Berlin, xviii, 7, 10, 18, 36
Treaty of St. Germain, 12, 36
Treaty of Versailles, xviii
Triandaf, Aurel, 81, 83–84
Trifa, Viorel, 55
Trihati, 222, 231; massacre of Gypsies at, 230, 235–236
Truelle, Jacques, 38–39, 89, 169–170, 180
Tudose, D., 139–140, 152
Tulbure, Emil, 66, 69, 86
Tulcin District, 198, 200, 201, 204–205, 215f, 222f, 255, 279; massacres of Jews in, 190–191
Turks, 5, 28
Turnu Severin camp, 66, 111
Tutova District, 9

UER. *See* Union of Romanian Jews.
Ukraine, xxii, 116–117, 119–122; Transnistria created, 122; under German occupation, 195, 205, 224, 247, 284
Ukrainians, 12, 38f, 236f, 281; Jews in Bessarabia/Bukovina massacred by, 99f, 108; Jews in Transnistria massacred by, 176, 177, 182–187. *See also* Jews, Ukrainian.
Union of Romanian Jews (UER), xix, 15f, 34, 44, 50f, 143, 276
United States, 53, 171; relations with Romania, 89–90, 168–169, 245, 256–257, 282, 284
Uniunea Evreilor Pămînteni, 15
Uniunea Evreilor Romani. *See* Union of Romanian Jews.
USSR. *See* Soviet Union.

Vapniarka camp, 205, 210, 217, 220, 250–251, 254, 255–256, 257, 279, 291
Vartic, Gheorghe, 100–101, 102f

Vasilinovo, massacres of Jews in, 188, 191, 200
Vasiliu, C. Z., 261–262, 268, 278–279, 284; anti-Semitism of, 64, 91, 104; and deportations of Jews/Gypsies, 92, 174, 198, 226–227, 228, 285; execution, 4, 287; and Regat deportation plans, 245f; and repatriation plans, 251–252, 253–255, 256
Vaslui District, 9, 49
Vatican, relations with Romania, 243, 246, 292
Văşcăuţi: camp at, 123; massacre of Jews in, 100
Vertujeni transit camp, 121–134 passim, 135–137, 142f, 144–146, 149–150, 152, 201–202, 291
Vetu, Ion, 117
Vijniţa, 125, 278f; massacre of Jews in, 100
Vilavca, massacre of Jews in, 100
Viteazul, Mihai, 5
Voda, Aron, 5
Voicu, George, xxiv
Voiculescu, General (Governor of Bessarabia), 92–93, 139, 147, 150, 152ff, 273
Voiculescu, Vasile, 248
Volcineţ, massacre of Jews in, 117

Walachia, 12, 50; deportation/internment of Jews in, 35, 64, 111, 118, 121, 174, 190, 200, 218; deportation plans for, 239, 242, 245–248, 258, 264, 274, 282, 292, 294; Jewish culture in, xx, 5, 13; nineteenth-century repression of Jews in, 8–9; number of Jews in, 13, 18; number of Transnistria survivors from, 255; repatriation to, 249–250, 252–253; Revolution of 1848 in, 6
Wannsee Conference, 239
War Refugee Board, 256–257, 258, 292
Weck, René de, 258
Weiss, Aureliu, 248, 271–272, 283
Weissman, Mişu, xx
Weizsäcker, Ernst von, 243

Woermann, Ernst, 243
World War I, xviii, 11f, 14, 62

Yellow star, 31–34, 119, 141–142, 262,
    275
Yiddish, xx, 11, 14f, 19

Zăhărești, massacre of Jews in, 40
Zaharia, Gheorghe, 86
Zaharovca, massacre of Jews in, 188f
Zamfir, Mihai, xxiv
Zavadovca, massacre of Jews in, 189
Zăvoianu, Stefan, 55
Zionism, xix–xx, 15f, 86, 171, 284

A NOTE ON THE AUTHOR

Radu Ioanid was born in 1953 in Bucharest, Romania, and grew up there. He studied at the University of Bucharest; at the University of Cluj, where he received a Ph.D.; and at the École des Hautes Études en Sciences Sociales in Paris, where he received a doctorate in history. He has also written *Urbanization in Romania* and *The Sword of the Archangel: Fascist Ideology in Romania,* as well as numerous articles and contributions to collections of essays. Mr. Ioanid has been a Starkoff Fellow at the American Jewish Archives and is the Associate Director of the International Programs Division at the United States Holocaust Memorial Museum. He is now a United States citizen.